8.95

Accounting for BTEC

Frank Wood, BSc(Econ), FCA and
Joe Townsley, BCom, FCA

Lorraine J Liddle

CBNP2.

PITMAN PUBLISHING
128 Long Acre, London WC2E 9AN

©Frank Wood and Joe Townsley 1987

First published in Great Britain 1987

ISBN 0 273 02922 3

Printed and bound in Great Britain.

GW00691442

Contents

1

Bank Reconciliation Statements

Let us assume that we have just written up our cash book. We call at the bank on 30 June 19-5 and obtain from the bank manager a copy of our bank statement. On our return we tick off in our cash book and on the bank statement the items that are similar. A copy of our cash book (bank columns only) and of our bank statement are now shown as Exhibit 1.1.

Exhibit 1.1

Cash Book (bank columns only)

19-5			£	19-5			£
June	1 Balance b/f	✓	80	June 27	I. Gordon	✓	35
,,	28 D. Johnson	✓	100	,, 29	B. Tyrell		40
				,, 30	Balance c/d		105
			180				180
July	1 Balance b/d		105				

Bank Statement

19-5		Dr	Cr	Balance
		£	£	£
June 26	Balance b/fwd	✓		80 CR
,, 28	Banking	✓	100	180 CR
,, 30	I. Gordon	✓ 35		145 CR

By comparing the cash book and the bank statement, it can be seen that the only item that was not in both of these was the cheque payment to B. Tyrell £40 in the cash book.

The reason this was in the cash book, but not on the bank statement, is simply one of timing. The cheque had been posted to B. Tyrell on 29 June, but there had not been time for it to be banked by Tyrell and pass through the banking system. Such a cheque is called an 'unpresented cheque' because it has not yet been presented at the drawer's bank.

To prove that, although they are different figures the balances are not different because of errors, a bank reconciliation statement is drawn up. This is as follows:

Bank Reconciliation Statement
as at 30 June 19-5

	£
Balance in Hand as per Cash Book	105
Add unpresented cheque: Tyrell	40
Balance in Hand as per Bank Statement	145

It would have been possible for the bank reconciliation statement to have started with the bank statement balance:

Bank Reconciliation Statement
as at 30 June 19-5

	£
Balance in Hand as per Bank Statement	145
Less unpresented cheque: Tyrell	40
Balance in Hand as per Cash Book	105

You should notice that the bank account is shown as a debit balance in the firm's cash book because to the firm it is an asset. In the bank's books the bank account is shown as a credit balance because this is a liability of the bank to the firm.

We can now look at a more complicated example in Exhibit 1.2. Similar items in both cash book and bank statement are shown ticked.

Exhibit 1.2

Cash Book

19-5		£	19-5		£
Dec 27 Total b/fwd		2,000	Dec 27 Total b/fwd		1,600
,, 29 J. Potter	√	60	,, 28 J. Jacobs	√	105
,, 31 M. Johnson (B)		220	,, 30 M. Chatwood (A)		15
			,, 31 Balance c/d		560
		2,280			2,280
19-6					
Jan 1 Balance b/d		560			

Bank Statement

			Dr	Cr	Balance
19-5			£	£	£
Dec 27 Balance b/fwd					400 CR
,, 29 Cheque	✓			60	460 CR
,, 30 J. Jacobs	✓		105		355 CR
,, ,, Credit transfers: L. Shaw (C)				70	425 CR
,, ,, Bank Charges (D)			20		405 CR

The balance brought forward in the bank statement £400 is the same figure as that in the cash book, i.e. totals b/fwd £2,000−£1,600 = £400. However, items (A) and (B) are in the cash book only, and (C) and (D) are on the bank statement only. We can now examine these in detail:

(A) This is a cheque sent by us yesterday to Mr Chatwood. It has not yet passed through the banking system and been presented to our bank, and is therefore an 'unpresented cheque'.

(B) This is a cheque banked by us on our visit to the bank when we collected the copy of our bank statement. As we handed this banking over the counter at the same time as the bank clerk gave us our bank statement, naturally it has not yet been entered on the statement.

(C) A customer, L. Shaw has paid his account by instructing his bank to pay us direct through the banking system, instead of paying by cheque. Such a transaction is usually called a 'Bank Giro Transfer'. The term previously used was 'Credit Transfer'.

(D) The bank has charged us for the services given in keeping a bank account for us. It did not send us a bill: it simply takes the money from our account by debiting it and reducing the amount of our balance.

We can show these differences in the form of a table. This is followed by bank reconciliation statements drawn up both ways. This is for illustration only; we do not have to draw up a table or prepare two bank reconciliation statements. All we need in practice is one bank reconciliation statement, drawn up whichever way we prefer.

			Adjustment required to one balance to reconcile it with the other	
Items not in both sets of books	*Effect on Cash Book balance*	*Effect on Bank Statement*	*To Cash Book balance*	*To Bank Statement balance*
1. Payment M. Chatwood £15	reduced by £15	none − not yet entered	add £15	deduct £15
2. Banking M. Johnson £220	increased by £220	none − not yet entered	deduct £220	add £220
3. Bank Commission £20	none − not yet entered	reduced by £20	deduct £20	add £20
4. Credit Transfers £70	none − not yet entered	increased by £70	add £70	deduct £70

Bank Reconciliation Statement as on 31 December 19-5

	£	£
Balance in hand as per Cash Book		560
Add unpresented cheque	15	
Credit transfers	70	85
		645
Less Bank commission	20	
Bank lodgement not yet entered on bank statement	220	240
Balance in hand as per bank statement		405

Bank Reconciliation Statement as on 31 December 19-5

	£	£
Balance in hand as per bank statement		405
Add Bank commission	20	
Bank lodgement not yet entered on bank statement	220	240
		645
Less Unpresented Cheques	15	
Traders Credit Transfers	70	
		85
Balance in Hand as per Cash Book		560

Standing Orders and Direct Debits

A firm can instruct its bank to make regular payments of fixed amounts at stated dates to certain persons or firms. These are standing orders. These payments would be automatically effected by the bank without the firm having to make out cheques or doing anything else once the instructions have been given to the bank. At a particular date such a payment might have been made by the bank, but the payment might not have been shown in the firm's cash book on that date. Such standing orders can only be altered by the paying firm.

There are also payments which have to be made, and where the authority to get the money is given to the firm to whom the money is to be paid, instead of giving one's bank the instructions to pay certain amounts. Instead of one's bank remembering to make the payment, the creditor can automatically charge one's bank account with the requisite amount. These are called 'direct debits'.

Writing up the Cash Book Before Attempting a Reconciliation

It will soon become obvious that in fact the best procedure is to complete entering up the cash book before attempting the reconciliation, this being done by finding out the items that are on the bank statement but not in the cash book and making entries for them in the cash book. By this means the number of adjustments needed in the reconciliation statement are reduced. However, in examinations the questions sometimes ask for the reconciliation to take place before completing the cash book entries.

If, in Exhibit 1.2, the cash book had been written up before the bank reconciliation statement had been drawn up, then the cash book and reconciliation statement would have appeared as follows in Exhibit 1.3.

Exhibit 1.3

Cash Book

19-5		£	19-5		£
Dec	27 Total b/fwd	2,000	Dec	27 Total b/fwd	1,600
,,	29 J. Potter	60	,,	28 J. Jacobs	105
,,	31 M. Johnson	220	,,	30 M. Chatwood	15
,,	31 Credit transfers		,,	31 Bank commission	20
	L. Shaw	70	,,	31 Balance c/d	610
		2,350			2,350
19-6					
Jan	1 Balance b/d	610			

Bank Reconciliation Statement as on 31 December 19-5

	£
Balance in hand as per cash book	610
Add unpresented cheque	15
	625
Less Bank lodgement not yet entered on bank statement	220
Balance in hand as per bank statement	405

Bank Overdrafts

The adjustments needed to reconcile the bank overdraft according to the firm's books with that shown in the bank's books are the complete opposite of that needed when the account is not overdrawn. It should be noticed that most banks show that an account has been overdrawn by putting the letters O/D after the amount of the balance; this is obviously the abbreviation for overdraft.

Exhibit 1.4 shows a cash book fully written up to date, and the bank reconciliation statement needed to reconcile the cash book and bank statement balances.

Exhibit 1.4

Cash Book

19-4		£	19-4		£
Dec	5 I. Howe	308	Dec	1 Balance b/f	709
,,	24 L. Mason	120	,,	9 P. Davies	140
,,	29 K. King	124	,,	27 J. Kelly	63
,,	31 G. Cumberbatch	106	,,	29 United Trust	77
,,	,, Balance c/f	380	,,	31 Bank Charges	49
		1,038			1,038

Bank Statement

19-4		Dr £	Cr £	Balance £
Dec	1 Balance b/f			709 O/D
,,	5 Cheque		308	401 O/D
,,	14 P. Davies	140		541 O/D
,,	24 Cheque		120	421 O/D
,,	29 K. King: Credit Transfer		124	297 O/D
,,	29 United Trust: Standing order	77		374 O/D
,,	31 Bank Charges	49		423 O/D

Bank Reconciliation Statement as on 31 December 19-4

	£
Overdraft as per cash book	380
Add Bank Lodgements not on bank statement	106
	486
Less Unpresented cheque	63
Overdraft per bank statement	423

Dishonoured cheques

When a cheque is received from a customer and paid into the bank, it is recorded on the debit side of the cash book. It is also shown on the bank statement as a banking by the bank. However, at a later date it may be found that the cheque has not gone through the account of the drawer, in other words his bank has failed to 'honour' the cheque, the cheque therefore is known as a 'dishonoured' cheque.

There are several possible reasons for this. Let us suppose that J. Hewitson gave us a cheque for £5,000 on May 20th 19-2. We bank it, but a few days later our bank return the cheque to us. Typical reasons are:

(a) Hewitson had put £5,000 in figures on the cheque, but had written it in words as five thousand five hundred pounds. You will have to give the cheque back to Hewitson for amendment.

(b) Normally cheques are considered 'stale' six months after the date on the cheque, in other words the banks will not 'honour' cheques over six months old. If Hewitson had put the year 19-1 on the cheque instead of 19-2, then the cheque would be returned to us by our bank.

(c) Hewitson simply did not have sufficient funds in his bank account. Suppose he had previously only got a £2,000 balance, and his bank would not allow him an overdraft. In such a case the cheque would be dishonoured. The bank would write on the cheque 'refer to drawer', and we would have to get in touch with Hewitson to see what he was going to do to put matters right.

In all of these cases the bank would automatically show the original banking as being cancelled by showing the cheque paid out of our bank account. As soon as this happens they will notify us, and we will then also show the cheque as being cancelled by a credit in the cash book. We will then debit that amount to his account.

When Hewitson originally paid his account our records would appear as:

J. Hewitson

19-2	£	19-2	£
May 1 Balance b/d	5,000	May 20 Bank	5,000

Bank Account

19-2	£
May 20 J. Hewitson	5,000

After our recording the dishonour, the records will appear as:

J. Hewitson

19-2	£	19-2	£
May 1 Balance b/d	5,000	May 20 Bank	5,000
May 25 Bank: cheque dishonoured	5,000		

Bank Account

19-2	£	19-2	£
May 20 J. Hewitson	5,000	May 25 J. Hewitson: cheque dishonoured	5,000

In other words Hewitson is once again shown as owing us £5,000.

Assignment Exercises

Note: *Questions without the suffix 'A' have answers shown at the back of this book. Questions with the suffix 'A' do not have answers in the book, so that teachers/lecturers can set the questions for classwork or homework.*

1.1. From the following details draw up a bank reconciliation statement from details as on 31 December 19-6:

	£
Cash at bank as per bank column of the Cash Book	678
Unpresented cheques	256
Cheques received and paid into the bank, but not yet entered on the bank statement	115
Credit transfers entered as banked on the bank statement but not entered in the Cash Book	56
Cash at bank as per bank statement	875

1.2A. Draw up a bank reconciliation statement, after writing the cash book up-to-date, ascertaining the balance on the bank statement, from the following as on 31 March 19-9:

	£
Cash at bank as per bank column of the cash book (Dr)	3,896
Banking made but not yet entered on bank statement	606
Bank charges on bank statement but not yet in cash book	28
Unpresented cheques C. Clarke	117
Standing order to A.B.C. Ltd entered on bank statement, but not in cash book	55
Credit transfer from A. Wood entered on bank statement, but not yet in cash book	189

1.3. The following are extracts from the cash book and the bank statement of J. Roche.

You are required to:
(a) Write the cash book up-to-date, and state the new balance as on 31 December 19-5, and
(b) Draw up a bank reconciliation statement as on 31 December 19-5.

Cash Book

19-5	Dr.	£	19-5	Cr.	£
Dec	1 Balance b/f	1,740	Dec	8 A. Dailey	349
Dec	7 T. J. Masters	88	Dec	15 R. Mason	33
Dec	22 J. Ellis	73	Dec	28 G. Small	115
Dec	31 K. Wood	249	Dec	31 Balance c/d	1,831
Dec	31 M. Barrett	178			
		2,328			2,328

Bank Statement

19-5		Dr.	Cr.	Balance
		£	£	£
Dec	1 Balance b/f			1,740
Dec	7 Cheque		88	1,828
Dec	11 A. Dailey	349		1,479
Dec	20 R. Mason	33		1,446
Dec	22 Cheque		73	1,519
Dec	31 Credit transfer: J. Walters		54	1,573
Dec	31 Bank Charges	22		1,551

1.4A. The bank columns in the cash book for June 19-7 and the bank statement for that month for C. Grant are as follows:

Cash Book

19-7	Dr	£	19-7	Cr	£
Jun	1 Balance b/f	2,379	Jun	5 D. Blackness	150
Jun	7 B. Green	158	Jun	12 J. Gray	433
Jun	16 A. Silver	93	Jun	16 B. Stephens	88
Jun	28 M. Brown	307	Jun	29 Orange Club	57
Jun	30 K. Black	624	Jun	30 Balance c/d	2,833
		3,561			3,561

Bank Statement

19-7		Dr	Cr	Balance
		£	£	£
Jun	1 Balance b/f			2,379
Jun	7 Cheque		158	2,537
Jun	8 D. Blackness	150		2,387
Jun	16 Cheque		93	2,480
Jun	17 J. Gray	433		2,047
Jun	18 B. Stephens	88		1,959
Jun	28 Cheque		307	2,266
Jun	29 U.D.T. standing order	44		2,222
Jun	30 Brown & Black: trader's credit		90	2,312
Jun	30 Bank Charges	70		2,242

You are required to:

(*a*) Write the cash book up-to-date to take the above into account, and then
(*b*) Draw up a bank reconciliation statement as on 30 June 19-7.

1.5. Following is the cash book (bank columns) of E. Flynn for December 19-3.

19-3	Dr	£	19-3	Cr	£
Dec	6 J. Hall	155	Dec	1 Balance b/f	3,872
Dec	20 C. Walters	189	Dec	10 P. Wood	206
Dec	31 P. Miller	211	Dec	19 M. Roberts	315
Dec	31 Balance c/d	3,922	Dec	29 P. Phillips	84
		4,477			4,477

The bank statement for the month is:

19-3		Dr. £	Cr. £	Balance £
Dec	1 Balance			3,872 O/D
Dec	6 Cheque		155	3,717 O/D
Dec	13 P. Wood	206		3,923 O/D
Dec	20 Cheque		189	3,734 O/D
Dec	22 M. Roberts	315		4,049 O/D
Dec	30 Mercantile: standing order	200		4,249 O/D
Dec	31 K. Saunders: trader's credit		180	4,069 O/D
Dec	31 Bank charges	65		4,134 O/D

You are required to:
(a) Write the cash book up-to-date to take the necessary items into account, and
(b) Draw up a bank reconciliation statement as on 31 December 19-3.

1.6A. The bank statement for G. Greene for the month of March 19-6 is:

19-6		Dr. £	Cr. £	Balance £
Mar	1 Balance			5,197 O/D
Mar	8 L. Tulloch	122		5,319 O/D
Mar	16 Cheque		244	5,075 O/D
Mar	20 A. Bennett	208		5,283 O/D
Mar	21 Cheque		333	4,950 O/D
Mar	31 M. Turnbull: trader's credit		57	4,893 O/D
Mar	31 B.K.S.: standing order	49		4,942 O/D
Mar	31 Bank Charges	28		4,970 O/D

The cash book for March 19-6 is:

19-6	Dr.	£	19-6	Cr.	£
Mar	16 N. Marsh	244	Mar	1 Balance b/f	5,197
Mar	21 K. Alexander	333	Mar	6 L. Tulloch	122
Mar	31 U. Sinclair	160	Mar	30 A. Bennett	208
Mar	31 Balance c/d	5,280	Mar	30 J. Shaw	490
		6,017			6,017

You are required to:
(a) Write the cash book up-to-date and
(b) Draw up a bank reconciliation statement as on 31 March 19-6.

2

Errors Not Affecting Trial Balance Agreement

In double entry it was seen that if someone followed these rules:

Every debit entry needs a corresponding credit entry
Every credit entry needs a corresponding debit entry

and entered up his books using these rules, then when he extracted the trial balance its totals would agree, i.e. it would 'balance'.

Suppose he correctly entered cash sales £70 to the debit of the cash book, but did not enter the £70 to the credit of the sales account. If this was the only error in the books, the trial balance totals would differ by £70. However, there are certain kinds of errors which would not affect the agreement of the trial balance totals, and we will now look at in this chapter. These are:

1. Errors of omission − where a transaction is completely omitted from the books. If we sold £90 goods to J. Brewer, but did not enter it in either the sales or Brewer's personal account, the trial balance would still 'balance'.

2. Errors of commission − this type is where the correct amount is entered but in the wrong person's account, e.g. where a sale of £11 to C. Green is entered in the account of K. Green. It will be noted that the correct class of account was used, both the accounts concerned being personal accounts.

3. Errors of principle − where an item is entered in the wrong class of account, e.g. if a fixed asset such as a motor van is debited to an expenses account such as motor expenses account.

4. Compensating errors − where errors cancel out each other. If the sales account was added up to be £10 too much and the purchases account also added up to be £10 too much, then these two errors would cancel out in the trial balance. This is because totals both of the debit side of the trial balance and of the credit side will be £10 too much.

5. Errors of original entry − where the original figure is incorrect, yet double-entry is still observed using this incorrect figure. An instance of this could be where there were sales of £150 goods but an error is made in calculating the sales invoice. If it was calculated as £130, and £130 was credited as sales and £130 debited to the personal account of the customer, the trial balance would still 'balance'.

6. Complete reversal of entries − where the correct accounts are used but each item is shown on the wrong side of the account. Suppose we had paid a cheque to D. Williams for £200, the double-entry of which is Cr Bank £200, Dr D. Williams £200. In error it is entered as Cr D. Williams £200, Dr Bank £200. The trial balance totals will still agree.

Correction of Errors

When these errors are found they have to be corrected. The entries have to be made in the double entry accounts. In addition, an entry should be made in The Journal, to explain the correction. We can now look at one of these for each type of error.

1. Error of Omission

The sale of goods, £59 to E. George, has been completely omitted from the books. We must correct this by entering the sale in the books.

The Journal

	Dr	Cr
	£	£
E. George	59	
Sales account		59
Correction of omission of Sales Invoice No.		
from sales journal.		

2. Error of Commission

A purchase of goods, £44 from C. Simons, was entered in error in C. Simpson's account. To correct this, it must be cancelled out of C. Simpson's account, and then entered where it should be in C. Simon's account. The double-entry will be:

C. Simpson

19-5	£	19-5	£
Sept 30 C. Simons: Error corrected	44	Sept 30 Purchases	44

C. Simons

		19-5	£
		Sept 30 Purchases: Entered originally in C. Simpson's A/c	44

The Journal entry will be:

The Journal

	Dr	Cr
	£	£
C. Simpson	44	
C. Simons		44

Purchase Invoice No. . . . . . . entered in wrong personal
account, now corrected

3. Error of Principle

The purchase of a machine, £200, is debited to Purchases account instead
of being debited to a Machinery account. We therefore cancel the item out
of the Purchases account by crediting that account. It is then entered where
it should be by debiting the Machinery account.

The Journal

	Dr	Cr
	£	£
Machinery account	200	
Purchases account		200

Correction of error purchase of fixed asset debited to
purchases account.

4. Compensating Error

The sales account is overcast by £200, as also is the wages account. The
trial balance therefore still 'balances'. This assumes that these are the only
two errors found in the books.

The Journal

	Dr	Cr
	£	£
Sales Account	200	
Wages Account		200

Correction of overcasts of £200 each in the sales account
and the wages account which compensated for each
other.

5. Error of Original Entry

A sale of £98 to A. Smailes was entered in the books as £89. It needs another
£9 of sales entering now.

The Journal

	Dr	Cr
	£	£
A. Smailes	9	
Sales Account		9

Correction of error whereby sales were understated by
£9.

6. Complete Reversal of Entries

A payment of cash of £16 to M. Dickson was entered on the receipts side
of the cash book in error and credited to M. Dickson's account. This is
somewhat more difficult to adjust. First must come the amount needed to
cancel the error, then comes the actual entry itself. Because of this, the
correcting entry is double the actual amount first recorded. We can now
look at why this is so:

    What we should have had:

Cash

		£
	M. Dickson	16

M. Dickson

	£	
Cash	16	

Was entered as:

Cash

	£	
M. Dickson	16	

M. Dickson

		£
	Cash	16

We can now see that we have to enter double the original amount to correct
the error.

Cash

	£		£
M. Dickson	16	M. Dickson (error corrected)	32

M. Dickson

	£		£
Cash (error corrected)	32	Cash	16

Overall, when corrected, the cash account showing £16 debit and £32 credit means a net credit of £16. Similarly, Dickson's account shows £32 debit and £16 credit, a net debit of £16. As the final (net) answer is the same as what should have been entered originally, the error is now corrected. The Journal entry appears:

The Journal

	Dr	Cr
	£	£
M. Dickson	32	
Cash		32

Payment of cash £16 debited to cash and credited to M.
Dickson in error on . . . . Error now corrected.

Casting

You will often notice the use of the expression 'to cast', which means 'to add up'. Overcasting means incorrectly adding up a column of figures to give an answer which is greater than it should be. Undercasting means incorrectly adding up a column of figures to give an answer which is less than it should be.

Assignment Exercises

2.1. Show the journal entries necessary to correct the following errors:

(a) A sale of goods £678 to J. Harris had been entered in J. Hart's account.
(b) The purchase of a machine on credit from L. Pyle for £4,390 had been completely omitted from our books.
(c) The purchase of a motor van £3,800 had been entered in error in the Motor Expenses account.
(d) A sale of £221 to E. Fitzwilliam had been entered in the books, both debit and credit, as £212.
(e) Commission received £257 had been entered in error in the Sales Account.
(f) A receipt of cash from T. Heath £77 had been entered on the credit side of the cash book and the debit side of T. Heath's account.
(g) A purchase of goods £189 had been entered in error on the debit side of the drawings account.
(h) Discounts Allowed £366 had been entered in error on the debit side of the Discounts Received account.

2.2A. Show the journal entries needed to correct the following errors:

(*a*) Purchases £699 on credit from K. Ward had been entered in H. Wood's account.

(*b*) A cheque of £189 paid for advertisements had been entered in the cash column of the cash book instead of in the bank column.

(*c*) Sale of goods £443 on credit to B. Gordon had been entered in error in B. Gorton's account.

(*d*) Purchase of goods on credit K. Isaacs £89 entered in two places in error as £99.

(*e*) Cash paid to H. Moore £89 entered on the debit side of the cash book and the credit side of H. Moore's account.

(*f*) A sale of fittings £500 had been entered in the Sales Account.

(*g*) Cash withdrawn from bank £100, had been entered in the cash column on the credit side of the cash book, and in the bank column on the debit side.

(*h*) Purchase of goods £428 has been entered in error in the Fittings Account.

3

Suspense Accounts and Errors

In Chapter 2 errors were looked at where the trial balance totals were not thrown out of agreement. However, there are many errors which will mean that the trial balance will not 'balance'.

We can now look at some of these. It is assumed that there are no compensating errors.

1. Incorrect additions, either totals too great or too small, in any account.

2. Entering an item on only one side of the books. For instance, if the debit entry is made but not the credit entry, or a credit entry but no debit entry.

3. Entering one figure on the debit side of the books but another figure on the credit side. For instance, if £80 for cash received from M. Brown is entered in the cash book, but £280 is entered in respect of it in Brown's account.

Every effort should be made to find the errors immediately, but especially in examinations it is assumed that for one reason or other this is not possible. Making this assumption, the trial balance totals should be made to agree with each other by inserting the amount of the difference between the two sides in a Suspense Account. This occurs in Exhibit 3.1 where there is a £40 difference.

Exhibit 3.1

Trial Balance as on 31 December 19-5

	Dr	Cr
	£	£
Totals after all the accounts have been listed	100,000	99,960
Suspense Account		40
	100,000	100,000

Suspense Account

		19-5	£
		Dec 31 Difference per	
		trial balance	40

If the errors are not found before the final accounts are prepared, the balance of £40, being a credit balance, will be shown on the capital and liabilities side of the balance sheet. This, however, should never occur if the figure is a large one: the error must always be found. If the item is small, however, it may be added to current liabilities if it is a credit balance, or to current assets if it is a debit balance.

When the error(s) are found they must be corrected. For each correction an entry must be made in The Journal describing the correction.

Assume that the error of £40 as shown in Exhibit 3.1 is found in the following year on 31 March 19-6. The error was that the sales account was undercast by £40. The balance on the suspense account should now be cancelled. The sales account should be credited to increase the account that had been understated. The accounts will appear:

Suspense Account

19-6	£	19-5	£
Mar 31 Sales	40	Dec 31 Difference per	
		trial balance	40

Sales

		19-6	£
		Mar 31 Suspense	40

This can be shown in journal form as:

The Journal

	Dr	Cr
19-6	£	£
Mar 31 Suspense	40	
Sales		40
Correction of undercasting of sales by £40 in last year's accounts		

We can now look at Exhibit 3.2 where the suspense account difference was caused by more than one error.

Exhibit 3.2

The trial balance at 31 December 19-7 showed a difference of £77, being a shortage on the debit side. A suspense account is opened, and the difference of £77 is entered on the debit side of the account.

On 28 February 19-8 all the errors from the previous year were found.

(*a*) A cheque of £150 paid to L. Bond had been correctly entered in the cash book, but had not been entered in Bond's account.

(*b*) The purchases account had been undercast by £20.

(*c*) A cheque of £93 received from K. Smith had been correctly entered in the cash book, but had not been entered in Smith's account.

These are corrected as follows:

Suspense Account

19-8		£	19-8		£
Jan 1	Balance b/fwd	77	Feb 28	L. Bond	150
Feb 28	K. Smith	93	,, 28	Purchases	20
		170			170

L. Bond

19-8		£
Feb 28	Suspense	150

Purchases

19-8		£
Feb 28	Suspense	20

K. Smith

	19-8		£
	Feb 28	Suspense	93

The Journal		*Dr*	*Cr*
19-8		£	£
Feb 28	L. Bond	150	
	Suspense		150
	Cheque paid omitted from Bond's account		
Feb 28	Purchases	20	
	Suspense		20
	Undercasting of purchases by £20 in last year's accounts		
Feb 28	Suspense	93	
	K. Smith		93
	Cheque received omitted from Smith's account		

Only those errors which do throw the trial balance totals out of balance have to be corrected via the Suspense Account.

The Effect of Errors on Reported Profits

When errors are not discovered until a later period, it will often be found that the gross and/or net profits will have been incorrectly stated for the earlier period when the errors were made but had not been found.

Exhibit 3.3 shows a set of accounts in which errors have been made.

Exhibit 3.3

K. Black

Trading and Profit and Loss Account for the year ended 31 December 19-5

	£	£
Sales		8,000
Less Cost of Goods Sold:		
Opening Stock	500	
Add Purchases	6,100	
	6,600	
Less Closing Stock	700	5,900
Gross Profit		2,100
Add Discounts Received		250
		2,350
Less Expenses:		
Rent	200	
Insurance	120	
Lighting and Heating	180	
Depreciation	250	750
		1,600

Balance Sheet as at 31 December 19-5

	£	£
Fixed Assets		
Fixtures	2,200	
Less Depreciation to date	800	1,400
Current Assets		
Stock	700	
Debtors	600	
Bank	340	
	1,640	
Less Current Liabilities		
Creditors	600	
Working Capital		1,040
Suspense Account		60
		2,500

Financed by:		
Capital		
Balance as at 1.1.19-5	1,800	
Add Net Profit	1,600	
	3,400	
Less Drawings	900	2,500
		2,500

Now suppose that there had only been one error found on 31 March 19-6, and that was that sales had been overcast £60. The correction appears as:

Suspense

19-6		£	19-6	£
Jan 1 Balance b/d		60	Mar 31 Sales	60

Sales

19-6	£
Mar 31 Sales	60

The Journal

	Dr	Cr
19-6	£	£
Mar 31 Sales	60	
Suspense		60

Overcasting of sales by £60 in last year's accounts.

If a statement of corrected net profit for the year ended 31 December 19-5 is drawn up it will be shown in Exhibit 3.4.

Exhibit 3.4

K. Black

Statement of Corrected Net Profit for the year ended 31 December 19-5

	£
Net profit per the accounts	1,600
Less Sales overcast	60
Corrected net profit for the year	1,540

If instead there had been 4 errors in the accounts of K. Black, found on 31 March 19-6, their correction can now be seen. Assume that the net difference had also been £60.

(a)	Sales overcast by	£70
(b)	Rent undercast by	£40
(c)	Cash received from a debtor entered in the Cash Book only	£50
(d)	A purchase of £59 is entered in the books, debit and credit entries, as £95	

The entries in the suspense account, and the journal entries will be as follows:

Suspense

19-6		£	19-6		£
Jan	1 Balance b/d	60	Mar 31 Sales		70
Mar 31 Debtor		50	,, 31 Rent		40
		110			110

The Journal

		Dr	Cr
19-6		£	£
Mar 31 Sales		70	
	Suspense		70
	Sales overcast of £70 in 19-5		
Mar 31 Rent		40	
	Suspense		40
	Rent expense undercast by £40 in 19-5		
Mar 31 Suspense		50	
	Debtor's account		50
	Cash received omitted from debtor's account in 19-5		
Mar 31 Creditor's account		36	
	Purchases		36
	Credit purchase of £59 entered both as debit and credit as £95 in 19-5		

N.B. Note that (*d*), the correction of the understatement of purchases, does not pass through the suspense account.

Exhibit 3.5 shows the statement of corrected net profit.

Exhibit 3.5

K. Black

Statement of Corrected Net Profit for the year ended 31 December 19-5

		£
Net profit per the accounts		1,600
Add Purchases overstated		36
		1,636
Less Sales overcast	70	
Rent undercast	40	110
Corrected net profit for the year		1,526

Error (*c*), the cash not posted to a debtor's account, did not affect profit calculations.

Assignment Exercises

3.1. Your book-keeper extracted a trial balance on 31 December 19-4 which failed to agree by £330, a shortage on the credit side of the trial balance. A Suspense Account was opened for the difference.

In January 19-5 the following errors made in 19-4 were found:

1. Sales day book had been undercast by £100.
2. Sales of £250 to J. Cantrell had been debited in error to J. Cochrane's account.
3. Rent account had been undercast by £70.
4. Discounts Received account had been undercast by £300.
5. The sale of a motor vehicle at book value had been credited in error to Sales Account £360.

You are required to:

(a) Show the journal entries necessary to correct the errors.
(b) Draw up the suspense account after the errors described have been corrected.
(c) If the net profit had previously been calculated at £7,900 for the year ended 31 December 19-4, show the calculation of the corrected net profit.

3.2A. You have extracted a trial balance and drawn up accounts for the year ended 31 December 19-6. There was a shortage of £292 on the credit side of the trial balance, a suspense account being opened for that amount.

During 19-7 the following errors made in 19-6 were located:

1. £55 received from sales of old Office Equipment has been entered in the sales account.
2. Purchases day book had been overcast by £60.
3. A private purchase of £115 had been included in the business purchases.
4. Bank charges £38 entered in the cash book have not been posted to the bank charges account.
5. A sale of goods to B. Cross £690 was correctly entered in the sales book but entered in the personal account as £960.

You are required to:

(a) Show the requisite journal entries to correct the errors.
(b) Write up the suspense account showing the correction of the errors.
(c) The net profit originally calculated for 19-6 was £11,370. Show your calculation of the correct figure.

3.3. F. W. Low's trial balance at 31 December 19-4 did not agree. He opened a suspense account for the difference, prepared his trading and profit and loss account and drew up the following balance sheet:

Balance Sheet

	£	£		£	£
Fixed Assets			Capital (1.1.19-4)	6,093	
Furniture and Fittings	470		Add Net Profit	2,970	
Motor Vans	1,430	1,900		9,063	
Current Assets			Less Drawings	2,500	6,563
Stock	3,146		Sundry creditors		2,475
Sundry Debtors	2,142		Suspense Account		12
Cash in hand and					
Balance at Bank	1,862	7,150			
		9,050			9,050

The following errors which accounted for the difference in the trial balance were subsequently discovered:

1. Bank charges £7 had been entered in the cash book but the double entry had not been completed.
2. Loss on the sale of an old motor van £12 had been correctly entered in the motor van account but had been charged to depreciation account as £21.
3. A cheque £86 for the purchase of a new typewriter had been correctly entered in the cash book but entered in the furniture and fittings account as £66.
4. A sale of goods to F. J. Bell £46 was correctly entered in the sales book but was posted to Bell's account as £64.
5. A credit note £17 received from R. Tate, a creditor, had been correctly entered in the subsidiary records but posted to Tate's account as £19.
6. The debt balance of £122 on R. S. Muir's account in the sales ledger, at 31 December 19-4 had been carried down as £132 and included in the trial balance at this figure.

You are required:
(a) To make the journal entries now required to correct the above errors;
(b) To show your calculation of the correct net profit in account form;
(c) To draw up a corrected balance sheet as at 31 December 19-4.

3.4A. Black and Co. have produced a trial balance for the year ended 31 March 19-0, which does not balance. A suspense account was opened for the difference. An examination of the company's books in the following year disclosed the following errors:

1. An invoice from J. Jones amounting to £100, for goods purchased, had been omitted from the purchase day book but has been posted direct to purchases account in the nominal ledger but not to Jones' account in the purchase ledger.
2. The sales day book had been undercast by £240 and posted to the sales account accordingly.
3. Discount allowed for the month of March amounting to £489 has not been posted to the nominal ledger.

4. Goods received from CRT Ltd. on 31 March 19-0, costing £2,410, have been included in stock but the invoice has not yet been received.

5. A cheque for £192 received from J. Crank, a debtor, has been posted direct to the sales account in the nominal ledger.

6. Sales account in the nominal ledger has been credited with a credit note for £250 being trade-in allowance given on a company van.

You are required:

(a) To give the journal entries, where necessary, to correct the errors, or if no journal entry is required, state how they will be corrected.

(b) To prepare a statement showing the effect the corrections would have on the company's profit for the year. The net profit before the corrections are made is £20,000.

(c) All the errors have now been found. What was the opening balance on the Suspense Account?

4

Control Accounts

When all the accounts were kept in one ledger a trial balance could be extracted as a test of the arithmetical accuracy of the accounts. It must be remembered that certain errors were not revealed by such a trial balance. If the trial balance totals disagreed, the number of entries for such a small business being relatively few, the books could easily and quickly be checked so as to locate the errors. However, when the firm has grown and the accounting work has been so subdivided that there are several or many ledgers, a trial balance the totals of which did not agree could result in a great deal of unnecessary checking before the errors were found. What is required in fact is a type of trial balance for each ledger, and this requirement is met by the Control Account. Thus it is only the ledgers whose control accounts do not balance that need detailed checking to find errors.

The principle on which the control account is based is simple, and is as follows. If the opening balance of an account is known, together with information of the additions and deductions entered in the account, the closing balance can be calculated. Applying this to a complete ledger, the total of opening balances together with the additions and deductions during the period should give the total of closing balances. This can be illustrated by reference to a sales ledger:

	£
Total of Opening Balances, 1 January 19-6	3,000
Add total of entries which have increased the balances	9,500
	12,500
Less total of entries which have reduced the balances	8,000
Total of closing balances should be	4,500

Because totals are used the accounts are often known as Total Accounts. Thus a control account for a sales ledger could be known either as a Sales Ledger Control Account or as a Total Debtors Account. Similarly, a control account for a purchases ledger could be known either as a Purchases Ledger Control Account or as a Total Creditors Account.

It must be emphasized that control accounts are not necessarily a part of the double entry system. They are merely arithmetical proofs performing the same function as a trial balance to a particular ledger.

It is usual to find them in the same form as an account, with the totals of the debit entries in the ledger on the left-hand side of the control account, and the totals of the various credit entries in the ledger on the right-hand side of the control account.

Exhibit 4.1 shows an example of a sales ledger control account for a ledger in which all the entries are arithmetically correct.

Exhibit 4.1

	£
Sales Ledger No. 3	
Debit balances on 1 January 19-6	1,894
Total credit sales for the month	10,290
Cheques received from customers in the months	7,284
Cash received from customers in the month	1,236
Returns Inwards from customers during the month	296
Debit balances on 31 January as extracted from the sales ledger	3,368

Sales Ledger Control

19-6		£	19-6		£
Jan	1 Balances b/f	1,894	Jan	31 Bank	7,284
,,	31 Sales	10,290	,,	,, Cash	1,236
			,,	,, Returns Inwards	296
			,,	,, Balances c/d	3,368
		12,184			12,184

On the other hand Exhibit 4.2 shows an example where an error is found to exist in a purchases ledger. The ledger will have to be checked in detail, the error found, and the control account then corrected.

Exhibit 4.2

	£
Purchases Ledger No. 2	
Credit balances on 1 January 19-6	3,890
Cheques paid to suppliers during the month	3,620
Returns outwards to suppliers in the month	95
Bought from suppliers in the month	4,936
Credit balances on 31 January as extracted from the purchases ledger	5,151

Purchases Ledger Control

19-6		£	19-6		£
Jan 31	Bank	3,620	Jan 1	Balances b/f	3,890
,, ,,	Returns Outwards	95	,, 31	Purchases	4,936
,, ,,	Balances c/d	5,151			
		8,866*			8,826*

*There is a £40 error in the purchases ledger.

Other Advantages of Control Accounts

Control accounts have merits other than that of locating errors. Normally the control accounts are under the charge of a responsible official, and fraud is made more difficult because transfers made (in an effort) to disguise frauds will have to pass the scrutiny of this person.

For management purposes the balances on the control account can always be taken to equal debtors and creditors without waiting for an extraction of individual balances. Management control is thereby aided, for the speed at which information is obtained is one of the prerequisities of efficient control.

Exhibit 4.3

Sales Book

Date	Details	Total		Ledgers	
			A–F	G–O	P–Z
19-6		£	£	£	£
Feb 1	J. Archer	58	58		
,, 3	G. Gaunt	103		103	
,, 4	T. Brown	116	116		
,, 8	C. Dunn	205	205		
,, 10	A. Smith	16			16
,, 12	P. Smith	114			114
,, 15	D. Owen	88		88	
,, 18	B. Blake	17	17		
,, 22	T. Green	1,396		1,396	
,, 27	C. Males	48		48	
		2,161	396	1,635	130

The Sources of Information for Control Accounts

To obtain the totals of entries made in the various ledgers, analytical journals and cash books are often used. Thus a firm with sales ledgers split on an alphabetical basis might have a sales book as per Exhibit 4.3. The totals of the A–F column will be the total sales figures for the sales ledger A–F control account, the total of the G−O column for the G−O control account and so on.

In electronic or machine accounting the control account is usually built in as an automatic by-product of the system.

Other Transfers

Transfers to bad debts accounts will have to be recorded in the sales ledger control account as they involve entries in the sales ledgers.

Similarly, a contra account whereby the same firm is both a supplier and a customer, and inter-indebtedness is set off, will also need entering in the control accounts. An example of this follows: G. Carter has supplied the firm with £880 goods, and the firm has sold him £600 goods. In the firm's books the £600 owing by him is set off against the amount owing to him, leaving a net amount owing to Carter of £280.

Sales Ledger
G. Carter

	£
Sales	600

Purchases Ledger
G. Carter

	£
Purchases	880

The set-off now takes place.

Sales Ledger
G. Carter

	£		£
Sales	600	Set-off: Purchases Ledger	600

Purchases Ledger
G. Carter

	£		£
Set-off: Sales Ledger	600	Purchases	880
Balance c/d	280		
	880		880
		Balance b/d	280

The transfer of the £600 will therefore appear on the credit side of the sales ledger control account and on the debit side of the purchases ledger control account.

Exhibit 4.4 shows a worked example of a more complicated control account.

Exhibit 4.4

19-6		£
Aug	1 Sales ledger − debit balances	3,816
,,	1 Sales ledger − credit balances	22
,,	31 Transactions for the month:	
	Cash received	104
	Cheques received	6,239
	Sales	7,090
	Bad Debts written off	306
	Discounts allowed	298
	Returns inwards	164
	Cash refunded to a customer who had overpaid his account	37
	Dishonoured cheques	29
	At the end of the month:	
	Sales ledger − debit balances	3,879
	Sales ledger − credit balances	40

Sales Ledger Control Account

19-6		£	19-6		£
Aug	1 Balances b/d	3,816	Aug	1 Balances b/d	22
,,	31 Sales	7,090	,,	31 Cash	104
,,	,, Cash refunded	37	,,	,, Bank	6,239
,,	,, Cash; dishonoured		,,	,, Bad debts	306
	cheques	29	,,	,, Discounts allowed	298
,,	,, Balances c/d	40	,,	,, Returns inwards	164
			,,	,, Balances c/d	3,879
		11,012			11,012

Control Accounts as Part of Double Entry

The control accounts may be treated as being an integral part of the double entry system, the balances of the control accounts being taken for the purpose of extracting a trial balance. In this case the personal accounts are being used as subsidiary records.

Self-Balancing Ledgers and Adjustment Accounts

Because ledgers which have a control account system are proved to be correct as far as the double entry is concerned they are sometimes called self-balancing ledgers. The control accounts where such terminology is in use are then often called 'Adjustment Accounts'.

Assignment Exercises

4.1. You are required to prepare a sales ledger control account from the following for the month of May:

19-6		£
May 1 Sales Ledger Balances		4,936
Totals for May:		
Sales Journal		49,916
Returns Inwards Journal		1,139
Cheques and Cash received from customers		46,490
Discounts allowed		1,455
May 31 Sales Ledger Balances		5,768

4.2. You are required to prepare a purchases ledger control account from the following for the month of June. The balance of the account is to be taken as the amount of creditors as on 30 June.

19-6		£
June 1 Purchases Ledger Balances		3,676
Totals for June:		
Purchases Journal		42,257
Returns Outwards Journal		1,098
Cheques paid to suppliers		38,765
Discounts received from suppliers		887
June 30 Purchases Ledger Balances		?

4.3. The trial balance of Barrel & Cask Ltd. revealed a difference in the books. In order that the error(s) could be located it was decided to prepare purchases and sales ledger control accounts.

From the following prepare the control accounts and show where an error may have been made:

19-5		£
Jan 1 Purchases Ledger Balances		21,926
Sales Ledger Balances		37,404
Totals for the year 19-5:		
Purchases Journal		302,196
Sales Journal		401,384
Returns Outwards Journal		5,044
Returns Inwards Journal		9,212
Cheques paid to suppliers		290,600
Petty Cash paid to suppliers		99
Cheques and Cash received from customers		374,216
Discounts allowed		10,984
Discounts received		4,216
Bad Debts written off		605
Customers' cheques dishonoured		88
Balances on the Sales Ledger set off		
against balances in the Purchases Ledger		2,916

Dec 31 The list of balances from the purchases ledger shows a total of £21,247 and that from the sales ledger a total of £40,643.

4.4A. There is an error in the trial balance of Jug & Bottle Ltd. The accountant tells you that it can be found in either the sales or the purchases ledger. From the following information ascertain the location and the amount of the error.

	£
19-8	
Sept 1 Sales Ledger Balances	109,872
Purchases Ledger Balances	107,352
Totals for the month:	
Sales Journal	99,832
Purchases Journal	84,514
Returns Inwards Journal	2,278
Returns Outwards Journal	2,196
Cheques paid to suppliers	77,530
Cash received from customers	70
Cheques received from customers	93,910
Discounts allowed	2,910
Bad Debts written off	198
Discounts received	1,774
Customers' cheques dishonoured	830
Balance on the Sales Ledger set off against balances in the Purchases Ledger	518
Sept 30 Sales Ledger Balances	110,867
Sales Ledger: Credit Balances	47
Purchases Ledger Balances	109,848

5

Single Entry and Incomplete Records

For every small shopkeeper, market stall or other small business to keep its books using a full double-entry system would be ridiculous. First of all, a large number of the owners of such firms would not know how to write up double-entry records, even if they wanted to.

It is far more likely that they would enter down details of a transaction once only, that is why we would call it single-entry. Also many of them would have failed to record every transaction, and these therefore would be incomplete – the reason why we would call these 'incomplete records'.

It is perhaps only fair to remember that accounting is after all supposed to be an aid to management, it is not something to be done as an end in itself. Therefore, many small firms, especially retail stores, can have all the information they want by merely keeping a cash book and having some form of record, not necessarily in double entry form, of their debtors and creditors.

Probably the way to start is to recall that, barring an introduction of extra cash or resources into the firm, the only way that capital can be increased is by making profits. Therefore, the most elementary way of calculating profits is by comparing capital at the end of last period with that at the end of this period. If it is known that the capital at the end of 19-4 was £2,000 and that at the end of 19-5 it has grown to £3,000, and that there have been no drawings during the period, nor has there been any fresh introduction of capital, the net profit must therefore be £3,000−£2,000 = £1,000. If on the other hand the drawings had been £700, the profits must have been £1,700 calculated thus:

Last year's Capital+Profits−Drawings=this year's Capital
£2,000 +   ?   −£700   =   £3,000

Filling in the missing figure by normal arithmetical deduction:

£2,00+£1,700−£700=£3,000.

Exhibit 5.1 shows the calculation of profit where insufficient information is available to draft a trading and profit and loss account, only information of assets and liabilities being known.

Exhibit 5.1

H. Taylor provides information as to his assets and liabilities at certain dates.

At 31 December 19-5. *Assets:* Motor van £1,000; Fixtures £700; Stock £850; Debtors £950; Bank £1,100; Cash £100. *Liabilities:* Creditors £200; Loan from J. Ogden £600.

At 31 December 19-6. *Assets:* Motor van (after depreciation) £800; Fixtures (after depreciation) £630; Stock £990; Debtors £1,240; Bank £1,700; Cash £200. *Liabilities:* Creditors £300; Loan from J. Ogden £400; Drawings were £900.

First of all a Statement of Affairs is drawn up as at 31 December 19-5. This is the name given to what would have been called a balance sheet if it had been drawn up from a set of records. The capital is the difference between the assets and liabilities.

Statement of Affairs as at 31 December 19-5

	£	£
Fixed Assets		
Motor Van		1,000
Fixtures		700
		1,700
Current Assets		
Stock	850	
Debtors	950	
Bank	1,100	
Cash	100	
	3,000	
Less Current Liabilities		
Creditors	200	
Working Capital		2,800
		4,500
Financed by		
Capital (difference)		3,900
Long Term Liability		
Loan from J. Ogden		600
		4,500

A statement of affairs is now drafted up at the end of 19-6. The formula of Opening Capital + Profit − Drawings = Closing Capital is then used to deduce the figure of profit.

Statement of Affairs as at 31 December 19-6

		£	£
Fixed Assets			
Motor van			800
Fixtures			630
			1,430
Current Assets			
Stock		990	
Debtors		1,240	
Bank		1,700	
Cash		200	
		4,130	
Less Current Liabilities			
Creditors		300	3,830
			5,260
Financed by:			
Capital			
Balance at 1.1.19-6		3,900	
Add Net Profit	(C)	?	
	(B)	?	
Less Drawings		900 (A)	?
Long Term Loan			
Loan from J. Ogden			400

Deduction of Net Profit.
Closing Capital + Net Profit − Drawings = Closing Capital. Finding the missing figures (A) (B) and (C) by deduction,
(A) is the figure is needed to make the balance sheet totals equal, i.e. £4,860.
(B) is therefore £4,860 + £900 = £5,760.
(C) is therefore £5,760 − £3,900 = £1,860.
To check:

Capital		3,900		
Add Net Profit	(C)	1,860		
	(B)	5,760		
Less Drawings		900	(A)	4,860

Obviously, this method of calculating profit is very unsatisfactory as it is much more informative when a trading and profit and loss account can be drawn up. Therefore, whenever possible the comparisons of capital method of ascertaining profit should be avoided and a full set of final accounts drawn up from the available records. When doing this it must be remembered that the principles of calculating profit are still those as described in the compilation of a double entry trading and profit and loss account. Assume that there are two businesses identical in every way as to sales, purchases, expenses, assets and liabilities, the only difference being that one proprietor keeps a full double entry set of books while the other keeps his on a single entry basis. Yet when each of them draws up his final accounts they should be identical in every way. Exhibit 5.2 shows the method for drawing up final accounts from single entry records.

Exhibit 5.2

The accountant discerns the following details of transactions for J. Frank's retail store for the year ended 31 December 19-5:

1. The sales are mostly on a credit basis. No records of sales have been made, but £10,000 has been received, £9,500 by cheque and £500 by cash, from persons to whom goods have been sold.
2. Amount paid by cheque to suppliers during the year = £7,200.
3. Expenses paid during the year: By cheque, Rent £200, General Expenses £180; by cash, Rent £50.
4. J. Frank took £10 cash per week (for 52 weeks) as drawings.
5. Other information is available:

	At 31.12.19-4 £	At 31.12.19-5 £
Debtors	1,100	1,320
Creditors for goods	400	650
Rent Owing	–	50
Bank Balance	1,130	3,050
Cash Balance	80	10
Stock	1,590	1,700

6. The only fixed asset consists of fixtures which were valued at 31 December 19-4 at £800. These are to be depreciated at 10 per cent per annum.

The first step is to draw up a statement of affairs as at 31 December 19-4.

Statement of Affairs as at 31 December 19-4

	£	£
Fixed Assets		
Fixtures		800
Current Assets		
Stock	1,590	
Debtors	1,100	
Bank	1,130	
Cash	80	
	3,900	
Less Current Liabilities		
Creditors	400	
Working Capital		3,500
		4,300
Financed by:		
Capital (difference)		4,300
		4,300

All of these opening figures are then taken into account when drawing up the final accounts for 19-5.

Next a cash and bank summary is drawn up:

	Cash	Bank		Cash	Bank
	£	£		£	£
Balances 31.12.19-4	80	1,130	Suppliers		7,200
Receipts from debtors	500	9,500	Rent	50	200
			General Expenses		180
			Drawings	520	
			Balances 31.12.19-5	10	3,050
	580	10,630		580	10,630

J. Franks

Trading and Profit and Loss Account for the year ended 31 December 19-5

	£	£
Sales (note 2)		10,220
Less Cost of Goods Sold:		
Stock at 1.1.19-5	1,590	
Add Purchases (note 1)	7,450	
	9,040	
Less Stock at 31.12.19-5	1,700	7,340
Gross Profit		2,880
Less Expenses:		
Rent (note 3)	300	
General Expenses	180	
Depreciation: Fixtures	80	560
Net Profit		2,320

Note 1. In double entry, purchases means the goods that have been bought in the period irrespective of whether they have been paid for or not during the period. The figure of payments to suppliers must therefore be adjusted to find the figures of purchases.

	£
Paid during the year	7,200
Less payments made, but which were for goods which were purchases in a previous year (creditors 31.12.19-4)	400
	6,800
Add purchases made in this year, but for which payment has not yet been made (creditors 31.12.19-5)	650
Goods bought in this year, i.e. purchases	7,450

The same answer could have been obtained if the information had been shown in the form of a total creditors account, the figure of purchases being the amount required to make the account totals agree.

Total Creditors

	£		£
Cash paid to suppliers	7,200	Balances b/f	400
Balances c/d	650	Purchases (missing figures)	7,450
	7,850		7,850

Note 2. The sales figure will only equal receipts where all the sales are for cash. Therefore, the receipts figures need adjusting to find sales. This can be done by constructing a total debtors account, the sales figures being the one needed to make the totals agree.

Total Debtors

	£		£
Balances b/f	1,100	Receipts: Cash	500
		Cheque	9,500
Sales (missing figures)	10,220	Balances c/d	1,320
	11,320		11,320

Note 3. Expenses are those consumed during the year irrespective of when payment is made. A rent account can be drawn up, the missing figure being that of rent for the year.

Rent Account

	£		£
Cheques	200	Rent (missing figure)	300
Cash	50		
Accrued c/d	50		
	300		300

The balance sheet can now be drawn up as in Exhibit 5.3.

Exhibit 5.3

Balance Sheet as at 31 December 19-5

Fixed Assets	£	£	£
Fixtures at 1.1.19-5		800	
Less Depreciation		80	720
Current Assets			
Stock		1,700	
Debtors		1,320	
Bank		3,050	
Cash		10	
		6,080	
Less Current Liabilities			
Creditors	650		
Rent Owing	50	700	
Working Capital			5,380
Financed by:			6,100
Capital			
Balance 1.1.19-5 (per Opening Statement of Affairs)			4,300
Add Net Profit			2,320
			6,620
Less Drawings			520
			6,100

Incomplete Records and Missing Figures

In practice, part of the information relating to cash receipts or payments is often missing. If the missing information is in respect of one type of payment, then it is normal to assume that the missing figure is the amount required to make both totals agree in the cash column of the cash and bank summary. This does not happen with bank items owing to the fact that another copy of the bank statement can always be obtained from the bank. Exhibit 5.4 shows an example when the drawings figure is unknown, Exhibit 5.5 is an example where the receipts from debtors had not been recorded.

Exhibit 5.4

The following information of cash and bank receipts and payments is available:

	Cash	Bank
	£	£
Cash paid into the bank during the year	5,500	
Receipts from debtors	7,250	800
Paid to suppliers	320	4,930
Drawings during the year	?	–
Expenses paid	150	900
Balances at 1.1.19-5	35	1,200
Balances at 31.12.19-5	50	1,670

	Cash	Bank		Cash	Bank
	£	£		£	£
Balances 1.1.19-5	35	1,200	Banking C	5,500	
Received from debtors	7,250	800	Suppliers	320	4,930
Bankings C		5,500	Expenses	150	900
			Drawings	?	
			Balances 31.12.19-5	50	1,670
	7,285	7,500		7,285	7,500

The amount needed to make the two sides of the cash columns agree is £1,265. Therefore, this is taken as the figure of drawings.

Exhibit 5.5

Information of cash and bank transactions is available as follows:

	Cash	Bank
	£	£
Receipts from debtors	?	6,080
Cash withdrawn from the bank for business use (this is the amount which is used besides cash receipts from debtors to pay drawings and expenses)		920
Paid to suppliers		5,800
Expenses paid	640	230
Drawings	1,180	315
Balances 1.1.19-5	40	1,560
Balance 31.12.19-5	70	375

	Cash	Bank		Cash	Bank
	£	£		£	£
Balances 1.1.19-5	40	1,560	Suppliers		5,800
Received from debtors	?	6,080	Expenses	640	230
Withdrawn from			Withdrawn from		
Bank C	920		Bank C		920
			Drawings	1,180	315
			Balances 31.12.19-5	70	375
	1,890	7,640		1,890	7,640

Receipts from debtors is, therefore, the amount needed to make each side of the cash column agree, £930.

It must be emphasized that balancing figures are acceptable only when all the other figures have been verified. Should for instance a cash expense be omitted when cash received from debtors is being calculated, then this would result in an understatement not only of expenses but also ultimately of sales.

Where there are Two Missing Pieces of Information

If both cash drawings and cash receipts from debtors were not known it would not be possible to deduce both of these figures. The only source lying open would be to estimate whichever figure was more capable of being accurately assessed, use this as a known figure, then deduce the other figure. However, this is a most unsatisfactory position as both of the figures are no more than pure estimates, the accuracy of each one relying entirely upon the accuracy of the other.

Assignment Exercises

5.1. B. Arkwright started in business on 1 January 19-5 with £10,000 in a bank account. Unfortunately he did not keep proper books of account.

He is forced to submit a calculation of profit for the year ended 31 December 19-5 to the Inspector of Taxes. He ascertains that at 31 December 19-5 he had stock valued at cost £3,950, a motor van which had cost £2,800 during the year and which had depreciated by £550, debtors of £4,970, expenses prepaid of £170, bank balance £2,564, cash balance £55, trade creditors £1,030, and expenses owing £470.

His drawings were: cash £100 per week for 50 weeks, cheque payments £673. Draw up statements to show the profit or loss for the year.

5.2A. J. Kirkwood is a dealer who has not kept proper books of account. At 31 August 19-6 his state of affairs was as follows:

	£
Cash	115
Bank Balance	2,209
Fixtures	4,000
Stock	16,740
Debtors	11,890
Creditors	9,052
Motor Van (at valuation)	3,000

During the year to 31 August 19-7 his drawings amounted to £7,560. Winnings from a football pool £2,800 were put into the business. Extra fixtures were bought for £2,000.

At 31 August 19-7 his assets and liabilities were: Cash £84, Bank Overdraft £165, Stock £21,491, Creditors for goods £6,002, Creditors for expenses £236, Fixtures to be depreciated £600, Motor Van to be valued at £2,500, Debtors £15,821, Pre-paid Expenses £72.

Draw up a statement showing the profit or loss made by Kirkwood for the year ended 31 August 19-7.

5.3. Following is a summary of Kelly's bank account for the year ended 31 December 19-7:

	£		£
Balance 1.1.19-7	405	Payments to creditors	
Receipts from debtors	37,936	for goods	29,487
Balance 31.12.19-7	602	Rent	1,650
		Rates	890
		Sundry Expenses	375
		Drawings	6,541
	38,943		38,943

All of the business takings have been paid into the bank with the exception of £9,630. Out of this, Kelly has paid wages of £5,472, drawings of £1,164 and purchase of goods £2,994.

The following additional information is available.

	31.12.19-6	31.12.19-7
Stock	13,862	15,144
Creditors for goods	5,624	7,389
Debtors for goods	9,031	8,624
Rates Prepaid	210	225
Rent Owing	150	–
Fixtures at valuation	2,500	2,250

You are to draw up a set of final accounts for the year ended 31 December 19-7. Show all of your workings.

5.4A. J. Evans has kept records of his business transactions in a single entry form, but he did not realise that he had to record cash drawings. His bank account for the year 19-4 is as follows:

	£		£
Balance 1.1.19-4	1,890	Cash withdrawn from bank	5,400
Receipts from debtors	44,656	Trade Creditors	31,695
Loan from T. Hughes	2,000	Rent	2,750
		Rates	1,316
		Drawings	3,095
		Sundry Expenses	1,642
		Balance 31.12.19-4	2,648
	48,546		48,546

Records of cash paid were. Sundry Expenses £122, Trade Creditors £642. Cash sales amounted to £698.

The following information is also available:

	31.12.19-3 £	31.12.19-4 £
Cash in Hand	48	93
Trade Creditors	4,896	5,091
Debtors	6,013	7,132
Rent Owing	–	250
Rates in Advance	282	312
Motor Van (at valuation)	2,800	2,400
Stock	11,163	13,021

You are to draw up a Trading and Profit and Loss Account for the year ended 31 December 19-4, and a Balance Sheet as at that date. Show all of your workings.

5.5. You are to draft a set of budgeted final accounts for the year ended 31 December 19-6 for F. Oliver from the following information:
1. Net Profit to be 16⅔% of the balance on the Capital Account as at 1 January 19-6.
2. Gross Profit as a percentage of Sales to be 30%.
3. Gross Profit to be £30,000.
4. Fixed Assets which had cost £80,000 had been depreciated by 50% at the start of the year. Of the reduced balance a further 12½% is to be treated as depreciation for 19-6.
5. Closing Stock to be 40% of the Purchases figure for the year.
6. Purchases to be equal in value to 50% the Sales figure.
7. Discounts Received to be 2% of Purchases.
8. Discounts Allowed to be 1% of Sales.
9. Expenses, as a percentage of Sales, to be Selling Expenses 10%; Administration Expenses 7%.
10. Drawings to be 60% of the Net Profit.
11. At 31 December 19-6 creditors to be 35% of Purchases; debtors to be 12½% of Sales.
12. Bank Balance to be that necessary to finance the above.

5.6A. Draft a set of budgeted final accounts for the year ended 31 December 19-8 for Z. Hopper from the following information:
1. Purchase to be 66% of the Sales figure. (confirmed 66% not 66⅔%)
2. Closing Stock to be 33⅓% of the Purchases figure.
3. Gross Profit as a percentage of sales to be 24%.
4. Gross Profit to be £60,000.
5. Net Profit to be 20% of the balance on the Capital Account as at 1 January 19-8.
6. Discounts Received to be 80% of Discounts Allowed.
7. Discounts Allowed to be 1% of Sales.
8. Fixed Assets, which had cost £60,000 had been depreciated by 33⅓% by the start of the year. Depreciation on the reduced balance is to be 10%.
9. Drawings to be 70% of the Net Profit.
10. Selling Expenses to be 4% of Sales.
11. Administration Expenses to be 75% greater than the Selling Expenses.
12. At 31 December 19-8 creditors to be 20% of the Purchases figure.
13. Debtors to be 30% of the Sales Figure.
14. Bank Balance to be that which is necessary to agree the balance sheet totals.

5.7. S. Agnew has lost his records of sales, and you will have to deduce the sales figure. The summary of his bank account for the year ended 31 December 19-6 is as follows:

	£		£
Receipts from debtors	67,595	Balance 1.1.19-6	2,059
Extra capital introduced	3,000	Suppliers for goods	49,382
		Motor Expenses	4,624
		Rent & Rates	3,728
		General Expenses	846
		Fixtures bought	3,500
		Drawings	1,364
		Balance 31.12.19-6	5,092
	70,595		70,595

A cash loan of £500 had been received on 1 July 19-6. Interest is to be paid on this at the rate of 16% per annum. Cash payments were as follows:

Drawings	6,070
Suppliers	406
General Expenses	707

Motor vans owned by the firm had cost £8,000 in January 19-4, and depreciation should be written off at 25% using the reducing balance method. Fixtures costing £2,000 had been bought in January 19-3 and depreciation is being written off at the rate of 10%, using the straight-line method.

The following information is also given:

	31.12.19-5	31.12.19-6
	£	£
Stock	10,500	11,370
Cash in Hand	165	112
Creditors for goods	6,238	4,187
Debtors	16,840	19,385
Motor Expenses Owing	123	238
Rent paid in advance	115	–
Rent Owing	–	230

You are required to draw up a Trading and Profit and Loss Account for the year to 31 December 19-6 and a Balance Sheet as at that date.

6

Departmental Accounts

Accounting information varies in its usefulness. For a retail store with five departments, it is obviously better to know that the store has made £10,000 gross profit than to be completely ignorant of this fact. The figure of £10,000 gross profit unfortunately does not give the owners the insight into the business necessary to control it much more effectively. What would be far more meaningful would be the knowledge of the amount of gross profit or loss for each department. Assume that the gross profits and losses for the departments were as follows:

Department	Gross profit	Gross loss
	£	£
A	4,000	
B	3,000	
C	5,000	
D		8,000
E	6,000	
	18,000	8,000

Gross profit of the firm, £10,000.

Ignoring the overhead expenses for the sake of simplicity, although in practice they should never be ignored, can any conclusions be drawn from the above? It may well appear that if department D was closed down then the store would make £18,000 gross profit instead of £10,000. This could equally well be true or false depending on circumstances. Department D may be deliberately run at a loss so that its cheap selling prices may attract customers who, when they come to the store, also buy goods in addition from departments A, B, C and E. If department D were closed down perhaps most of the customers would not come to the store at all. In this case all the other departments would only have small gross profits because of the falls in sales and if this happened the gross profits might well be −

departments: A £1,000, B £500, C £2,500 and E £2,000, a total of £6,000. Therefore department D operating at a loss because of cheap prices would have increased the gross profit of the firm.

The converse could, however, hold true. If department D were closed down the sales in the other departments might rise. Department D could be a wine and spirits department at the entrance to the store through which all customers have to walk to the other departments. Teetotallers may therefore avoid the store because they would not like to be seen going into a department where alcohol was being sold. To close down the department, leaving it merely as an access route to the other departments, may result in higher sales in these other departments because the teetotallers who had previously shunned the store might now become customers. The effect on the existing non-teetotal customers could also be considered as well as the possibility of the re-location of the wine and spirits department.

Accounting information therefore seldom tells all the story. It serves as one measure, but there are other non-accounting factors to be considered before a relevant decision for action can be made.

The various pros and cons of the actions to be taken to increase the overall profitability of the business cannot therefore be efficiently considered until the departmental gross profits or losses are known. It must not be thought that departmental accounts refer only to departmental stores. They refer to the various facets of a business. Consider the simple case of a barber who does shaving and haircutting. He may find that the profit from shaving is very small, and that if he discontinues shaving he will earn more from extra haircutting because he does not have to turn customers away because of lack of time. The principle of departmental accounts is concerned just as much with the small barber's shop as with a large department store. The reputation of many a successful businessman has been built up on his ability to utilize the departmental account principle to guide his actions to increase the profitability of a firm. The lesson still has to be learned by many medium-sized and small firms. It is one of accounting's greatest, and simplest, aids to business efficiency.

Expenses

The expenses of the firm are often split between the various departments, and the net profit for each department then calculated. Each expense is divided between the departments on what is considered to be the most logical basis. This will differ considerably between businesses. An example of a Trading and Profit and Loss Account drawn up in such a manner is shown in Exhibit 6.1.

Exhibit 6.1

Northern Stores have three departments in their store:

	(a) Jewellery	(b) Ladies hairdressing	(c) Clothing
	£	£	£
Stock of goods or materials, 1 January 19-8	2,000	1,500	3,000
Purchases	11,000	3,000	15,000
Stock of goods or materials, 31 December 19-8	3,000	2,500	4,000
Sales and work done	18,000	9,000	27,000
Wages of assistants in each department	2,800	5,000	6,000

The following expenses cannot be traced to any particular department:

	£
Rent	3,500
Administration expenses	4,800
Air conditioning and lighting	2,000
General expenses	1,200

It is decided to apportion rent together with air conditioning and lighting in accordance with the floor space occupied by each department. These were taken up in the ratios of (a) one-fifth, (b) half, (c) three-tenths. Administration expenses and general expenses are to be split in the ratio of sales and work done.

The Northern Stores
Trading and Profit and Loss Account for the year ended 31 December 19-8

	(a) Jewellery £	£	(b) Hairdressing £	£	(c) Clothing £	£
Sales and Work Done		18,000		9,000		27,000
Cost of Goods or Materials:						
Stock 1.1.19-8	2,000		1,500		3,000	
Add Purchases	11,000		3,000		15,000	
	13,000		4,500		18,000	
Less Stock 31.12.19-8	3,000	10,000	2,500	2,000	4,000	14,000
Gross Profit		8,000		7,000		13,000
Less Expenses:						
Wages	2,800		5,000		6,000	
Rent	700		1,750		1,050	
Administration expenses	1,600		800		2,400	
Air conditioning and lighting	400		1,000		600	
General expenses	400	5,900	200	8,750	600	10,650
Net Profit/Loss		2,100		(1,750)		2,350

This way of calculating net profits and losses seems to imply a precision that is lacking in fact, and would often lead to an interpretation that the hairdressing department has lost £1,750 this year, and that this amount would be saved if the department was closed down. It has already been stated that different departments are very often dependent on one another, therefore it will be realized that this would not necessarily be the case. The calculation of net profits and losses are also dependent on arbitrary division of overhead expenses. It is by no means obvious that the overheads of department (b) would be avoided if it were closed down. Assuming that the sales staff of the department could be discharged without compensation, then £5,000 would be saved in wages. The other overhead expenses shown under department (b) would not, however, necessarily disappear. The rent may still be payable in full even though the department were closed down. The administration expenses may turn out to be only slightly down, say from £4,800 to £4,600, a saving of £200; air conditioning and lighting down to £1,500, a saving of £500; general expenses down to £1,100, a saving of £100. Therefore the department, when open, costs an additional £5,800 compared with when the department is closed. This is made up as follows:

	£
Administration expenses	200
Air conditioning and lighting	500
General expenses	100
Wages	5,000
	5,800

But when open, assuming this year is typical, the department makes £7,000 gross profit. The firm is therefore £1,200 a year better off when the department is open than when it is closed, subject to certain assumptions. These are:

(a) That the remaining departments could not be profitably expanded into the space vacated to give greater proportionate benefits than the hairdressing department.

(b) That a new type of department which would be more profitable than hairdressing could not be set up.

(c) That the department could not be leased to another firm at a more profitable figure than that shown by hairdressing.

There are also other factors which, though not easily seen in an accounting context, are still extremely pertinent. They are concerned with the possible loss of confidence in the firm by customers generally; what appears to be an ailing business does not usually attract good customers. Also the effect on the remaining staff should not be ignored. The fear that the dismissal of the hairdressing staff may mirror what is also going to happen to themselves may result in the loss of staff, especially the most competent members who could easily find work elsewhere, and so the general quality of the staff may decline with serious consequences for the firm.

A far less misleading method of drafting departmental accounts is by showing costs which are in the nature of direct costs allocated entirely to the department, and which would not be payable if the department was closed down, in the first section of the Trading and Profit and Loss Account. The second section is left to cover those expenses which need arbitrary apportionment or which would still be payable on the closing of the department. The surpluses brought down from the first section represent the 'contribution' that each department makes to cover the expenses and profit. The contributions can thus be seen to be the results of activities which are under a person's control, in this case the departmental managers concerned. The sales revenue has been generated by the workforce, etc., all under their control, and the costs charged have been under their control, so that the surpluses earned (or deficits incurred) are affected by the degree of their control. The other costs in the second section are not, however, under their control. The departmental managers cannot directly affect to any great extent the costs of rent or of air conditioning and lighting, so that the contributions from the sections of the business must more than cover all these expenses if the business is to earn a profit. From the figures given in Exhibit 6.1 the accounts would appear as shown in Exhibit 6.2.

Exhibit 6.2

The Northern Stores

Trading and Profit and Loss Account for the year ended 31 December 19-8

	(a) Jewellery		(b) Hairdressing		(c) Clothing	
	£	£	£	£	£	£
Sales and work done		18,000		9,000		27,000
Less Cost of goods or materials:						
Stock 1.1.19-8	2,000		1,500		3,000	
Add Purchases	11,000		3,000		15,000	
	13,000		4,500		18,000	
Less Stock 31.12.19-8	3,000		2,500		4,000	
	10,000		2,000		14,000	
Wages	2,800	12,800	5,000	7,000	6,000	20,000
Surpluses c/d		5,200		2,000		7,000

All Departments

		£
Surpluses b/d:		
Jewellery	5,200	
Hairdressing	2,000	
Clothing	7,000	14,200
Less:		
Rent and rates	3,500	
Administration expenses	4,800	
Air conditioning and lighting	2,000	
General expenses	1,200	11,500
Net Profit		2,700

The balance sheet

The Balance Sheet does not usually show assets and liabilities split between different departments.

Inter-departmental transfers

Purchases made for one department may be subsequently sold in another department. In such a case the items should be deducted from the figure for Purchases of the original purchasing department, and added to the figure for Purchases for the subsequent selling department.

Assignment Exercises

6.1. From the following you are to draw up the Trading Account for Charnley's Department Store from the following for the year ended 31 December 19-8.

Stocks:	1.1.19-8	31.12.19-8
	£	£
Electrical Department	6,080	7,920
Furniture Department	17,298	16,150
Leisure Goods Department	14,370	22,395

Sales for the year:	£
Electrical Department	29,840
Furniture Department	73,060
Leisure Goods Department	39,581

Purchases for the year:	
Electrical Department	18,195
Furniture Department	54,632
Leisure Goods Department	27,388

6.2. J. Spratt is the proprietor of a shop selling books, periodicals, newspapers and children's games and toys. For the purposes of his accounts he wishes the business to be divided into two departments:

Department A   Books, periodicals and newspapers.
Department B   Games, toys and fancy goods.

The following balances have been extracted from his nominal ledger at 31 March 19-6:

	Dr	Cr
	£	£
Sales Department A		15,000
Sales Department B		10,000
Stocks Department A, 1 April 19-5	250	
Stocks Department B, 1 April 19-5	200	
Purchases Department A	11,800	
Purchases Department B	8,200	
Wages of sales assistants Department A	1,000	
Wages of sales assistants Department B	750	
Newspapers delivery wages	150	
General office salaries	750	
Rates	130	
Fire insurance − buildings	50	
Lighting and air conditioning	120	
Repairs to premises	25	
Internal telephone	25	
Cleaning	30	
Accountancy and audit charges	120	
General office expenses	60	

Stocks at 31 March 19-6 were valued at:
Department A   £300
Department B   £150

The proportion of the total floor area occupied by each department was:

Department A   One-fifth
Department B   Four-fifths

Prepare J. Spratt's Trading and Profit and Loss Account for the year ended 31 March 19-6, apportioning the overhead expenses, where necessary, to show the Department profit or loss. The apportionment should be made by using the methods as shown:

Area − Rates, Fire Insurance, Lighting and Air Conditioning, Repairs, Telephone, Cleaning; Turnover − General Office Salaries, Accountancy, General Office Expenses.

6.3A. From the following list of balances you are required to prepare a departmental trading and profit and loss account in columnar form for the year ended 31 March 19-0, in respect of the business carried on under the name of Ivor's Superstores:

		£	£
Rent and rates			4,200
Delivery expenses			2,400
Commission			3,840
Insurance			900
Purchases:	Dept. A	52,800	
	B	43,600	
	C	34,800	
			131,200
Discounts received			1,968
Salaries and wages			31,500
Advertising			1,944
Sales:	Dept. A	80,000	
	B	64,000	
	C	48,000	192,000
Depreciation			2,940
Opening Stock:	Dept. A	14,600	
	B	11,240	
	C	9,120	
			34,960
Administration and general expenses			7,890
Closing stock:	Dept. A	12,400	
	B	8,654	
	C	9,746	
			30,800

Except as follows, expenses are to be apportioned equally between the departments.

Delivery expenses – proportionate to sales.
Commission – two per cent of sales.
Salaries and wages; Insurance – in the proportion of 6:5:4.
Discounts received – 1.5 per cent of purchases.

7

Columnar Day Books

Purchases Analysis books

Provided firms finish up with the items needed for display in their final accounts, the actual manner in which they do it is completely up to them. Some firms use one book to record all items got on credit. These consist not only of the Purchases, but also of items such as Motor Expenses, Stationery, Fixed Assets, Carriage Inwards and so on. The idea is that all invoices for items which will not be paid for on the day that the item is received will be entered in this book. However, all of the various types of items are not simply lumped together, as the firm needs to know how much of the items were for Purchases, how much for Stationery, how much for Motor Expenses, etc., so that the relevant expense accounts can have the correct amount of expenses entered in them. This is achieved by having a set of analysis columns in the book, all of the items are entered in a Total Column, but then they are analysed as between the different sorts of expenses, etc.

Exhibit 7.1 shows such a Purchases Analysis book drawn up for a month from the following list of items got on credit:

19-5		£
May	1 Bought goods from D. Watson Ltd on credit	296
,,	3 Bought goods on credit from W. Donachie & Son	76
,,	5 Motor van repaired, received invoice from Barnes Motors Ltd	112
,,	6 Bought stationery from J. Corrigan	65
,,	8 Bought goods on credit from C. Bell Ltd	212
,,	10 Motor lorry serviced, received invoice from Barnes Motors Ltd	39
,,	13 Bought stationery on credit from A. Hartford & Co	35
,,	16 Bought goods on credit from M. Doyle Ltd	243
,,	20 Received invoice for carriage inwards on goods from G. Owen	58
,,	21 Bought goods on credit from B. Kidd & Son	135
,,	24 Bought goods on credit from K. Clements	122
,,	24 Received invoice for carriage inwards from Channon Haulage	37
,,	26 Bought goods on credit from C. Bell Ltd	111
,,	28 Bought stationery on credit from A. Hartford & Co.	49
,,	29 Bought goods on credit from B. Kidd & Son	249
,,	31 Received invoice for petrol for the month, to be paid for in June, from Barnes Motors Ltd	280

Exhibit 7.1

Purchases Analysis Book

Date	Name of Firm	PL Folio	Total	Purchases	Stationery	Motor Expenses	Carriage Inwards
19-5			£	£	£	£	£
May 1	D. Watson Ltd	129	296	296			
,, 3	W. Donachie & Son	27	76	76			
,, 5	Barnes Motors Ltd	55	112			112	
,, 6	J. Corrigan & Co	88	65		65		
,, 8	C. Bell Ltd	99	212	212			
,, 10	Barnes Motors Ltd	55	39			39	
,, 13	A. Hartford & Co	298	35		35		
,, 16	M. Doyle Ltd	187	243	243			
,, 20	G. Owen	222	58				58
,, 21	B. Kidd & Son	188	135	135			
,, 24	K. Clements	211	122	122			
,, 24	Channon Haulage	305	37				37
,, 26	C. Bell Ltd	99	111	111			
,, 28	A. Hartford & Co	298	49		49		
,, 29	B. Kidd & Son	188	249	249			
,, 31	Barnes Motors Ltd	55	280			280	
			2,119	1,444	149	431	95
				GL 77	GL 97	GL 156	GL 198

Exhibit 7.1 shows that the figure for each item is entered in the Total column, and is then also entered in the column for the particular type of expense. At the end of the month the arithmetical accuracy of the additions can be checked by comparing the total of the Total column with the sum of totals of all of the other columns. These two grand totals figures should equal each other. In this case 1,444 + 149 + 431 + 95 = 2,119. The total column will also be useful for Control Accounts; examined in Chapter 4.

It can be seen that the total of Purchases for the month of May was £1,444 and therefore this can be debited to the Purchases Account in the General Ledger; similarly the total of Stationery bought on credit in the month can be debited to the Stationery Account in the General Ledger and so on. The folio number of the page to which the relevant total has been debited is shown immediately under the total figure for each column, e.g. under the column for Purchases is GL 77, meaning that the item has been entered in the General Ledger page 77. The entries can now be shown:

General Ledger

Purchases Account Page 77

19-5		£
May 31 Purchases Analysis		
105		1,444

Stationery Page 97

19-5		£
May 31 Purchases Analysis		
105		149

	Motor Expenses		Page 156

19-5	£		
May 31 Purchases Analysis			
105	431		

	Carriage Inwards		Page 198

19-5	£		
May 31 Purchase Analysis			
105	95		

The individual accounts of the creditors, whether they be for goods or for expenses such as Stationery or Motor Expenses, can be kept to gether in a single Purchases Ledger. There is no need for the Purchases Ledger simply to have accounts only for creditors for Purchases. Perhaps there is a slight misuse of the name Purchases Ledger where this happens, but it is common practice amongst a lot of firms. It is often called the 'Bought Ledger'.

To carry through the double entry involved with Exhibit 7.3 the Purchases Ledger is now shown.

Exhibit 7.3

Purchases Ledger

	W. Donachie & Son		Page 27
	19-5		£
	May 3 Purchases	PB 105	76

	Barnes Motors Ltd		Page 55
	19-5		£
	May 5 Purchases	PB 105	112
	,, 10 ,,	PB 105	39
	,, 31 ,,	PB 105	280

	J. Corrigan & Co.		Page 88
	19-5		£
	May 6 Purchases	PB 105	65

	C. Bell Ltd		Page 99
	19-5		£
	May 8 Purchases	PB 105	212
	,, 26 ,,	PB 105	111

	D. Watson Ltd		Page 129
	19-5		£
	May 1 Purchases	PB 105	296

M. Doyle Ltd		Page 187
19-5		£
May 16 Purchases	PB 105	243

B. Kidd & Son		Page 188
19-5		£
May 21 Purchases	PB 105	135
,, 29 ,,	PB 105	249

K. Clements		Page 211
19-5		£
May 24 Purchase	PB 105	122

G. Owen		Page 222
19-5		£
May 20 Purchases	PB 105	58

A. Hartford & Co		Page 298
19-5		£
May 13 Purchases	PB 105	35
,, 28 ,,	PB 105	49

Channon Haulage		Page 305
19-5		£
May 24 Purchases	PB 105	37

The reader has just been shown how to draw up Purchases Analysis Books. The basic idea of having a total column, and analysing the items under various headings, can be carried one stage further. This could be the case where it was desired to ascertain the profits of a firm on a departmental basis.

In such a case the Purchases Analysis Books already described could have additional columns so that the purchase of goods for each department could be easily ascertained. Taking the Purchases Analysis Book per Exhibit 7.1, assume that the firm had three departments, Sports Department, Household Department and Electrical Department. Instead of one column for Purchases there could be three columns, each one headed with the title of a Department. When the invoices for purchases were being entered in the enlarged Purchases Analysis Book, the amount of each invoice could be split as between each department, and the relevant figures entered in each column. The total figure of all the three columns would represent the total for Purchases, but it would also be known how much of the Purchases were for each department. This would help when the final accounts were being drafted in a departmental fashion. The Purchases Analaysis Book per Exhibit 7.1 might appear instead as follows in Exhibit 7.2

Exhibit 7.2

				Purchases Analysis Book						Page 105
Date 19-5	Name of Firm		PL Folio	Total	Sports	House-hold	Elec-trical Dept.	Station-ery Dept.	Motor Exps.	Carriage Inwards
				£	£	£	£	£	£	£
May	1	D. Watson Ltd	129	296	80	216				
,,	3	W. Donachie & Son	27	76	76					
,,	5	Barnes Motors Ltd	55	112					112	
,,	6	J. Corrigan & Co	88	65				65		
,,	8	C. Bell Ltd	99	212	92		120			
,,	10	Barnes Motors Ltd	55	39					39	
,,	13	A. Hartford & Co	298	35				35		
,,	16	M. Doyle Ltd	187	243			243			
,,	20	G. Owen	222	58						58
,,	21	B. Kidd & Son	188	135	135					
,,	24	K. Clements	211	122	70		52			
,,	24	Channon Haulage	305	37						37
,,	26	C. Bell Ltd	99	111		111				
,,	28	A. Hartford & Co	298	49				49		
,,	29	B. Kidd & Son	188	249	60	103	86			
,,	31	Barnes Motors Ltd	55	280					280	
				2,119	513	430	501	149	431	95
					GL 77	GL 77	GL 77	GL 97	GL 156	GL 198

The Purchases Account in the General Ledger could also have three columns, so that the purchases for each department could be entered in separate columns. Then, when the Trading Account is drawn up the respective totals of each department could be transferred to it.

Of course, a Purchases Day Book could be kept, strictly for Purchases only, without the other expenses, such as Stationery, Motor Expenses and Carriage Inwards. In this case there would simply be the total column with an analysis column for each separate department's purchase.

With Purchases, the use of an analysis book with columns for other expenses is very useful. When looking at Sales, however, the need to split Sales between departments is not usually accompanied by the need to show analysis columns for other items of income. Involved in the expenditure of a firm are many items of expense besides Purchases. With income, the main part of income is represented by the Sales. The amount of transactions in such items as the selling of a fixed asset are relatively few. The Sales Analysis Book, or Columnar Sales Book as it might be called, therefore usually consists of the sales of goods only.

A columnar Sales Book for the same firm as in Exhibit 7.2 might appear as in Exhibit 7.3.

Exhibit 7.3

Columnar Sales Day Book

Date	Name of Firm	SL Folio	Total	Sports Dept.	Household Dept.	Electrical Dept.
19-5			£	£	£	£	£
May 1	N. Coward Ltd	87	190		190	
,, 5	L. Olivier	76	200	200		
,, 8	R. Colman & Co	157	307	102		205
,, 16	Aubrey Smith Ltd	209	480			480
,, 27	H. Marshall	123	222	110	45	67
,, 31	W. Pratt	66	1,800		800	1,000
			3,199	412	1,035	1,752
				GL 88	GL 88	GL 88

The Sales Account, and the Purchases Account, in the General Ledger could be in columnar form. From Exhibits 7.4 and 7.5 the Purchases and Sales Accounts would appear as:

General Ledger

Sales   page 88

		Sports Dept. £	Household Dept. £	Electrical Dept. £
	19-5			
	May 31 Credit Sales for the month	412	1,035	1,752

page 77   Purchases

	Sports Dept. £	Household Dept. £	Electrical Dept. £
19-5			
May 31 Credit Purchases for the month	513	430	501

The Purchases and Sales Accounts would then accumulate the figures for these items, so that when the final accounts were being drawn up the total figures for each department could be transferred to the Trading Account. There is, of course, nothing to stop a firm having one account for Purchases (Sports Dept.), another for Purchases (Household Dept.) and so on. The Stock Account could be kept in a columnar fashion as well, to aid the transfer of stock values to the respective departmental columns in the Trading Account.

The personal accounts in the Sales and Purchases Ledgers would not be in columnar form. As an instance of this, the personal account of W. Pratt in the Sales ledger would simply be debited with £1,800 in respect of the goods sold to him, there being no need to show the analysis between Household and Electrical Departments in his account. If the firm wanted to have columnar personal accounts then there is nothing to stop them keeping them, but this would not normally be the case.

Sales Analysis Books and VAT

All that would be needed would be an extra column for VAT. In the gross example that follows the debtors would be charged up with the gross amounts, whilst the VAT £184 would be credited to the VAT Account, and the Sales figures of £1,040, £410 and £390 credited to the Sales Account.

Columnar Sales Day Book

Date	Name of Firm	SL Folio	Total	VAT	Furniture Dept.	Hardware Dept.	General Dept.
19-4			£	£	£	£	£
May 1	H. Smedley	133	220	20	200		
,, 6	T. Sarson	297	528	48	210	100	170
,, 16	H. Hartley Ltd	444	286	26		110	150
,, 31	H. Walls	399	990	90	630	200	70
			2,024	184	1,040	410	390
				GL 65	GL 177	GL 177	GL 177

Books as Collection Points

We can see that the various Sales and Purchases Journals, and the ones for returns, are simply collection points for the data to be entered in the accounts of the double-entry system. There is nothing by law that says that, for instance, a Sales Journal has to be written up. What we could do is to look at the Sales Invoices and enter the debits in the customers' personal accounts from them. Then we could keep all the Sales Invoices together in a file. At the end of the month we could use an adding machine to add up the amounts of the Sales Invoices, and then enter that total to the credit of the Sales Account in the General Ledger.

That means that we would have done without the Sales Journal. As the debits in the customers' accounts are made, not by looking at the Sales Journal, but by looking at the Sales Invoices (we could say that these are 'slips' or paper), the system would be known as a 'slip' system. Such a system could lead to more errors being made and not being detected. It could also mean that book-keepers could more easily commit fraud as it would be more difficult for proprietors to see what was going on. The 'slip' system could also be used for Purchases and for Returns.

Assignment Exercises

7.1. C. Taylor, a wholesale dealer in electrical goods, has three departments: (a) Hi Fi, (b) TV, and (c) Sundries. The following is a summary of Taylor's Sales Invoices during the period 1 to 7 February 19-7:

	Customer	Invoice No.	Depart-ment	List price less trade discount	VAT	Total invoice price
				£	£	£
Feb 1	S. Markham	261	TV	2,600	260	2,860
2	F. Clarke	262	Hi Fi	1,800	180	1,980
3	C. Willis	263	TV	1,600	160	1,760
5	C. Mayall	264	Sundries	320	Nil	320
7	F. Clarke	265	TV	900	90	990
	S. Markham	266	Hi Fi	3,400	340	3,740

(a) Record the above transactions in a columnar book of original entry and post to the General Ledger in columnar form.

(b) Write up the Personal Accounts in the appropriate ledger.

N.B. – Do NOT balance off any of your ledger accounts.

*N.B. VAT was 10% rate

7.2. Enter up a Purchases Analysis Book with columns for the various expenses for M. Barber for the month from the following information on credit items.

19-6		£
July	1 Bought goods from L. Ogden	220
,,	3 Bought goods from E. Evans	390
,,	4 Received electricity bill (lighting & heating from North Electricity Boards)	88
,,	5 Bought goods from H. Noone	110
,,	6 Motor lorry repaired, received bill from Kirk Motors	136
,,	8 Bought stationery from Avon Enterprises	77
,,	10 Motor van serviced, bill from Kirk Motors	55
,,	12 Gas bill received from North Gas Board (lighting & heating)	134
,,	15 Bought goods from A. Dodds	200
,,	17 Bought light bulbs (lighting & heating) from O. Aspinall	24
,,	18 Goods bought from J. Kelly	310
,,	19 Invoice for carriage inwards from D. Adams	85
,,	21 Bought stationery from J. Moore	60
,,	23 Goods bought from H. Noone	116
,,	27 Received invoice for carriage inwards from D. Flynn	62
,,	31 Invoice for motor spares supplied during the month received from Kirk Motors	185

7.3. Enter up the relevant accounts in the Purchases and General Ledgers from the Purchases Analysis Book you have completed for question 7.2.

8

Bills of Exchange

When goods are supplied to someone on credit, or services performed for him, then that person becomes a debtor. The creditor firm would normally wait for payment by the debtor. Until payment is made the money owing is of no use to the creditor firm as it is not being used in any way. This can be remedied by factoring the debtors, which involves passing the debts over to a finance firm. They will pay an agreed amount for the legal rights to the debts.

Another possibility is that of obtaining a bank overdraft, with the debtors accepted as part of the security on which the overdraft has been granted.

Yet another way that can give the creditor effective use of the money owing to him is for him to draw a bill of exchange on the debtor. This means that a document is drawn up requiring the debtor to pay the amount owing to the creditor, or to anyone nominated by him at any time, on or by a particular date. He sends this document to the debtor who, if he agrees to it, is said to 'accept' it by writing on the document that he will comply with it and appends his signature. The debtor then returns the bill of exchange to the creditor. This document is then legal proof of the debt. The debtor is not then able to contest the validity of the debt but only for any irregularity in the bill of exchange itself. The creditor can now act in one of three ways:

1.   He can negotiate the bill to another person in payment of a debt. That person may also renegotiate it to someone else. The person who possesses the bill at maturity, i.e. the date for payment of the bill, will present it to the debtor for payment.

2.   He may 'discount' it with a bank. 'Discount' here means that the bank will take the bill of exchange and treat it in the same manner as money deposited in the bank account. The bank will then hold the bill until maturity when it will present it to the debtor for payment. The bank will make a charge to the creditor for this service known as a discounting charge.

3.   The third way open to the creditor is for him to hold the bill until maturity when he will present it to the debtor for payment. In this case, apart from having a document which is legal proof of the debt and could

therefore save legal costs if a dispute arose, no benefit has been gained from having a bill of exchange. However, action 1 or 2 could have been taken if the need had arisen.

The creditor who draws up the bill of exchange is known as the *Drawer*. The debtor on whom it is drawn is the *Drawee,* when accepted he becomes the *Acceptor,* while the person to whom the bill is to be paid is the *Payee*. In fact it may be recognized that a cheque is a special type of bill of exchange where the drawee is always a bank and in addition is payable on demand. This chapter, however, refers to bills of exchange other than cheques.

To the person who is to receive money on maturity of the bill of exchange the document is known as a 'bill receivable', while to the person who is to pay the sum due on maturity it is known as a 'bill payable'.

Dishonoured Bills

When the debtor fails to make payment on maturity the bill is said to be dishonoured. If the holder is someone other than the drawer then he will have recourse against the person who has negotiated the bill to him, that person will then have recourse against the one who negotiated it to him, and so on until final recourse is had against the drawer of the bill for the amount of money due on the bill. The drawer's right of action is then against the acceptor.

On dishonour a bill is often 'noted'. This means that the bill is handed to a lawyer acting in his capacity as a notary public, who then re-presents the bill to the acceptor. The notary public then records the reasons for it not being discharged. The notary public's fee is known as a 'noting charge'. With a foreign bill, in addition to the bill being noted, it is necessary to 'protest' the bill in order to preserve the holder's rights against the drawer and previous endorsers. 'Protest' is the term which covers the legal formalities needed.

The action to be taken by the drawer depends entirely upon circumstances. Often the lack of funds on the acceptor's part is purely temporary. In this case the drawer is will negotiate with the acceptor and agree to draw another bill, or substitute several bills of smaller amounts with different maturity dates, for the amount owing, frequently with an addition for interest to compensate for the extended period of credit. Negotiation is the keynote; it must not be thought that acceptors are always sued when they fail to make payment. They are customers, and where future dealings with them are expected to be profitable harsh measures are certainly to be avoided. Legal action should be the last action to be considered. Any interest charged to the acceptor would be debited to his account and credited to an Interest Receivable Account.

Discounting Charges and Noting Charges

From the acceptor's point of view the discounting of a bill is a matter wholly for the drawer or holder to decide. He, the acceptor, has been allowed a term of credit and will pay the agreed price on the maturity of the bill. Therefore the discounting charge is not one that he should suffer; this should be borne wholly by the person discounting the bill.

On the other hand, the noting charge has been brought about by the acceptor's default. It is equitable that his account should be charged with the amount of the expense of noting and protesting.

Retired Bills

Instead of waiting until maturity, bills may be retired, i.e. not allowed to run until maturity. They may be paid off before maturity, in which case a rebate is often allowed because the full term of credit has not been taken; or else renewed by fresh bills being drawn and the old ones cancelled, the new bills often including interest because the term of credit has been extended.

Exhibit 8.1
Drawer's Books

Goods had been sold by D. Jarvis to J. Burgon on 1 January 19-6 for £400. A bill of exchange is drawn by Jarvis and accepted by Burgon on 1 January 19-6, the date of maturity being 31 March 19-6. The following accounts show the entries necessary:

(*a*) If the bill is held by the drawer until maturity when the drawee makes payment.

J. Burgon

19-6		£	19-6		£
Jan	1 Sales	400	Jan	1 Bill Receivable	400

Bills Receivable

19-6		£	19-6		£
Jan	1 J. Burgon	400	Mar 31	Bank	400

Bank

19-6		£
Mar 31	Bills Receivable	400

(*b*) Where the bill is negotiated to another party by the drawer, in this case to I.D.T. Ltd on 3 January 19-6.

J. Burgon

19-6		£	19-6		£
Jan	1 Sales	400	Jan	1 Bill Receivable	400

Bills Receivable

19-6		£	19-6		£
Jan	1 J. Burgon	400	Jan	3 I.D.T. Ltd	400

(*c*) If the bill is discounted with the bank, in this case on 2 January 19-6, the discounting charges being £6.

J. Burgon

19-6		£	19-6		£
Jan	1 Sales	400	Jan	1 Bill Receivable	400

Bills Receivable

19-6		£	19-6		£
Jan	1 J. Burgon	400	Jan	2 Bank	400

Bank

19-6		£	19-6		£
Jan	2 Bills Receivable	400	Jan	2 Discounting Charges	6

Discounting Charges

19-6		£
Jan	2 Bank	6

Acceptor's Books

The instances (*a*), (*b*) and (*c*) in the drawer's books will result in similar entries in the acceptor's books. From the acceptor's point of view two things have happened, (1) The acceptance of the bill, and (2) its discharge by payment. The fact that (*a*), (*b*) and (*c*) would result in different payees is irrelevant as far as the acceptor is concerned.

D. Jarvis

19-6		£	19-6		£
Jan 1	Bills Payable	400	Jan 1	Purchases	400

Bills Payable

19-6		£	19-6		£
Mar 31	Bank	400	Jan 1	D. Jarvis	400

Bank

		19-6		£
		Mar 31	Bill Payable	400

Dishonoured Bills and Accounting Entries

These can be illustrated by reference to Exhibit 8.2

Exhibit 8.2

On 1 April 19-7 A. Grant sells goods for £600 to K. Lee, a bill with a maturity date of 30 June 19-7 being drawn by Grant and accepted by Lee on 2 April 19-7. On 30 June 19-7 the bill is presented to Lee, but he fails to pay it and it is therefore dishonoured. The bill is noted, the cost of £2 being paid by Grant on 7 July 19-7.

The entries needed will depend on whether or not the bill had been discounted by Grant.

(a) Drawer's Books

(i) *Where the Bill had not been discounted or renegotiated*

K. Lee

19-7		£	19-7		£
Apl 1	Sales	600	Apl 2	Bill Receivable	600
Jun 30	Bill Receivable – dishonoured	600			
July 7	Bank: Noting Charge (A)	2			

Bills Receivable

19-7		£	19-7		£
Apl 2	K. Lee	600	June 30	K. Lee – bill dishonoured	600

Bank

		19-7		£
		July 7	Noting Charges – K. Lee (A)	2

Note:

(A) As the noting charges are directly incurred as the result of Lee's default, then Lee must suffer the cost by his account being debited with that amount.

(ii) *Where the Bill had been discounted with a bank*

The entries can now be seen as they would have appeared if the bill had been discounted on 5 April 19-7, discounting charges being £9.

K. Lee

19-7		£	19-7		£
Apl	1 Sales	600	Apl	2 Bill Receivable	600
June 30	Bank − bill dis-honoured (C)	600			
July	7 Bank: Noting Charge	2			

Bills Receivable

19-7		£	19-7		£
Apl	2 K. Lee	600	Apl	5 Bank	600

Bank

19-7		£	19-7		£
Apl	5 Bills Receivable	600	Apl	5 Discounting Charges (B)	9
			June 30	K. Lee − bill dis-honoured (C)	600
			July	7 Noting Charges − K. Lee	2

Discounting Charges

19-7		£
Apl	5 Bank (B)	9

Notes:

(B) The discounting charges are wholly an expense of A. Grant. They are therefore charged to an expense account. Contrast this with the treatment of the noting charges.

(C) On maturity the bank will present the bill to Lee. On its dishonour the bank will hand the bill back to Grant, and will cancel out the original amount shown as being deposited in the bank account. This amount is then charged to Lee's personal account to show that he is still in debt.

(b) Acceptor's Books

The entries in the acceptor's books will not be affected by whether or not the drawer had discounted the bill.

A. Grant

19-7		£	19-7		£
Apl 1 Bill Payable		600	Apl 1 Purchases		600
			June 30 Bill Payable – dishonoured		600
			July 7 Noting Charge (D)		2

Bills Payable

19-7		£	19-7		£
Jun 30 A. Grant – bill dishonoured		600	Apl 1 A. Grant		600

Noting Charges

19-7		£
July 7 A. Grant (D)		2

Note:

(D) The noting charges will have to be reimbursed to A. Grant. To show this fact A. Grant's account is credited while the Noting Charges Account is debited to record the expense.

Bills Receivable as Contingent Liabilities

The fact that bills had been discounted, but had not reached maturity by the Balance Sheet date, could give an entirely false impression of the financial position of the business unless a note to this effect is made on the Balance Sheet. That such a note is necessary can be illustrated by reference to the following Balance Sheets.

Balance Sheet as at 31 December 19-7

	£	(a) £	£	(b) £
Fixed Asses		3,500		3,500
Current Assets:				
Stock	1,000		1,000	
Debtors	1,200		1,200	
Bills Receivable	1,800		–	
Bank	500		2,300	
	4,500		4,500	
Less Current Liabilities	3,000		3,000	
Working Capital		1,500		1,500
		5,000		5,000
		£		£
Financed by:				
Capital		5,000		5,000

Balance Sheet (*a*) shows the position if £1,800 of bills receivable were still in hand. Balance Sheet (*b*) shows the position if the bills had been discounted, ignoring discounting charges. To an outsider, Balance Sheet (*b*) seems to show a much stronger liquid position with £2,300 in the bank. However, should the bills be dishonoured on maturity the bank balance would slump to £500. The appearance of Balance Sheet (*b*) is therefore deceptive unless a note is added, e.g. *Note:* There is a contingent liability of £1,800 on bills discounted at the Balance Sheet date. This note enables the outsider to view the bank balance in its proper perspective of depending on the non-dishonour of the bills discounted.

Assignment Exercises

8.1. N. Gudgeon sells goods to two companies on July 1 19-7.

To R. Johnson Ltd	£2,460
To B. Scarlet & Co. Ltd.	£1,500

He draws bills of exchange on each of them and they are both accepted.

He discounts both of the bills with the bank on July 4 19-7, and suffers discounting charges of £80 on Johnson's bill and £65 on Scarlet's bill. On September 1 19-7 the bills mature and Johnson Ltd. meets its liability. Scarlet's bill is dishonoured and is duly noted on September 4, the noting charge being £6.

Show the above in the necessary accounts:

(*a*) In the books of Gudgeon.

(*b*) In the books of Scarlet Ltd. and of Johnson Ltd.

8.2A. P. Cummings buys goods from T. Victor Ltd. on January 21 19-7 for £2,900 and from C. Bellamy & Co. for £4,160. Bills are drawn on him and he accepts them.

T. Victor Ltd. discount their bill with their bank on January 29, the discounting charge being £110.

C. Bellamy & Co. simply keep their bill waiting for maturity.

On maturity of the bills on April 21 19-7, Cummings duly meets (pays) Bellamy's bill. He is unable to pay Victor's bill and it is accordingly dishonoured. Victor duly has it noted on April 28 19-7 the noting charge being £10.

Show the entries necessary in:

(a) The books of P. Cummings.
(b) The books of T. Victor Ltd.
(c) The books of C. Bellamy & Co.

8.3. K. C. owed T.M. £960. K.C. accepted a Bill of Exchange at three months date for this amount T.M. discounted it for £948.

Before the due date of the bill T.M. was informed that K.C. was unable to meet the bill and was offering a composition of 37½ per cent of each £ to his creditors. This offer was accepted and cash equivalent to the composition was received.

Show the ledger entries to record the above in T.M.'s ledger.

8.4. Draw up a Sales Ledger Control Account for the month of August 19-6 from the following:

19-6	£
Aug 1 Balances (Dr)	12,370
Balances (Cr)	105
Totals for the month:	
Sales Journal	16,904
Returns Inwards Journal	407
Cheques Received from customers	15,970
Bills receivable accepted	1,230
Cash received from customers	306
Bad Debts written off	129
Cash discounts allowed	604
Bill receivable dishonoured	177
Aug 31 Balances (Cr)	88
Balances (Dr)	?

8.5A. A Purchases Ledger Control Account should be drawn up for February 19-7 from the following:

19-7		£
Feb 1	Balances (Dr)	33
	Balances (Cr)	8,570
	Totals for the month:	
	Purchases Journal	11,375
	Returns Outwards Journal	568
	Bills Payable accepted by us	1,860
	Cheques paid to suppliers	9,464
	Cash paid to suppliers	177
	We were unable to meet a bill payable on maturity and it was therefore dishonoured	800
	We agreed to suffer noting charge on dishonoured bill	20
Feb 28	Balances (Dr)	47
	Balances (Cr)	?

8.6A. Indicate by Journal entries how the following would appear in the ledger accounts of (a) Noone, (b) Iddon.

19-8

Jan 1 Iddon sells goods £420 to Noone, and Noone sends to Iddon a three months' acceptance for this amount.

,, 1 Iddon discounts the acceptance with the Slough Discount Co. Ltd, receiving its cheque for £412.

Feb 29 One third of Noone's stock, valued at £3,600, is destroyed by fire. Noone claims on the underwriters at Lloyds with whom he is insured.

Apr 1 The underwriters admit the claim for £3,000 only as the total stock was only insured for £9,000.

,, 4 In view of Noone's difficulties Iddon meets the acceptance due today by giving his cheque for £420 to the Slough Discount Co. Ltd.; he draws on Noone a further bill for one month for £430 (to include £10 interest) which Noone accepts.

,, 9 Noone receives cheque from the underwriters in settlement of the admitted claim.

May 7 Noone's bank honours the acceptance presented by Iddon as due today.

8.7A. Enter the following in the appropriate ledger accounts of R. Smith:

19-0

Jan 5 R. Smith sold goods to P. Thomas, £320, and Thomas accepted Smith's bill for three months for this amount.

,, 6 R. Smith discounted Thomas's bill at the London Discount Co. for £304, and pays this amount into his account at the bank.

Apr 8 The London Discount Co. notified Smith that Thomas's bill had been dishonoured. Smith at once set cheque to the London Discount Co. for the full amount of the bill plus £3 charges.

,, 14 Smith agreed that Thomas's bankers should accept a further bill for one month for the total amount owing plus £10 interest, and received the new acceptance.

May 18 Smith's bank informed him the new bill had been paid.

9

Funds Flow Statements:
An Introduction

A profit and loss account discloses the net profit (or loss) resulting from the business during a period. A balance sheet simply lists the balances remining after the profit and loss account has been prepared. The balance sheet balances will however normally be quite different from those of last year's balance sheet. A funds flow statement endeavours to show the connection between the items in the two successive balance sheets. Whereas the profit and loss account will disclose the result of trading etc., the funds statement gives information as to the other types of activity which have occurred during the period, e.g. what fixed assets have been bought or sold, what loans have been obtained etc.

Further information from various forms of funds statements would enable the answers to be found such as:

Why has the bank balance fallen?
Where have the profits gone to?
Why has the working capital increased?

In 1975 Statement of Standard Accounting Practice (SSAP 10) was issued. All companies, except very small ones, have to prepare a 'Statement of Sources and Application of Funds'. In the SSAP 10 'funds' are working capital, although elsewhere there have been a wider interpretation of the meaning of 'funds'. Anyone later taking professional accounting examinations will need to study SSAP 10 in detail. The present chapter looks at simple funds statements, without restricting itself to the 'working capital' definition of funds.

For this simple approach the definition of funds will be that of 'resources' with the same meaning as when the accounting equation was first introduced.

Before actually performing the mechanics of constructing simple funds statements it must be stressed that:

1. The statement supplements the information given in the Profit and Loss Account and Balance Sheet,
2. The funds statement is a period statement which shows the main changes which have taken place in the financial structure of the business as a result of *all* activities, i.e. not just the trading activities.

3. The technique used when preparing the statement is the comparison of two successive balance sheets to bring out the changes which have taken place in the period in between. Illustrations are now given of a sole trader's business.

Balance Sheet (1st date)		*Balance Sheet (2nd date)*	
	£		£
Premises	8,000	Premises	8,000
Stock	10,000	Stock	13,000
Bank	2,000	Bank	2,000
	20,000		23,000
		Capital	20,000
Capital	20,000	Creditors	3,000
			£23,000

At date 1 the funds supplied by the owner are represented by the resources of Premises, Stock and Bank, totalling £20,000.

Stock £3,000 is then bought on credit so that the balance sheet is changed to that shown of the 2nd date.

By comparing balance sheet 1 with balance sheet 2 it can be seen that the increase in stocks was financed by the credit allowed by the creditors. The Funds Statement can now be prepared.

Statement of Source and Application of Funds
for period from 1st date to 2nd date

	£
Source of Funds	
Creditors	3,000
Application of Funds	
Increase in Stock	3,000

Before the 3rd date £2,000 of the stock is sold on credit for £3,400. Then before the 4th date £1,500 was received from debtors and £1,200 of it is used to pay creditors.

Balance Sheet (3rd date)			*Balance Sheet (4th date)*		
	£	£		£	£
Premises		8,000	Premises		8,000
Stock		11,000	Stock		11,000
Debtors		3,400	Debtors		1,900
Bank		2,000	Bank		2,300
		24,400			23,200
Capital:	20,000		Capital:		21,400
Add Profit	1,400	21,400			
Creditors	—	3,000	Creditors		1,800
		24,400			23,200

By comparing balance sheet 2 and 3, it can be seen that stock has been reduced by £2,000 and the sale produced funds of that amount plus a further £1,400 in profit. This source of £3,400 is represented by a increase in debtors of the same amount. The second funds statement will accordingly show this.

By comparing balance sheet 3 and 4 it can be seen that debtors have provided funds of £1,500, represented partly by an increase in cash and partly by a reduction in creditors. The third funds statement will reveal that situation.

Statement of Source and Application of Funds for period 2nd date to 3rd date	£	*Statement of Source and Application of Funds for period 3rd date to 4th date*	£
Source of Funds		Source of Funds	
Profit	1,400	Decrease in debtors	1,500
Decrease in stock	2,000		
	3,400		
		Application of Funds	
Application of Funds		Increase in bank	300
Increase in debtors	3,400	Decrease in creditors	1,200
			1,500

Adjustments Needed to Net Profit

When net profit is included as a source of funds, we usually have to adjust the net profit figure to take account of items included which do not involve a flow of funds. This will be illustrated by reference to balance sheets at 5th date and 6th date.

On the day that the balance sheet at the 5th date is being drawn up, extra Capital of £3,000 cash is brought in by the owner, and Fixtures are bought for £1,600, payment being made immediately.

Between then and the 6th date £3,200 stock is sold for £5,000 cash and the Fixtures are to be depreciated by £80. For the period the profit is therefore £1,800 − £80 = £1,720.

Balance Sheet (5th date)		£	*Balance Sheet (6th date)*		£
Premises		8,000	Premises		8,000
Fixtures		1,600	Fixtures	1,600	
Stock		11,000	Less Depreciation	80	1,520
Debtors		1,900	Stock		7,800
Bank		3,700	Debtors		1,900
		26,200	Bank		8,700
					27,920
Capital	21,400				
Add Cash			Capital	24,400	
Introduced	3,000	24,400	Add Net Profit	1,720	26,120
Creditors		1,800	Creditors		1,800
		26,200			27,920

When drawing up the Funds Statement for the period from date 4 to date 5 the purchase of Fixtures £1,600 will be shown as an application of funds. In the following period, date 5 to date 6, £80 is shown as depreciation of Fixtures and accordingly has also been deducted in calculating net profit. However the purchase of Fixtures in the previous period has already been treated as an application of Funds. As this has already been counted, depreciation should not also be counted as an outflow of funds. To get to the correct figure of profit as a source of funds, the depreciation figure should accordingly be added back to the net profit figure.

Statement of Source and Application of Funds for period 4th date to 5th date		*Statement of Source and Application of Funds for period 5th date to 6th date*	
	£		£
Source of Funds	3,000	Source of Funds: Net Profit	1,720
		Add Depreciation	80
Application of Funds		Total generated from	
Fixtures bought	1,600	operations	1,800
Increase in bank	1,400	Decrease in stock	3,200
	3,000		5,000
		Application of Funds	
		Increase in Bank	5,000
			5,000

Similarly, there are other non-cash items which would need adjusting to the net profit figure. These could be such items as provisions for bad debts or a book loss on the sale of a fixed asset. These can now be considered.

Between the 6th date and the 7th date £3,000 stock is sold for £5,100 to various customers on credit. As on the 7th date it is decided to make a provision for bad debts of £140. It is also decided to write off another £80 depreciation from fixtures. The net profit for the period will therefore be calculated as £5,100 − £3,000 = £2,100 less provision £140 and depreciation £80 = £1,880.

Between the 7th date and the 8th date, the Premises were sold for £7,750, proceeds being received immediately. The £250 loss on sale was written off to profit and loss. Stock costing £2,300 was sold for £3,950 on credit. £1,100 is paid off amounts owing to creditors. For this period another £80 depreciation is to be written off fixtures. The net profit is therefore £3,950 − £2,300 = £1,650 less loss on premises £250 and depreciation £80 = £1,320. Note that the provision for bad debts has remained at £140.

Balance Sheet (7th date)			*Balance Sheet (8th date)*		
		£			£
Premises		8,000	Fixtures	1,440	
Fixtures	1,520		Less Depreciation	80	1,360
Less Depreciation	80	1,440	Stock		2,500
Stock		4,800	Debtors	10,950	
Debtors	7,000		Less Provision	140	10,810
Less Provision	140	6,860			
Bank		8,700	Bank		15,350
		29,800			30,020
Capital	26,120		Capital	28,000	
Add Net Profit	1,880	28,000	Add Net Profit	1,320	29,320
Creditors		1,800	Creditors		700
		29,800			30,020

Statement of Source and Application of Funds for period 6th date to 7th date			*Statement of Source and Application of Funds for period 7th date to 8th date*		
		£			£
Source of Funds			Source of Funds: Net Profit		1,320
Net Profit		1,880	Add Depreciation	80	
Add Depreciation	80		,, Loss on Premises	250	330
,, Provision for Bad Debts	140	220	Total Generated from Operations		1,650
Total Generated from Operations		2,100	Sale of Premises		7,750
Decrease in Stock		3,000	Decrease in Stock		2,300
		5,100			11,700
Application of Funds			Application of Funds		
Increase in Debtors		5,100	Increase in Bank		6,650
			Increase in Debtors		3,950
			Decrease in Creditors		1,100
					11,700

Alternative Presentation

In the first year of your course the proposition that an accountant is a communicator was examined. Funds flow statements can be used to help communicate accounting information to those who are not well versed in Accounting, so that they may gain a better understanding of the financial statements.

Exhibit 9.1 gives two consecutive balance sheets of a business.

Exhibit 9.1

<table>
<tr><td colspan="3">A. Jackson
Balance Sheet as at
31 December 19-5</td><td colspan="3">A. Jackson
Balance Sheet as at
31 December 19-6</td></tr>
<tr><td></td><td>£</td><td>£</td><td></td><td>£</td><td>£</td></tr>
<tr><td>Fixed Assets</td><td></td><td></td><td>Fixed Assets</td><td></td><td></td></tr>
<tr><td>Premises at cost</td><td></td><td>50,000</td><td>Premises at cost</td><td></td><td>57,500</td></tr>
<tr><td>Motor Vehicles at</td><td></td><td></td><td>Motor Vehicles at</td><td></td><td></td></tr>
<tr><td>cost</td><td>24,000</td><td></td><td>cost</td><td>24,000</td><td></td></tr>
<tr><td>Less Depreciation</td><td>6,000</td><td>18,000</td><td>Less Depreciation</td><td>7,200</td><td>16,800</td></tr>
<tr><td></td><td></td><td>68,000</td><td></td><td></td><td>74,300</td></tr>
<tr><td>Current Assets</td><td></td><td></td><td>Current Assets</td><td></td><td></td></tr>
<tr><td>Stock</td><td>27,500</td><td></td><td>Stock</td><td>46,500</td><td></td></tr>
<tr><td>Debtors</td><td>15,700</td><td></td><td>Debtors</td><td>13,150</td><td>59,650</td></tr>
<tr><td>Bank</td><td>8,200</td><td>51,400</td><td></td><td></td><td>133,950</td></tr>
<tr><td></td><td></td><td>119,400</td><td></td><td></td><td></td></tr>
<tr><td>Capital</td><td></td><td></td><td>Capital</td><td></td><td></td></tr>
<tr><td>Balance at 1.1.19-5</td><td></td><td>108,800</td><td>Balance at 1.1.19-6</td><td></td><td>113,100</td></tr>
<tr><td>Add Net Profit</td><td></td><td>12,800</td><td>Add Net Profit</td><td></td><td>17,500</td></tr>
<tr><td></td><td></td><td>121,600</td><td></td><td></td><td>130,600</td></tr>
<tr><td>Less Drawings</td><td></td><td>8,500</td><td>Less Drawings</td><td></td><td>9,200</td></tr>
<tr><td></td><td></td><td>113,100</td><td></td><td></td><td>121,400</td></tr>
<tr><td>Current Liabilities</td><td></td><td></td><td>Current Liabilities</td><td></td><td></td></tr>
<tr><td>Creditors</td><td></td><td>6,300</td><td>Creditors</td><td>4,250</td><td></td></tr>
<tr><td></td><td></td><td></td><td>Bank Overdraft</td><td>8,300</td><td>12,550</td></tr>
<tr><td></td><td></td><td>119,400</td><td></td><td></td><td>133,950</td></tr>
</table>

A. Jackson asks his accountant to explain

(a) Why he now has a bank overdraft when last year he had money in the bank, and has run the business at a profit?

(b) Why his working capital has decreased during the year.

The accountant might draft his fund flow statements as follows:

	(a)			(b)	

A. Jackson

Statement of Source and Application of Funds for the year ended 31 December 19-6

	£
Source of Funds	
Net Profit	17,500
Add Depreciation	1,200
Total Generated from Operations	18,700
Reduction in Debtors	2,550
	21,250
Application of Funds	
Drawings	9,200
Extra Premises bought	7,500
Increase in Stock	19,000
Decrease in Creditors	2,050	37,750
Reduction in Bank Funds	(16,500)
Bank Balance 31.12.19-5	8,200
Bank Overdraft 31.12.19-6	8,300	16,500

A. Jackson

Statement of Source and Application of Funds for the year ended 31 December 19-6

	£
Source of Funds	
Net Profit	17,500
Add Depreciation	1,200
	18,700
Application of Funds	
Purchase of Extra Premises	7,500
Drawings	9,200	16,700
	2,000
Increase/(Decrease) in Working Capital	
Increase in Stock	19,000
Decrease in Debtors	(2,550)
Decrease in Creditors	2,050
Decrease in Bank	(16,500)
	2,000

Assignment Exercises

9.1. The last two balance sheets for B. Luckman are as follows:

Balance Sheet as at 31 December 19-3

		£		£
Fixed Assets		50,000	Capital	69,000
Current Assets			Loan	4,000
Stock	16,000		Creditors	13,000
Debtors	9,500			
Bank	10,500	36,000		
		86,000		86,000

Balance Sheet as at 31 December 19-4

	£			£
Fixed Assets	71,000	Capital		
Current Assets		Balance 1.1.19-4	69,000	
Stock	8,500	Add net profit	13,500	
Debtors	6,500		82,500	
Bank	2,000	17,000	Less Drawings	8,000	74,500
			Loan		9,000
			Creditors		4,500
		88,000			88,000

Mr Luckman is puzzled. He has made £13,500 profit, he has borrowed extra money, and yet his bank balance has fallen dramatically.

You are to set out a statement showing how the money has been spent. Note: The fixed assets were depreciated £4,000 during the year.

9.2A. **John Shaw**
Balance Sheet as at 31 December 19-3

	£		£
Buildings	45,000	Capital 1 January 19-3	54,000
Fixtures	7,000	Add net profit	13,500
Stock	7,500		
Debtors	3,500		67,500
Bank	2,500	Less drawings	7,500
Cash in hand	500		
			60,000
		Trade creditors	6,000
	66,000		66,000

Balance Sheet as at 31 December 19-4

	£		£
Buildings	45,000	Capital 1 January 19-4	60,000
Fixtures	9,000	Add net profit	12,000
Stock	14,000		
Debtors	8,700		72,000
Cash in hand	300	Less drawings	8,000
			64,000
		Trade creditors	8,900
		Bank overdraft	4,100
	77,000		77,000

Study the Balance Sheets shown above.

(*a*) Calculate the working capital on 31 December 19-3 and on 31 December 19-4.
(*b*) Calculate the percentage of net profit on capital at the beginning of each year.
(*c*) Draw up a statement explaining why it has become necessary to raise an overdraft during 19-4.

9.3. The Balance Sheets of a sole trader for two successive years are given below. You are required to calculate the variation in working capital and to explain how the variation has arisen.

Balance Sheets — as on 31 December

	19-3	19-4		19-3	19-4
	£	£		£	£
Land and Premises			Capital Account:		
(cost £3,000)	2,600	2,340	1 January	4,200	4,700
Plant and Machinery			*Add* Net Profit for		
(cost £2,000)	1,500	—	the year	1,800	2,200
(cost £3,000)	—	2,300		6,000	6,900
Stocks	660	630	Deduct Drawings	1,300	1,500
Trade Debtors	1,780	1,260			
Bank	—	710		4,700	5,400
			Trade Creditors	1,200	840
			Bank Overdraft	640	—
			Loan (repayable		
			December 19-0)	—	1,000
	6,540	7,240		6,540	7,240

9.4A. **John Flynn**

Balance Sheets as at 31 December

	19-8	19-9		19-8	19-9
	£	£		£	£
Buildings	5,000	5,000	Capital at 1 January	15,500	16,100
Fixtures			Add Cash Introduced	—	2,500
less depreciation	1,800	2,000	,, Net Profit for year	6,800	7,900
Motor				22,300	26,500
less depreciation	2,890	5,470	Less Drawings	6,200	7,800
Stock	3,000	8,410		16,100	18,700
Debtors	4,860	5,970			
Bank	3,100	—	Creditors	2,900	2,040
Cash	350	150	Bank Overdraft	—	1,260
			Loan (repayable 19-5)	2,000	5,000
	21,000	27,000		21,000	27,000

From the balance sheets above draw up a statement showing how the variation in working capital has arisen. Fixtures bought during the year amounted to £400, and a motor was bought for £4,000.

10

Final Accounts of Partnerships

If the sales, stock and expenses of a partnership were exactly the same as that of a sole trader then the trading and profit and loss account would be identical with that as prepared for the sole trader. However, a partnership would have an extra section shown under the profit and loss account. This section is called the profit and loss appropriation account, and it is in this account that the distribution of profits is shown. The heading to the trading and profit and loss account does not include the words 'appropriation account'. It is purely an accounting custom not to include it in the heading.

Exhibit 10.1

Taylor and Clarke are in partnership sharing profits and losses in the ratio of Taylor 3/5ths, Clarke 2/5ths. They are entitled to 5 per cent per annum interest on capitals, Taylor having £2,000 capital and Clarke £6,000. Clarke is to have a salary of £500. They charge interest on drawings, Taylor being charged £50 and Clarke £100. The net profit, before any distributions to the partners, amounted to £5,000 for the year ended 31 December 19-7.

The trading and profit and loss account of Taylor and Clarke from the details given would appear:

Taylor and Clarke

Trading and Profit and Loss Account for the year ended 31 December 19-7

Trading Account − same as for sole trader

£

Profit and Loss Account − same as for sole trader

	£	£	£
Net Profit			5,000
Interest on drawings:			
Taylor		50	
Clarke		100	150
Less:			
Interest on capitals			
Taylor	100		
Clarke	300	400	
Salary: Clarke		500	900
			4,250
Balance of profits shared:			
Taylor $^3/_5$ ths		2,550	
Clarke $^2/_5$ ths		1,700	4,250

Fixed and Fluctuating Capital Accounts

There is a choice open in partnership accounts of:

(a) Fixed Capital Accounts Plus Current Accounts

The capital account for each partner remains year by year at the figure of capital put into the firm by the partners. The profits, interest on capital and the salaries to which the partner may be entitled are then credited to a separate current account for the partner, and the drawings and the interest on drawings are debited to it. The balance of the current account at the end of each financial year will then represent the amount of undrawn (or withdrawn) profits. A credit balance will be undrawn profits, while a debit balance will be drawings in excess of the profits to which the partner was entitled.

For Taylor and Clarke, capital and current accounts, assuming drawings of £2,000 each, will appear:

Taylor − Capital

			£
Jan	1 Balance b/d		2,000

Clarke − Capital

			£
Jan	1 Balance b/d		6,000

Taylor — Current Account

	£			£
Dec 31 Cash: Drawings	2,000	Dec 31 Profit and Loss		
,, Profit and Loss		Appropriation		
Appropriation:		Account:		
Interest on		Interest on Capital	100
Drawings	50	Share of Profits	2,550
,, 31 Balance c/d	600			
	2,650			2,650
				£
		Jan 1 Balance b/d		600

Clarke — Current Account

	£			£
Dec 31 Cash: Drawings	2,000	Dec 31 Profit and Loss		
,, 31 Profit and Loss		Appropriation		
Appropriation:		Account:		
Interest on		Interest on Capital	300
Drawings	100	Share of Profits	1,700
,, 31 Balance c/d	400	Salary	500
	2,500			2,500
				£
		Jan 1 Balance b/d		400

Notice that the salary of Clarke was not paid to him, it was merely credited to his account. If in fact it was paid in addition to his drawings, the £500 cash paid would have been debited to the current account changing the £400 credit balance into a £100 debit balance.

(b) Fluctuating Capital Accounts

The distribution of profits would be credited to the capital account, and the drawings and interest on drawings debited. Therefore the balance on the capital account will change each year, i.e. it will fluctuate.

If Fluctuating Capital Accounts had been kept for Taylor and Clarke they would have appeared:

Taylor — Capital

	£			£
Dec 31 Cash: Drawings	2,000	Jan 1 Balance b/d		2,000
,, 31 Profit and Loss		Dec 31 Profit and Loss		
Appropriation		Appropriation		
Account:		Account:		
Interest on		Interest on Capital		100
Drawings	50	Share of Profits		2,550
,, 31 Balance c/d	2,600			
	4,650			4,650
		Jan 1 Balance b/d		2,600

Clarke — Capital

	£			£
Dec 31 Cash: Drawings	2,000	Jan 1 Balance b/d		6,000
,, 31 Profit and Loss		Dec 31 Profit and Loss		
Appropriation		Appropriation		
Account:		Account:		
Interest on		Interest on Capital		300
Drawings	100	Salary		500
,, 31 Balance c/d	6,400	Share of Profit		1,700
	8,500			8,500
		Jan 1 Balance b/d		6,400

Fixed Capital Accounts Preferred

The keeping of fixed capital accounts plus Current Accounts is considered preferable to fluctuating capital accounts. When partners are taking out greater amounts than the share of the profits that they are entitled to, this is shown up by a debit balance on the current account and so acts as a warning.

The Balance Sheet

The capital part side of the balance sheet will appear:

Balance Sheet as at 31 December 19-7

		£	£
Capitals:	Taylor	2,000	
	Clarke	6,000	8,000

Current Accounts	*Taylor*	*Clarke*	
	£	£	
Interest on Capital	100	300	
Share of profits	2,550	1,700	
Salary	–	500	
	2,650	2,500	
Less Drawings	2,000	2,000	
Interest on drawings	50	100	
	600	400	1,000

If one of the current accounts had finished in debit, for instance if the current account of Clarke had finished up as £400 debit, the abbreviation Dr would appear and the balances would appear net in the totals column:

	Taylor	*Clarke*	
	£	£	£
Closing balance	600	400 *Dr*	200

If the net figure turned out to be a debit figure then this would be deducted from the total of the capital accounts.

Assignment Exercises

10.1A. Dent, Bishop and White are in partnership. They share profits and losses in the ratio 3:2:1 respectively. Interest is charged on drawings at the rate of 10 per cent per annum and credited at the same rate in respect of the balances on the partners' capital accounts.

Bishop is to be credited with a salary of £2,000 per annum.

In the year to 31 December 19-4 the net profit of the firm was £50,400. The partners drawings of Dent £8,000; Bishop £7,200; White £4,800 were taken in two equal instalments by the partners on 1 April 19-4 and 1 October 19-4.

The balances of the partner's accounts at 31 December 19-3 were as follows:
(all credit balances)

	Capital Accounts £	Current Accounts £
Dent	30,000	750
Bishop	28,000	1,340
White	16,000	220

You are required to:

(a) Prepare the firm's profit and loss appropriation account for the year ended 31 December 19-4,

(b) Show how the partners' capital and current accounts are shown in the balance sheet as at 31 December 19-4.

10.2. Mendez and Marshall are in partnership sharing profits and losses equally. The following is their trial balance as at 30 June 19-6:

	Dr. £	Cr. £
Buildings at cost	50,000	
Fixtures at cost	11,000	
Provision for Depreciation: Fixtures		3,300
Debtors	16,243	
Creditors		11,150
Cash at Bank	677	
Stock at 30 June 19-5	41,979	
Sales		123,650
Purchases	85,416	
Carriage Outwards	1,288	
Discounts Allowed	115	
Loan Interest: King	4,000	
Office Expenses	2,416	
Salaries and Wages	18,917	
Bad Debts	503	
Provision for Bad Debts		400
Loan from J. King		40,000
Capitals: Mendez		35,000
Marshall		29,500
Current Accounts: Mendez		1,306
Marshall		298
Drawings: Mendez	6,400	
Marshall	5,650	
	244,604	244,604

Prepare a trading and profit and loss appropriation account for the year ended 30 June 19-6, and a balance sheet as at that date.
(i) Stock, 30 June 19-6 £56,340.
(ii) Expenses to be accrued: Office Expenses £96; Wages £200.
(iii) Depreciate fixtures 10 per cent on reducing balance basis Buildings £1,000.
(iv) Reduce provision for bad debts to £320.
(v) Partnership salary: £800 to Mendez. Not yet entered.
(vi) Interest on drawings: Mendez £180; Marshall £120.
(vii) Interest on capital account balances at 10 per cent.

10.3. You are required to prepare a trading and profit and loss account for the year ended 31 December 19-5, and a balance sheet as at that date from the following:

Trial Balance as at 31 December 19-5

	Dr	Cr
	£	£
Drawings:		
Perkins	1,750	
Hodson	1,429	
Capital:		
Perkins		9,000
Hodson		4,800
Current accounts as at 1 January 19-5:		
Perkins		880
Hodson	120	
Motor vehicles	1,870	
Stock−1 January 19-5	2,395	
Returns inwards and outwards	110	286
Sales		28,797
Purchases	19,463	
Wages and salaries	4,689	
Carriage inwards	216	
Delivery expenses	309	
Rent and rates	485	
Insurances	116	
Debtors and creditors	3,462	1,899
Cash in hand	180	
General expenses	204	
Loan−T. Farthingale		2,000
Discounts allowed and received	392	404
Motor expenses	635	
Cash at bank	241	
	48,066	48,066

Notes at 31 December 19-5:

1. Stock £5,623
2. Depreciate motors 10 per cent on reducing balance basis

3. Insurance prepaid £12
4. Rates owing £57
5. Included in salaries is a salary to Hodson for the year £300
6. Allow 5 per cent interest on capitals
7. Charge interest on drawings: Perkins £58; Hodson £39
8. Goods value £75 have been taken by Perkins for his own use, no entry having been in the books
9. Profit shared: Hodson 2/5ths; Perkins 3/5ths (calculations to nearest £)
10. Loan interest owing £140
11. Make a provision for bad debts £320.

10.4A. Oscar and Felix are in partnership. They share profits on the ratio: Oscar 60 per cent; Felix 40 per cent. The following trial balance was extracted as at 31 March 19-6:

	Dr. £	Cr. £
Office Equipment at cost	6,500	
Motor Vehicles at cost	9,200	
Provisions for depreciation at 31.3.19-5:		
Motor Vehicles		3,680
Office Equipment		1,950
Stock 31 March 19-5	24,970	
Debtors and Creditors	20,960	16,275
Cash at Bank	615	
Cash in Hand	140	
Sales		90,370
Purchases	71,630	
Salaries	8,417	
Office Expenses	1,370	
Discounts Allowed	563	
Current Accounts at 31.3.19-5:		
Oscar		1,379
Felix		1,211
Capital Accounts: Oscar		27,000
Felix		12,000
Drawings: Oscar	5,500	
Felix	4,000	
	153,865	153,865

Draw up a set of final accounts for the year ended 31 March 19-6 for the partnership. The following notes are applicable at 31 March 19-6.
(i) Stock 31 March 19-6 £27,340.
(ii) Office Expenses owing £110.
(iii) Provide for depreciation: Motors 20 per cent of cost, Office Equipment 10 per cent of cost.
(iv) Charge Interest on capitals at 10 per cent.
(v) Charge Interest on drawings: Oscar £180; Felix £210.

11

Goodwill

When a firm has been in existence for some time, then if the owner(s) wanted to sell the business, they may well be able to obtain more for the business as a going concern than they would if the assets shown on the Balance Sheet were sold separately. To simplify matters, imagine that a man has a small engineering works, of which he was the orginator, and that the business was started by him some twenty years ago. He now wishes to sell the business. If sold separately, the assets on the balance sheet would fetch a total of £40,000, being £12,000 for machinery, £25,000 for premises and the stock £3,000. As a complete going concern a purchaser may be willing to pay a total of £50,000 for it. The extra £10,000 that the purchaser will pay over and above the total saleable values of the identifiable assets is known in accounting as goodwill. This is a technical term used in accounting, it must not be confused with the meaning of goodwill in ordinary language usage.

The reasons why the purchaser would be willing to pay £10,000 for goodwill are not always capable of being identified with precision, nor is it often possible to place any particular value on any of the reasons which have induced him to make this offer. One fact only is obvious, and that is that no rational person would be willing to pay a higher figure for the entire going concern than he would pay for buying the identifiable assets separately, unless the expected rate of return on the purchase money spent was greater in the case of the entire going concern. While it is not possible to list all of the factors which induce purchasers to pay for goodwill, it may be useful to examine some possible motives.

(a) The business may have enjoyed some form of monopoly, either nationally or locally. There may not be sufficient trade for two such engineering firms to be carried on profitably. If the purchaser buys this firm then no one may set up in competition with him. On the other hand, if he buys the other assets separately and sets up his own firm, then the original business will still be for sale and the owner may well fix a price that will induce someone to buy it. Many prospective entrants would therefore be prepared to pay an extra amount in the hope of preserving the monopoly position. The monopoly may possibly be due to some form of governmental licence not otherwise easily available.

(b) The purchaser could continue to trade under the same name as that of the original firm. The fact that the firm was well known could mean that new customers would be attracted for this reason alone. The seller would probably introduce the purchaser to his customers. The establishment of a nucleus of customers is something that many new firms would be willing to pay for, as full profits could be earned from the very start of the business instead of waiting until a large enough body of customers is built up. There could be profitable contracts that were capable of being taken over only by the purchaser of the firm.

(c) The value of the labour force, including management skills other than that of the retiring proprietor. The possession of a skilled labour force, including that of management, is an asset that Balance Sheets do not disclose. To recruit and train a suitable labour force is often costly in money and effort, and the purchaser of a going concern would obviously normally be in a position to take over most of the labour force.

(d) The possession of trade marks and patents. These may have cost the original owner little or nothing, not be shown on the Balance Sheet, and could be unsaleable unless the business is sold as a going concern.

(e) The location of the business premises may be more valuable if a particular type of business is carried on rather than if the premises were sold to any other kind of business firm.

(f) The costs of research and development which have brought about cheaper manufacturing methods or a better product may not have been capitalized, but may have been charged as revenue expenditure in the periods when the expenditure was incurred. For any new firm starting up it could well cost a considerable amount of money to achieve the same results.

The amount which someone is prepared to pay for goodwill therefore depends on their view of the future profits which will accrue to the business due to the factors mentioned, or similar assets difficult to identify. The seller of the business will want to show these additional assets to their best advantage, while the buyer will discount those that he feels are inappropriate or over-stressed. The figure actually paid for goodwill will therefore often be a compromise.

The economic state of the country, and whether or not a boom or a recession is in the offing, together with the effects of a credit squeeze or of reflation, plus the relative position of the particular industry, trade or profession, will all affect people's judgements of future profits. In addition the shortage of funds or relatively easy access to finance for such a purchase will, together with the factors already mentioned, lead to marked differences of money paid for goodwill of similar firms at different points in time.

There are also instances where the amount that could be obtained for an entire going concern is less than if all the assets were sold separately. This, contrary to many a person's guess is not 'badwill', as this is just not an accounting term, but would in fact be negative goodwill. The owner would, if he was a rational man, sell all the assets separately, but it does not always hold true. The owner may well have a pride in his work, or a sense of duty to the community, and may elect to sell only to those who would carry on in the same tradition despite the fact that higher offers for the assets had been made. Someone who has had to sell his business quickly may also be forced to accept less than he would wish. In accounting it is well to remember that figures themselves only tell part of the story.

Methods of Valuing Goodwill

Custom plays a large part in the valuation of goodwill in many sorts of businesses. Goodwill exists sometimes only because of custom, because if a somewhat more scientific approach was used in certain cases it would be seen that there was no justification for a figure being paid for goodwill. However, justification or not, goodwill exists where the purchaser is willing to pay for it.

The mere calculation of a figure for goodwill does not mean that someone will be willing to pay this amount for it. As with the striking of any bargain there is no certainty until the price is agreed.

A very important factor to take into account in the valuation of goodwill is based on the 'momentum' theory of goodwill. This can be stated to be that the profits accruing to a firm from the possession of the goodwill at a point in time will lose momentum, and will be gradu ally replaced by profits accruing from new goodwill created later on. Thus the old goodwill fades away or loses momentum, it does not last for ever, and new goodwill is gradually created. Therefore in a business goodwill may always exist, but it will very rarely be either of the same value or composed of the same factors.

Some of the methods used in goodwill valuation can now be looked at. The rule of thumb approach can be seen in particular in methods (i), (ii) and (iii) which follow. However, the accountant's role has often been not necessarily to find any 'true' figure which could be validated in some way, but has instead been to find an 'acceptable' figure, one which the parties to a transaction would accept as the basis for settlement. In particular trades, industries and professions, these methods while not necessarily 'true' have certainly been acceptable as the basis for negotiations.

(i) In more than one type of retail business it has been the custom to value goodwill at the average weekly sales for the past year multiplied by a given figure. The given figure will, of course, differ as between different types of businesses, and often changes gradually in the same types of businesses in the long term.

(ii) With many professional firms, such as accountants in public practice, it is the custom to value goodwill as being the gross annual fees times a given number. For instance, what is termed a two years' purchase of a firm with gross fees of £6,000 means goodwill = 2 × £6,000 = £12,000.

(iii) The average net annual profit for a specified past number of years multiplied by an agreed number. This is often said to be x years purchase of the net profits.

(iv) The super-profits basis.

(a) The Traditional View

The net profits are taken as not representing a realistic view of the 'true' profits of the firm. For a sole trader, no charge has been made for his services when calculating net profit, yet obviously he is working in the business just as is any other employee. If the net profit is shown as £5,000, can he say that he is better off by £5,000 than he would otherwise have been? The answer must be negative, since if he had not owned a business he could have been earning money from some other employment. Also, if he had not invested his money in the business he could have invested it somewhere else. If these two factors are taken into account, the amount by which he would have been better off is given the name of 'super-profit'.

Exhibit 11.1

Hawks, a chemist, has a shop from which he makes annual net profits of £4,300. The amount of his capital invested in the business was £10,000. If he had invested it elsewhere in something where the element of risk was identical he would have expected a 5 per cent return per annum. If, instead of working for himself, he had in fact taken a post as a chemist he would have earned a salary of £1,800 per annum.

	£	£
Annual net profits		4,300
Less Remuneration for similar work	1,800	
,, Interest on capital invested £10,000 at 5 per cent	500	2,300
Annual Super-profits		2,000

If it is expected that super-profits can be earned for each of the next five years, then the value of the goodwill is the value of receiving £2,000 extra for each of the next five years.

Sometimes the goodwill is calculated as x years purchase of the super-profits. If this were an eight-year purchase of super-profits of £5,000, then the goodwill would be stated to be worth £40,000.

(b) The Discounted Momentum Value Method

The momentum theory of goodwill has already been discussed briefly. The benefits to be gained from goodwill purchased fall as that goodwill gradually ceases to exist, while other benefits are gained from new goodwill created by the new firm. The principle may be further illustrated by reference to the fact that old customers die or may leave the firm, and new ones coming along to replace them are likely to be due to the efforts of the new proprietors. Therefore when buying a business the goodwill should be assessed as follows:

(i)   Estimate the profits that will accrue from the firm if the existing business is taken over.

(ii)   Estimate the profits that would be made if, instead of buying the existing business, identical assets are bought (other than the goodwill) and the firm starts from scratch.

The difference in the profits to be earned will therefore be as a result of the incidence of the goodwill.

Exhibit 11.2

Years	Estimated profits if existing business taken over	Estimated profits if new business set up	Excess profits caused by goodwill taken over
	£	£	£
1	10,000	4,000	6,000
2	11,000	6,000	5,000
3	11,500	8,500	3,000
4	12,000	11,000	1,000
5	12,000	12,000	–
(and later years will show no difference in profits)			
			15,000

Sole Trader's Books

It would not be normal for goodwill to be entered in a sole trader's books unless he had actually bought it. Therefore the very existence of goodwill in the Balance Sheet would result in the assumption that the sole trader had bought the business from someone previously and was not himself the founder of the business.

Partnership Books

The partners may make any specific agreement between themselves concerning goodwill. There is no limit as to the ways that they may devise to value it or to enter it in the books, or to make adjusting entries in the books without opening a Goodwill Account. Whatever they agree will therefore take precedence over anything written in this chapter.

However, failing any agreement to the contrary, it is possible to state that a partner in a firm will own a share in the goodwill in the same ratio which he shares profits. Thus if A take one-quarter of the profits, then he will be the owner of one-quarter of the goodwill. This will hold true whether or not a Goodwill Account is in existence. Should a new partner be introduced who will take a share of one-third of the profits, he will, subject to there being any contrary agreement, be the owner of one-third of the goodwill. It is therefore essential that he should either pay something for goodwill when he enters the firm, or else an amount should be charged to his Capital Account.

This can probably be seen more clearly if a simple example is taken. A and B are in partnership sharing profits one-half each. A new partner, C, is admitted and A, B and C will now take one-third share of the profits, and therefore each will now own one-third of the goodwill. As A and B used to own one-half of the goodwill each they have therefore given part of the asset to C. A few months later the business is sold to a large company and £30,000 is obtained for good will. A, B and C will thus receive £10,000 each for their respective shares of the goodwill. If C had not been charged for goodwill, or had paid nothing for it, then A and B would have surrendered part of their ownership of the firm to C and received nothing in return.

Any change in profit sharing will, unless specifically agreed to the contrary, mean that the ownership of the goodwill will also change. As some partners give up their share, or part of their share, of an asset while other partners gain, it is therefore essential that some payment or adjustment be made whenever profit sharing is altered. This will take place whenever any of the following events occur:

1. There is a change in the profit-sharing ratios of existing partners.

2. A new partner is introduced.

3. A partner dies or retires.

Unlike a sole trader, a partnership may therefore have a Goodwill Account opened in its books even though the goodwill has never been purchased from an outside source. For instance, a Goodwill Account may be opened just because the partners have changed profit-sharing ratios even though they were the partners that were the founders of the firm, and had not therefore ever paid anything to an outsider for goodwill.

Depreciation of Goodwill

Opinion has always been split between two main schools of thought. One school considers that purchased goodwill should be written off directly and should not be maintained as an asset. The other school took the view that goodwill should be depreciated through the profit and loss account year by year over its useful life.

Limited Companies

In January 1985 Statement of Standard Accounting Practice No. 22 (SSAP 22) 'Accounting for Goodwill' was issued. This relates to companies and groups of companies.

A brief summary is as follows:

1. Purchased goodwill should normally be eliminated as an asset from the books on acquisition.

2. In some companies where special needs are appropriate, the purchased goodwill can be 'amortised' (i.e. depreciated) year by year over its useful economic life.

3. Goodwill which has not been bought, but has been created within the company (inherent goodwill) should never be brought into the books.

4. Where there is 'negative goodwill', this should be added to the reserves in the balance sheet of the company.

12

Accounting Ratios

Accounting information summarises the economic performance and situation of a business. In order to make use of this information the user needs to analyse and interpret its meaning. When confronted with information it is useful to have a framework of analysis available to make an attempt to distil what is important from the mass of less important data.

A mechanic confronted with a car that is refusing to start has a set of routine checks which will by elimination help to identify the problem. Someone without the appropriate knowledge can feel helpless faced with the complex array of electrical and mechanical parts under the bonnet of a car.

A business is in many ways more complex than a motor car. In a car cause and effect can be traced through a mechanical sequence. A thorough check will show the fault and a repair can be made. If a business's sales decline however, the cause may be clearly identifiable on the other hand the problem may be due to a variety of causes, some of which are human problems and may not be so easily diagnosed. A business consists of people interacting amongst themselves as well as with the mechanical means of production at their disposal. The human behaviour element may not always lend itself to logical and systematic analysis.

Having said this however the first stage in analysis is the development of a systematic review of the accounting data. In this respect accounting ratios are relationships which bring together the results of activity which experience shows identify the key areas for success of the business.

The choice of ratios will be determined by the needs of the user of the information. In this chapter the ratios which are illustrated are divided into main groups which may be identified with the requirements of particular users. However this division whilst it is useful as an aid to our memory and in developing a logical approach should not be taken as a set of rigid rules. A supplier of goods on credit to a firm, will mainly be interested in his customers immediate ability to repay him, which will be measured by liquidity ratios, but he will also be interested in the overall future and prospects of the customer measured by the Profitability and other ratios.

The main parties interested in accounts include shareholders and potential shareholders, creditors, lenders, the Government for taxation and statistical purposes, potential take over bidders, employees particularly though their trade unions, as well as management. The interests of the various parties have been summarised in Exhibit 12.1 which divides the types of ratio into five main categories. In this book it is not possible to show all possibly useful ratios since these can run to many hundreds, rather generally useful common ratios are illustrated. In practice it is sensible to calculate as many ratios as appear useful for the required objective.

Exhibit 12.1

Examples of Parties with an immediate interest	*Type of Ratio*
Potential Suppliers of goods on credit; Lenders, e.g. Bank managers and debenture holders; Management.	*Liquidity (Credit Risk):* Ratios indicating how well equipped the business is to pay its way.
Shareholders (Actual and Potential); Potential take-over bidders; Lenders; Management; Competitive firms; Tax Authorities; Employees.	*Profitability:* How successfully is the business trading.
Shareholders (Actual and Potential); Potential take-over bidders; Management; Competitive Firms; Employees.	*Use of Assets:* How effectively are the assets of the firm utilised.
Shareholders (Actual and Potential); Potential take-over bidders; Management; Lenders and Creditors in assessing MSK.	*Capital Structure:* How does the capital structure of the firm affect the cost of capital and the return to shareholders.
Shareholders (Actual and Potential); Potential take-over bidders; Management.	*Investment:* Show how the market prices for a share reflect a company's performance.

Exhibit 12.2 shows a set of accounts prepared for The Rational Company Ltd. The various types of ratio mentioned in Exhibit 12.1 will be illustrated using the data for The Rational Company Ltd.

Exhibit 12.2

The Rational Co. Ltd.
(Abridged) Balance Sheet at 31st December, 19-1

Fixed Assets			£	Share Capital		£
	Cost	Aggregate		150,000 £1		
Land		depreciation	Net	Ordinary Shares		150,000
& Buildings	500,000	150,000	350,000	8% Preference Shares		30,000
Plant	40,000	—	40,000			180,000
	540,000	150,000	390,000	Reserves		
				Profit and Loss Account		120,000
						300,000
Current Assets				Mortgage Debentures 7%		210,000
Stock in Trade		90,000		Current Liabilities		
Debtors		105,000		Trade Creditors	21,000	
Cash at Bank		15,000				
			210,000	Bank Overdraft	30,000	
				Current Taxation	39,000	90,000
			600,000			600,000

(Abridged) Trading and Profit and Loss Account
for the year ending 31st December, 19-1

	£	£
Sales		900,000
Cost of goods sold		780,000
Gross Profit		120,000
General and Administrative Expenses	18,600	
Sales Expenses	8,400	
Depreciation	30,000	57,000
Net Operating Profit		63,000
Debenture Interest	14,700	
Bank Interest	1,000	15,700
		47,300
Income from Royalties		4,700
Profit for the year before taxation		52,000
Corporation Tax		22,000
Net Profit for the year after taxation		30,000
Dividends:		
Preference Shares (8 per cent)	2,400	
Ordinary Shares (10 per cent)	15,000	17,400
		12,600
Balance from previous years		107,400
		120,000

The Market Price of an Ordinary Share at 31st December, 19-1 was £3.

Liquidity Ratios

The analysis of credit risk was the historic starting point for formal ratio analysis. With widely scattered markets a firm is frequently asked to trade with companies it has little or not knowledge of. The risks of supplying goods on credit to a strange company are fairly obvious and in practice can be very hazardous. Many small businesses have themselves been forced to wind up because a large customer has failed to pay its debt. It is hardly surprising that firms specializing in giving advice on credit risks should have come into existence. These firms started the consistent use of ratios to analyze company balance sheets. Usually they are operating as outsiders and therefore have to rely on published information, in contrast to the management of a business who can obtain much more detailed information about that business. The following ratios are useful in the measurement of liquidity:

The Current Ratio

The Current Ratio measures Current Assets: Current Liabilities. In general terms we are comparing assets which will become liquid in approximately twelve months with liabilities which will be due for payment in the same period. This ratio was described in the previous chapter.

Referring to Exhibit 12.2 the Current Ratio is 210,000:90,000=2.3:1. This may also be conveniently expressed by $\dfrac{210,000}{90,000} = 2.3$ times.

The Acid Test Ratio

In order to refine the analysis of the Current Ratio another ratio is used which takes only those current assets which are cash or will convert very quickly into cash. This will normally mean Cash and Debtors or Current Assets less Stock in Trade. The Acid Test Ratio may, therefore, be stated as:

Current Assets less Stock in Trade : Current Liabilities.

The ratio calculated from Exhibit 12.2 is: 1.3:1 or

$$\frac{120,000}{90,000} = 1.3 \text{ times.}$$

This shows that provided Creditors and Debtors are paid at approximately the same time, the company has sufficient liquid resources to meet its current liabilities. If a large proportion of the Current Assets had been in the form of Stock in Trade the liquid position might have been dangerously low.

The ratios shown under Credit Risk have been concerned with liquidity. A useful supplement to this type of analysis is provided by Cash Flow Statements which have been dealt with in another chapter. From the point of view of management, the forecast cash flow statement is the most useful statement for control of credit. For those outside the firm, however, this information is not usually available and they must rely on the ratios.

Profitability Ratios

Profitability is the end product of the policies and decisions taken by a firm, and is its single most important measure of success.

Gross Profit/Sales

From Exhibit 12.2 the ratio for the Rational Company Ltd. is

$$\frac{120,000}{900,000}$$

$= .133$ or as a percentage on sales $= 13.3$ per cent.

It is impossible to state a rule of thumb for this figure which will vary considerably from firm to firm and industry to industry.

Net Profit (after Tax)/Sales

The same comments apply to Net Profit/Sales as to Gross Profit/Sales. The difference between the two ratios will be explained by measuring the ratios of sales to the Expenses in the Profit and Loss Account. The ratio from Exhibit 12.2 in $\dfrac{30,000}{900,000} = .033 = 3.3$ per cent. This percentage of 3.3 indicates by how much the profit margin can decline before the firm makes losses.

Return on Capital Employed

Great care must be exercised in measuring ratios of profit to Capital Employed. These are no standard definitions and thus for comparability it is necessary to ensure that the same method is used over time for the same firm or between different firms. Another problem is inherent in comparing profit which arises over a period of time, with Capital Employed which is taken from the Balance Sheet and is thus measured at one point of time. For a proper evaluation the Capital Employed needs to be an average figure for the accounting period in which the profit was calculated. As an external analyst the only data available is at the beginning and end of the accounting period. Since the year end is by no means likely to be representative of the average for a period any calculated figure must be taken with caution. If for examples an analyst knows that a major investment in fixed assets took place mid-way through the year he would tend to average the opening and closing figures. If little change has taken place then the year end figure may be used.

Net Profit (After Tax)/Total Assets

In this calculation of Return on Capital Employed the Total Assets are defined as all Fixed and other Non-Current Assets plus Working Capital.

Working Capital is simply the figure reached by deducting Current Liabilities from Current Assets, (assuming that Current Assets exceed Current Liabilities). Using the data from Exhibit 12.2, the working capital is Current Assets £210,000 less Current Liabilities £90,000 = £120,000. The Total Assets are therefore Fixed Assets £390,000 + Working Capital £210,000 = £600,000 and the return is

$$\frac{\text{Net Profit (after tax)}}{\text{Total Assets}} = \frac{30,000}{600,000} = 5\%$$

One of the problems with using this approach to Return on Capital is that Net Profit after tax will already have had interest on debentures, loans and overdrafts changed against it and thus if this interest is significant the return on assets will be understated.

Similarly if the Assets of the business include items of an intangible nature such as Goodwill it is often felt that the return on assets is better related to tangible assets alone, since the accounting valuation of intangibles varies so much.

To answer these problems the following ratio is often used:

Net Operating Profit/Operating Assets

The aim here is to be take the operating profit which is the outcome of operations before interest charges are made or any investment income is included. This profit will then be taken over Operating Assets which are the tangible assets used in the generation of the Operating Income. Operating Assets will not include intangibles nor investments in shares or other securities outside the firm, whether shown under a separate hearing or as Current Assets.

As with the previous calculation of Total Assets it is appropriate to take Working Capital as part of Operating Assets but in this definition it is frequently appropriate to exclude Bank Overdraft from Current Liabilities. Although from a legal point of view and from the Banks intention it is a Current Liability, since repayment can be demanded at short notice, in practice for a well run business the bank is usually happy to maintain an overdraft over extended periods of time. Unlike most of the other Current Liabilities interest is chargeable on overdrafts.

Thus this definition of Return on Capital Employed is Net Operating Profit: Tangible Operating Fixed Assets + (Working Capital + Overdraft). Referring to Exhibit 12.2 this is equal to £390,000 + £120,000 + £30,000 = £540,000. Which is equivalent to:

Share Capital £180,000 + Reserves £120,000 + Debentures £210,000 + Bank overdraft £30,000 = £540,000

The Net Operating Profit which in Exhibit 12.2 = £63,000 is the profit obtained from the Capital Employed before paying interest or dividends to any of these sources of capital. This return on Capital Employed in the Rational Company Ltd. is therefore $\dfrac{63,000}{540,000}$ = 11.7 per cent.

Net Profit (After Taxes)/Owners Equity

In this case the net profit after tax (less Preference Dividends) is compared with Ordinary Shareholders stake in the business, i.e. share capital plus reserves. From Exhibit 12.2 the ratio is

$$\frac{£27,600}{£270,000} = 10.2 \text{ per cent.}$$

In contrast to the previous ratio this one is not an overall measure of profitability but is specially concerned with the return an ordinary shareholder might expect.

Use of Assets Ratios

Although the way assets are utilized will effect profitability, these particular ratios deserve to be evaluated separately as they are of great importance. In effect they show how effectively management has been using the assets at their disposal.

A straightforward ratio between Assets and Sales can be used by the external analyst. For the Rational Co. Ltd we should show:

Land and Buildings	: Sales	350,000 : 900,000 = 1 :	2.6
Plant	: Sales	40,000 : 900,000 = 1 :	22.5
Total Fixed Assets	: Sales	390,000 : 900,000 = 1 :	2.3
Stock in Trade	: Sales	90,000 : 900,000 = 1 :	10.0
Debtors	: Sales	105,000 : 900,000 = 1 :	8.6
Cash at Bank	: Sales	15,000 : 900,000 = 1 :	60.0
Total Current Assets	: Sales	210,000 : 900,000 = 1 :	4.3

It is often convenient to express these ratios in terms of 'per £1,000 of sales' to avoid too much 'rounding off'. For example Land and Buildings per £1,000 of sales would be £388.9 i.e. (350,000 ÷ 900).

A number of these activity ratios are sufficiently important to merit special mention and in some cases detailed development.

Sales/Fixed Assets

The ratio of Sales to Fixed Assets measures the utilisation a firm is obtaining from its investment in fixed plant. If the ratio is low it indicates that management may not be utilizing its plant very effectively. In the illustration from Exhibit 12.2, the ratio is = 2.3 times, or £433.3 per £1,000 of sales.

Stock Turnover

This important ratio is measured in the first instance by dividing Sales by Stock in Trade. Since Sales are at Selling Prices, the Stock should also be measured at selling price. Usually an easier way is to divide Sales at Cost Price (which is the Cost of Goods Sold total) by Stock in Trade at cost value. The stock figure used should be an average figure for the year. Whilst the true average will be known to management it will often not be available to outsiders. In this situation a very rough approximation is used by taking the average of the opening and closing stocks. If in the example in Exhibit 12.2, the stock at 1 January had been £50,000 and the stock at 31st December is £90,000 the average would be taken as

$$\frac{50,000+90,000}{2} = £70,000.$$

The Stock turnover therefore is

$$\frac{\text{Cost of Goods Sold}}{\text{Stock in Trade}} = \frac{780,000}{70,000} = 11.1 \text{ times.}$$

If the cost of Goods Sold is not know, it may be necessary to use the Sales figure instead. Although this is not a satisfactory basis, it may be better than nothing if like is compared with like. Notice that in this example Stock turnover = 12.9 times if the Sales figure is used.

Collection Period for Debtors

The resources tied up in debtors is an important ratio subject. We have already calculated the relationships of debtors to sales which in the example is 1:8.6. This means that for every £8.6 sold there is £1 of debtors outstanding.

This relationship is often translated into the length of time a debtor takes to pay. If we assume that the sales for Rational Ltd. are made over the whole of one year i.e. 365 days this means that on average a debt is outstanding for $365 \times \frac{1}{8.6} = 42.4$ days.

Notice that it is assumed sales take place evenly over the year, and we have ignored holidays. However it is useful to know that our customers take about 6 weeks to pay!

In recent years the interest in productivity measurement has raised interest in many ratios which combine information which is not essentially part of the accounts with accounting data. Published Accounts for example are now required to show as supplementary information the average number of people employed by a limited Company. This information may be related to Sales to give an index of Sales per employee. For example if the average number employed by the Rational Company were 215 then sales per employee would be $\dfrac{900,000}{215}$ = £4,186. This example is given as an illustration of the development of this type of measurement which may be a useful guide to assessment of a company's performance.

Capital Structure Ratios

The Capital Structure of a business is important because it has a significant influence on the risk to lenders, and on the return to shareholders.

In the first instance it is worthwhile to express the Balance Sheet in percentage terms. For the Rational Company using the main sub-totals it would be as follows:

Balance Sheet at 31 December 19-1

	%		%
Fixed Assets	65.0	Ordinary Shares	25.0
Current Assets	35.0	8% Preference Shares	5.0
		Reserves	20.0
			50.0
		Debenture	35.0
		Current Liabilities	15.0
	100.0		100.0

Net Worth/Total Assets

From this can be seen immediately that Ordinary Shares and Preference Shares with the Reserves, which total is often called Net Worth is providing 50 per cent of the financing of Fixed and Current Assets. Thus the ratio Net Worth: Fixed Assets + Current Assets is an important measure of the shareholder stake in a business. (300,000: 390,000 + 210,000 = 1:2).

Fixed Assets/Net Worth

From the Balance Sheet it is also easy to see that a high proportion of the assets (65%) are Fixed Assets. A comparison of the Fixed Assets with Net Worth shows whether the longer term investment usually involved in Fixed Assets is provided by Shareholders. In our example the ratio is £390,000 : £300,000 (or 65%:50%) = 1:0.77. This ratio shows that shareholders are not providing all the investment required to finance the fixed assets quite apart from current assets. The remainder of the funding of assets is provided by borrowing. The important thing here is to ensure that the borrowing is sufficiently long term to match the investment in fixed assets. If the company has to repay borrowing whilst all its resources are locked into assets which cannot easily be converted into cash it can only make repayment by fresh borrowing or new capital issues which may cause problems.

Fixed Assets/Net Worth and Long Term Loan

Provided the Mortgage Debenture has a reasonably long life the Rational Company provides reasonable cover of its Fixed Assets since Fixed Assets: Net Worth + Long Term Loan are in the ratio 1:1.31.

Coverage of Fixed Charges

This relationship is obtained by dividing net profit by any fixed interest charges or rentals. Since these charges are allowable expenses for tax purposes, the profit before tax will be used. From Exhibit 12.2 the interest charges are £15,700 with no rental expense. The available profit before tax is £52,000 + £15,700 = £67,700. The Fixed Charges are, therefore, covered

$$\frac{\text{Profit before tax} + \text{Fixed Charges}}{\text{Fixed Charges}} \quad \frac{67,000}{15,700} = 4.3 \text{ times.}$$

This is low enough to indicate a company which is high geared.

High Geared means a company which has a high proportion of borrowing to net worth. A company with no gearing has all its funds provided by the ordinary shareholder. Gearing has also been measured indirectly in the ratio of Net Worth: Total Assets. The lower the proportion of funds provided from Net Worth, the higher the borrowing and hence gearing.

The coverage of fixed charges gives a very important measure of the extent to which the profit may decline before the company is not able to earn enough to cover the interest etc. it is legally obliged to pay. If charges are not paid legal steps will be taken against the company which usually end in it being taken over or wound up.

Borrowing/Net Worth

This ratio is the most direct measure of gearing since it indicates the proportions in which all funds are provided for the business. Borrowing is taken as all the long term and current liabilities of the business and Net Worth as Share Capital and Reserves. In this definition Preference Shares are included in net worth. Although the return to Preference Shareholders is fixed like interest there is no legal obligation for the company to pay it, hence the inclusion with Net Worth. If you are however looking at the effect of gearing on the return to ordinary shareholders it may then be appropriate to treat Preference Share Dividends as a fixed change.

The Ratio for Rational Co. Ltd. is thus

£210,000 + £90,000 : 300,000 = 1:1.

Investment Ratios

These ratios are important for the investor and financial manager who is interested in the market prices of the shares of a company on the Stock Exchange.

Dividend Yield

This measures the real rate of return on an investment in shares, as distinct from the declared dividend rate which is based on the nominal value of a share. The Yield is calculated as follows, illustrated from Exhibit 12.2:

$$\frac{\text{The Dividend per Share}}{\text{Market Price per Share}} = \frac{£1 \times 10 \text{ per cent}}{£3} = 3.3 \text{ per cent.}$$

Dividend Cover for Ordinary Shares

This indicates the amount of profit for an ordinary dividend and indicates the amount of profit retained in the business. The cover is:

$$\frac{\text{Net Profit for the year after Tax} - \text{Preference Dividend}}{\text{Dividend on Ordinary Shares}}$$
$$= \frac{£30,000 - 2,400}{15,000} = 1.8 \text{ times.}$$

Earnings Per Ordinary Share

As is implied by the name this ratio is

$$\frac{\text{Net Profit for the year after tax} - \text{Preference Dividend}}{\text{Number of Ordinary Shares}}$$
$$= \frac{£30,000 - 2,400}{150,000} = £0.18 \text{ per share}$$

The calculation of this important ratio is now covered by the Statement of Standard Accounting Practice 3.

The Price Earnings Ratio

Finally the Price Earnings Ratio relates the earnings per share to the price the shares sell in the market. From Exhibit 12.2 the ratio is:

$$\frac{\text{Market Price}}{\text{Earnings per Share}} = \frac{£3}{£.18} = 16.7$$

This relationship is an important indicator to investor and financial manager of the market's evaluation of a share, and is very important when a new issue of shares is due since it shows the earnings the market expects in relation to the current share prices.

Summary of Ratios

Type of Ratio	*Method of Calculation*
Liquidity	
Current Ratio	$$\dfrac{Current\ Assets}{\text{Current Liabilities}}$$
Acid Test Ratio	$$\dfrac{Current\ Assets\ less\ Stock\ in\ Trade}{\text{Current Liabilities}}$$
Profitability	
Gross Profit/Sales	$$\dfrac{Gross\ Profit}{\text{Sales}}$$
Net Profit after Tax/Sales	$$\dfrac{Net\ Profit\ after\ Tax}{\text{Sales}}$$
Return on Capital Employed	
Net Profit After Tax/Total Assets	$$\dfrac{Net\ Profit\ After\ Tax}{\text{Fixed and Other Assets} + \text{Working Capital}}$$
Net Operating Profit/Operating Assets	$$\dfrac{Net\ Operating\ Income}{\text{Tangible Operating Fixed Assets} + \text{Working Capital and Overdraft}}$$
Net Profit (after tax)/Owners Equity	$$\dfrac{Net\ Profit\ after\ tax\ less\ Preference\ Dividend}{\text{Ordinary Share Capital} + \text{Reserves}}$$
Use of Assets	
Asset/Sales	$$\dfrac{Individual\ Asset\ Totals}{\text{Sales}}$$
Sales/Fixed Assets	$$\dfrac{Fixed\ Assets}{\text{Sales}}$$
Stock Turnover	$$\dfrac{Cost\ of\ Goods\ Sold}{\text{Average Stock in Trade}}$$
Collection Period for Debtors	$$365 \times \dfrac{Debtors}{\text{Sales}}$$
Capital Structure	
Net Worth/Total Assets	$$\dfrac{Ordinary\ Share\ Capital + Preference\ S.C.\ + Reserves}{\text{Fixed Assets} + \text{Other Assets} + \text{Current Assets}}$$
Fixed Assets/Net Worth	$$\dfrac{Fixed\ Assets}{\text{Net Worth}}$$
Fixed Assets/Net Worth and Long Term Loan	$$\dfrac{Fixed\ Assets}{\text{Net Worth} + \text{Long Term Loan}}$$

Coverage of Fixed Charges	$\dfrac{\textit{Net Profit before tax and Fixed Charges}}{\text{Fixed Charges}}$
Borrowing/Net Worth	$\dfrac{\textit{Long Term + Current Liabilities}}{\text{Net Worth}}$

Investment

Dividend Yield	$\dfrac{\textit{Dividend per Share}}{\text{Market Price per Share}}$
Dividend Cover for Ordinary Shares	$\dfrac{\textit{Net Profit after tax - Pref. Div.}}{\text{Ordinary Share Dividend}}$
Earnings per Ordinary share	$\dfrac{\textit{Net Profit after tax - Pref. Div.}}{\text{Number of Ordinary Shares}}$
Price Earnings Ratio	$\dfrac{\textit{Market Price per Share}}{\text{Earnings per Share}}$

Assignment Exercises

12.1A. Describe the five main groups of ratios and indicate who may be interested in each type.

12.2. Explain what you think the following ratios indicate about a firm:
(a) Acid Test ratio.
(b) Net Operating Profit/Capital Employed.
(c) Collection Period for Debtors.
(d) Net Worth/Total Assets.
(e) Dividend Cover for Ordinary Shares.

12.3A. Stock Turnover is sometimes calculated by dividing sales by the average of the opening and closing stock in trade figures. What is wrong with this method of computation?

12.4. For each of the following items select the lettered item(s) which indicate(s) its effect(s) on the company's accounts. More than one item may be effected.
1. Declaration and payment of a dividend on Preference Share Capital.
2. Declaration of a proposed dividend ordinary shares due for payment in one month.
3. Purchase of stock in trade for cash.
4. Payment of creditors.
5. Bad Debt written off against an existing provision for Bad and Doubtful Debts.

108

Effect
A. Reduces working capital.
B. Increases working capital.
C. Reduces current ratio.
D. Increases current ratio.
E. Reduces acid test ratio.
F. Increases acid test ratio.

12.5A. Describe four ratios which might help you to assess the profitability of a company and explain their significance.

12.6. A limited company with 100,000 £1 Ordinary Shares as its Capital earns a profit after tax of £15,000. It pays a dividend of 10 per cent. The Market price of the shares is £1.50. What is the:
(a) Yield on Ordinary Shares?
(b) Earnings per share?
(c) Price/Earnings ratio?

12.7A. What ratios might be of particular interest to a potential holder of debentures in a limited company?

12.8. The following is a Trading and Profit and Loss Account of a small limited company engaged in manufacturing for the year ending 31 December 19-2:

	£'000		£'000
Opening Stock	20	Sales (credit)	150
Purchases (credit)	120		
	140		
Less Closing Stock	40		
	100		
Direct Manufacturing Expenses	20		
Overhead Expenditure	10		
Net Profit	20		
	150		150

Balance Sheet at 31 December, 19-2

	£
Authorised and Issued Share Capital	100
Reserves	40
	140
5 per cent Debentures	60
	200

Fixed Assets:	*Cost*	*Aggreg. depr.*	
Freehold Property	100	–	100
Plant and Machinery	40	20	20
	140	20	120
Current Assets:			
Stocks at cost		40	
Debtors		50	
Quoted Investments at cost		60	
Bank		20	
		170	
Less Current Liabilities:			
Corporation Tax	10		
Bills Payable	20		
Tax Creditors	60	90	80
			200

Required

Select five major ratios and apply them to the above accounts and comment upon their relevance.

12.9A. Ironsides Limited
Balance Sheet as at 31 December, 19-8

	£			£
Fixed Assets at cost	7,200,000	*Authorised Share Capital*		
Depreciation	2,000,000	2,500,000 Ordinary £1		2,500,000
	5,200,000			
		Issued and Fully paid		
		Share Capital		
Current Assets		2,400,000 Shares of £1		
Stock	1,200,000	each		2,400,000
Debtors	800,000	General Reserve		1,600,000
Investments	600,000			4,000,000
Cash	200,000 2,800,000			
		6% Debenture	800,000	
		5% Mortgage	2,000,000	2,800,000
				6,800,000
		Bank Loan 8%		400,000
		Creditors	280,000	
		Taxation	520,000	800,000
	£8,000,000			£8,000,000

Condensed Profit and Loss Account for year ended 31 December, 19-9.

		£
Sales		12,000,000
Cost of Production		10,320,000
GROSS PROFIT		1,680,000
Other Expenses:		
Administration	120,000	
Selling	68,000	
Rent	112,000	
Depreciation	400,000	700,000
		980,000
Less Interest—		
Bank	32,000	
Mortgage	100,000	
Debenture	48,000	180,000
		800,000
Less Corporation Tax 45%		360,000
		440,000
Less Dividend		400,000
To General Reserve	£	40,000

You are required to calculate for Ironsides Ltd. ten significant ratios and comment on their meaning.

12.10. The annual accounts of the Wholesale Textile Company Limited have been summarized for 19-1 and 19-2 as follows:

	Year 19-1		Year 19-2	
Sales	£	£	£	£
Cash	60,000		64,000	
Credit	540,000	600,000	684,000	748,000
Cost of sales		472,000		596,000
Gross margin		128,000		152,000
Expenses				
Warehousing		26,000		28,000
Transport		12,000		20,000
Administration		38,000		38,000
Selling		22,000		28,000
Debenture interest		—		4,000
		98,000		118,000
Net profit		30,000		34,000

	On 31 Dec. 19-1		On 31 Dec. 19-2	
	£	£	£	£
Fixed assets				
(*less* depreciation)		60,000		80,000
Current assets				
Stock	120,000		188,000	
Debtors	100,000		164,000	
Cash	20,000	240,000	14,000	366,000
Less Current liabilities				
Trade creditors		100,000		152,000
Net current assets		140,000		214,000
		200,000		294,000
Share Capital		150,000		150,000
Reserves and undistributed profit		50,000		84,000
Debenture loan		—		60,000
		200,000		294,000

You are informed that:

1. All sales were from stocks in the company's warehouse.
2. The range of merchandise was not changed and buying prices remained steady throughout the two years.
3. Budgeted total sales for 19-2 were £780,000.
4. The debenture loan was received on 1 January, 19-2, and additional fixed assets were purchased on that date.

You are required to state the internal accounting ratios that you would use in this type of business to assist the management of the Company in measuring the efficiency of its operation, including its use of capital.

Your answer should name the ratios and give the figures (calculated to one decimal place) for 19-1 and 19-2, together with possible reasons for changes in the ratios for the two years. Ratios relating to capital employed should be based on the capital at the year end. Ignore taxation.

12.11A. The following data relate to the financial results of the Gazco Ltd. for the years ended 31 December, 19-1, 19-2 and 19-3:

	Balance Sheets as at:		
	31 Dec., 19-3	31 Dec., 19-2	31 Dec., 19-1
Fixed Assets	£(million)	£(million)	£(million)
Land	2	2	2
Buildings	24	22	19
Plant and Equipment	115	105	91
Mineral Deposits	1	1	1
Oil and Gas Properties—			
Producing	9	8	8
Oil and Gas Leaseholds—			
Undeveloped	1	1	1
Accumulated Depreciation	(71)	(60)	(51)
Accumulated Depletion	(3)	(3)	(3)
	78	76	68

Current Assets			
Inventories	19	17	15
Accounts Receivable	20	17	15
Marketable Securities	17	15	11
Cash	4	3	3
Development Expenses	3	2	2
	£141	£130	£114
	£(million)	£(million)	£(million)

Share Capital and Reserves			
Share Capital			
Authorised, Issued and Fully Paid in Ordinary Shares of £1 each	6	6	6
Capital Reserves			
Share Premium Account	40	36	32
Revenue Reserves			
Retained Earnings	32	30	27
	78	72	65
Long Term Liabilities			
Debentures	40	39	30
Bank Loans	3	2	2
Current Liabilities			
Accounts Payable and Accruals	12	12	11
Current Taxation	7	4	5
Bank Overdraft	1	1	1
	£141	£130	£114

Profit and Loss Accounts for the Year ended

	31 Dec., 19-3	31 Dec., 19-2	31 Dec., 19-1
	£(million)	£(million)	£(million)
Income:			
Net sales	119	106	93
Other Income	1	1	1
	120	107	94
Deductions:			
Cost of Goods Sold	85	76	67
Selling and Administration	18	15	13
Interest on long-term liabilities	1	1	1
Other	1	1	1
Profit before Taxation	15	14	12
Provision for Taxation	7	6	5
Profit after Taxation	£8	£8	£7

(a) Prepare the following analyses of the company's liquidity at the end of 19-3 and 19-2:

   (i)   Amount of Working Capital;

   (ii) Current ratio;

   (iii) Acid test ratio.

(b) Prepare the following analyses of the company's operations: for 19-3 and 19-2:

   (i)   Rate of return after tax on capital employed at end of each year;

   (ii) Rate of return after tax on shareholders' equity; at end of each year;

   (iii) Turnover rate for fixed assets; at end of each year;

   (iv) Percentage of profit before tax to sales revenue;

   (v) Number of times fixed interest charge is covered.

   (vi) Earnings per share.

12.12. The Balance Sheet and Profit and Loss Account for Goodmark Ltd. are shown below:

Balance Sheet at 31 December 19-1

		£	£
Fixed Assets:	Land & Buildings (net)		300
	Plant (net)		1,880
			2,180
Current Assets			
	Stock in Trade	710	
	Debtors	340	
	Cash	140	1,190
			3,370
Share Capital			
	£1 Ordinary Shares		520
	£1 10% Preference Shares		100
			620
Reserves			
	Retained Profits		1,000
			1,620
Debentures			1,270
Current Liabilities			
	Trade Creditors	450	
	Current Taxation	30	480
			£3,370

Profit and Loss Account for Year Ending 31 December 19-1

	£
Sales	3,640
Cost of Goods Sold	2,350

	£	1,290
Selling and Administration Expenses	810	
Depreciation	170	
Interest	60	
		1,040

Net Profit before Taxation	250
Taxation	100
Net Profit after Taxation	£150

Calculate

(a) Acid Test Ratio.

(b) Times Fixed Charges (i.e. Interest) Covered.

(c) Profit after Tax on Owners Equity Ratio.

(d) Collection period for Debtors.

(e) Stock Turnover.

13

Interpretation of Final Accounts

The Interpretation of Final Accounts through the use of ratios can conveniently be divided into two parts. Firstly there is analysis by those outside the firm who are seeking to understand more from the published accounting data. On the other side there is management wishing to interpret a much fuller range of internal information in a meaningful way. In both situations current information will be assessed in relation to past trends of the same business and with comparative information for similar firms.

Comparisons Over Time

One of the most helpful ways in which accounting ratios can be used is to compare them with previous periods ratios for the same organisation. Taking as an example Net Profit after Tax/Sales the results for the Rational Co. Ltd are as follows:

	This year	1	2	3	4	5
			Years ago			
Net Profit after Tax/Sales	3.3	3.8	3.1	3.4	3.4	3.5

This years result acquires much more significance when compared to the previous five years. The appreciation of the trends is usually assisted by graphing the results as in Exhibit 13.1.

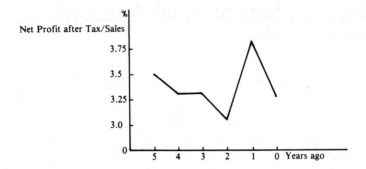

Exhibit 13.1

This graph very clearly illustrates how the net profit margin has fluctuated. In this type of case the ratio which is a comparative number is not expected to 'grow' in the way that an expanding firm expects its Sales to grow. Thus for ratios an ordinary graph would normally be appropriate.

However when the ratio points have been plotted it can be helpful to insert a line of best fit to these points. Thus on the graph we drew of Net Profit After Tax/Sales a line of best fit gives a useful idea of the past trends of the ratio as an Exhibit 13.2.

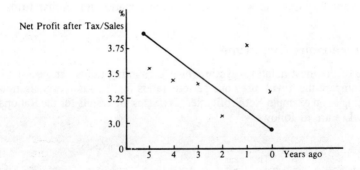

Exhibit 13.2

This can be drawn either by eye or better by using a statistical technique such as least squares.

It is very tempting to extend these trend lines into the future as a form of forecast. Past trends should not be used mechanically to predict the future. Only if you are sure that all conditions influencing a ratio are likely to remain constant next year should you extend the trend. Notice that in the graph we have just plotted the linear trend is relatively little influenced by the upturn in the current year. This improvement may in fact represent the start of an upward movement if we had sufficient information to explain it. Thus great care must be taken with predictions.

As with the interpretation of all ratios the best approach is to structure the analysis in an orderly fashion. The pyramid type of structuring explained later in the chapter is a useful model since it links together a set of ratios, in a way that helps to develop understanding — one ratio being explained by other more detailed ratios.

It is also often helpful to combine with the comparison of ratios over time, some information about the trends in the real accounting data. In the example we have just examined of the Net Profit after Tax/Sales ratio it is likely to be helpful for someone interpreting the accounts to have alongside his graphical analysis of the ratio other graphs showing the sales in £ and Net Profit after Tax in £. The ratio analysis must always be kept in the perspective of the real accounting results. The graphs of key figures from the Profit and Loss Account for example can usefully be developed on logarithmic scales to emphasise trends.

Comparisons with other firms

Comparisons over time are useful since they give a perspective on trends developing within a firm. However since firms operate in a competitive environment it is always necessary to have some basis of comparison with other organisations particularly those in the same type of business.

Whilst in principle inter-firm comparisons are very worthwhile there are considerable practical differences. Firstly in many cases organisations are not directly comparable with others in size or in the exact nature of business carried on. A large multinational company can be involved in a wide range of industries and countries of operation, as a whole therefore it is probably unique. Size can in itself have an important bearing on ratios. For example the Capital Structure Ratios of a large public company are not comparable with one which is small and privately owned. Secondly inter-company comparisons are frequently made misleading by differences in accounting methods and factors such as the age structure and location of assets.

Most of the difficulties mentioned can be overcome by a properly structured scheme of inter-firm comparison. Here firms agree to pool data and employ experts to ensure comparability of the data. However this type of scheme is only available internally for the management. For the external analyst relying on published data the development of accounting standards is helping to ensure a better basic source of information. The external analyst must by necessity look at the overall ratios for more general guidelines to a firm's performance.

External Analysis

The outsider is at some disadvantage in undertaking ratio analysis since he will have relatively little information about the underlying bases of accounting. He will, however, be able to obtain information which is now published, showing ratios by industry. These are calculated from the published accounts of public companies, and more limited information on accounts of private companies. This information would tend to be in a form similar to that shown in Exhibit 13.3, which is an abbreviated form of a broad schedule of ratios.

Using some information from Exhibit 12.2 in Chapter 12, let us set up the information we have available to assess the Rational Co. Ltd. which is a Building and Civil Engineering Firm.

The ratios shown are the median figures for the companies in the sample. In practice it would be common to show the two quartile figures as well.

Ratio	Rational Co. Ltd.		Industry Median for Building and Civil Engineering	
	19-0	19-1	19-0	19-1
Operating Profit/Capital Employed	13.2	11.7	14.5	14.8
Net Profit after Tax/Sales	3.8	3.3	3.9	4.6
Sales/Fixed Assets	3.1	2.3	7.7	7.0
Sales/Stock	13.5	12.9	10.1	7.3
Current Assets/Current Liabilities	2.2	2.3	1.32	1.36
Liquid Assets/Current Liabilities	1.1	1.3	.96	.93

Exhibit 13.3

Illustration of Published Ratios by Industry
Quoted Companies Year 19x0 and 19x1

Industry Classification	Year	Financial Performance				Credit Control	
		P/CE %	NP/S %	S/FA times	S/ST times	CA/CL times	LA/CL times
Building and Civil	19-0	14.5	3.9	7.7	10.1	1.32	.96
Engineering	19-1	14.8	4.6	7.0	7.3	1.36	.93
Specialist Constr-	19-0	14.5	5.3	6.0	9.8	1.55	1.15
uction Contrac-	19-1	17.8	6.0	6.3	12.1	1.66	1.08
tors							

Notes: P.=Net Operating Profit   S.T. =Stock in Trade
N.P.=Net Profit After Tax   C.A. =Current Assets
C.E.=Capital Employed   C.L. =Current Liabilities
S.=Sales   L.A. =Liquid Assets or Current
  Assets
F.A.=Fixed Assets   Less Stock

Whilst it must be appreciated that we are working with only a few ratios and that ideally we would look at least at five year's information we might draw some tentative conclusions:

Operating Profit/Capital Employed is lower than the median figure for the industry. Looking further we see that Sales/Fixed Asset Ratio is considerably below average. The two ratios are closely linked since Sales is an important contributor to Profit and Fixed Assets are part of Capital Employed. Net Profit after tax to Sales is also below average but the company is utilizing its stock above the average level. Both the liquidity ratios are above average, which may mean from the company's point of view that too much resources are tied up in non-productive cash or debtor balances, which would also contribute to a low return on capital employed.

In practice we could also look at the quartile figures in addition to the median. Our conclusions from the analysis can only be tentative but there is an impression which develops even from the limited information we have looked at that all is not right with the Rational Co. Ltd. Profitability is below average and the explanation seems to lie in a low net profit margin, and low utlization of fixed assets plus too many liquid assets. The trend of profitability figures cannot be assessed from two years, and it would have been useful to see information covering as many years back such as will give a reasonable guide. In preparing the graphs of trends over time for the ratios it is often very useful to show the Industry Data on the same graph as that for the firm. Using the example previously illustrated the graph for the Rational Co. Ltd. Profit after Tax/Sales would be improved by adding the Industry Median figures as in Exhibit 13.4

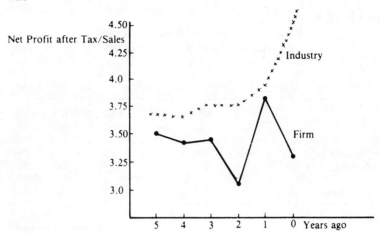

Exhibit 13.4

Internal Analysis

From a management point of view very useful information can be drawn from a detailed ratio analysis between companies using a full range of information not normally published. The Centre for Inter-firm Comparisons is a specialist organisation undertaking this work, maintaining secrecy as to the identity of participating firms, but ensuring that all firms taking part prepare their information on a comparable basis. Several Trade Association and Professional Bodies run similar schemes for their members. The Centre for Inter-firm Comparison have developed what is known as the 'pyramid' approach to ratios. This simply means that a key ratio at the top of the pyramid is explained by more detailed ratios which branch our below. One example is shown in Exhibit 13.5 developed from the key ratio Operating Profit/Operating Assets. Not that

$$\frac{\text{Operating Profit}}{\text{Operating Assets}} \text{ is the same as } \frac{\text{Sales}}{\text{Operating Assets}} \times \frac{\text{Operating Profit}}{\text{Sales}}$$

(cancelling out Sales in the multiplication).

In a working scheme very many detailed ratios would be developed from the framework illustrated in this chapter. The main benefit usually arises by the more general comparison, but the detail allows backup research if things are going wrong.

The ratios are as follows:

Ratio	Last Year	This Year
Return on assets		
1. Operating profit/Operating assets (%)	8.2	11.1
Profit margin on sales and turnover of assets		
2. Operating profit/sales (%)	6.7	5.8
3. Sales/Operating assets (times per year)	2.5	1.7
Departmental costs (as a percentage of sales)		
4. Production	71.0	70.9
5. Distribution and marketing	16.3	18.2
6. Administration	6.0	5.1
Asset utilisation (£'s per £1,000 of sales)		
3a. Operating assets	703	653
10. Current assets	593	480
11. Fixed assets	102	101
Current asset utilisation (£'s per £1,000 of sales)		
12. Material stocks	142	141
13. Work in progress	156	152
14. Finished stocks	152	94
15. Debtors	143	103

The results of our firm can now be appraised alongside the other companies in the sample. Our firm is identified by 'C'.

THE INTERFIRM COMPARISON

Ratio	A	B	C	D	E
Return on assets					
1. Operating profit/Operating assets (%)	17.2	14.5	11.1	8.6	3.9
Profit margin on sales and turnover of assets					
2. Operating profit/sales (%)	14.0	14.3	5.8	7.9	2.0
3. Sales/Operating assets (times per year)	1.3	1.1	1.7	1.0	2.4
Departmental costs (as a percentage of sales)					
4. Production	74.0	70.5	70.9	71.7	77.0
5. Distribution and marketing	8.5	12.2	18.2	14.2	16.0
6. Administration	3.5	3.0	5.1	6.2	5.0
Asset utilisation (£'s per £1,000 of sales)					
3a. Operating assets	842	908	653	1030	500
10. Current assets	616	609	480	800	370
11. Fixed assets	250	320	101	241	160
Current asset utilisation (£'s per £1,000 of sales)					
12. Material stocks	131	120	141	172	84
13. Work in progress	148	120	132	175	140
14. Finished stocks	203	164	94	259	68
15. Debtors	134	205	123	194	78

Interpreting the Inter-firm Comparison we are able to see that our firm is below two other firms in return on operating assets. This can be traced to Operating Profit/Sales. Note that total departmental costs + operating profit as per cent sales = 100 per cent. The main factor in the profit being below firms A and B is high distribution and marketing costs. Action can be taken on these costs if appropriate.

Since firm C will have details of the general size and description of all the firms in the sample (although the names of firms are confidential) and knows that the Centre for Inter-firm Comparison makes sure that the figures used are comparable, very valuable information can be drawn for management.

When several periods data is available this type of information is much more readily appreciated in graphical form.

Exhibit 13.5

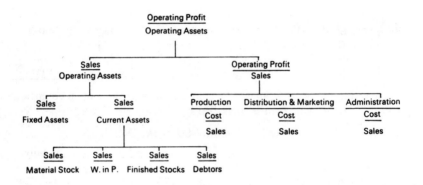

The Limitations of Ratio Analysis

The Advantages of ratio analyses which have been brought out in this text are that they provide a consistent and disciplined approach to the analysis of accounts. In addition they are a convenient method of comparing the performance of a particular firm with others and of seeing trends over time. Nonetheless there are dangers in accepting answers which appear to be put forward by ratio in too rigid a manner. The following points are relevant:

1. Accounting Statements present a limited picture only of the business. The information included in accounts does not cover all aspects of the business.

2. The problem associated with differing bases of accounting are nowhere more important than in ratio analysis. In particular differences in valuing fixed assets, depreciation methods and in valuation of stock-in-trade can be mentioned. As you will appreciate from your study of accounting there is usually a variety of accounting methods which may be appropriate to a particular firm.

3. The accounts of large organisations frequently aggregate operations in different industries and an external analyst will not be able to split up the results of one sector from another.

4. Comparison of a firm which finances its fixed plant through rental, thus not showing it as an asset, with a firm which purchases its own assets will be difficult.

5. External analysis of balance sheets can be misleading because the picture at that particular moment of time may not be representative of the year as a whole. For example firms frequently take stock when their stock levels are lowest. Average figures should be used but are not available externally.

6. Interpretation of a change in a ratio needs careful examination of changes in both numerator and denominator. Without a very full and detailed investigation some wrong conclusions can be drawn.

7. There is room for considerable difference between individual companies. It is wrong to lay down too rigid guidelines since what may be good for one successful firm may be wrong for another.

8. In general it is incorrect to compare small firms with very large firms. Many of the general industrial analyes of ratios are overall averages, and are, therefore, not strictly comparable to any particular firm.

The lesson is that whilst ratios are useful in indicating areas for investigation they cannot be relied upon to answer all the questions raised. Many of the limitations may, however, be reduced if a properly supervised scheme of inter-firm comparison is introduced.

Interpretation of Accounts for Employees

The interpretation which has been reviewed so far in this chapter has been for people with a good knowledge of the basis of accounting. Many firms have realised in recent years that it can be of great interest to their employees, if they attempt to make important features of the accounts generally available. Experience has tended to show that the average employee is very easily put off if too much detail is presented to him. Most firms attempt therefore to give a much more limited amount of information and to present it as imaginatively as possible in a special employee report. It is always far better to get over a limited amount of important information than to include so much detail that the message is obscured. Those who are interested can look for more detail in the main published accounts.

Firms have developed many different approaches in preparing their reports to employees. Many succeed by capturing interest through good graphics and design. Care must be taken however not to make these reports appear too trivial or condescending. Some examples of graphical illustrations which are also used in the main published accounts are shown below, however their is a very wide range of approach between different firms many of which include cartoons and 'comic-strip' types of presentation to capture interest. Space is not available here to do justice to this type of presentation. Try to find examples of company reports in libraries.

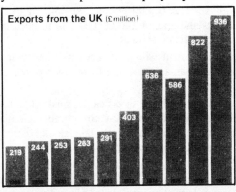

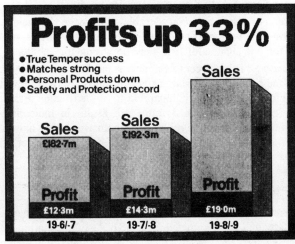

Exhibit 13.6

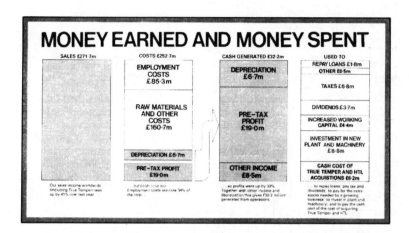

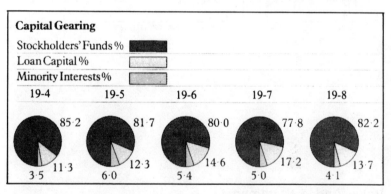

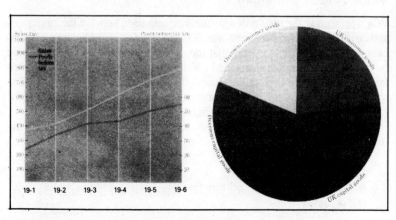

Exhibit 13.7

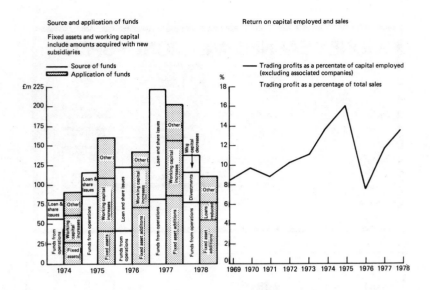

Source and application of funds

Fixed assets and working capital
include amounts acquired with new
subsidiaries

Return on capital employed and sales

Value Added Statements

When presenting the results of a business organisation both for the employees
and investors, particularly one which is involved in manufacturing, it has
been proposed in recent years that the statement of Profit and Loss could
be restated in terms of 'value added'. Value added is defined as Sales Income
less materials and services purchased from outside the organisation. The
total value added by the organisation is used to provide wages, dividends,
interest, taxes and funds for new investment.

The basic Value-Added Statement will thus include the following
information:

	£
Sales	XXX
less Bought in materials and services	XXX
Value Added	XXX

Applied as follows:

To pay employees:		
wages and pensions		xxx
To pay provider of capital:		
interest on loans	xxx	
dividends on shares	xxx	xxx
To pay government:		
corporation tax		xxx
To provide for maintenance and expansion of assets:		
depreciation	xxx	
retained profits	xxx	xxx
Value Added		

As an example the abridged Profit and Loss Account of Growth Manufacturers Ltd. will be restated in Value Added terms as shown below:

Growth Manufacturers Ltd.
Profit and Loss Account
for the year ended 31 December 19-1 (abridged)

	£
Sales	12,000,000
Costs (details as below)	8,400,000
Operating Profit	3,600,000
Interest	1,200,000
Profit before Taxation	2,400,000
Corporation Tax	1,100,000
Profit after Taxation	1,300,000
Dividend on Ordinary Shares	500,000
Profit Retained	800,000

Note: Costs include:

	£
Wages, pensions and other employee benefits	3,200,000
Depreciation	750,000
All other costs were bought in from outside.	4,450,000
	8,400,000

Growth Manufacturers Ltd.
Value Added Statement
for the year ended 31 December 19-1

	£
Sales	12,000,000
less Bought in materials and services	4,450,000
Value Added	7,550,000

Applied as follows:

		£
To pay employees wages, pensions and other benefits		3,200,000
To pay providers of capital: interest	1,200,000	
dividends on shares	500,000	1,700,000
To pay government corporation tax		1,100,000
To provide for maintenance and expansion of assets: depreciation	750,000	
retained profit	800,000	1,550,000
Value Added		7,550,000

Assignment Exercises

13.1A. Describe the sources from which an external investor might obtain financial information about a company in which he is interested.

13.2A. In order to judge the performance of a business it may be necessary to set standards for comparison. How should such standards be established? Describe some of the standards which may be adopted.

13.3A. Explain clearly the advantages and limitations of ratio analysis.

13.4. What is meant by the term a 'pyramid' of ratios? What is the object of this kind of presentation?

13.5A. What advantages might arise from using the services of the Centre for Inter-Firm Comparisons?

13.6A. During 19-3 the comparative financial data for three companies in the same industrial sector were as follows:

	Z.A. Ltd.	X.B. Ltd.	C.L. Ltd.
	£	£	£
Issued Capital—			
6 per cent £1 Preference	10,000	40,000	—
£1 Ordinary Shares	70,000	60,000	120,000
Revenue Reserves	60,000	40,000	—
	140,000	140,000	120,000

Represented by—			
Fixed Assets (net)	52,000	76,000	54,000
Current Assets—			
Stock	48,000	40,000	64,000
Debtors	30,000	56,000	80,000
Cash	42,000	24,000	16,000
	172,000	196,000	214,000
Less Current Liabilities			
Creditors	(24,400)	(44,600)	(64,000)
Proposed Dividends	(7,600)	(11,400)	(30,000)
	140,000	140,000	120,000
Average Stock	50,000	72,000	60,000
Sales	250,000	240,000	800,000
Gross Profit	50,000	60,000	80,000
Net Profit	30,000	30,000	30,000

You are required:

(a) to write a report analysing and comparing the performance of the three companies;

(b) to advise a client with £5,000 to invest in shares of one of the three companies which company and which type of share to select.

13.7. Using the data which is attached to question 13.12 you are given the following data for the same company for the previous 4 years. Analyse the trends disclosed.

Years Ago:	4	3	2	1
Current Ratio	1.6	1.5	2.2	2.9
Acid Test Ratio	0.78	0.69	1.00	1.22
Times Interest Charges Covered	5.0	5.6	5.5	5.0
Net Profit after Tax/Owners Equity	21%	21%	16%	11%
Collection Period for Debtors (days)	29	30	39	35
Stock Turnover (times)	5.8	4.9	3.5	3.4

13.8A. The Directors of Handbags Ltd. have asked you to assess the situation of their Company.

Preliminary investigations show the following results and median data from an Interfirm Association acting for the bag making industry of which Handbags Ltd. is a member.

	19-1 Interfirm % of Total	Handbags Ltd. £000's £	19-2 Interfirm % of Total	Handbags Ltd. £000's £	19-3 Interfirm % of Total	Handbags Ltd. £000's £
Land and Buildings at Current Valuation	20	300	25	300	30	240
Plant and Machinery at Current Valuation	20	60	25	54	40	45
Stocks at cost						
Materials	20	45	15	90	10	90
Finished Goods	20	45	25	90	10	135
Debtors	10	45	10	60	5	90
Cash	10	45	—	6	5	—
	100%	£540	100%	£600	100%	£600
REPRESENTED BY						
Share Capital	40	300	40	300	30	300
Capital Reserve	—	—.	—	—	—	30
Reserves and P. & L.	10	90	20	60	30	—
10% Debentures	—	—	—	150	—	150
Creditors	50	150	40	90	40	120
	100%	£540	100%	£600	100%	£600

Note: Handbags Ltd. sold land (cost £60,000) for £90,000 in 19-3 to provide extra working capital.

PROFIT AND LOSS ACCOUNT DATA	19-1 Handbags Ltd.		19-2 Handbags Ltd.		19-3 Handbags Ltd.	
	Interfirm % of Sales	£000's £	Interfirm % of Sales	£000's £	Interfirm % of Sales	£000's £
COST OF SALES						
Materials Consumed	20	180	20	165	15	150
Wages (Direct)	40	342	30	393	15	318
Depreciation of Plant and Machinery (charged by a machine hour rate)	2	18	8	15	10	9
Power (fixed charge per unit consumed)	1	9	3	9	5	6
Other Variable Overheads (e.g. Salesmen's Commission)	2	18	4	15	5	12
Light, heat, salaries, rates, etc.	14	135	18	129	18	144
Depreciation of premises	1	9	2	9	2	6
OTHER DEBITS:						
Interest on Loan Capital	—	—	—	15	—	15
Taxation	8	84	6	—	12	—
Dividends	8	60	8	—	15	—
TOTAL DEBITS	96	855	99	750	97	660
SALES	100	900	100	720	100	600
DEFICIT for year	—	—	—	30	—	60
SURPLUS for year	4	45	1	—	3	—
BALANCES b/fwd	*	45	*	90	*	60
BALANCES cd./fwd.	*	90	*	60	*	—
Bags sold	300,000		210,000		150,000	
Average price per bag	£3		£3		£2.15	

*Note it is not realistic to show interfirm balances as a per cent on sales.

Discuss the trends indicated and the preliminary conclusions you would draw from this data.

13.9. Read the following data, then attempt the questions shown at the end.

The Portroy Chemical Co. Ltd.

Balance Sheets

	30 June, 19-1		30 June, 19-2	
	£'000	%	£'000	%
Share Capital (£1 Shares)				
Ordinary	50,000	17.2	50,000	16.9
5% Preference	25,000	8.6	25,000	8.4
Reserves				
Profit and Loss	115,000	39.5	117,000	39.5
	190,000	65.3	192,000	64.8
8% Debentures	56,000	19.2	55,000	18.6
Current Liabilities				
Trade Creditors	35,000	12.0	36,000	12.2
Taxation	1,800	.6	2,500	.8
Bank overdrafts	8,200	2.9	10,500	3.6
Total Current Liabilities	45,000	15.5	49,000	16.6
	291,000	100.0	296,000	100.0

	£'000	%	£'000	%
Fixed Assets				
Land, Buildings, Plant and Equipment at cost	249,000	85.6	250,000	84.5
Aggregate depreciation	(126,000)	43.3	(128,000)	43.2
	123,000	42.3	122,000	41.3
Investments	14,000	4.8	15,500	5.2
Current Assets				
Stock in Trade	86,000	29.6	85,000	28.7
Debtors and Prepayments	58,000	19.9	58,000	19.6
Cash	10,000	3.4	15,500	5.2
Total Current Assets	154,000	52.9	158.500	53.5
	291,000	100.0	296,000	100.0

Portroy Chemical Co. Ltd.
Profit and Loss Accounts

	19-1 £'000	%	19-2 £'000	%
Sales	1,250,000	100.0	1,260,000	100.0
Cost of Goods Sold	1,150,000	92.0	1,149,120	91.2
Gross Profit	100,000	8.0	110,880	8.8
Operating Expenses				
Depreciation	11,250	0.9	10,080	0.8
Selling and Administration	68,750	5.5	70,560	5.6
General Expenses	15,000	1.2	12,600	1.0
Total Operating Expense	95,000	7.6	93,240	7.4
Operating Profit	5,000	0.4	17,640	1.4
Other Income	3,750	0.3	2,520	0.2
Total Income	8,750	0.7	20,160	1.6
Interest Charges	1,250	0.1	2,520	0.2
Net Profit before Taxation	7,500	0.6	17,640	1.4
Corporation Tax	2,500	0.2	6,300	0.5
Net Profit after Taxation	5,000	0.4	11,340	0.9

Additional information for the year ended 30 June, 19-2.
Stock Exchange Prices for Ordinary Shares ranged from £1.25 to £1.75.
Ordinary Dividend declared 5 per cent.

Inter Firm Comparisons
P represents the Portroy Company Ltd.
A, B and C are competitive firms of a similar size.

	19-0	19-1	19-2
Gross Profit per cent Sales			
A	10.2	9.7	10.4
B	6.3	5.9	6.1
C	8.4	9.6	9.3
P	9.3	8.0	—
Net Profit per cent Sales			
A	0.4	1.2	1.0
B	0.2	(0.2)	(0.1)
C	0.9	0.8	0.8
P	0.8	0.4	—

Current Ratio

A	2.3	1.9	1.7
B	4.4	4.3	3.9
C	4.1	3.5	3.5
P	3.0	3.4	—

Acid Test Ratio

A	0.9	0.8	0.8
B	2.4	2.3	2.2
C	1.8	1.8	1.7
P	1.4	1.5	—

Debtors — Collection Period in Days

A	10.5	12.4	12.3
B	18.2	19.6	20.4
C	16.5	15.3	16.4
D	15.2	16.9	—

Stock Turnover (based on Cost of Goods Sold and assuming closing stock represents the average)

A	14.8	14.7	14.7
B	13.2	13.5	13.4
C	14.7	14.7	14.6
P	13.9	13.4	—

Net Worth as per cent of Total Assets

A	58.2	55.9	55.7
B	55.0	53.0	56.0
C	68.7	66.5	66.4
P	68.4	65.3	—

Number of Times Fixed Charges Earned

A	3.8	15.8	15.5
B	3.9	(2.0)	0.3
C	6.2	5.2	5.1
P	4.3	7.0	—

Operating Profit/Capital Employed

A	1.5	5.3	3.2
B	1.0	—	—
C	4.2	3.1	3.4
P	3.2	2.0	—

Earnings per Ordinary Share

A	£.06	0.32	0.29
B	£.02	(0.5)	(0.3)
C	£.33	0.26	0.26
P	£.15	0.08	—

Price Earnings Ratio (based on average of high and low price for the year)

A	75.0	14.2	0.29
B	45.0	—	—
C	12.0	19.2	17.0
P	17.6	19.8	—

Dividend Yield (based on average of high and low price for the year)

A	4.1	3.4	3.5
B	—	—	—
C	3.5	3.2	3.2
P	3.6	3.3	—

You are required to:
1. Calculate and fill in 19-2 ratios for the Portroy Co. Ltd.
2. What conclusions can be drawn from the data given?

13.10A. From the following information for Growquick Ltd. prepare a Value Added Statement.

	£	
Sales		30,000,000
Sundry costs:		
Wages, persons and benefits	5,000,000	
Depreciation	1,000,000	
Other items bought in from outside	8,000,000	14,000,000
Operating Profit		16,000,000
Interest charges		1,500,000
		14,500,000
Taxation — Corporation tax		7,000,000
Profit after Taxation		7,500,000
Dividend on Ordinary Shares		3,000,000
Retained Profit		4,500,000

14

Accounting as an Information System

So far this book has been concerned primarily with the recording function of accounting, often called book-keeping, and the drafting of the final accounts of different types of organizations, such as partnerships or limited companies. The term generally used for this is Financial Accounting. Much of it is concerned with legal requirements, such as complying with the provisions of the Companies Acts when drafting final accounts, or keeping an accounting record of a customer's legal indebtedness, i.e. a debtor's account. With companies the final accounts represent the account given to the shareholders by the directors of their running of the company during a particular year, in other words it is a statement of the directors' 'stewardship'. These accounts are also given to other interested parties such as the bankers to the firm, creditors, Inspectors of Taxes etc.

Whilst Financial Accounting is necessary from a legal point of view, it cannot be said to be ideal from the point of view of controlling the activities of a firm. Your studies would therefore be incomplete if you had seen only the 'stewardship' function of accounting. The use of accounting for controlling the activities of a firm is probably more important, therefore the rest of this book is concerned mainly with accounting for 'Management Control' purposes. The word 'management' does not necessarily mean that the firm is a limited company, although most of the large organisations in the private sector of industry would in fact be limited companies. It means instead the people who are managing the affairs of the firm, whether they are directors, partners, sole traders or 'managers' classified as those employees who are in charge of other employees.

Before starting to examine Accounting for Management Control let us look first at the deficiencies of Financial Accounting when we want to control the activities of an organization. Its first deficiency is that it deals with operations that have already occurred: it deals with the past, not the future. It is possible to control something whilst it is happening, and control can be arranged for something that is going to happen, but when it has already happened without being controlled then the activity has ended and we are too late to do anything about control. In this way if a company incurs a loss and we do not realize it until long after the event then the loss cannot be prevented. What we really want to do is to control affairs so that a loss is not incurred if at all possible, and we should be able to call on accounting techniques to help in the control of activities. However, it certainly does not mean that we are not interested in the past. We can learn lessons from the past which can be very useful in understanding what is going on now, and what is likely to be happening in the future.

The second deficiency of Financial Accounting is that it is concerned with the whole of the firm. Thus the Trading Account of a firm may show a gross profit of £60,000, and whilst it is better to know that than to have no idea at all of what the gross profit is, it does not tell management much about past transactions. Suppose that in fact the firm manufactures three products — watches, pens and cigarette lighters. Some possibilities of how much profit (or loss) was attributable to each of the products might be as in Exhibit 14.1.

Exhibit 14.1

Various possibilities of profits and loss for each product

	1	2	3	4
Watches	20,000	5,000	30,000	(30,000)*
Pens	20,000	70,000	28,000	65,000
Lighters	20,000	(15,000)*	2,000	25,000
Total Gross Profit	£60,000	£60,000	£60,000	£60,000

*Losses are shown in brackets

These are only some of the possible figures of profit and loss for each product which could result in an overall gross profit of £60,000. Just the figure of total gross profit would give you very few clues as to what lessons can be learned from studying the past to help you control the firm in the future. If possibility number 2 was in fact the correct solution then it would stimulate further discussion and investigation as to why these results had occurred. It could result in the closing down of the section of the firm which makes cigarette lighters if, after investigation, it was found to be in the interests of the firm to cease manufacturing them. Many more lessons can therefore be learned from events if the firm's activities can be examined for each part of its activities instead of just the whole of its activities.

This means that Financial Accounting is of little use by itself for Management Control purposes. It does not mean that it is of no use at all for control purposes, as for instance the Financial accounting system may reveal that the debtors at a point in time are £50,000. Management need to know this if they are to control their finances properly, but although this is true of some accounting figures in Financial Accounting many of the other accounting figures may not be much use in controlling the business. For example if a building was bought in 1930 for £20,000 it may well be worth £200,000 today, whilst if we rented a similar building now it might cost us £30,000 a year. We would surely not use the original cost of £20,000 as the deciding factor as to what we will do now with the building. The original cost is now completely irrelevant for the control of the business now or in the future.

Objectives of the Firm

Before we can discuss Management Control we have to ask ourselves what it is for, we cannot really have control unless it is for a purpose. It would be generally agreed that Management Control is needed in guiding the firm so that it achieved its objectives. Before any plans can be drawn up in financial terms the objectives of the firm should be defined quite clearly by the director or owners of a firm. It must not be thought that to make as much profit as possible is the objective of every firm. It would still beg the question of whether it was maximum profit in the long term or the short term that was most important.

In fact it is very rare for the objectives of a firm to be spelled out clearly and unambiguously. Just because in theory it would be a good idea if all firms were to write down their objectives, so that misunderstandings could be cleared up more easily does not mean that it is done. In every walk of life there is a great deal of muddled thinking, and boards of directors and owners of firms are no exception to the general rule. There is a great deal of 'muddling through' without any really clear ideas of in which direction the firm is heading. If the objectives are uncertain then management control must also be uncertain, and the muddled thinking will penetrate downwards from the board of directors to the shop floor.

Objectives could be expressed in terms of profit and in addition other factors could be brought in. Instances could be the size of the share of the market the firm wished to achieve, the quality of the goods manufactured, the sense of obligation to its employees or the duty of the firm to the community at large. As to whether or not a firm has good management control this can only be found by looking at how effective the management control system was in guiding the firm towards its objectives. Thus a firm making artificial limbs might conceivably set itself a much lower profit target than it could make, because the directors put product quality before profit. The management control system in that case is concerned more with quality than it would be with profit. But the directors may well have stipulated a profit figure they must achieve, even though it is lower than they could manage if they let quality slide, and therefore the management control system would have as its task the maintaining of the highest quality product possible whilst still achieving the profit target.

People and Management Control

It is also important to point out that the most important resource of any firm are the people who work on it. A danger exists that a great deal of care and attention may be given to designing a management control system and operating it, but this is absolutely of no use to management if it does not result in action by the human beings in the firm. Systems and figures do not themselves do anything, instead it is the people in the firm who take (or do not take) the necessary action.

You must bear in mind that figures thrown up by systems are only part of the evidence available when a decision has to be made as to the necessary action. A particular department may be incurring losses now, but the sales manager may give as his considered opinion that sales will increase soon and that the department will become profitable. If people accepted accounting figures as the only criteria on which action should be based then there would be some very bad actions by management. Many of the now very successful products have started off by incurring losses in the early stages, and have been eventually successful because the firm has persevered with the product because they had the faith that it would eventually make the grade.

If it was possible to have exactly the same system of management control in three different firms, it might be found in firm A that the control system was useless because no one acted on the data produced. In firm B the control system might result in damage being done to the firm because management used the data as though it was the only criteria in gauging the actions it should take. In firm C it might be an extremely good system because the management saw the data as a useful guide in the planning and control of the firm, and had also made certain that the rest of the organization took the same view.

How human beings react to a management control system is therefore right at the heart of the problem of ensuring that an effective management control system is in use.

Management Information

Part of this book is about information which is intended to be used by the management of an organisation. For a small and simple organisation the information needs of management may be limited and can be obtained by direct observation — using eyes to look and the voice to ask questions. For example a person managing a greengrocery stall on a market can often operate effectively without formal records to help him. What he buys is determined by the goods available in the local wholesale market and his personal knowledge of what his customers are prepared to buy at a given price. His records will probably centre around the recording of cash and the details of his sales and expenditures in order to prepare financial accounts. However apart from the essential requirement of maintaining proper cash levels these records do not help him in the day to day management of his business operations.

If in contrast we look at the manager responsible for buying greengrocery for a large supermarket chain certain differences emerge. The basic decision about what to buy at a given price remains the same. However in the large organisation there is a much wider choice of where and how to buy than in the small organisation. The large buyer may for example be able to enter into contracts directly with growers and to enter forward contracts for the supply of produce (for example a farmer agrees to sell all his potatoes at the end of the summer to the firm at a fixed price).

In the large organisation the buyer will not be in direct contact with the many different sales outlets and therefore needs written information to keep him in touch with demand. He does not have to listen to complaining customers! Similarly because the sources of supply are likely to be much wider for the big firm he needs more formal information to keep him in touch with market prices.

One of the other features about the large organisation which distinguishes it from the small, is that responsibility for running the business is shared between many different people. In order to ensure that the operations of the firm are carried out efficiently and effectively there needs to be some criteria to measure the performance of the managers. In a small firm the inadequate proprietor will either make a very poor living or become a bankrupt.

Thus his success or failure is clearly his own responsibility. In a large firm the same things can happen overall, but the situation may be obscured by a swings and roundabouts effect of some good sections making up for some bad. A management information system should help identify these problems in an organisation.

The Management Process

The way that management operates in an organisation may be conveniently described by a division into three areas:

1. Forecasting and Planning
2. Controlling Operations
3. Evaluating Performance

1. Forecasting and Planning is the process by which Senior Management decide on major overall issues concerning what the business is going to do, and how it is going to do it. It involves an assessment of information about the future which is called forecasting. When the forecast has been prepared then the company can plan how to achieve the objectives set by management based on the forecast. Planning is the process of co-ordinating the resources available to attain an objective.

2. Controlling Operations involves management in a number of processes and requires several different kinds of information. It involves converting top management plans into an operating pattern which matches the parts into which a company is divided. This changes the overall plan into detailed operating plans which relate to the management structure of the company. This process is called budgeting.

When actual events occur then the information recording the events needs to be measured in such a way that it can be compared with the plan.

This important process of management gives a feedback on the success of the plan to those who set it in the first instance.

Controlling operations effectively also requires information designed to help managers take the decisions which their jobs require. For example information about the profit produced by one product as compared to another will enable a decision about how many of each product to make.

3. Evaluating Performance involves the analysis and assessment of actual results. This is partly a process of comparison with plans but not exclusively. The information on which plans were based may have been wrong. Thus the analysis of performance whilst involving comparison of actual with planned results needs considerable judgement as to what the plan should have been had all the facts been known in advance.

The three elements we have described are by no means completely independent. One way of looking at them is as a cycle in which information is circulating continually from one area to another as in Exhibit 14.2.

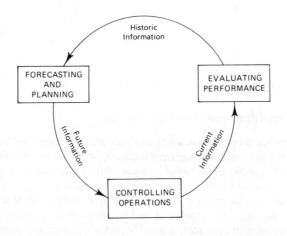

Exhibit 14.2

In this diagram information is shown to flow around from one part into the other. Thus for example forecasts in one period may be improved by taking account of the analysis of what happened last period.

The diagram we have just prepared only looks at internal information. In practice information is being fed into the process from outside. Top management will have to take into account all the information it can about the outside environment such as competition, economic cutbacks etc. The Control of Operations also receive information about actual events.

It is also useful to add to the diagram a time dimension as in Exhibit 14.3 Forecasting and Planning must relate to the future. Controlling

Operations relates to concurrent events — the here and now. Evaluating Performance can only be retrospective or historically based

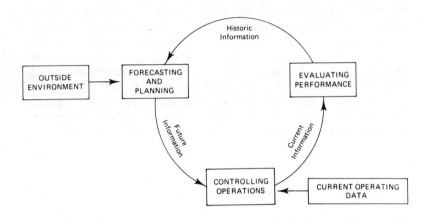

Exhibit 14.3

Types of Management Information

So far in this chapter no attempt has been made to describe the nature of the information which management requires. Information may come in many shapes and forms. In this book we are only concerned with information which is capable of being expressed in numerical terms, which in other words may be 'quantified'. Information of a more general nature about peoples' 'feelings' or 'views' may be very useful to management but cannot be quantified, and therefore is usually part of the informal rather than the formal information systems.

Within the body of quantified information it is normal to identify that part which can be measured in money terms. This is the part of the information system which is called Accounting Information. Accounting information is a very important element in the whole system since the organisation is basically an economic unit which must survive in conditions of economic scarcity and competition. In other words an organisation which does not meet its economic objectives will eventually fail or be taken over. Hence the central importance of accounting information.

However other quantified information may be very important for management. For example if you are a farmer you will measure the yield of milk from your cows in the first instance as gallons. A production manager will be very concerned to monitor the tonnages produced on his machines.

Quantitative Methods in the Information System

A modern management information system collects all the data together (into what is called a data bank) and issues that part which is important to each manager. Thus the distinction between accounting and other types of management information has tended to become less meaningful in modern data processing systems. The techniques of quantitative analysis (or statistics) apply to all the data in this system whether it be accounting data or not.

Assignment Exercises

14.1. Complete the following sentences by listing the missing words on a piece of paper:
(a) Most of the larger organisations in the private sector of industry are _____ _____.
(b) Financial Accounting is of _____ use by itself for management control purposes.
(c) Before we can discuss management control we must establish the _____ of the business.
(d) An effective management control system can only be judged by looking at how _____ the system was in guiding the firm towards its _____.

14.2A. Complete the following sentences by listing the missing words on a piece of paper:
(a) Management Control states _____ shall be done, sees that it _____ done, checks _____ it has been done.
(b) A management control system is of no use if it does not _____ _____ _____ by the human beings in the firm.
(c) An accountant in management should cater for the _____ of _____.
(d) Accounting information is not the only _____ on which action should be based.

14.3. In respect of the following statements write down whether you think they are TRUE or FALSE.
(a) An accountant can find all the solutions to the problems of the business in his textbooks, if he has a big enough library.
(b) The management control system of the business is concerned only with objectives which can be expressed only in terms of profits.
(c) Financial Accounting is normally of little use by itself for management control purposes.
(d) The majority of firms do not spell out their objectives clearly and objectively.

14.4A. In respect of the following statements write down whether you think they are TRUE or FALSE.
(a) A firm might deliberately set itself a lower profit target than it could achieve.
(b) A management control system can function effectively even if the people in the firm do not react to control in the right way.

(c) Much information needed for management control will be in non-accounting terms.

(d) Quality may be more important than profits in some firms.

14.5A. A department store has four departments — (A) Clothing, (B) Furniture, (C) General, (D) Restaurant. A Trading Account has been drawn up which shows that the following gross profits or losses have been made:

(A)	Clothing Department	£10,000 gross profit
(B)	Furniture Department	£15,000 gross profit
(C)	General Department	£16,000 gross profit
(D)	Restaurant	£4,000 gross loss

What would you advise the management to do?

15

Elements of Costing

Cost Accounting is needed so that there can be an effective management accounting system. Without a study of costs such a system could not exist. Before entering into any detailed description of costs it is better if we ask ourselves first of all what use we are going to make of information about costs in the business. This can best be done by referring to something which is not accounting, and then relating it to accounting. Suppose that your employer asked you to measure the distance between Manchester and London, but walked away from you without giving any further information. As you thought about his request the following thoughts might go through your head:

1. *HOW* does he want the distance measuring? Some possibilities are:
   (a) From the southern outskirts of Manchester to the northern outskirts of London.
   (b) From the accepted geographical centre of London, to the accepted geographical centre of Manchester.
   (c) To the centres of the two cities calculated as mathematically precise points.
   (d) By road, this could be just major roads, just minor roads, or could be either major or minor roads the main requirement being the quickest route by road or the shortest route by road.
   (e) By canal.
   (f) By air; allowance may or may not be made for the distance covered by the aircraft which would include climbing to an altitude of 5,000 feet or perhaps 40,000 feet, or might ignore the distance travelling in achieving an altitude.

2. The *COST* of obtaining the information. Measuring distances (or measuring costs) is not costless itself. Using very sophisticated instruments to get accurate measurement can be very expensive indeed. On the other hand it might just be a matter of measuring the distance on a map with a rule and converting it into miles — this would cost hardly anything at all.

3. What is the *PURPOSE* for which the measurement will be used? This has been deliberately left as the last point, but in fact it should have been the first question that came into your mind. Illustrations of the use could have been as follows:

(a) He is going to drive from Manchester to London by car and wants a rough idea of the mileage so that he can gauge what time to set off if he is to arrive before dark in London.

(b) He might conceivably want to walk it.

(c) Perhaps he wants to send goods by canal.

(d) He might be an amateur pilot who want to fly from Manchester Airport to London Airport.

(e) He might be submitting a tender for the building of a motorway by the shortest possible route, cutting tunnels through ranges of hills.

The lesson to be learned from this is that measurement depends entirely on the use that is to be made of the data. Far too often firms make measurements of financial and other data without looking first at the use that is going to be made of it. In fact it could be said that 'information' is useful data that is provided for someone. Data given to someone which is not relevant to the purpose required is just not information. Data which is provided for a particular purpose, and which is completely wrong for the purpose, is worse than having no data at all. At least when there is no data the manager knows that he is making a guess, when useless data is collected it first of all has cost money to collect, in itself a waste of money; secondly it often gets taken to be useful data and misleads a manager into taking steps which are completely wrong and would not have happened if he had relied instead on his own hunches. Third it clogs up the communication system within a firm, so that other data is not acted on properly because of the general confusion that has been caused.

How is all this reflected in a study of costs?

1. What is the data on costs wanted for? It might be needed for the financial accounts, for management control or for decision making. Different data on costs are wanted for different purposes.

2. How are the costs to be measured? Only when the purpose for which the costs are to be used has been decided can the measurement process be decided. Financial accounting for instance needs a certain precision in calculating costs which is often not needed in management accounting, where sometimes the nearest thousand pounds will be good enough for the purpose.

3. The cost of obtaining costing data should not exceed the benefits to be gained from having it. This does not refer to some cost data which is needed to comply with various provisions of the law. Some cases of the benefits exceeding the costs could well be data which costs £1 to obtain but will be used as a basis for pricing many of the products of the firm — if the cost had been 'guessed' instead of being found an error could have meant large losses for the firm if the prices had been set too low because of this. On the other hand to spend £10,000 to find data on sales which the sales manager will toss into the waste-paper basket because it is not the type of data he wants, is money wasted. Similarly, a great deal of the time spent in precise calculations can be wasted, e.g. if the managing director to know the figure of stock-in-trade for the financial accounts he will want to know that it is £2,532,198, but if he wants to know the figure for the

purpose of having a general chat with the bank manager the figure of £2½ million will be quite accurate enough.

When it is known what the costs are for, how much is to be spent on studying the costs, then subsequently the way costs are to be measured can proceed further.

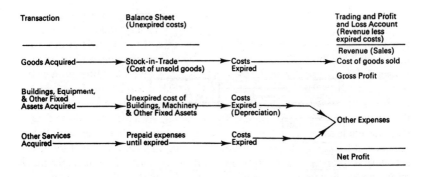

Transaction	Balance Sheet (Unexpired costs)		Trading and Profit and Loss Account (Revenue less expired costs)
			Revenue (Sales)
Goods Acquired	Stock-in-Trade (Cost of unsold goods)	Costs Expired	Cost of goods sold
			Gross Profit
Buildings, Equipment, & Other Fixed Assets Acquired	Unexpired cost of Buildings, Machinery & Other Fixed Assets	Costs Expired (Depreciation)	Other Expenses
Other Services Acquired	Prepaid expenses until expired	Costs Expired	
			Net Profit

Exhibit 15.1

Here the costs are concerned with the past and are found for the purpose of calculating the gross and net profits, or to put it in a rather more academic way the purpose was that of the measurement of income.

Past costs in Trading Companies

Past costs — often aptly called historic costs — are part of the ordinary Financial Accounting done in firms. Here the 'original cost' concept is used. A diagram — Exhibit 15.1 shows costs flowing through Financial Accounts.

Past Costs in Manufacturing Companies

The costs flowing through the firm are analysed in a different fashion than Trading Companies because of the extra dimension, the fact that the firm manufacturers goods and then trades in them — thus the manufacturing elements is the extra dimension. Exhibit 15.2 shows costs flowing through a Manufacturing Company.

148

Exhibit 15.2

The flow of costs through a manufacturing company

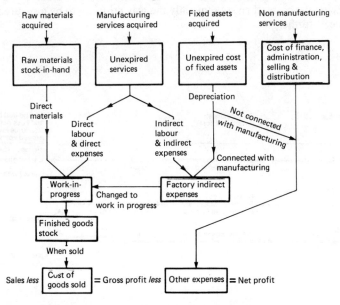

Direct materials are those materials which become part of the finished good, subject to the proviso that the expense involved in tracing the cost is worthwhile. Some items, usually of insignificant amounts, are treated as indirect materials even though they are part of the finished product because the cost cannot be ascertained easily.

Direct Labour are those labour cost which are applied to convert the direct materials into the finished good, also subject to the proviso that the expense involved in tracing this cost is worthwhile.

Direct Expenses are those expenses which can be traced direct to the product being manufactured. These are fairly rare, but an instance would be a royalty where the production of each item resulted in say £1 being due to the owner of a patent.

Prime Cost: The total of Direct Materials + Direct Labour + Direct Expenses is called Prime Cost.

Naturally there will be disagreement between accountants as to whether certain costs are worth tracing as being of a Direct type, as it will often be a matter of judgement which defies any easy proof whether or not the expense of tracing the cost exceeds the benefit from so doing. You should get used to the idea in accounting that disagreement will often occur, which will only be settled by a compromise or appeal to someone in higher authority to settle the argument. This obviously relates to many things in accounting beside the decision as to whether an item is of a direct type or not.

Factory Indirect Expenses or Manufacturing Overhead are all those other expenses concerned with the manufacturing process which have not been treated as of the direct type. Because there is no easily traceable direct connection with the goods being manufactured these costs must be apportioned between the goods being manufactured in a logical fashion. The word 'logical' must be stressed, remember that the accounting functions should be suited to the purpose in hand rather than the organization of the firm suited to meet the accounting system. As the saying goes 'The tail should not wag the dog', meaning that the tail and accounting can be given the same meaning here.

Production Cost: The total of Prime Cost + Factory Indirect Expenses is called Production Cost.

Administration, Selling and Distribution and Finance Expenses are common to both trading and manufacturing firms.

Total Cost: If we add together Production Cost and Administration, Selling and Distribution, and Finance Expenses, the resultant figure is known as Total Cost. To summarise:

	Direct Materials
ADD	Direct Labour
ADD	Direct Expenses
Gives:	PRIME COST
ADD	Factory Indirect Expenses
Gives:	PRODUCTION COST
ADD	Administration Expenses
ADD	Selling and Distribution Expenses
ADD	Finance Expenses
Gives:	TOTAL COST

Exhibit 15.3 is a list of typical types of expenses found in a manufacturing firm. These can be analysed as to whether they are Direct Materials, Direct Labour, Direct Expenses, Factory Indirect Expenses, Administration Expenses, Selling and Distribution Expenses, or Finance Expenses. See how well you can do yourself by covering up the right-hand column with a piece of paper, then sliding your paper down to reveal one answer at a time after you have mentally analysed it yourself.

Exhibit 15.3

Cost	*Cost Analysis*
1. Raw Materials for goods—identifiable with product made.	Direct Materials
2. Rent of Factory Buildings.	Factory Indirect Expenses
3. Salesmen's Salaries.	Selling and Distribution
4. Wages of Machine Operators in Factory.	Direct Labour
5. Wages of Accounting Machine Operators in Office.	Administration Expenses
6. Depreciation of Lathes in Factory.	Factory Indirect Expenses
7. Depreciation of Typewriters in Office.	Administration Expenses

8. Depreciation of Fixtures in Sales Showrooms.	Selling and Distribution Expenses
9. Foremen's Wages in Factory.	Factory Indirect Expenses
10. Royalty paid for each item manufactured.	Direct Expenses
11. Works Manager's salary: he reckons that he spends ¾ of his time in the factory and ¼ in general administration of the firm.	¾ Factory Indirect Expenses ¼ Administration Expenses
12. Raw Materials incorporated in goods sold, but too difficult to trace to the goods being made.	Indirect Expenses
13. Depreciation of Motor Vehicles used for delivery of finished goods to customers.	Selling and Distribution Expenses
14. Interest on Bank Overdraft.	Finance Expenses
15. Wages of crane drivers in factory.	Factory Indirect Expenses
16. Discounts Allowed.	Finance Expenses
17. Company Secretary's salary.	Administration Expenses
18. Advertising.	Selling and Distribution Expenses
19. Wages of Staff of Canteen used by Factory Staff only.	Factory Indirect Expenses
20. Cost of hiring special machinery for use in manufacturing one special item.	Direct Expenses

Assignment Exercises

15.1A. If someone asked you to obtain a new type of cost data for them, what would you want to know before you commenced to work?

15.2. From the following information work out:

(a) Prime Cost

(b) Production Cost

	£
(c) Total Cost	
Salaries of employees in the Administrative Block	80,000
Wages of indirect labour force in the factory	110,000
Expenses of running firm's canteen attended by all workers, ¾ work in the factory, ¼ in other parts of the firm	8,000
Interest on loans and overdraft	2,000
Wages: drivers of lorries used for distribution	2,500
Salaries: Salesmen	7,000
Commission on sales: paid to salesmen	1,200
Raw Materials used in production	210,000
Depreciation: Machinery in Factory	6,000
Accounting Machinery	500
Delivery Vehicles	1,500
Showroom Equipment	100
Labour costs directly connected with manufacture	120,000
Other Factory Indirect Expenses	66,000

15.3A. From the following information work out:

(a) Prime Cost

(b) Production Cost

(c) Total Cost

		£
Wages and Salaries of Employees:		
In Factory (60 per cent is directly concerned with units being manufactured)		150,000
In Sales Force		15,000
In Administration		26,000
Carriage Costs: On Raw Materials brought into the firm		1,800
On finished goods delivered to customers		1,100
Rent and Rates: Of Factory Block	4,900	
Of Sales Department and Showrooms	1,000	
Of Administrative Block	1,100	7,000
Travelling Expenses: Salesmen	3,400	
Administrative staff	300	
Factory Workers not connected directly with production	200	3,900
Raw Materials: Stock at start of period		11,400
Bought in the period		209,000
Stock at close of the period		15,600
Royalties: payable per unit of production		400
Depreciation: Salesmens' cars	500	
Vehicles used for deliveries to customers	300	
Cars of administrative staff	400	
Machinery in Factory	1,800	
Office Machinery	200	3,200
Interest Costs on Borrowed Money		800
Other Factory Indirect Expenses		6,000
Other Administrative Expenses		4,000
Other Selling Expenses		1,000

15.4. Analyse the following costs between:

1. Direct Materials
2. Direct Labour
3. Factory Indirect Expenses
4. Administration Expenses
5. Selling and Distribution Expenses
6. Finance Expenses

   (a) Wages of men maintaining machines in factory
   (b) Wages of man maintaining accounting machinery
   (c) Expenses of canteen run exclusively for factory workers
   (d) Expenses of canteen run exclusively for administrative workers
   (e) Grease used for factory machinery
   (f) Cost of raw materials
   (g) Carriage inwards on fuel used in factory boiler-house
   (h) Carriage inwards on raw material
   (i) Wages of managing director's chauffeur

(j) Wages of cleaners in factory
(k) Discounts Allowed
(l) Rent of salesrooms
(m) Wages of lathe operators in factory
(n) Wages of security guards; The area of the factory buildings is four times as great as the other buildings
(o) Debenture interest
(p) Rent of annexe used by accounting staff
(q) Managing director's remuneration
(r) Salesmen's salaries
(s) Running costs of salesmen's cars
(t) Repairs to factory buildings
(u) Audit fees
(v) Power for machines in factory
(w) Rates: ¾ for factory buildings and ¼ for other buildings
(x) Rent of internal telephone system in factory
(y) Bank Charges
(z) Costs of advertizing products on television.

15.5A. Analyse the following costs between

1. Direct Materials
2. Direct Labour
3. Factory Indirect Expenses
4. Administration Expenses
5. Selling and Distribution Expenses
6. Finance Expenses

(a) Interest on bank overdraft
(b) Factory Storekeepers Wages
(c) Hire of Rolls-Royce for managing director's use
(d) Repairs to factory roof
(e) Hotel bills incurred by salesmen
(f) Motor tax for vans used for delivering goods to customers
(g) Chief Accountant's salary
(h) Lubricants for factory machinery
(i) Cost of paper-tape for firm's computer
(j) Helicopter hire charges re special demonstration of company's products
(k) Debt collection costs
(l) Costs of painting advertising signs on London buses
(m) Cost of airplane tickets for salesmen
(n) Wages of painters engaged in production
(o) Wages of time-keepers in factory
(p) Postal charges for letters
(q) Wages of office boy in general office
(r) Postal charges — parcels sent to customers
(s) Repairs to vans used for taking goods to customers
(t) Cost of raw materials included in product
(u) Wages for charwomen engaged in administration block
(v) Carriage inwards on raw materials
(w) Repairs to neon sign in Piccadilly Circus
(x) Advertising agency fees
(y) Wages of crane drivers in factory
(z) Power costs of accounting machinery.

15.6 From the following information work out:

(a) Prime Cost
(b) Production Cost
(c) Total Cost

		£
Wages and Salaries of Employees:		
In Factory (70 per cent is directly concerned with units being manufactured)		220,000
Salaries: Salesman		8,000
Commission on Sales paid to Salesman		1,400
Salaries of administrative staff		72,000
Travelling Expenses:		
Salesmen	2,900	
Factory Workers not directly concerned with production	100	
Administrative Staff	200	3,200
Haulage costs on raw material bought		4,000
Carriage costs on goods sold		7,800
Depreciation: Factory Machinery	38,000	
Accounting & office machinery	2,000	
Motor Vehicles:		
Salemens cars	3,800	
Administrative staff	1,600	
Sales display equipment	300	45,700
Royalties payable per unit of production		1,600
Canteen costs used by all the workers, ⅔ work in the factory, ⅓ in other parts of the firm		6,000
Raw materials: Stock at start of period		120,000
Stock at close of period		160,000
Bought in the period		400,000
Interest on Loans and Overdrafts		3,800
Other Factory Indirect Expenses		58,000
Other Administrative Expenses		42,000
Other Selling Expenses		65,000

15.7. Analyse the following costs between:

1. Direct Materials
2. Direct Labour
3. Factory Indirect Expenses
4. Administrative Expenses
5. Selling and Distribution Expenses
6. Finance Expenses

   (a) Costs of electricity for office duplicating equipment
   (b) Hotel costs of salesmen
   (c) Haulage costs bringing materials to factory
   (d) Wages of drilling machine operators in factory
   (e) Raw material costs
   (f) Hiring hoardings for sale posters
   (g) Cost Accountant's salary
   (h) Legal costs re debt collection

(i) Repairs to drilling machinery
(j) Shipping cost of sending goods overseas
(k) Chairman's remuneration
(l) Rent of stand at an exhibition
(m) Repairs to factory cranes
(n) Salary of Secretary to managing director
(o) Repairs to showrooms
(p) Bank overdraft interest
(q) Wages of lathe operators
(r) Discounts Allowed
(s) Printing sales brochures
(t) Wages of service department apprentices in the factory
(u) Costs of accounting stationery
(v) Salary of nurse in factory accident room
(w) Wages of women assembling goods
(x) Fire Insurance of factory
(y) Fees of management consultants reorganising office routines
(z) Diesel oil for running factory machinery.

16

Manufacturing Accounts

In a manufacturing account the production cost of goods completed during an accounting period is calculated. This means that all the items of Production Cost are charged to the manufacturing account. Administration and selling and distribution expenses are charged to the profit and loss account.

You should note that it is the production cost of goods *completed* in the period, irrespective as to when the work started on them. Because of this fact goods partly completed, known as work in progress, have to be taken into account.

Two exhibits are now given. In the first of these, 16.1, a case is shown of a firm without any work in progress, either at the beginning or the end of the accounting period.

Exhibit 16.1

The following are details of production cost for the year ended 31 December 19-4.

1 January 19-4, stock of raw materials	800
31 December 19-4, stock of raw materials	1,200
Purchase of raw materials	9,000
Manufacturing (direct) wages	15,000
Royalties	400
Indirect wages	8,000
Rent of factory (excluding administration and selling and distribution departments)	1,080
Factory rates	340
General indirect expenses	430
Depreciation of works machinery	550

Manufacturing Account for the year ended 31 December 19-4

	£	£
Stock of Raw Materials 1.1.19-4		800
Add Purchases		9,000
		9,800
Less Stock of Raw Materials 31.12.19-4		1,200
Cost of Raw Materials Consumed		8,600
Manufacturing Wages		15,000
Royalties		400
Prime Cost		24,000
Factory Overhead Expenses		
Rent	1,080	
Rates	340	
Indirect Wages	8,000	
Depreciation	550	
General Expenses	430	10,400
Product Cost of Goods Completed c/d		34,400

When the production cost of goods completed is known, it is carried down to the trading account, in the place where normally the purchases are shown. Sometimes a firm will additionally also buy goods for resale, and in this case the trading account will have both figures included.

Work in Progress

If there is work in progress i.e. goods only part completed at the beginning and end of an accounting period, then an adjustment will be needed. To calculate the production cost of goods completed during the period, the value of the work in progress at the beginning must be brought in as it is work which normally will be finished within the period. Likewise work in progress at the end of the period must be carried forward to the next period, as it will be completed during that next period. The adjustments are made by adding the value of work in progress at the beginning to the total production cost for the period, and the closing work in progress is deducted. This is shown in Exhibit 16.2.

Exhibit 16.2

	£
1 January 19-3 Stock of raw materials	900
31 December 19-3 Stock of raw materials	1,250
1 January 19-3 Work-in-progress	460
31 December 19-3 Work-in-progress	540
For the year ended 31 December 19-3:	
Wages: Direct	5,440
Indirect	3,060
Raw Materials Purchased	12,800
Power and Fuel	520
Direct Expenses	260
Carriage inwards on raw materials	170
Factory rent and rates	840
Depreciation of factory machinery	360
Insurance of factory buildings	120
General factory expenses	390

Manufacturing Account for the year ended 31 December 19-3

	£	£
Stock of Raw Materials 1.1.19-7		900
Add Purchases		12,800
,, Carriage Inwards		170
		13,870
Less Stock of Raw Materials 31.12.19-7		1,250
Cost of Raw Materials Consumed		12,620
Direct Wages		5,440
Direct Expenses		260
Prime Cost		18,320
Factory Overhead Expenses		
Power and Fuel	520	
Indirect Wages	3,060	
Rent and Rates	840	
Depreciation of Machinery	360	
Insurance	120	
General Factory Expenses	390	5,290
		23,610
Add Work-in-Progress 1.1.19-3		460
		24,070
Less Work-in-Progresses 31.12.19-3		540
		23,530
Production Cost of Goods Completed c/d		23,530

The trading account deals with finished goods. If in Exhibit 16.2 there had been £4,800 stock of finished goods at 1 January 19-3 and £5,600 at 31 December 19-3, and also assuming that the sales of finished goods amounts to £37,000, the trading account would appear as follows:

Trading Account for the year ended 31 December 19-3

	£	£
Sales		37,000
Less Cost of Goods Sold		
Stock of Finished Goods 1.1.19-3	4,800	
Add Production Cost of Goods Completed	23,530	
	28,330	
Less Stock of Finished Goods 31.12.19-3	5,600	22,730
Gross Profit c/d		14,270

The Profit and Loss Account is then drawn up in the normal way, and the expenses charged these will be Administration Expenses, Selling and Distribution Expenses and Finance Expenses. The items referring to stocks and work in progress will appear as follows in the Balance Sheet as at 31 December 19-3.

Current Assets

Stocks:

Raw Materials	1,250
Finished Goods	5,600
Work in Progress	540

Assignment Exercises

16.1. Prepare Manufacturing, Trading and Profit and Loss Accounts from the following balances of Logan Ltd for the year ended 31 December 19-7.

	£
Stocks at 1 January 19-7:	
Raw Materials	18,450
Work in Progress	23,600
Finished Goods	17,470
Purchases: Raw Materials	64,300
Carriage on Raw Materials	1,605
Direct Labour	65,810
Office Salaries	16,920
Rent and Rates	2,700
Office Lighting and Heating	5,760
Depreciation: Works Machinery	8,300
Office Equipment	1,950
Sales	200,600
Factory Fuel & Power	5,920

Rent and Rates are to be apportioned: Factory ⅔rds : Office ⅓. Stocks at 31 December 19-7 were: Raw Materials £20,210, Work in Progress £17,390, Finished Goods £21,485.

16.2A. From the following details you are to draw up a Manufacturing, Trading and Profit and Loss Account for the year ended 30 September 19-4.

	30.9.19-3	30.9.19-4
	£	£
Stocks of Raw Materials, at cost	8,460	10,970
Work in Progress	3,070	2,460
Finished Goods Stock	12,380	14,570

For the year:	£
Raw Materials Purchased	38,720
Manufacturing Wages	20,970
Factory Expenses	12,650
Depreciation:	
Plant & Machinery	7,560
Delivery Vans	3,040
Office Equipment	807
Factory Power	6,120
Advertising	5,080
Office and Administration Expenses	5,910
Salesmens' Salaries and Expenses	6,420
Delivery Van Expenses	5,890
Sales	134,610
Carriage Inwards	2,720

16.3. D. August is a manufacturer. His trial balance at 31 December 19-6 is as follows:

	£	£
Delivery Van Expenses	2,500	
Light & Heat: Factory	2,859	
Office	1,110	
Manufacturing Wages	45,470	
Advertising	1,866	
General Expenses: Office	1,950	
Factory	5,640	
Salesmen: Commission	7,860	
Purchase of Raw Materials	39,054	
Rates: Factory	4,800	
Office	2,200	
Machinery (cost £50,000)	32,500	
Office Equipment (cost £15,000)	11,000	
Office Salaries	6,285	
Debtors	28,370	
Creditors		19,450
Bank	13,337	
Sales		136,500
Premises at Cost	40,000	
Stocks at 31 December 19-5:		
Raw Materials	8,565	
Finished Goods	29,480	
Drawings	8,560	
Capital		137,456
	293,406	293,406

Prepare the Manufacturing, Trading and Profit and Loss Accounts for the year ended 31 December 19-6 and a Balance Sheet as at that date. Give effect to the following adjustments:

1. Stocks at 31 December 19-6, Raw Materials £9,050, Finished Goods £31,200. There is no Work in Progress.
2. Depreciate Machinery £2,000, Office Equipment £1,500.
3. Manufacturing Wages due but unpaid at 31 December 19-6 £305, Advertising prepaid £108.

16.4A. B. Little has a manufacturing business. His trial balance as on 31 December 19-7 was as follows:

	£	£
Carriage Outwards	2,760	
Rent and Rates: Office	990	
Factory	4,850	
Office Machinery (cost £6,000)	4,200	
Bank		14,360
Debtors	28,972	
Sales		184,715
Machinery (cost £50,000)	28,000	
Salaries to Salesmen	8,570	
Raw Material Purchases	57,245	
Sundry Expenses: Factory	1,362	
Office	898	
Creditors		15,477
Stocks at 31 December 19-6:		
Raw Materials	15,872	
Finished Goods	51,897	
Office Salaries	8,416	
Advertising	4,278	
Manufacturing Wages	64,371	
Light & Heat: Office	1,475	
Factory	4,896	
Drawings	9,900	
Capital		84,400
	298,952	298,952

You are to draw up a Manufacturing, Trading and Profit and Loss Account for the year ended 31 December 19-7, and a Balance Sheet as on that date. Give effect to the following adjustments:

(a) Depreciate Machinery £5,000, Office Machinery £800.
(b) The following were due but unpaid at 31 December 19-7, Advertising £188, Light & Heat:- Office £125, Factory £488.
(c) The factory rent had been prepaid £250 at 31 December 19-7.
(d) Stocks at 31 December 19-7, Raw Materials £13,820, Finished Goods £56,842.

17

Product Costs and Period Costs

Product costs are those costs which are allocated to the units of goods manufactured. In fact product costs make up Production Cost. Such costs are charged up to the cost of goods manufactured in the Trading Account, and would normally be part of the valuation of unsold goods if the goods to which they refer had not been sold by the end of the period. Product costs are therefore matched up against revenue as and when the goods are sold and not before.

Period costs are those of a non-manufacturing nature and represent the selling and distribution, administration and the financial expenses. They are treated as expenses of the period in which they were incurred irrespective of the volume of goods sold.

Past Costs: Trading and Manufacturing Compared

There is a very important difference between costs in a Trading concern with that in a Manufacturing concern. In a Trading concern such items as wages, depreciation and indirect expenses are treated as period costs, i.e. they are charged to the Profit and Loss Account. In a manufacturing concern the wages, depreciation and indirect expenses are treated as part of the Production Cost, and the unsold goods at the end of the period are normally valued at Production Cost. These items, therefore, affect the closing valuation of stock-in-hand in the manufacturing firms but not in the trading concern, and different figures for stock-in-trade mean that the reported profits are different. Exhibit 17.1 gives and example of the first year of (a) a trading concern and (b) a manufacturing concern where total costs are the same but profits calculated are different because of the inclusion of a proportion of Indirect Expenses when Stock-in-Trade was valued at the end of each period in the manufacturing firm.

Exhibit 17.1

Retailing Firm—Expenses:	£	£	£	£
Purchases—1,000 units		90,000		
Wages and Salaries		13,000		
General Expenses		17,000		
Finance Expenses		2,000		
(Same total as Manufacturing Firm)		122,000		
Sales: 800 units			£120,000	

Manufacturing Firm—Expenses:	£	£	£	£
Cost of Raw Materials Used to make 1,000 units		50,000		
Wages: Direct Labour	20,000			
Factory Indirect Labour	12,000			
Salaries and Wages: Administration and Selling	8,000	40,000		
Other Factory Indirect Expenses	20,000			
Other Selling and Administration Expenses	10,000	30,000		
Finance Expenses		2,000		
(Same total as Retail Firm)		122,000		
Sales: 800 units			£120,000	

Closing Stocks of Goods
Retailing Firm: Valued at cost

200 units in hand which cost $\dfrac{200}{1,000} \times £90,000 = £18,000$

Manufacturing Firm: Valued at Production Cost
200 units in hand which cost $\dfrac{200}{1,000} \times$ (Raw Materials 50,000 + Wages 32,000 +

Factory Indirect Expenses 20,000)
$= \dfrac{200}{1,000} \times £102,000 = £20,400$

Retailing Firm's Trading and Profit and Loss Account

	£		£
Purchases	90,000	Sales	120,000
Less Closing Stock	18,000		
Cost of Goods Sold	72,000		
Gross Profit c/d	48,000		
	120,000		120,000

Wages and Salaries	13,000	Gross Profit b/d	48,000
General Expenses	17,000		
Finance Expenses	2,000		
Net Profit	16,000		
	48,000		48,000

Manufacturing Firm's Manufacturing and Trading and Profit and Loss Account

Cost of Materials Used	50,000	Production Cost of Goods	
Direct Labour	20,000	Completed c/d	102,000
Prime Cost	70,000		

Factory Indirect Expenses

Indirect Labour	12,000			
Other Indirect Expenses	20,000			
		32,000		
		102,000		102,000

	£		£
Production Cost of Goods			
Completed b/d	102,000	Sales	120,000
Less Closing Stock			
(see calculation)	20,400		
Cost of Goods Sold	81,600		
Gross Profit c/d	38,400		
	120,000		120,000

Salaries and Wages	8,000	Gross Profit b/d	38,400
Other Administration and			
Selling Expenses	10,000		
Finance Expenses	2,000		
Net Profit	18,400		
	38,400		38,400

The difference between the net profits of the two firms of £2,400 can be seen to be equal to the difference between the closing stocks, i.e. £20,400 and £18,000. The difference in profit calculations can be seen to be due to the different treatment of costs as product costs and period costs in the two firms.

You have now looked at the various elements of cost as far as the whole of the firm is concerned. Such a classification of costs is necessary so that the overall production cost can be ascertained in the case of a manufacturing company with its effect on the valuation of the closing stock of finished goods and of work-in-progress. What most businesses want to know is how much each item has cost to make. This means that the total costs for the whole firm are not sufficient, and so these costs must be analysed further.

Any costing system must bring about the better control of the firm in guiding it towards its objectives, and the benefits to be derived from the costing system must be greater than the expense of operating the costing system. We must, therefore, look at the possible advantages to be gained in carrying on further analyses of cost:

(a)   Because expenditure is traced down to each item produced, or each batch of items, it becomes possible to ascertain the contribution of each item towards the profitability of the business. The desirability of stopping unprofitable activities can then be assessed.

(b)   Once the profitability of each item is known the reasons for increases or decreases in profits can be seen more clearly.

(c)   It becomes easier to forecast future results if we know more about the operations of all the various parts of the business. When forecasted results are not achieved it becomes possible to highlight the reasons for the failure to achieve the forecasted results.

(d)   Estimates and tenders can be prepared in future with far greater confidence — previously such calculations as were done must have been largely guesswork. Fewer errors should be made because of the greater knowledge gained via the costing system.

(e)   Improvements in various activities of the firm may come about because of the more relevant information that can be supplied. Thus a machine which had always been though to be quite cheap to use may turn out to be very expensive to use. This may bring about an investigation which would not otherwise have happened, and it may consequently be found that a simple attachment to the machine costing £10 brings about a saving of £100 a year.

(f)   As will shortly be described, a very important advantage is the control of expenditure, and it can be achieved because an individual can be made responsible for the expenditure under his control.

The possible advantages which can be gained from having a costing system can be seen to be quite considerable. It is, however, now a convenient point to remind you that accounting techniques themselves do not solve problems. Instead it is people within the firm who, when armed with the information that accounting techniques can provide, are far more able to make sensible decisions about what should be done to aid the progress of the firm towards its objectives. Imagine trying to decide which item to stop producing out of twelve items made by a firm if you have little information as to the contribution of each item towards the profitability of the firm. Very often the solution will be that a new layout in the factory is needed; special training given to certain employees; changes made in the system of remunerating employees and so on. The information provided by accounting is, therefore, only one part of the whole story for any problem. It is important to remember that often it will be the least important information available to the decision-taker.

The Control of Costs

One of the most important features of cost accounting is its use for control purposes, meaning in this context the control of expenditure. But control of expenditure is possible only if you can trace the costs down to employees who are responsible for such costs. An area of responsibility is called a 'responsibility centre'. (For costing products the costs are allocated first to convenient areas known as 'cost centres'. Often 'cost centres' are also 'responsibility centres' but not necessarily since a manager's responsibility may only be for part of a cost centre or for more than one.) In a manufacturing firm all direct materials, direct labour and direct expenses are traced to cost centres, in this case they would be known as 'product centres'. A product centre may be such as a single machine used for jobbing work, i.e. quite a lot of separate jobs performed specially to conform with the customer's specifications. It could, however, be a group of similar machines or a production department.

In comparison factory indirect expenses by definition, i.e. because they are 'indirect' expenses, cannot be traced (or it is not worthwhile tracing them) to product centres. These are traced to cost centres which give service rather than being concerned with work directly on the products, and such cost centres are, therefore, known as 'service centres'. Examples of service centres would be the factory canteen or the maintenance department. The costs from these service centres will then need allocating to the product centres in a logical fashion.

In practice there are a number of possible ways of allocating costs to cost centres. What must not be lost sight of is the endeavour to trace costs to a person responsible for the expenditure as well as to the product so that the costs can be controlled.

Costing: Manufacturing firms compared with retailing or wholesale firms

It is quite wrong to think that costing is concerned only with manufacturing firms. Both text-books and examinations papers often give the impression that only in manufacturing is costing needed or found. This is quite incorrect, as costing is just as relevant to retailing and wholesaling firms as it is to those in manufacturing. It is simply that manufacturing, which usually has more complex sorts of activities because of the manufacturing element, has attracted greater attention than other types of firms. There are, in addition, many other forms of organisations such as farming, shipping, banking and even charitable organisations where costing can aid management control. It would indeed be difficult to find any organisation which could not use some form of costing system profitably.

Assignment Exercises

17.1. From the following information draw up a Trading and Profit and Loss Account for C. Dean's retail business, and a Manufacturing and Profit and Loss Account for D. Warren's manufacturing business. These businesses were both started on 1 January, 19-3, accordingly neither of them had opening Stock-in-Trade, and the accounts are for the year ended 31 December, 19-3.

C. Dean	£	
Purchases: 5,000 units	100,000	
Wages and Salaries	50,000	
Rent and Rates	9,000	
Other Expenses	40,000	
Finance Expenses	1,000	
	£200,000	
Sales: 4,200 units at £50 each =	£210,000	

D. Warren		£
Cost of Raw Materials from which 5,000 units are manufactured during the year		100,000
Wages: Factory Direct	28,000	
Wages: Factory Indirect	8,000	
Salaries: Administration	10,000	
Salaries: Salesmen	4,000	
		50,000
Other Factory Indirect Expenses	38,000	
Other Selling and Administrative Expenses	11,000	
		49,000
Finance Expenses		1,000
		£200,000
(N.B. There is no work-in-progress.)		
Sales: 4,200 units at £50 each =		£210,000

(Keep your answer, you may need it for question 17.3.)

17.2A. Draw up a Trading and Profit and Loss Account for J. Knight, a retail firm, and a Manufacturing, Trading and Profit and Loss Account for J. Hanson, a manufacturing firm for the year ended 31 December, 19-7. Both firms have just completed their first year of activity.

J. Knight	£
Purchases: 2,000 units	40,000
Selling and Distribution Expenses	30,000
Administration Expenses	7,000
Finance Expenses	3,000
	£80,000
Sales: 1,500 units at £52 each =	£78,000

J. Hanson	£
Cost of Raw Materials from which 2,000 units have been made	50,000
Direct Labour	10,000
Factory Indirect Expenses	12,000
Administration Expenses	5,000
Selling Expenses	1,200
Finance Expenses	1,800
	£80,000

(N.B. There is no work-in-progress).

Sales: 1,500 units at £52 each =	£78,000

(Keep your answer, you may need it for question 17.4).

17.3. This question is a continuation of 17.1. You are to bring forward the closing stocks goods at 31 December, 19-3 which become the opening stocks for the year ended 31 December, 19-4.

C. Dean's retail business and D. Warren's manufacturing businesses have now each completed their second year of operations. You are required to draw up a Trading and Profit and Loss Account for C. Dean and a Manufacturing, Trading and Profit and Loss Account for D. Warren, each for the year ended 31 December, 19-4.

C. Dean	£
Purchases during the year 6,000 units	120,000
Wages and Salaries	53,000
Rent and Rates	9,000
Other Expenses	42,000
Finance Expenses	2,000
	£226,000
Sales: 5,600 units at £50 each =	£280,000

D. Warren		£
Cost of Raw Materials from which 6,000 units have been manufactured during the year		120,000
Wages: Factory Direct	30,000	
Wages: Factory Indirect	9,000	
Salaries: Administrative Staff	10,000	
Salaries: Salesmen	4,000	53,000
Other Factory Indirect Expenses	39,000	
Other Selling Expenses	8,000	
Other Administrative Expenses	4,000	51,000
Finance Expenses		2,000
		£226,000
Sales: 5,600 units at £50 each =		£280,000

(N.B. There is no work-in-progress.)

17.4A. This question is a continuation of 17.2A. You are to bring forward the closing stocks at 31 December, 19-7 which become the opening stocks for the year ended 31 December, 19-8.

J. Knight's retail business and J. Hanson's manufacturing business have now each completed their second year of operations. You are required to draw up a Trading and Profit and Loss Account for J. Knight, and a Manufacturing, Trading and Profit and Loss Account for J. Hanson, both for the year ended 31 December, 19-8.

J. Knight	£
Purchases during the year: 2,500 units	50,000
Selling and Distribution Expenses	36,000
Administration Expenses	9,000
Finance Expenses	2,000
	£97,000
Sales: 2,200 units at £52 each =	£114,400

J. Hanson	
Cost of Raw Materials from which 2,500 units have been made during the year	62,500
Direct Labour	12,500
Factory Indirect Expenses	14,000
Administration Expenses	5,000
Selling Expenses	2,000
Finance Expenses	1,000
	£97,000
Sales: 2,200 units at £52 each =	£114,400

17.5A. What advantages can be gained by operating a costing system?

18

Accounting for Materials

It may seem a simple matter that when materials are used in production they should be charged to the cost centre at 'cost price'. Before we look at other problems connected with materials, the ways in which these 'cost prices' can be determined will be considered first. It should be mentioned that there are more methods than are described in this chapter, including the way in which they are calculated under standard costing — this is looked at in Chapter 29, but this chapter limits its survey to the other main methods in use.

First of all a word of warning. Students often confuse the actual physical issue of the goods or materials to production etc. with the attempt to put a price on the issue of the goods. Suppose that we had always bought a particular type of item for £1 each ever since the firm began. When these are used in production the cost centre will be charged up with £1 for each item used. On the other hand this country, and the world generally, has experienced inflation for quite a few years now. This has meant that for most items the price per item has been increasing steadily over the past few decades. On the other hand some items have been falling in price. An instance of this are ballpoint pens which were about £3 each for the cheapest type when they were first produced around the year 1943. They now cost a few pence for the cheapest type. With other items the price fluctuates up and down. After all in a free society the price is the interaction of supply and demand. Physically you may have to follow a chronological pattern of issuing goods to production on the basis of the first goods to be received are the first to be issued to production. This could well be the case with perishable foodstuffs as, for instance, meat being put into meat pies. On the other hand it may not matter at all as to the order in which the goods received by the firm are issued to production, it may be an item such as a plastic clip which would not deteriorate at all with age. What we are going to consider is the calculation of the price of the item which is to be charged to production. For this purpose we will ignore in the first instance which goods were actually issued to production, instead we will concentrate on which goods were 'deemed' to be issued to production. Often a firm will know only how many items were issued, it may not know at all when the various items were received by the firm as, for instance, in the case of the plastic clips it does not matter to the firm at all in which order the goods are issued. If it does not benefit a firm to know the chronological order in which goods are received then it will surely not bother to go to the expense of finding out the information.

Let us now look at the mechanics of finding the price at which goods are charged out to production, or in a retail firm are priced to find the cost of goods sold. We will use the same basic information and find the cost of goods issued by the three main methods in use. The information is that the goods issued and received are as follows:

Received	*Number and cost per item*
19-1	
January	10 at £15 each = £150
March	10 at £17 each = £170
August	20 at £20 each = £400
Issued	*Number issued*
19-1	
April	8
December	24

First In, First Out method (abbreviated as FIFO)

With this method the first goods received are deemed to be issued first, Goods from earlier receipts are treated as being issued before any of the goods from later receipts.

In this case the cost of the goods issued is stated to be £120 + £440 = £560.

	Received	Issue Price	Stock after each transaction
January	10 at £15 each		10 at £15 each = £150
March	10 at £17 each		10 at £15 each = £150 10 at £17 each = £170 = £320
April		8 at £15 each = £120	2 at £15 each = £30 10 at £17 each = £170 = £200
August	20 at £20 each		2 at £15 each = £30 10 at £17 each = £170 20 at £20 each = £400 = £600
December		2 at £15 each = £30 10 at £17 each = £170 12 at £20 each = £240 = £440	8 at £20 each = £160

Last In, First Out method (abbreviated as LIFO)

This method treats each issue of goods as being made from the last lot of goods received previous to the date of issue. If that lot of goods is not enough then the balance of the issue is treated as being made from the next previous lot still unissued, and so on.

	Received	Issue Price	Stock after each transaction
January	10 at £15 each		10 at £15 each = £150
March	10 at £17 each		10 at £15 each = £150 10 at £17 each = £170 = £320
April		8 at £17 each = £136	10 at £15 each = £150 2 at £17 each = £34 = £184
August	20 at £20 each		10 at £15 each = £150 2 at £17 each = £34 20 at £20 each = £400 = £584
December		20 at £20 each = £400 2 at £17 each = £34 2 at £15 each = £30 = £464	8 at £15 each = £120

In this case the cost of the goods issued is stated to be £136 + £464 = £600.

Average cost method

Each time there is a receipt of goods the average cost of the goods held in stock is recalculated. Any issues then made are at that price until another receipt of goods when the price is recalculated for further issues, and so on.

	Received	Issued	Average Cost per unit of stock held £	Number of units in stock	Total value of stock £
January	10 at £15 each		15	10	150
March	10 at £17 each		16	20	320
April		8 at £16 each = £128	16	12	192
August	20 at £20 each		18.5	32	592
December		24 at £18.5 each = £444	18.5	8	148

In this case the cost of the goods issued is stated to be £128 + £444 = £572.

Periodic inventory valuation methods

So far we have looked at materials or goods being issued and the records being kept on a perpetual basis, meaning by this that each issue or sale was compared with the receipts strictly on a chronological basis and the price of issue calculated accordingly. The record was, therefore, being maintained perpetually throughout the year. For accounting purposes, however, especially in financial accounting, the calculation of the cost of the goods issued or sold may not be determined until the end of the accounting year. When this is done the exact date of issue or sale during the year is ignored — it is just looked at from the point of view of the total issued or sold. Using the average cost method the issue price is the average cost for the whole year rather than the different averages at different points in time. The LIFO method assumes that the last goods to come in during the year are the first to be issued, instead of the last to be received before the issue was made. The FIFO method will, however, give the same answer no matter whether the perpetual or the periodic method is used.

An illustration of the way the two methods can give different answers is shown in Exhibit 18.1.

The following details are relevant to the receipt and issue of goods. There was no opening stock of goods.

Exhibit 18.1

	Receipts		*Issues*	
19-1	January	9 at £20 each	May	5 items
	July	6 at £30 each	November	4 items

Perpetual inventory — average cost

	Received	Issued	Average Cost per unit of stock held	Number of units in stock	Total value of stock
					£
January	9 at £20		20	9	180
May		5 at £20	20	4	80
July	6 at £30		26	10	260
November		4 at £26	26	6	156

Periodic inventory — average cost

Received			
	9 at £20 =	180	
	6 at £30 =	180	
	15	£360	

Fifteen items cost a total of £360, therefore the average cost at which issues will be priced is £360/15 = £24 each. As 9 items have been issued the total price that they will be charged out as cost of goods sold or materials used is 9 × £24 = £216. Compare this with the issue price of 5 × £20 plus 4 × £26 = £204 using the perpetual inventory method. The closing stocks are 6 × £24 = £144 under the periodic inventory method and £156 under the perpetual inventory method.

Similarly the LIFO method of pricing issues will give different answers, in fact 5 × £20 plus 4 × £30 = £220 with the perpetual method and 6 × £30 plus 3 × £20 = £240 with the periodic method. The FIFO method will give the same answer under both methods, that of 9 × £20 = £180 for the cost of the issues.

Assignment Exercises

18.1. From the following figures calculate the closing stock-in-trade that would be shown using (i) FIFO, (ii) LIFO, (iii) AVCO methods on a perpetual inventory basis.

Bought			*Sold*	
January	10 at £30 each	April	8 for £46 each
March	10 at £34 each	December	12 for £56 each
September	20 at £40 each		

18.2. For question 18.1 draw up the Trading Account for the year showing the gross profits that would have been reported using (i) FIFO, (ii) LIFO, (iii) AVCO methods on a perpetual inventory basis.

18.3A. From the data in questions 18.1 what would the answers have been if the periodic inventory method had been used for the valuation of stock-in-trade?

18.4A. From the figures in question 18.3A draw up the Trading Accounts using (i) FIFO, (ii) LIFO, (iii) AVCO methods on a periodic inventory basis.

18.5. What does the relationship have to be between the physical issue of goods and the pricing out of goods?

18.6A. Receipts and issues of a good are as follows:

Receipts			*Sales*	
January	20 at £30 each	June	6 for £45 each
May	10 at £33 each	August	22 for £46 each
July	16 at £38.5 each	December	10 for £48 each
October	12 at £39 each		

There was no opening stock-in-hand.

(a) Using the perpetual inventory method you are required to calculate the closing stock-in-trade using (i) FIFO, (ii) LIFO, (iii) AVCO.

(b) Draw up the Trading Account showing the different reported gross profits from the figures given in (a).

(c) Using the periodic inventory method you are required to calculate the closing stock-in-trade using (i) FIFO, (ii) LIFO, (iii) AVCO.

(d) Draw up the Trading Accounts showing the different reported gross profits calculated from the figures given in (c).

18.7. (a) From the following figures calculate the closing stock-in-trade that would be shown using (i) FIFO, (ii) LIFO, (iii) AVCO methods on a perpetual inventory basis.

Bought			*Sold*	
January	24 at £10 each	June		30 at £16 each
April	16 at £12.50 each	November		34 at £18 each
October	30 at £13 each			

(b) Draw up Trading Accounts using each of the three methods.

19

Comparison of FIFO, LIFO and Average Cost Methods

The fact that accounts can be constructed to give widely differing answers and yet be within the law is a constant source of amazement to the general public. They feel, instinctively, that balance sheets should be 'correct', and that for a firm only one answer is possible in the form of a Trading and Profit and Loss Account and Balance Sheet. We have already seen that issues of goods to production or as cost of goods sold can be on differing bases. There are many other factors which can be shown quite differently, a prime example of this are depreciation provisions as there are quite a number of ways of calculating depreciation, and in any event even where firms use the same method, e.g. the straight line method for similar assets, one firm may fix an asset life of five years and another ten years, one firm may estimate a residual value of £1,000 and the other firm may estimate it at £100.

The point that has to be brought home to the reader is that Final Accounts are concerned very much with matters of opinion. As matters are at present it would be impossible to get perfect uniformity between firms, as the opinions of one board of directors can never be exactly the same as the opinions of a board of directors of a similar firm, there are bound to be differences no matter how small. The late 1960s saw many disputes, especially where a firm had been taken over, because the accounts prior to the takeover were drafted on completely different bases than would have been used by the directors of the firm that had made the takeover bid. The figures involved have often been quite large, in one case the opinions of the figure that should have been included as stock varied by as much as four million pounds. The professional accountancy bodies have moved towards greater standardization in stock valuation.

To illustrate this further we will now look at the accounts of three firms for the first three years of operation. Each firm has exactly the same transactions, but they each use different methods of pricing out issues of goods with a corresponding effect on their stock valuations at the end of each year.

A worked example

Each firm starts with Capital of £200 in the bank. All sales are cash sales and all purchases and expenses are paid for immediately. Each of the firms is in the same sort of retail trade. Receipts of goods are shown in chronological order, the periodic method of inventory control being used instead of the perpetual method.

	Receipts	Sales	General Expenses
Year 1	20 at £10 each	30 at £14 each	£50
	20 at £12 each		
Year 2	10 at £13 each	32 at £16 each	£60
	20 at £14 each		
Year 3	12 at £18 each	36 at £24 each	£80
	30 at £21 each		

We can now look at the calculation of the prices at which goods have been issued (sold in this case), then the Final Accounts are shown for each firm. The first firm uses Average Cost (AVCO), the second firm First In First Out (FIFO), and the third firm Last In First Out (LIFO).

Average cost method (AVCO)

	Receipts	£	Average Cost	Issues	Stock end of year
Year 1:	20×£10 each	=200			
	20×£12 each	=240			
	40	440	£440÷40 = £11	30×£11 = £330	10×£11 = £110
Year 2: Stock b/f:	10×£11 each	=110			
	10×£13 each	=130			
	20×£14 each	=280			
	40	520	£520÷40 = £13	32×£13 = £416	8×£13 = £104
Year 3: Stock b/f:	8×£13 each	=104			
	12×£18 each	=216			
	30×£21 each	=630			
	50	950	£950÷50 = £19	36×£19 = £684	14×£19 = £266

First In First Out method (FIFO)

	Receipts £	Issues £	Stock end of year
Year 1:	20×£10 each =200	20×£10 each =200	
	20×£12 each =240	10×£12 each =120	10×£12 each = £120
	40 440	30 320	
Year 2:			
Stock b/f:	10×£12 each =120	10×£12 each =120	
	10×£13 each =130	10×£13 each =130	
	20×£14 each =280	12×£14 each =168	8×£14 each = £112
	40 530	32 418	
Year 3:			
Stock b/f:	8×£14 each =112	8×£14 each =112	
	12×£18 each =216	12×£18 each =216	
	30×£21 each =630	16×£21 each =336	14×£21 each = £294
	50 958	36 664	

Last In First Out method (LIFO)

	Receipts £	Issues £	Stock end of year
Year 1:	20×£10 each =200	20×£12 each =240	
	20×£12 each =240	10×£10 each =100	10×£10 each = £100
	40 440	30 340	
Year 2:			
Stock b/f:	10×£10 each =100	20×£14 each =280	
	10×£13 each =130	10×£13 each =130	
	20×£14 each =280	2×£10 each = 20	8×£10 each = £80
	40 510	32 430	
Year 3:			
Stock b/f:	8×£10 each = 80	30×£21 each =630	
	12×£18 each =216	6×£18 each =108	6×£18 each = £108
	30×£21 each =630		8×£10 each = £80
	50 926	36 738	= £188

Now we can look at the Trading and Profit and Loss Accounts and Balance Sheets for each of the three years. For simplicity we can assume that all goods were bought for cash and all sales were cash sales.

Trading and Profit and Loss Accounts − Year 1

	AVCO		FIFO		LIFO	
	£	£	£	£	£	£
Sales		420		420		420
Less Cost of Goods Sold:						
Purchases	440		440		440	
Closing Stock	110	330	120	320	100	340
		90		100		80
Less Expenses		50		50		50
Net Profit		40		50		30

Balance Sheets − Year 1

	AVCO	FIFO	LIFO
	£	£	£
Stock	110	120	100
Bank	130	130	130
	240	250	230
Capital	200	200	200
Add Net Profit	40	50	30
	240	250	230

	AVCO	FIFO	LIFO
Net Profit expressed as Return on Capital Employed	$\frac{40}{240} \times \frac{100}{1} =$ 16.7%	$\frac{50}{250} \times \frac{100}{1} =$ 20%	$\frac{30}{230} \times \frac{100}{1} =$ 13%

Trading and Profit and Loss Accounts − Year 2

	AVCO		FIFO		LIFO	
	£	£	£	£	£	£
Sales		512		512		512
Less Cost of Goods Sold:						
Opening Stock	110		120		100	
Add Purchases	410		410		410	
	520		530		510	
Less Closing Stock	104	416	112	418	80	430
Gross Profit		96		94		82
Less Expenses		60		60		60
Net Profit		36		34		22

Balance Sheets − Year 2

	AVCO	FIFO	LIFO
	£	£	£
Stock	104	112	80
Bank	172	172	172
	276	284	252
Capital	240	250	230
Net Profit	36	34	22
	276	284	252

	AVCO	FIFO	LIFO
Net Profit expressed as Return on Capital Employed	$\dfrac{36}{276} \times \dfrac{100}{1} =$	$\dfrac{34}{284} \times \dfrac{100}{1} =$	$\dfrac{22}{252} \times \dfrac{100}{1} =$
	13%	12%	8.7%

Trading and Profit and Loss Accounts − Year 3

	AVCO		FIFO		LIFO	
	£	£	£	£	£	£
Sales		864		864		864
Less Cost of Goods Sold:						
Opening Stock	104		112		80	
Add Purchases	846		846		846	
	950		958		926	
Less Closing Stock	266	684	294	664	188	738
Gross Profit		180		200		126
Less Expenses		80		80		80
Net Profit		100		120		46

Balance Sheets − Year 3

	AVCO	FIFO	LIFO
	£	£	£
Stock	266	294	188
Bank	110	110	110
	376	404	298
Capital	276	284	252
Net Profit	100	120	46
	376	404	298

	AVCO	FIFO	LIFO
Net Profit expressed as Return on Capital Employed	$\dfrac{100}{376} \times \dfrac{100}{1} =$	$\dfrac{120}{404} \times \dfrac{100}{1} =$	$\dfrac{46}{298} \times \dfrac{100}{1} =$
	26.6%	29.7%	15.4%

It will probably be easier to see the differences in reported profits using different cost methods of pricing our goods if a diagram is used. This can be shown as Exhibit 19.1

Exhibit 19.1

Reported profits if different pricing methods used

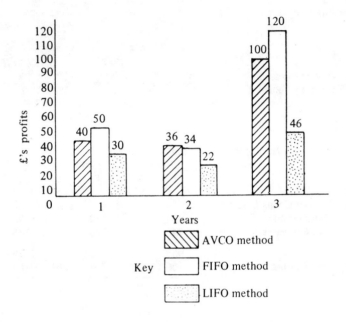

Accounting practice and stock valuation

You may well think that the worked example (*see* 19.1) was an artificial example in that in practice the same method would have been used by the three firms. This is far from the truth — surveys have shown that similar types of firms use different methods. Practice is very much conditioned by the high rates of taxation suffered by firms, this will be examined more closely in later chapters. Apart from the fact that accounting practice is so much affected by the desire to make the tax burden easier the other main reason is probably that of ease of calculation. Custom plays a part in some industries and very often it is found that a firm prices out goods, and therefore values stock, in a particular manner for no better reason than the accountant had used a particular method at his last firm and now puts it in use in his new firm.

Rising prices and pricing methods including NIFO

In a period of rising prices, as is indeed the case in the worked example (*see* 19.1), the LIFO method will tend to delay profit recognition as compared with the FIFO method. The AVCO method will usually lead to results in between the LIFO and FIFO methods. On the other hand, in a period of falling prices FIFO would tend to record lesser profits more quickly.

A variation of LIFO using prices based on the next prices at which units will be bought is called Next In First Out (NIFO). The adoption of the next price at which goods would be bought rather than the last price at which they were actually bought moves further towards charging current replacement costs against current sales. The problem with NIFO, as with LIFO, is that the stock-in-trade balance will be valued at outdated prices. A more comprehensive replacement cost method is described below and is generally preferable to NIFO.

What should govern choice of method?

The overriding consideration is the need to give a 'true and fair view' of the state of the affairs of the organization as on the Balance Sheet date, and of the trend of the organization's trading results. There is as yet, however, no precise definition of 'true and fair view', and it therefore rests on the judgement of the people concerned. Just as a large group of people could never agree as to which is the best football team in Great Britain, so also will it be impossible unless some very firm guidelines are laid down as to which would be the best method, i.e. LIFO, NIFO, FIFO or AVCO, to keep to the 'true and fair view'. Especially since the movement towards Current Costs in Financial Accounts many firms have moved away from historic costs towards current cost values for inventory records. The following illustration shows the approach of Current Cost Accounting to periodic inventory valuation.

Replacement cost method

Under this method (called CCA for Current Cost Accounting) the balance of inventory is revalued to its current replacement value at the year end. The issues of material are also revalued at the average replacement value for the year. The revisions to the inventory values are transferred to an Inventory Revaluation Reserve Account. The gains arising from revaluation are gains from holding inventories rather than from manufacturing and are not included in the Net Operating Profit.

Using the data from the worked example (*see* 19.1) the following information is obtained in addition to that used in the historic cost accounts.

	Average Replacement Cost £	Year End Replacement Cost £
Year 1	11	12
2	13.50	14
3	20.00	22

The data will then be evaluated as follows:

	Receipts		Issue at Average Replacement Cost 1	£	Stock at Year End Replacement Cost 2	£	1+2 £	Adjustment to Revaluation Account £
Year 1	20×£10= 200							
	20×£12= 240							
	40	440	30×£11 =	330	10×£12 =	120	450	+ 10
Year 2								
Stock b/f	10×£12 =120							
	10×£13 =130							
	20×£14 =280							
	40	530	32×£13.50 =	432	8×£14 =	112	544	+ 14
Year 3								
Stock b/f	8×£14= 112							
	12×£18 =216							
	30×£21 =630							
	958		36×£20 =	720	14×£22 =	308	1,028	+ 70

Trading and Profit and Loss Accounts

	Year 1 £	Year 1 £	Year 2 £	Year 2 £	Year 3 £	Year 3 £
Sales		420		512		864
Less Cost of Goods Sold at current values:						
Opening Stock	–		120		112	
Add Purchases	440		410		846	
Revaluation	10		14		70	
	450		544		1,028	
Less Closing Stock at Current Value	120	330	112	432	308	720
Gross Operating Profit		90		80		144
Less Expenses		50		60		80
Net Profit		40		20		64

	Balance Sheets Year 1	Year 2	Year 3
	£	£	£
Stock	120	112	308
Bank	130	172	110
	250	284	418
Capital	200	250	284
Revaluation of Stock Reserve	10	14	70
Net Operating Profit	40	20	64
	250	284	418

Note by comparison the net profits for:

AVCO	40	36	100
FIFO	50	34	120
LIFO	30	22	46

In the first two years the FIFO profits of £50 and £34 are equivalent to the Net Operating Profit plus the Revaluation Reserve £40 + £10 = £50 and £20 + £14 = £34. In the third year a difference arises because the closing stock is valued at a replacement price of £22 per unit which is higher than any units actually bought in the year. Under FIFO the closing stock of 14 units is valued at £21 compared to £22 under CCA, which accounts for a difference of £1 per unit − in total £14. This is the difference between the two results, i.e. CCA £64 + 70 = £134 − 14 = FIFO £120. The CCA approach gives more information than the historic cost method as it distinguishes between 'holding gains' and 'operating profits'.

For costing on a perpetual basis where prices are changing frequently it would usually be more convenient to use Standard Costing methods which are shown in Chapter 29.

Assignment Exercises

19.1. D. Simon has been in business for 3 years, deals in only one product, and has used the FIFO method of valuing stock-in-trade on a perpetual inventory basis. The figures of receipts and sales are as follows:

		Receipts		*Sales*
Year 1	January	30 at £12 each	July	24 for £15.5 each
	May	30 at £14 each	November	16 for £18 each
Year 2	February	10 at £16 each	June	30 for £22 each
	April	10 at £18 each	December	20 for £23 each
	November	20 at £18 each		
Year 3	January	10 at £19 each	April	20 for £23 each
	March	20 at £20 each	July	10 for £24 each
	August	10 at £19 each	December	24 for £26 each
	November	20 at £21 each		

You are required to calculate the valuation of the closing stock-in-trade for each of the three years. Keep your answer, it will be used as a basis for later questions.

19.2. What would the stock-in-trade valuations have been at the end of each of the three years in 19.1 if the LIFO method had been used?

19.3. What would the stock-in-trade valuations have been at the end of each of the three years in 19.1 if the AVCO method had been used?

19.4. From the figures in 19.1 draw up the Trading Accounts for each of the three years assuming that the stock records were kept on a perpetual basis if (i) the FIFO method had been used, (ii) the LIFO method was used, (iii) the AVCO method was used. (Keep your answer — it will be used as the basis of a later question.)

19.5. If in 19.1 the periodic method had been in use rather than the perpetual method then what would the answer have been?

19.6. If in 19.2 the periodic method had been in use rather than the perpetual inventory method then what would the answer have been?

19.7. If in 19.3 the periodic method had been used rather than the perpetual inventory method then what would the answer have been?

19.8. If in 19.4 the periodic method had been used rather than the perpetual method then what would the answer have been? Keep your answer, it will be used as the basis of a later question.

19.9A. Using the answer in 19.4 (i), i.e. the FIFO method set of Trading Accounts, draft the Profit and Loss Accounts and Balance Sheets for the three years if the cash receipts and payments (includes the bank receipts and payments) were as follows (see note re depreciation at end of question):

Year 1

Capital Introduced	1,200	Fixed Assets bought	200
Cash Sales (all sales all for		Payments to Creditors for	
cash	660	goods (goods are bought	
		on credit)	500
		Expenses	100
		Drawings	80
		Balance carried forward	980
	£1,860		£1,860

Year 2

Balance brought forward	980	Payment to Creditors	750
Cash Sales	1,120	Expenses	110
		Drawings	190
		Balance carried forward	1,050
	£2,100		£2,100

Year 3

Balance brought forward	1,050	Payments to Creditors	900
Cash Sales	1,324	Expenses	130
		Drawings	240
		Balance carried forward	1,104
	£2,374		£2,374

You may assume that there was nothing owing for expenses at the end of each year. The Fixed Assets are to be depreciated £20 per annum.

19.10A. Using the same figures of cash as in 19.9 draft Profit and Loss Accounts and Balance Sheets for the three years to the answer in 19.4(ii), i.e. the LIFO method set of Trading Accounts.

19.11A. Using the same figures of cash as in 19.9 draft Profit and Loss Accounts and Balance sheets for the three years to the answer in 19.4 (iii), i.e. the AVCO set of Trading Accounts.

19.12A. Using your answer to 19.8(i) i.e. Trading Accounts using FIFO on a periodic inventory basis, and using the same figures of cash as in 19.9, draw up Profit and Loss Accounts and Balance Sheets for the three years.

19.13A. Using your answer to 19.8(ii), i.e. Trading Accounts using LIFO on a periodic inventory basis, and using the same figures of cash as in 19.9, draw up Profit and Loss Accounts and Balance Sheets for the three years.

19.14A. Using your answer to 19.8(iii), i.e. Trading Accounts using AVCO on a periodic inventory basis, and using the same figures of cash as in 19.9, draw up Profit and Loss Accounts and Balance Sheets for the three years.

19.15A. P. Paul has been in business for three years, deals in only one product, and has used the FIFO method of valuing stock-in-trade on a perpetual inventory basis. The figures of receipts and sales are as follows:

		Receipts		Sales
Year 1	January	28 at £10 each	March	11 for £16 each
	April	12 at £10 each	August	15 for £16 each
	November	14 at £11 each	December	10 for £16.5 each
Year 2	February	9 at £12 each	April	17 for £17 each
	June	10 at £13 each	July	8 for £17 each
	August	8 at £12 each	December	30 for £19 each
	November	20 at £13 each		
Year 3	January	15 at £15 each	February	15 for £19 each
	April	10 at £16 each	November	32 for £22 each
	June	10 at £17 each		
	October	20 at £19 each		

You are required to calculate the valuation of the closing stock-in-trade for each of the three years. Keep your answer, it will be used as a basis for later questions.

19.16A. What would the stock-in-trade valuations have been in 19.15 if the LIFO method had been used?

19.17A. What would the stock-in-trade valuations have been in 19.15 if the AVCO method had been used?

19.18A. From the figures 19.15 draw up the Trading Accounts for each of the three years assuming that the stock records were kept on a perpetual basis if (i) the FIFO method had been used, (ii) the LIFO method was used, (iii) the AVCO method was used.

19.19A. If in 19.16 the periodic inventory method had been in use instead of the perpetual inventory method, what would the answer have been?

19.20A. If in 19.17 the periodic inventory method had been in use instead of the perpetual inventory method, what would the answer have been? (nearest £)

19.21A. If in 19.18 the periodic inventory method had been in use instead of the perpetual inventory method, what would the answer have been?

19.22. Using the data from 19.1 and the following additional information on replacement costs, construct Trading Accounts for the three years using Replacement Cost Method.

	Average Replacement Cost	Year End Replacement Cost
	£	£
Year 1	13	15
2	18	18.50
3	19.50	21.00

19.23. Using the data from 19.22 and the following additional information on replacement costs, construct Trading Accounts for the three years using Replacement Cost Method.

	Average Replacement Cost	Year End Replacement Cost
	£	£
Year 1	23	26.50
2	28	30.00
3	31	31.00

19.24A. Using the data from 19.15A. and the following additional information on replacement costs construct Trading Accounts for the three years using Replacement Cost Method.

	Average Replacement Cost	Year End Replacement Cost
	£	£
Year 1	10.50	11.50
2	13.00	14.00
3	17.00	20.00

20

Wages and Salary Schemes

The calculation of wages or salaries payable to an employee, was shown in the preceding first year course book *Finance* and started from the gross amount that was due to the individual. The gross amount due to an individual is set out in the contract of employment to which every employed person is entitled. Some contracts specify a fixed amount payable, e.g. for each hour worked, often called a 'day rate', or on a calendar basis of 'per annum' or 'per month'. If someone's wage is based on an hourly rate of £4, all that needs to be recorded are the hours worked. If 40 hours are worked the gross wage will be £4 × 40 = £160. For people paid on a calendar basis it would be unusual to record the hours worked unless they are entitled to overtime, i.e. extra payment for hours worked in excess of an agreed basic number, e.g. £6 an hour overtime is payable on all hours worked in excess of 35 per week, so if 40 hours are worked, overtime is 5 hours × £6 = £30. The introduction of 'flexitime' systems which entitle employees to work non-standard hours is also often accompanied with a need to record hours worked even for a calendar-based system of payment. This is because it is impossible when people are working flexible hours for management to tell simply by 'inspection' whether an individual is working the contracted number of hours per week.

Many organizations decide to relate what they pay to some measure of work done such as units of output. Thus many wages, rather than being simply flat hourly rates, are variable depending on the amount of work done. Many people on flat wages or salaries also receive a 'bonus' if profits are good. Such methods of payment are intended to motivate people to work for the objectives of the organization.

The widest range of schemes occur in situations where the work being done is capable of easy measurement. The simplest schemes pay by the unit produced, e.g. if the rate is £2 per unit and ten units are produced, then the gross pay is £2 × 10 = £20. These are called *piece rate* systems. The advantages of piece rate schemes include the following:

(*a*) they are easy to understand;

(*b*) they are easy to administer provided the recording and checking of work done by each individual is properly organized;

(*c*) there is a very direct relationship between the work produced and the reward for it.

The problems of piece rate schemes include the following:

(*a*) careful checks are needed on quality as there is a clear incentive for the workers simply to produce as many units as possible;

(*b*) they can impose strong pressure on individuals to short-cut safety measures — in order to increase units produced — which can lead to accidents;

(*c*) trade unions are sometimes hostile to such schemes, often using arguments based on 'safety' and unfairness to individuals;

(*d*) individuals working may suffer loss of wage through no fault of their own, if the supply of work to them is delayed or otherwise disrupted due to problems in the organization;

(*e*) the group 'norms' in the workforce may discourage an individual from exceeding an acceptable level of output. If individuals are working in an environment which involves a high level of overhead cost, it becomes important to obtain high output levels, probably above the group 'norms'.

If, for example, the cost of a 'workstation' to produce computer typesetting material costs £1,000 per week, then consider the output of:

(*a*) Typesetter A who sets 50 pages.
The cost per page = 1,000/50 = £20.
(*b*) Typesetter B who sets 40 pages.
The cost per page = 1,000/40 = £25.

Typesetter B costs 25 per cent more than A in terms of the workstation overhead cost. It is clearly important to obtain as high an output as possible from expensive resources.

The disadvantages of very simple piecework systems (listed above) encourage organizations to devise schemes that encourage people to work more specifically in the organization's interests. As an example of such schemes, in relation to output performance it is often convenient to measure the output in hours. This can then be related to the hours of capacity of available resources. In order to do this a unit of output must be related to the time required to produce it. This requires the use of evaluation techniques, such as work study, which will be described later.

For example, one page of output of material to be typeset is evaluated at 0.5 standard hours work. The piece rate is set at one page = 0.5 standard hours = £7.50 per standard hour.

Using the previous example, the payment to the two workers would be:
(*a*) A sets 50 pages = 25 standard hours × £7.50 = £187.50.
(*b*) B sets 40 pages = 20 standard hours × £7.50 = £150.00.

In order to increase the effective standard hours produced, particularly as this will save the organization a considerable amount of overhead, the incentive scheme may be weighted to give higher or lower rewards for output above or below fixed levels.

Assume, for example, that the rate for typesetting at a standard of two pages per hour is £7.50. Typesetting at a rate below standard will be penalised by deducting ten per cent from the standard rate, whereas production above the standard will be rewarded by adding ten per cent to the standard rate.

During the week when standard hours amount to 40, the two typesetters produce the following:

(a) A — 90 pages.
(b) B — 70 pages.

Their pay will be:

(a) A — 90 pages = 45 standard hours × £7.50 = £337.50 × 110% = £371.25.
(b) B — 70 pages = 35 standard hours × £7.50 = £262.50 × 90% = £236.25.

At the base wage level A earns 337.5/262.5 = 129% of B's wage, whereas with weighting A earns 371.25/236.25 = 157% of B's wage.

Clearly, a scheme which actually penalised low production as well as rewarding high production may not be popular with employees. Many schemes simply reward high output without penalising low output. However, as was pointed out earlier, the low production situation is expensive in wasting productive capacity and therefore overheads! Agreements in particular industries have produced wide variations in the types of scheme in operation. Schemes which operate in practice often offer a guaranteed time-rate — which is in other words a minimum wage. This covers the situation where output may be at low levels through no fault of the employee, but it does also reduce the disincentive related to low production levels.

Premium bonus schemes

Adapted piecework systems

In any system which is designed to increase productivity, the benefit to the employer comes from spreading the fixed overheads over a greater number of units produced. In straight piecework the increase in production results in higher wages to employees and a smaller share of overhead per unit. In time-rate systems, if production is increased the labour cost remains unaltered in total and the employer benefits from lower wage cost per unit as well as from lower overhead cost per unit. There are two variants in piecework which are designed to share the benefits in a way which falls between the two extremes outlined above. They are named after their developers, Halsey and Rowan.

The Halsey system

Given a standard time for a unit of work done, it is possible to calculate how much time has been saved when the job is completed. It is this time saved, valued at the time-rate, which is shared between employee and employer. In the Halsey system the share is 50 per cent each. For example:

Allowed time/unit:	1 hour
Rate/hour:	£2
Actual time taken:	45 minutes
Proportion:	50 per cent

The rate of pay per unit is then calculated as:

Time rate £2 × ¾ =	£1.50
Bonus (1 − ¾) × £2 × 50%	
=	0.25
	————
	£1.75

The bonus formula is (time allowed − time taken) × rate of pay × percentage share agreed for the employee.

In this example the rate/unit of output is £1.75 for labour, rather than £2 in piecework.

In a variation called the Halsey—Weir system the saving is shared one-third to the employee and two-thirds to the employer. Using the same data as before the bonus would be:

$$\text{Bonus } (1-\tfrac{3}{4}) \times £2 \times \tfrac{1}{3} = 0.17$$

which compares to a bonus of 0.25 on the straight Halsey system.

The Rowan system

Here the system is designed to dampen down the bonus at higher levels of output and appeals to employers in situations where there are severe reservations about the accuracy of the standards. As in the Halsey system a bonus is calculated, but this time the share is given by the ratio of time taken to time allowed.

For example, using the same data as given for the Halsey example above, the rate of pay is now calculated as:

Rate/unit

Time-rate £2 × ¾ = £1.500

Bonus $(1-¾)×£2×\dfrac{45}{60} =$ 0.375

£1.875

Time taken is 45 minutes compared to the allowed 60 minutes hence the share of 45/60.

As the time saved increases, the bonus also increases until the job is being performed at twice the standard rate. After that any further saving in time would actually reduce the bonus. This can be demonstrated easily.

Let X be the time taken and Y the time allowed.

$$\text{Bonus, B} = (Y - X) \times \frac{X}{Y} \times £R$$

$$B = (X - \frac{X^2}{Y}) \times R \text{ where } Y \text{ and } R \text{ are constant}$$

Differentiating:

$$\frac{dB}{dX} = (1 - \frac{2X}{Y}) \times R \text{ and } \frac{dB}{dX} = 0 \text{ when } X = \frac{1}{2}Y$$

At this point the bonus is a maximum. Note that $\dfrac{d^2B}{dX^2} = -\dfrac{2R}{Y}$ which is negative, as it must be if the point $X = \dfrac{Y}{2}$ is to be a maximum.

For those whose mathematical ability is not their strongest point, this can be illustrated by using two cases where the time taken is (a) half an hour, (b) a quarter of an hour.

(a) Time rate £2 × ½ 1.00
Bonus $(1-½) \times £2 \times 30/60$ .50

£1.50

(b Time rate £2 × ¼ .50
Bonus $(1-¼) \times £2 \times 45/60$ .375

£0.875

Group bonus schemes

Not all workers can be associated with individual piecework schemes, either because their work is not easily measured in terms of production or because they work in teams and individual effort cannot be measured. In such cases a gang or team or larger group can be associated and share a group bonus between them. Such bonuses are calculated according to output achieved. Clearly the output must be definitely associated with the group, to avoid the confusion that could result from overlap.

These group bonus schemes can be extended to include the associated indirect workers, such as supervisors and store-keepers. Without these extensions, unfortunate anomalies can occur which are certain to cause considerable labour problems. It is a central feature of incentive schemes that they inevitably have a ripple effect throughout the firm's labour force.

A graphical illustration

A summary of the different systems is presented in graphical form in Exhibit 20.1. This shows the way in which weekly wages vary as productivity increases, according to the wage system used.

Exhibit 20.1

The different wages schemes

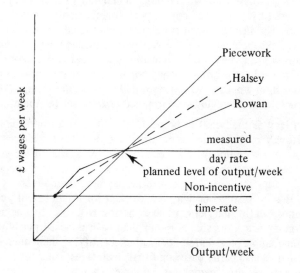

Whatever method of wage calculation is used, the management should have a plan, usually in the form of an attainable target. Whichever incentive wage method is employed it will tend to give the same results around this planned level and will only deviate markedly when productivity is widely away from it.

Profit-sharing schemes

Schemes which offer a bonus to employees based on profits are used in many organizations. The issues to be decided in such schemes are as follows.

(a) The amount of funds to be made available for bonus payments. This 'pool' will be established on a formula related to profits — at its simplest, X per cent of the year's profit, but often on a more detailed basis.

The main problem is to identify profit increases due to the efforts of employees during the year. If there has been major capital investment which has increased profit, rewarding labour on a percentage of total profit would be unfairly generous. It is therefore common to relate the 'pool' to a share of profit after a fair return on the average capital employed has been earned. It is also important to identify those items included in profit which are 'extra-ordinary'. In other words, profits or losses which are not due to employees' work or effort, e.g. a profit on selling surplus buildings, would normally be excluded from bonus calculations.

(b) How is the pool to be split between the individual beneficiaries? At its simplest it could be divided equally, but it is more often based on how much the individual contributes directly to profit, i.e. higher-level managers get more bonus. In addition, an individual's quality of performance is measured by a scheme scoring performance against objectives set for each job. The idea of rewards based on individual performance tends to apply at management levels. Even within management, however, it is common to group levels of responsibility together and allocate an overall level of reward to the group. Group bonus schemes are also commonly used for production workers, where rewards for particular groups are based on their success in achieving performance criteria set for them.

(c) How is the bonus to be paid? The simplest form of payment is in cash. However, some schemes offer holidays or gifts as an alternative. There are now many company schemes which offer shares in the company to employees. Many schemes are used as an incentive for employees to remain with the organization — by spreading payment over several years. This means that only someone who has worked for a number of years attains full bonus, and if that person leaves he/she will lose the backlog owing. The argument to give shares rather than cash is based partly on a belief in making employees shareholders, thus identifying their interest with the owners'. It is also partly based on fiscal advantages, since tax relief is given on properly set up schemes for employee shares.

The concept of linking employees' remuneration with profit sharing has attracted support from economists and politicians. It is seen as a way of overcoming excessive wage demands, since basic wages and salaries could be linked to low annual increases, in particular not above the level of inflation, plus a profit share — which would only apply if profits were sufficient to cover the extra amount. Significant increases in wages or salaries would only be paid if profits are good.

Whilst profit sharing would not cover those employed in the public and 'non-profit' sectors, there are considerable difficulties in drafting adequate schemes even in the 'profit sector'. The 'agency theory' approach to management emphasizes the possible conflict between managers and 'owners' which profit-sharing schemes can reinforce. In particular, managers may use their 'insider' information to obtain an unfair reward at the expense of the owners. There is also a tendency for such schemes to encourage managers to become over-cautious in avoiding risky situations — since the penalties on them may be considerable, not only in cash terms but also to their reputations.

Incentives for employees in indirect labour and administrative positions

Because it may be hard to measure the work output of people not on direct production yet at the same time controlling important elements of the business, schemes to provide rewards for good performance are often sought. 'Profit share' schemes can be used although the problem often arises that in these areas direct impact on profit earned may seem remote. In this situation the bonus may go up or down quite independently of the particular group's own efforts. Schemes which reward the area for its performance against budget may therefore be introduced. Merit-rating schemes which are described later in the chapter are used in this situation. If, for example, the section's actual costs for a period of, say, three months are less than budgeted costs, a bonus of five per cent on salary could be payable. These schemes may be worthwhile if clear and objective budget standards are available. There are, however, grave dangers that a department may, under such schemes, save costs in its department — irrespective of damage to total company profit — simply to earn a bonus.

Control of incentive schemes

The factor which is essential to the success of all bonus and incentive schemes is the presence of some procedure enabling the standards of performance on which the rewards are to be based to be fairly set and judged. This is a continual process which requires both monitoring and arbitration. The ability to set standards of performance varies both from industry to industry, organization to organization, and in different parts of the same business. The measurement of work in the production area has probably been studied more scientifically than other areas, in the process known as work study.

Work study

The techniques of work study cover two specific activities, Method Study and Work Measurement. Method study is concerned to study the detailed tasks which comprise the different jobs in a production environment. Production engineers are concerned to study the physical activities carried on by operatives as well as the environment in which they work, i.e. the layout of plant. Having recorded all the detail an analysis is made to improve the efficiency of the use of all resources involved, with the objective of reducing the cost of manufacturing a unit. Once the method has been studied and a solution agreed, the engineers then examine the tasks and activities with the object of timing them. This is known as Work Measurement and is the basis of establishing standard hours of work from which not only are piece rates agreed for wages, but also forms the basis of product costing. The time-study engineer has to take into account many factors in setting a time, which will allow for differences between operatives, working situations, the learning curve and the inclination of those being studied to go-slow when rates are being set. It requires sound judgement in addition to a very detailed understanding of the process concerned! It is also necessary in most organizations to obtain the agreement of the trade union representative who will be concerned to ensure that adequate time is built in for rest periods and for safety measures, etc.

Similar techniques to work study can be applied to routine clerical tasks in the processing of accounting data and other information. The term 'Organization and Methods' is used rather than Work Study and the techniques are those of the Systems Analyst rather than the Production Engineer. However in principle the objectives are similar even though the 'product' of an information system may not be as tangible as manufacturing products.

Merit rating

In jobs where Work Study is not appropriate because the work has a qualitative rather than a quantitative basis, the emphasis in rewarding good performance has to be assessed on the individual's own performance. The emphasis in Merit Rating is to score the individual's performance in carrying out his job. In order to do this a system has to be drawn up. The system will:

(a) Identify for each job what characteristics are required of a successful employee, e.g. enterprise, accuracy, politeness, reliability etc.

(b) The characteristics identified in (a) need to be weighted — so that a proper job description which shows what is wanted in each position can be prepared.

(c) Each employee can then be awarded points for his success in his job.

A system of merit rating can be used both for awarding salary and wage increases and in addition, where appropriate, profit sharing or bonus incentive payments.

Job evaluation

In a large organization it can be difficult to assign the appropriate rate of pay to different jobs. Very often there is a traditional structure which has developed historically and has been compounded by the structure of individual trade unions bargaining for different groups of employees within the organization. Job evaluation is used to describe the process of attempting to develop a coherent structure of rates for different jobs in the organization. The process followed is as follows:

(*a*) Evaluate the basic intelligence, skill and training together with any other relevant features which are required for a particular job. Also factors such as physical effort, mental effort and responsibility which are required of the employee should also be evaluated.

(*b*) Each factor established in (*a*) is awarded points on a set scale – say out of ten. Thus each job is split into factors which are then awarded points, e.g. the accountant may get nine (out of ten) points for responsibility, but may only get two points for physical effort.

(*c*) The total points for each job are related to a wage or salary scale.

Although job evaluation may seem a fair way of fixing wages, it often fails to take account of external supply and demand for skilled labour, as well as the effect of collective bargaining by trade unions.

Assignment Exercises

20.1. Brandlow plc remunerates its labour force by offering a minimum wage of £200 per week. In addition a bonus is paid of £2 for each hour of production time saved against standard. What wages would be paid to the following employees?

Employee No.	Hours works	Standard output of units per hour	Actual output in units
1002	35	50	2,000
1003	37	50	2,000
1005	35	50	1,650

20.2. The Magic Organisation uses a Halsey-Weir type of payment system with the time saved being divided one-third to the employee and two-thirds to the employer. The hourly rate of pay is £4. Calculate the wage payments for each of the following:

Employee No.	Hours worked	Standard time per unit	Units produced
205	40	1 hour	70
208	40	1 hour	50
226	36	1 hour	38

20.3. Using the data in question 20.2 what would the payments have been if the Rowan system had been in operation?

21

Overheads

Previous chapters have been concerned to look at the direct expenses of materials and labour. The definition of overhead cost is the total cost of indirect materials, indirect labour and indirect expenses. In other words, overheads covers all costs other than direct material and direct labour. So far as indirect material is concerned the initial system for ordering, receiving and stocking indirect material is no different in principle than for direct material. It may be that there are large numbers of small indirect material purchases which do not justify the cost of formal stock control. In this situation the cost of material would be expensed immediately. This is based on the concept of materiality, not because the item is 'indirect' and, indeed, exactly the same approach applies to direct material where small items would be expensed, or treated as indirect, i.e. as overhead.

As with material, indirect labour is recorded in exactly the same way as its direct counterpart. There is no real difference between the two other than in the relationship between the work done and the product or service being produced. The motivation and control of employees is equally important whether they are working on direct of indirect work. However, indirect work commonly does not have a tangible or easily measured output and is therefore harder to assess than direct work.

The other indirect costs cover a very wide range in that they relate to the whole of the rest of the business. They will be classified according to the main functional activities in the particular business, e.g.:

> Factory overheads
> Distribution overheads
> Warehousing overheads
> Administrative overheads
> Research and development
> Selling and marketing overheads
> Financial overheads

Within each of these functional activity heads the costs will be classified according to their nature, e.g.:

Indirect wages
Indirect material and supplies
Depreciation of buildings and equipment
Insurance of buildings and equipment
Rates
Electricity
Heating oil
and so on

The classification of overhead costs by reference to their nature and under broad functional headings is only a start in the process of breaking costs down into groupings that help generate appropriate information for management control and decisions. The essence of a sound management information system (of which the cost accounting system is part) is its ability to be flexible in order to be 'appropriate'. This in fact indicates a requirement to pay particular attention to the initial coding of cost classification for overhead costs. In modern systems, once it has been entered into the system it is relatively easy to break down the data. Computers are very efficient at this process — but they can only process information that is coded into the input. It is therefore very important when designing a system to anticipate the kind of analysis which may be needed in future.

For example, Timescare Co plc has three factories which are coded:

01	Glasgow
02	Manchester
03	London

Overhead expenses are classified in detail in an expenses code book, an extract from which shows:

151	Heating — oil
152	Heating — gas
153	Heating — electric

Functional areas of the business are classified as follows:

951	Factory
961	Warehouse
971	Administration
981	Selling

If an invoice is received for gas supplied for fuel for the heating boilers in the Glasgow warehouse it would be coded 01/152/961.

This represents a broad analysis of the location, type and functional use of overhead cost. It could easily be added to by extending the codes to cover other details which may specify more precisely the nature and end use of the overhead item.

Control of overhead costs

When looking at material and labour costs any organization needs to exercise considerable care in controlling the manner in which orders are placed or employees hired and paid. Since overheads include both material and labour the same must apply to that area also but, in addition, there is a wide range of other supplies and services which need careful control. All items supplied which are of material value should therefore form part of the system ensuring that purchases are properly authorized. This ensures that quotations are obtained to get competitive prices, and that opportunity for fraud is minimized.

Whilst requirements in the system may avoid loss of resource in the organization through bad buying policies they will not in themselves make sure that resources are used efficiently. Waste through poor control of overheads is difficult to prevent, particularly in large organizations. In a small business the owner tends to treat business costs as personal and takes particular care to avoid wasteful activities. One way that large organizations attempt to obtain a comparable personal involvement is to break down the whole structure into small units which correspond to defined areas of management responsibility. A 'responsibility centre' is defined as a unit or function of an organisation headed by a manager having direct responsibility for its performance.

For example, the Jones Corporation breaks down all its broad functional areas of management into responsibility centres. The manager in charge of each centre is required to manage the resources in the centre efficiently and effectively. In order to enable him to do this and to measure his success it is necessary to analyse the costs covered by each centre. As an illustration of this is the warehousing function which covers four areas of responsibility:

> Receiving and stacking
> Stockcheck and issue
> Records and stock control
> Packing

The four managers responsible receive an analysis of the cost for their respective areas showing all the costs by basic classification. The packing department's manager would receive a statement with the detail in Exhibit 21.1.

Exhibit 21.1

WAREHOUSING				
PACKING CENTRE: MANAGER . . . . Mr. W. Smith				
Cost Classification	Month £	Year to date £	Last year month £	Last year to date £
Direct material				
Direct labour				
Indirect material				
Indirect labour				
Depreciation:				
Building				
Machinery				
Insurances				
Rates				
Electricity				
Heating				

Reporting by responsibility centre is one way of attempting to control overhead cost. As such it is much improved where it is incorporated into the process of budgetary control and not only are current costs compared with last year but also with the expected (i.e. budget) figures. This approach will be developed later in budgetary control.

The control of overhead cost is not limited to the creation of responsibility centres which indeed will only help if they are administered by an enthusiastic and perceptive senior management. The application of work study methods to clerical routine usually called Organization and Methods can be effective. A management attitude which is always seeking efficient methods of working is probably the best prescription.

Overhead cost collection

The main requirement for the interpretation of overhead costs is that they are related to the manager's need to make decisions. In the preceding paragraphs this involved allocating costs to responsibility centres. In many organizations the process of cost allocation needs to go further than this. In particular, management need to know the costs involved in making products or providing services. They need to make the right decision when faced with alternatives. The whole range of situations requiring breakdowns of cost will become more evident the more time you spend studying as an accountant. At this stage the assumption is made that the need exists.

By definition direct costs can be traced to the product or service into which they are incorporated. In the case of overheads this is not necessarily the case. In a factory which only produces one product all the factory costs can be traced as direct expenses of that product. Where more than one product is made, however, the direct relationship breaks down. Consider a factory making two products Ug and Oz of which 200 and 500 units are made respectively. The factory rent is £7,000. How should this be attributed to the two products?

The solution to this question needs to be carefully considered and understood. For some purposes the answer might best be based on marginal analysis which asks questions about the impact on the rent cost of incremental changes in units produced. For example, if the plant is to double the production of Oz the effect on rent may vary between nothing, if the current space is sufficient, and say £2,000 which is the cost of an extra unit of rent where the current factory is at full capacity. This type of review is appropriate when planning changes for the future whether expansion or contraction. Note that the 'cost' of rent varies between £0 and £2,000.

If, on the other hand, what is required is a valuation of units of Ug and Oz based on their average factory cost then a different solution will be found. In order to work out the element of rent that relates to each product the situation within the factory needs to be known. If the products are made in distinct areas then the rent can be split based on the floor area used, e.g. Ug — 40 per cent = £2,800; Oz — 60 per cent = £4,200.

However, if the processes are intermingled floor area is not an adequate answer. A very crude split may then be based on the respective units produced, e.g. Ug — 200/700 = £2,000; Oz — 500/700 = £5,000.

Examples of commonly found bases for the apportionment of overheads are:

Apportionment basis	*Nature of expenditure*
Number of employees (i.e. personnel)	Canteen, welfare and medical, employer's liability insurance
Floor area (i.e. space)	Rent, rates, building repairs and insurance, lighting
Power consumption rating (i.e. activities)	Electricity, steam, oil.

Many other reasonable bases could well be thought of but whatever is used is only an approximation for convenience. In this area it is easy to adopt a spurious form of accuracy which by using a numerical calculation seems to invest the result with an air of apparent infallibility. Remember that attribution of overheads can only be valid if the assumptions on which the process is based are understood and acceptable for the purpose to which the information will be put. Calculating the average cost of a unit of stock-in-trade is required by all manufacturing organizations that hold stocks —

in order to calculate their profit. The inclusion of an overhead element in the cost will be based on what the management consider to be a 'true and fair basis'. This is a judgement, not an absolute prescription.

Whilst these warnings are relevant it is also important that a cost and management accountant should exercise great care to make sure that overheads are attributed on a well-considered and justifiable plan. A carefully worked out approximation must be a better basis than a wild guess or nothing at all!

With this in mind the methods of allocating and apportioning overheads will be considered in detail. In order to relate overheads to products or services, except for the unusual case of the single-product factory, it is necessary to subdivide the whole into sub-units. The sub-unit will be defined as some convenient part of the organization that logically and practically is suitable for the collection of costs in relationship to activities. It may be one machine or a workshop. It could be a robot-controlled assembly line or an office full of people. The sub-unit is called a cost centre. In Chartered Institute of Management Accounting CIMA official terminology a cost centre is defined as: 'A location, function or items of equipment in respect of which costs may be ascertained and related to cost units for control purposes.'

A cost centre is not the same as a responsibility centre which is defined as: 'A unit or function of an organization headed by a manager having responsibility for its performance.' The two types of centre are for different purposes but will often coincide since many cost centres are likely to be the responsibility of a manager. However, some responsibility centres may contain several cost centres. Although in some organizations the two terms may seem to be much the same, in practical application they are not the same and should never be confused.

The aim in creating cost centres is to break down the total organization cost from a large whole to a smaller part that can more readily be related to units produced. In order to achieve this breakdown of total cost there will need to be allocation and apportionment. Cost allocation is the charging of discrete identifiable items of cost to cost centres, e.g. material or labour that is used exclusively in that cost centre. Cost apportionment, on the other hand, is the division of costs amongst two or more cost centres in proportion to the estimated benefit received using a proxy, e.g. using floor area to apportion rent.

Cost centres can be distinguished between product cost centres and service cost centres. The product cost centres are the producing or operating departments so far as the items being produced are concerned. Service cost centres cover the rest of the organization and are supportive of product cost centres by providing services such as maintenance, canteen facilities or data processing. When attempting to relate costs to products therefore, it will be necessary to apportion the service cost centres' costs to product cost centres. The following example gives an illustration of how a service cost centre's cost will be apportioned to product cost centres.

A worked example

A firm has four production departments and a canteen. Statistics for the four production departments are:

	No. of employees	Average earnings £	Total earnings £
Cutting	10	1,800	18,000
Dressmaking	90	967	87,000
Coatmaking	90	967	87,000
Packing	10	800	8,000

and the cost of the canteen is £5,500.

If the number of employees is chosen as the basis, the apportionment is a simple arithmetical exercise of dividing the £5,500 between the production departments in proportion to the number of employees. The result would be as follows:

		£
Cutting	$10/200 \times 5,500 =$	275
Dressmaking	$90/200 \times 5,500 =$	2,475
Coatmaking	$90/200 \times 5,500 =$	2,475
Packing	$10/200 \times 5,500 =$	275
		5,500

The basis of division could have been relative total earnings instead of the number of employees.

In the example just given the problem was simplified by having only one service department. What happens if there is more than one? Exhibit 21.2 illustrates the situation.

Exhibit 21.2
Apportionment with more than one service centre

P1	P2	P3	S1	S2	
$£X_1$	$£X_2$	$£X_3$	$£X_4$	$£X_5$	Stage 1
$£X_1+$	$£X_2+$	$£X_3+$	$£X_4+$	0	Stage 2
$£X_1++$	$£X_2++$	$£X_3++$	0	£?	Stage 3

At stage 1 the five cost centres are shown. Three are product centres and the problem is to share the costs of the two service centres between these three product centres.

At stage 2 the second service centre has been reduced to nil.

At stage 3 the first service centre is in turn transferred to the other departments. Unfortunately, since service departments usually operate on behalf of the other service departments (witness the data processors use the canteen), some of the second transfer goes into service centre 2.

This process could go on indefinitely, although with ever reducing amounts being involved.

There are four approaches to dealing with this situation. The first has already been described above, but as soon as the figures are judged to be insignificant a cut-off is applied.

The step-down method is a first approximation to this, closing service departments in turn without allowing any form of 'echo back'. Once a service department has been closed, it is treated as being no longer in existence. The most significant cost centres are dealt with first.

The third method involves a cruder approximation, in which the service departments are regarded as providing useful service to product centres only. This means that the total for each service department is divided in some way between product centres and other service centres are ignored.

The fourth and final way is to set up the equations relating the departments to each other, that is using the proportions involved in apportioning. These may be solved in the usual algebraic way, or by use of matrix algebra in the more general case. It is questionable whether this procedure is justified in view of the somewhat arbitrary basis on which the original sharing has been conducted.

Allocation of factory overheads to jobs

The apportionment routine has collected all the factory overheads within the product cost centres. The final task is to allocate these to the jobs as they pass through the firm's operations.

This is done by calculating an overhead rate and applying this to the jobs. The need is to establish a relationship between something which has been measured directly to a unit of production and the indirect costs which have been apportioned to product centres. For instance, there is close measurement of direct labour hours, direct material consumed, machine hours utilised. Each of these will do according to circumstances. Additionally, derived measures such as direct labour cost fulfil the requirements.

Suppose that a specified period has these results:

	Department	
	A	B
Total overhead	£39,000	£36,000
Machine hours	20,000	1,000
Direct labour hours	9,500	36,000
Direct labour cost	£19,500	£72,000

Department A is machine dominated and for each machine hour used on the job £1.95 should be allocated i.e. $\left(\dfrac{39,000}{20,000}\right)$. In department B, labour predominates and overheads are allocated at the rate of 50 per cent of direct labour cost. This rate can alternatively be stated as £1.00 per direct labour hour.

Predetermined overheads

The normal procedure is to calculate these absorption rates in advance and then to use them throughout the ensuing year. If the information used is entirely historic then the allocation to jobs is the analysis of the total overheads apportioned to the product centre in the actual period. However, this has the disadvantage of being affected by seasonal variations. If costs of production are to be used to help in long-run decisions, then it would be helpful to iron out the seasonal differences. This is done by taking estimates of factory overheads over a complete season and dividing this by estimated direct labour hours or whatever is to be used. This provides a predetermined absorption rate.

The use of a rate known in advance of a month-end also speeds up the reporting process. This is a useful bonus, even though the value of information about average unit costs is strictly limited for control and decision-making purposes.

Additionally, the use of one rate saves the work of recalculating a rate for every month.

Under/over-absorption

It is not likely to happen that estimates will be exactly right, either more overheads will be charged to production (over-absorption) or the converse, under-absorption, will occur.

All that remains to be considered now is the treatment of the under/over-absorbed figure. There are three possibilities:

(a) transfer the over/under-absorption to the profit and loss account for the period;

(b) divide the amount proportionately to raw material stock, work-in-progress, finished goods and cost of goods sold; base the proportions on period-end balances;

(c) carry the difference forward to the next period.

The first method is applicable at the year-end if the difference is regarded as being due to failure or success in achievement. In the second case the original application rates are regarded as being wrong. The third way is for interim profit reports (i.e. monthly or quarterly) where it is expected that the normal seasonal variations will cancel out in future periods.

The process of apportionment and allocation can now be drawn together into a single illustration as shown in Exhibit 21.3. The amounts given in Exhibit 21.3 are estimates for the coming year, based on expectations of future costs, but naturally heavily influenced by the experience of past costs.

Exhibit 21.3

Illustration of overhead rates

Cost	Total	Production centres				Service centres	
		P1	P2	P3	P4	S1	S2
	£						
Indirect material	3,000	500	500	500	900	200	300
Indirect labour	5,000	600	700	700	1,000	1,500	500
Indirect expenses	4,000	500	500	600	400	1,000	1,000
	12,000	1,600	1,700	1,900	2,300	2,700	1,800
S1	–	700	800	500	500	(2,700)	200
S2	–	300	500	500	700	–	(2,000)
	12,000	2,600	3,000	2,900	3,500	–	–
Direct labour cost	£5,700	£1,500	£1,500	£1,700	£2,000		
Overhead rate as %age of direct labour cost		173%	200%	171%	175%		
Direct labour hours		2,000	4,000	5,800	1,000		
Overhead rate per direct labour hour		£1.3	£0.75	£0.50	£3.50		
Machine hours		10,000	12,000	5,000	7,000		
Overhead rate per machine hour		£0.26	£0.25	£0.58	£0.70		

Summary

In the absorption, or full cost, system all manufacturing overheads are included as part of the cost of the goods produced and are included in their value for profit calculating purposes. Unfortunately, not all costs can be directly associated with products and some have to be averaged out. The steps in this process are as follows:

(a) trace as many costs as is feasible to the products — these are direct;

(b) divide the firm into cost centres;

(c) apportion all the remaining, that is the indirect, costs between all the cost centres;

(*d*) reapportion the service centres amongst the product centres;

(*e*) apply a measure of activity to the totals in order to obtain an absorption rate.

This can be performed on a historic cost basis, but there are three major disadvantages to doing this. The process has to be repeated monthly, it is slow to produce reports and it does not cope automatically with seasonal fluctuations. The more usual process is to estimate the figure in advance and use a predetermined rate throughout the year. Of course, the amount absorbed using this rate will never equal the amount actually spent and it is necessary to handle amounts under/over-absorbed.

The information produced about unit costs is of limited value. It is only an average for the period and should not be used in making decisions about prices or levels of production. The information relevant for this will be discussed in later chapters. Nor can average costs of a product be of much use in control. Again they are averages of historic costs with some element of estimation in them. They lack information about standards and are divorced from such concepts as managerial responsibility and controllability, which, again, is something to be looked at later.

In conclusion, the information gained from fixed overhead absorption is of limited value only. Therefore, the cost of these procedures should always be related to the benefits gained. Refinements of method are not likely to be justified, since they almost invariably cost money and bring a spurious accuracy to results.

Assignment Exercises

21.1. The Thames Company has three product cost centres and two service cost centres. The company factory overheads budgeted for a period are as follows:

	£
Rent and rates	6,000
Heating	3,000
Power	10,000
Depreciation of machinery	10,000
Indirect labour cost	18,000
Miscellaneous	3,000

The following information is available for help in apportionment:

	P_1	P_2	P_3	S_1	S_2	Total
Floor space	2,000	2,000	2,000	1,000	1,000	8,000
Cubic capacity	20,000	20,000	15,000	5,000	5,000	65,000
Machine H.P.	150	60	30	50	10	300
Machine values (£)	50,000	20,000	20,000	30,000	130,000	250,000
Direct labour hours	2,000	2,000	3,000	1,000	1,000	9,000

Required: apportion the overheads to these five departments.

21.2. Use the information given below and the apportionment of 21.1 to reapportion the service centres to the cost centres.

The expense of S_1 and S_2 are apportioned as follows:

	P_1	P_2	P_3	S_1	S_2
S_1	40	20	20	–	20
S_2	30	30	30	30	–

21.3. Use the information from 21.1 and 21.2 to calculate the overhead cost for processes P_1, P_2 and P_3.

21.4. The Mersey Company has prepared the following budget for 19-5:

	£
Sales	100,000
Variable factory expenses	25,000
Fixed factory expenses	80,000
Stock change	NIL
	units
Production	50,000

During the year the actual expenditure of factory overheads was £110,000 and the over-absorption was £5,500. How many units were produced? Ignore work-in-progress.

21.5. The Severn Company reported the following data for the month of January 19-5.

	£
Sales	50,000
Cost of goods sold	40,000
Factory overhead spent	10,000
Factory overhead absorbed	9,700
Selling and administration expenses	4,000
Work-in-progress	1,000
Finished goods stock	10,000

Prepare the profit and loss account for January:
(a) assuming the under-absorbed overhead is carried forward to later periods;
(b) assuming it is immediately charged to the period.

22

Absorption and Marginal Costing

The most commonly accepted cost accounting theory used for purposes of the determination of profit is where all the Factory Indirect Expenses are allocated to the products manufactured. This is shown in Exhibit 17.1 where the Factory Indirect Expenses are seen as adding to the value of work-in-progress and thence to finished goods stock. The Production Cost of any article is thus comprised of Direct Materials, Direct Labour, any Direct Expenses and a share of Factory Indirect Expense.

After the financial year is over it is possible to look back and calculate what the Factory Indirect Expenses actually were, such as in Exhibit 17.1 where the Factory Indirect Expenses were seen to be £32,000. That firm had a calculation of the closing stock valuation which was:

$$\frac{\text{Unsold items}}{\text{Items produced}} \times \text{Production Cost of Goods Completed}$$

or in figures $\dfrac{200 \text{ units}}{1,000 \text{ units}} \times \text{Production Cost } £102,000 = \underline{\underline{£20,400}}$

Cost data is used for other purposes than valuing stock, and the question is, therefore, whether or not this method is suitable for all purposes in cost accounting. This method of allocating all the Factory Indirect Expenses to products is known as absorption costing or full costing.

A worked example

We can now look at a decision we might have to come to about a future action. This example shows a firm which has to make a decision about whether or not to take on an extra order.

Donald Ltd's factory has been making 1,000 units annually of a particular product for the past few years. Last year costs were:

	£
Direct Labour	2,000
Direct Materials	3,000
Factory Indirect Expenses	4,000
Production Cost	9,000
Administration and Other Expenses	1,000
	10,000

The 1,000 units had been sold for £12 each = £12,000. The production cost per unit can be seen to be £9,000 ÷ 1,000 = £9.

The current year is following exactly the same pattern of production and costs. Suddenly, part-way through the year, a foreign buyer says he will take 200 units if the price for him can be cut from £12 each to £8 each. A meeting is held and the managing director says, 'What a pity. This could have been our first export order, something we have been waiting to happen for several years. The selling price overseas has no bearing on our selling price at home. But it costs us £9 a unit in production costs alone. We just cannot afford to lose money so as to export. Our shareholders would not tolerate the profits of the company falling to less than £2,000.'

'I think that you are wrong,' says John the accountant. 'Let's look at this year's results (a) if we do not accept the order and (b) if the order is accepted.' He then drafts the following:

	(a) *Order not taken*		(b) *Order taken*	
	£			£
Sales 1,000×£12		12,000		
1,000×£12+200×£8				13,600
Less Expenses:				
Direct Labour	2,000		2,400	
Direct Materials	3,000		3,600	
Factory Indirect Expenses	4,000		4,200	
Other Expenses	1,000	10,000	1,000	11,200
Net Profit		2,000		2,400

'More profit. This means that we take the order,' says the sales director enthusiastically.

'Surely you've got your figures wrong, John,' says the managing director. 'Check your arithmetic.'

'There's nothing wrong with my arithmetic,' says John, 'but perhaps it will be a little more enlightening if I draft (b) Order taken, more fully.'

(b) *Order taken*

Sales		13,600
Less Costs which vary with production: Direct Labour. The men are on piece work of a type that means 20 per cent more production brings 20 per cent more wages (i.e. £2,000 for 1,000 units, £2,400 for 1,200 units).	2,400	
Direct Materials. 20 per cent greater production gives 20 per cent more materials (£3,000 + £600).	3,600	
Factory Indirect Expenses: Some would not change at all, e.g. Factory Rent, Factory Rates. Some would alter, e.g. cost of electric power because machines are used more. Of the Factory Indirect Expenses one-quarter is variable. For this part £1,000 costs for 1,000 units means £1,200 costs for 1,200 units.	1,200	7,200
Sales less Variable Costs		6,400
Fixed Costs; i.e. costs which will not alter at all if 200 more units are produced.		
Factory Indirect Expenses; fixed part	3,000	
Administration and Other Expenses	1,000	4,000
Net Profit		2,400

'We can do all this without borrowing any money,' says the managing director, 'so I'll phone now to tell them we will start production immediately. By the way, John, come to my office this afternoon and tell me more about variable and fixed costs.'

The lesson to be learned

We must not get lost in the technicalities of accounting. It is easy to think that calculations which look complicated must give the right answer. Logic must be brought to bear on such problems. This last case shows that different costs will often be needed when making decisions about the future than the costs which were used for calculating profit earned in the past. £9 per unit had been taken for stock valuation, but this case proves that a firm could still manufacture units and sell at less than £9 each and still increase profits. The reason for this state of affairs is the very essence of the differences between fixed and variable costs which we will now consider.

Fixed and variable costs

The division of costs into those that are fixed and those that are variable is not an easy matter. Even factory rent is not always a fixed cost, for if production had to be increased to a certain figure the firm might have to rent further premises. Such a change would not usually happen in the short-term, it would take a while to rent and set-up a new factory or extra premises before production could start. When fixed costs are mentioned it is normally assumed that this means costs which are fixed in the short-term.

In the firm Donald Ltd, the example assumed that variable costs were 100 per cent variable, by this meaning that if production rose 20 per cent then the cost would rise 20 per cent, if the production rose 47 per cent then the cost would also rise 47 per cent. This is not necessarily true. The cost of power may rise 20 per cent if production rose 20 per cent, but the cost of repairing and maintaining the machines may rise by only 10 per cent if production rose 20 per cent. In this case the machine maintenance would be a semi-variable cost, this being the term for a cost which varies with production but not at a proportionate rate.

Cost behaviour

Intelligent cost planning and control is dependent on the knowledge of how costs behave under certain conditions. What is important is how costs behave in a particular firm, there is no substitute for experience in this respect.

Raw materials are examples of variable costs which normally vary in strict proportion to the units manufactured. Labour costs, on the other hand, usually move in steps, thus the name 'step-variable' costs. For instance, a job may be done by two men, and then a slight increase in activity means that the two men cannot manage it so that a third man is added. In fact it may represent only 2⅓ men's work, but the acquisition of workers comes in indivisible chunks. There can still be a further increase in activity without any more workers, but then the time will come when a fourth man is needed. This is shown on the two graphs in Exhibit 22.1.

Exhibit 22.1

Variable cost behaviour

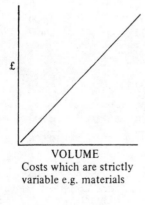

£

VOLUME
Costs which are strictly
variable e.g. materials

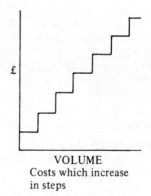

£

VOLUME
Costs which increase
in steps

Marginal costing and absorption costing contrasted

Where costing is used which takes account of the variable cost of products rather than the full production cost, then this is said to be Marginal Costing. We have seen that a marginal costing approach to the decision as to whether or not to accept the foreign order by Donald Ltd gave us the answer which increased the firm's profitability, whereas to use absorption costing of £9 a unit in a blind fashion would have meant rejecting the order and therefore passing up the chance to increase profits and break into the foreign market. Let us look now at what would happen if we used either marginal costing or absorption costing in the calculation of profits for a whole firm, i.e. income determination.

A worked example

The final accounts of a firm, Burke Ltd, are now shown drafted as if (A) Marginal Costing had been used, (B) Absorption Costing had been used. The following information is available:

1. All fixed factory overheads amounted to £4,000 per annum.
2. Variable overheads amounted to £2 per unit.
3. Direct labour and direct materials total £3 per unit.
4. Sales remain constant at 1,000 units per annum at £12 per unit.
5. Production in year 1 is 1,200 units, year 2 is 1,500 units and year 3 is 900 units.

Year 1	(A) Marginal Costing £		(B) Absorption Costing £	
Sales		12,000		12,000
Less Variable Costs:				
Direct Labour and Material, 1,200×£3	3,600		3,600	
Variable overheads, 1,200×£2	2,400		2,400	
Total Variable Cost	6,000			
Less in (A) Valuation Closing Stock				
$\frac{200}{1,200} \times £6,000$	1,000 *			
	5,000			
Fixed Factory Overhead	4,000	9,000	4,000	
Total Production Costs			10,000	
Less in (B) Valuation Closing Stock				
$\frac{200}{1,200} \times £10,000$			1,666*	8,334
Gross Profit		3,000		3,666

*see note later

Year 2

Sales		12,000		12,000
Less Variable Costs:				
Direct Labour and Material 1,500×£3	4,500		4,500	
Variable Overheads, 1,500×£2	3,000		3,000	
Total Variable Cost	7,500			
Add in (A) Opening Stock b/fwd	1,000			
	8,500			
Less in (A) Closing Stock				
$\frac{700}{1,500} \times £7,500*$	3,500			
	5,000			
Fixed Factory Overhead	4,000	9,000	4,000	
Total Production Costs			11,500	
Add Opening Stock in (B) b/fwd			1,666	
			13,166	
Less Closing stock in (B)*				
$\frac{700}{1,500} \times £11,500$			5,366	7,800
Gross Profit		3,000		4,200

*see note later

Year 3	(A) *Marginal Costing*		(B) *Absorption Costing*	
		£		£
Sales		12,000		12,000
Less Variable Costs:				
Direct Labour and Material, 900×£3	2,700		2,700	
Variable Overheads, 900×£2	1,800		1,800	
Total Variable Cost	4,500			
Add in (A) Opening Stock b/fwd	3,500			
	8,000			
Less in (A) Closing Stock				
$\frac{600}{900} \times £4,500$	3,000			
	5,000			
Fixed Factory Overheads	4,000	9,000	4,000	
			8,500	
Add in (B) Opening Stock b/fwd			5,366	
			13,866	
Less in (B) Closing Stock $\frac{600}{900} \times £8,500$			5,666	8,200
Gross Profit		3,000		3,800

Notes:

The Closing Stock each year for (A) is made up of:

$$\frac{\text{Unsold units}}{\text{No. of units produced in year}} \times \text{Total Variable Cost of that year}$$

Units produced year 1 1,200−sold 1,000 = Stock 200 units
Units produced year 2 1,500+200 opening stock − sales 1,000 = Closing Stock 700 units
Units produced year 3 900 units+700 opening stock − sales 1,000 = Closing Stock 600 units
So in year 1 unsold units are 200 units; units produced 1,200; total variable cost is £6,000, therefore stock valuation is

$$\frac{200}{1,200} \times £6,000 = \underline{£1,000}$$

The Closing Stock each year for (B) is made up of:

$$\frac{\text{Unsold units}}{\text{No. of units produced in year}} \times \text{Total Production Cost of that year.}$$

So in year 1 Stock valuation becomes $\frac{200}{1,200} \times £10,000 = £1,666.$

Exhibit 22.2 shows in diagrammatic form the reported profits shown in this example.

Exhibit 22.2

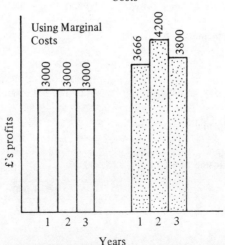

Profits under marginal and absorption costs

Comparison of reported gross profits using marginal cost and absorption cost methods – constant sales and uneven production

The worked example has illustrated that Burke Ltd, a firm which has had the same amount of sales each year at the same prices, and the variable costs per unit have not changed at all, shows quite different profit figures using a Marginal Costing approach compared with Absorption Costing. As these were the gross profits that were calculated let us assume that the selling, distribution, administration and finance expenses were £1,000 for each of these years. The net profits would therefore be as follows:

	(A) *Marginal Costing*	(B) *Absorption Costing*
	£	£
Year 1	2,000	2,666
Year 2	2,000	3,200
Year 3	2,000	2,800

Because of the Absorption Costing approach year 2 shows the biggest profit. As sales etc. are the same, only production being different, this means that the year which has the greatest closing stock has shown the greatest profit. Because of greater production the amount of fixed factory overhead is less. For instance in year 1 with 1,200 units produced and £4,000 fixed factory overhead this means £4,000 ÷ 1,200 = £3.3 per unit, year 2 £4,000 ÷ 1,500 = £2.7 per unit, year 3 £4,000 ÷ 900 = £4.4 per unit (only taken to one decimal place).

By calculating the value of closing stock bringing in fixed factory overhead means that less gets charged for fixed factory overhead when production is greatest, and thus there is a tendency for a greater profit to be shown.

Of course it gets more complicated because the closing stock of one year is the opening stock of the next year, and under absorption costing the values of units of stock will vary. Look at year 3: the opening stock of 700 units is shown as £5,366 = £7.7 approximately; the closing stock of 600 units is shown as £5,666 = £9.4 approximately. Yet these are exactly the same kind of things, and because we have made costs the same each year we have been ignoring inflation. To show a higher profit in a year when the closing stock is higher than usual is often dangerous. In fact the stock may be rising because we cannot sell the goods, we are really getting into trouble, yet the accounts sublimely show a higher profit!

Many experts have argued for or against the Marginal and the Absorption approach in income determination. The Marginal approach really states that fixed Factory Overhead is a function of time and should not be carried forward to the next period by including it in stock valuations. The Absorption approach states that such overhead is concerned with production and therefore the goods produced in that year, but not yet sold, should have such overhead brought into the calculation of their value carried forward to the next period. Put bluntly – do such costs 'attach' to the product or to time? Accountants are divided on this issue, perhaps what has been written in this chapter may have brought you down in favour of one side or the other. It does seem that the marginal approach will become used much more frequently than in the past, at least for internal management purposes.

Assignment Exercises

22.1. Drake Ltd's cost and revenues for the current year are expected to be:

		£
Direct Labour		6,000
Direct Materials		7,000
Factory Indirect Expenses:		
Variable	4,500	
Fixed	500	
		5,000
Administration Expenses		1,200
Selling and Distribution Expenses		600
Finance Expenses		200
		£20,000

It was expected that 2,000 units would be manufactured and sold, the selling price being £11 each.

Suddenly during the year two enquiries were made at the same time which would result in extra production being necessary. They were:

(A) An existing customer said that he would take an extra 100 units, but the price would have to be reduced to £9 per unit on this extra 100 units. The only extra costs that would be involved would be in respect of variable costs.

(B) A new customer would take 150 units annually. This would mean extra variable costs and also an extra machine would have to be bought costing £1,500 which would last for 5 years before being scrapped. It would have no scrap value. Extra running costs of this machine would be £600 per annum. The units are needed for an underdeveloped country and owing to currency difficulties the highest price that could be paid for the units was £10 per unit.

On this information, and assuming that there are no alternatives open to Drake Ltd, should the company accept or reject these orders? Draft the memo that you would give to the managing director of Drake Ltd.

22.2A. Hawkins Ltd. expects its costs per unit − assuming a production level of 100,000 per annum − to be:

	£
Direct Materials	2.8
Direct Labour	2.4
Factory Indirect Expenses: Variable	0.8
Fixed	0.4
Selling and Distribution Expenses	0.2
Administration Expenses	0.3
Finance	- 0.1
	£7.0

Selling prices is £7.5 per unit.

The following propositions are put to the managing director. Each proposition is to be considered on its own without reference to the other propositions.

(a) If the selling price is reduced to £7.4 per unit sales could be raised to 120,000 units per annum instead of the current 100,000 units. Apart from Direct Materials, Direct Labour and Factory Variable Expenses there would be not change in costs. 7.2

(b) If the selling price is put up to £7.2 per unit sales would be 80,000 per annum instead of 100,000. Apart from variable costs there would also be a saving of £2,000 per annum in Finance Costs.

(c) To satisfy a special order, which would not be repeated, 5,000 extra units could be sold at £6.3 each. This would have no effect on fixed expenses.

(d) To satisfy a special order, which would not be repeated, 3,000 extra units could be sold for £5.9 each. This would have no effect on fixed expenses.

Draft a memo stating what you would advise the managing director to do giving your reasons and workings.

22.3A. Assume that by coincidence two firms have exactly the same costs and revenue, but that Magellan Ltd. uses a marginal costing approach to the valuation of stock-in-trade in its final accounts, whilst Frobisher Ltd. has an absorption cost approach. Calculate the gross profits for each company for each of their first three years of operating from the following:

(a) All fixed factory overhead is £9,000 per annum.

(b) Direct Labour costs over each of the three years − £3 per unit.

(c) Direct Material costs over each of the three years − £5 per unit.

(d) Variable overheads which vary in direct ratio to production were £2 per unit.

(e) Sales are: Year 1 900 units: Year 2 1,200 units: Year3 1,100 units. The selliong price remained constant at £29 per unit.

(f) Production is at the rate of: Year 1 1,200 units: Year 2 1,300 units: Year 3 1,250 units.

22.4A. Gould Ltd. have been in business for three years and have always used an absorption cost approach to the valuation of stock-in-trade for their final accounts. They are approached by a take-over bidder who prefers to use a marginal cost approach. The price for the shares is agreed at a formula: Average Gross Profit for the three years calculated using the marginal cost approach times 5, add Gross Profit for year 3 using the absorption cost approach times 2 = Price to be given for all the shares of Gould Ltd.

The following informationis available:

(a) Sales were: Year 1   10,000 units: Year 2   12,000 units: Year 3   11,000 units.

(b) Production is at the rate of: Year 1   13,000 units: Year 2   11,000 units: Year 3   12,000 units.

(c) Direct Labour costs per unit were constant at £6 per unit.

(d) Direct Material costs per unit over three years were constant at £11 per unit.

(e) Variable Overheads which vary in direct proportion to production were £4 per unit.

(f) Fixed expenses are: factory overhead £80,000 per annum.

(g) Selling price remained constant at £30 per unit.

You are required to calculate the amount that would have to be paid for the shares of Gould Ltd. by the take-over bidder.

22.5. The costs and revenues for Garrick Limited for the present year are expected to be as follows:

	£
Direct Labour	16,000
Direct Materials	21,000
Factory Indirect Expenses*	9,000
Administration Expenses	3,000
Selling and Distribution Expenses	2,000
Finance Expenses	1,000
	52,000
Net profit	8,000
Sales: 4,000 units (at £15 each)	60,000

*Made up of one-third fixed and two-thirds variable expenses.

Towards the end of the year two additional projects come under consideration. Both of these would require extra production. They are:

(a) A new customer would take 200 units annually. The order would bring about extra variable costs in direct proportion to the extra production needed. In addition an extra machine would have to be bought for £3,000, it would last for four years before being scrapped, there being a scrap value of £200. The extra running costs of this machine would be £1,800 per annum. The highest price that could be paid by this customer, it is an overseas company, is £25 per unit.

(b) An existing customer says he will take 50 units additionally per annum, but the price would have to fall to £13 per unit on these 50 units.

Based on the information above, what advice would you give to your Managing Director? You are also to state how you would qualify your advice. Show all of your workings to substantiate your advice?

22.6. Your firm has been trading for three years. It has used a marginal costing approach to the valuation of stock-in-trade in its final accounts. Your directors are interested to know what the recorded profits would have been if the absorption cost approach had been used instead. Draw up the three year's accounts using both methods.

(a) Fixed factory overhead is £16,000 per annum.

(b) Direct Labour costs per unit over each of the three years £4 per unit.

(c) Direct Material costs over each of the three years £3 per unit.

(d) Variable overheads which vary in direct ratio to production were £5 per unit.

(e) Sales are: Year 1   9,000 units; Year 2   10,000 units; Year 3   15,000 units. All at £16 per unit.

(f) Production is at the rate of: Year 1   10,000 units; Year 2   12,000 units; Year 3   16,000 units.

23

Job and Process Costing

The earlier chapters on costing have been concerned mainly with the firm as a whole. You have seen the effects of Marginal and Absorption Costing if applied to the firm, and you have seen the flow of costs through manufacturing and retail businesses. Now we have to consider the use of these concepts in the application of costing in firms. So far there has been a certain amount of simplification just so that the concepts could be seen without too much detail obscuring your view. For instance it has been usually assumed in most of the Exhibits that the firms have been making only one kind of product, and that there has really been only one cost centre. Without stretching your imagination greatly you will realize that firms manufacture many different types of goods, and that there are many cost centres in most firms.

When looking at the costing systems in use it can be seen that they can usually be divided into two main types, (a) Job Costing, (b) Process costing. These two main types have either an absorption or marginal costing approach, they use FIFO or LIFO or AVCO methods of pricing issues etc. It is important to realize that Marginal Costing is not a costing system, it is instead an approach to costing which is used when Job or Processing Costing systems are used. The same applies to Absorption Costing.

The choice of job costing or process costing

Process costing is relevant where production is regarded as a continuous flow, and would be applicable to industries where production is repetitive and continuous. One example would be an oil refinery where crude oil is processed continually, emerging as different grades of petrol, paraffin, motor oil, etc. Another instance would be a salt works where brine (salt water) is pumped into the works, and the product is slabs or packets of salt. Salt works and oil refineries will have a repetitive and continuous flow of production and would, therefore, use Process Costing.

Contrasted with this would be production which consisted of separate jobs for special orders which could be just one item or of a batch of items. For instance where bodies of Rolls-Royce cars are made to each customers' specifications, each car can be regarded as a separate job. Compared with this would be a printer's business where books are printed, so that the printing of say 5,000 copies of a book can also be regarded as a job. The 'job' can thus be one item or a batch of similar items.

1. Job Costing

Each job will be given a separate job number, and direct materials and direct labour used on the job will be charged to the job. The accumulation of the costs will be done on a 'job cost sheet'. The materials will have been charged to the job on FIFO, or LIFO, or AVCO, etc., basis. The direct labour costs will be found by recording the number of direct labour hours of each type of direct worker, and multiplying by the labour cost per hour for each type.

The job is thus the cost centre, and direct labour and direct materials can be charged direct to the cost centre. The indirect expenses cannot be charged direct to the job, such costs are charged instead to a service cost centre and the cost of the service centre is then apportioned between the various jobs to give the cost of each job including indirect expenses. Now it is only after the accounting period is over that the exact costs of each service centre are known, but you will want to know how much each job costs as it is finished. You will not want to wait months to find out the cost of each job. This is solved by estimating the indirect expenses, and then fixing the method of apportioning these estimated expenses as described in Chapter 21.

A Worked Example:

Suppose there are three jobs being performed and these are in separate production departments, Departments A, B and C. There are also two service centres, Departments G and H. Some of the indirect labour expenses and other indirect expenses can be allocated direct to the production departments × for instance the wages of the foremen of each of Departments A, B and C, or items such as lubricating materials if each department used quite different lubricants. Other indirect labour can be traced to the two centres G and H as well as expenses. The problem then is that of apportioning the costs of G and H between Departments A, B and C. We can now look at Exhibit 23.1, and see what answer this firm came up with.

Exhibit 23.1

Indirect Labour Costs and Other Indirect Expenses have been allocated to Production Departments A, B and C and Service Departments G and H as follows:

	Production Departments			Service Departments	
	A	B	C	G	H
Indirect Labour	2,000	3,000	4,000	500	1,000
Other Expenses	1,000	2,000	3,000	1,500	2,000
	£3,000	£5,000	£7,000	£2,000	£3,000

The problem is to apportion the costs of G and H to the production departments. G was a department which maintained factory buildings whilst H maintained factory machinery. A study of the costs of G produced a very easy answer. There was no doubt that the costs were in direct relationship to the floor space occupied by each department. But it must not be overlooked that department H also needed the attention of G's workforce so that part of the costs of G would have to be apportioned to H. These costs would then increase the total of costs of department H which would then need apportioning to the production departments. Floor space in square feet was A 2,000, B 4,000, C 3,000, and H 1,000. The £2,000 costs were therefore apportioned:

$$\text{Each department:} \quad \frac{\text{Its floor space}}{\text{Total floor space}} \times £2,000$$

Therefore:

$$A \quad \frac{2,000}{10,000} \times £2,000 = £400 \quad : \quad B \quad \frac{4,000}{10,000} \times £2,000 = £800$$

$$C \quad \frac{3,000}{10,000} \times £2,000 = £600 \quad : \quad H \quad \frac{1,000}{10,000} \times £2,000 = £200$$

(Department H's costs have now increased by £200 and become £3,200).

Department H's costs presented a far more difficult problem. Consideration was given to apportionment based on numbers of machines, volumes of production, and types of machinery. It was, however, felt that there was a high relationship in this case (although this would certainly not always be true in other firms) between the values of machinery in use and the costs of maintaining them. The more costly equipment was very complicated and needed a lot of attention. Consequently it was decided to apportion H's costs between A, B and C on the basis of the value of machinery in each department. This was found to be A £3,000; B £6,000; C £7,000. The costs were therefore apportioned:

$$\frac{\text{Value of machinery in department}}{\text{Total value of machinery in all 3 departments}} \times £3,200$$

Therefore:

A $\dfrac{3,000}{16,000} \times £3,200 = £600$: B $\dfrac{6,000}{16,000} \times £3,200 = £1,200$

C $\dfrac{7,000}{16,000} \times £3,200 = £1,400$

The costs and their apportionment can, therefore, be shown:

	Production Departments			Service Departments	
	A	B	C	G	H
Indirect Labour	2,000	3,000	4,000	500	1,000
Other Expenses	1,000	2,000	3,000	1,500	2,000
	3,000	5,000	7,000	2,000	3,000
Department G's costs apportioned	400	800	600	(2,000)	200
					3,200
Department H's costs apportioned	600	1,200	1,400		(3,200)
	£4,000	£7,000	£9,000	–	–

Now we have the estimated overhead for each department for the ensuing accounting period. We now have another problem as to how the overhead is going to be taken into the calculation of the cost of each job in these departments. After investigation the conclusion is that in departments A and B there is a direct relationship between direct labour hours and overhead, but in department C the guiding fact is machine hours. If the total overhead of departments A and B are therefore divided by estimated number of direct labour hours this will give the overhead rate per direct labour hour, whilst in department C the total overhead will be divided by the estimated machine hours. The calculation of the overhead rates are therefore:

	Production Departments		
	A	B	C
Direct Labour hours	5,000	4,000	
Machine hours			6,000
Overhead rate per Direct Labour hour	$\dfrac{£4,000}{5,000}$	$\dfrac{£7,000}{4,000}$	
	= £0.8	= £1.75	
Overhead rate per Machine hour			$\dfrac{£9,000}{6,000}=$ £1.5

We can now calculate the costs of four jobs performed in this factory:

Job A/70/144
Department A
Started 1.7.19-2.   Completed 13.7.19-2.
Cost of Direct Materials £130.
Number of Direct Labour hours 100.
Cost rate of direct labour per hour £0.9.

Job B/96/121
Department B
Started 4.7.19-2.   Completed 9.7.19-2.
Cost of Direct Materials £89.
Number of Direct Labour hours 40.
Cost rate of direct labour per hour £1.1.

Job C/67/198
Department C
Started 8.7.19-2. Completed 16.7.19-2.
Cost of Direct Materials £58.
Number of Direct Labour hours 50.
Cost rate of direct labour per hour £1.0.
Number of machine hours 40.

Job AC/45/34
Departments A and C
Started in A 3.7.19-2. Passed on to C 11.7.19-2. Completed in
C 16.7.19-2.Cost of Materials £115.
Number of Direct Labour hours (in dept. A) 80.
Number of Direct Labour hours (in dept. C) 90.
Cost rate per direct labour hour dept. A £0.9.
dept. C £1.0.
Number of machine hours, dept. C 70.

Job Cost Sheet.   Job No. A/70/144.

Started 1.7.19-2   Completed 13.7.19-2

			£
Materials			130
	Hours	*Rates £*	
Direct Labour	100	0.9	90
Factory Overhead	100	0.8	80
Total Job Cost			£300

Job Cost Sheet. Job No. B/96/121

Started 1.7.19-2.   Completed 9.7.19-2.

			£
Materials			89
	Hours	*Rates £*	
Direct Labour	40	1.1	44
Factory Overhead	40	1.75	70
Total Job Cost			£203

Job Cost Sheet. Job No. C/67/198

Started 8.7.19-2. Completed 16.7.19-2.

	Hours	Rates £	£
Materials			58
Direct Labour	50	1.0	50
Factory Overhead	40	1.5	60
Total Job Cost			£168

Job Cost Sheet. Job No. AC/45/34

Started 3.7.19-2. Completed 16.7.19-2.

	Hours	Rates £	£
Materials			115
Direct Labour (dept. A)	80	0.9	72
Direct Labour (dept. C)	90	1.0	90
Factory Overhead (dept. A)	80	0.8	64
Factory Overhead (dept. C)	70	1.5	105
Total Job Cost			£446

In the Exhibit and when the job costs were worked out it has not been stated whether or not this is using a marginal or absorption costing approach. Assume that in fact an absorption approach has been used in that overhead is deemed to include both fixed and variable overhead. If instead a marginal costing approach was to be used then the overhead brought into the calculations of job costs would exclude fixed overhead, so that the overhead rate would be a variable overhead rate.

Cost Centres – Job Costing and Responsibility

It must be pointed out that a cost centre for job costing is not necessarily the same as tracing the costs down to the individual who is responsible for controlling them. There are two questions here (a) Finding the cost of a job to check on its profitability and (b) Controlling the costs by making someone responsible for them so that he will have to answer for any variations from planned results. Many firms therefore keep separate records of costs to fulfil each of these functions.

2. Process Costing

Job costing treats production as a number of separate jobs being performed, whereas process costing sees production as a continuous flow. In process costing there is correspondingly no attempt to allocate costs to specific units being produced.

There is, however, usually more than one process in the manufacture of goods. We can take for an example a bakery producing cakes. There are three processes: (a) The mixing of the cake ingredients, (b) The baking of the cakes, (c) The packaging of the cakes. Each process is treated as a cost centre, and therefore costs for (a), (b) and (c) are collected separately. Overhead rates are then calculated for each cost centre in a similar fashion to that in job costing.

In the case of the bakery each accounting period would probably start and finish without any half-mixed or half-baked cakes, but some types of firms which use process costing have processes which take rather longer to complete than baking cakes. A typical case would be the brewing of beer. At the beginning and end of each period there would be partly processed units. It is a matter of arithmetic to convert production into 'equivalent production'. For instance, production during a particular period may be as in Exhibit 23.2.

Exhibit 23.2

Started in previous year ¾ completed then, and ¼ completed in current period, 400 units, 400 × ¼	100
Started and completed in current period	680
Started in current period and ⅛ completed by end of period, 160 units, 160 × ⅛	20
Equivalent Production	800 units

If the total costs of the cost centre amounted to £4,000 then the unit cost would be $\frac{£4,000}{800} = £5$.

In fact process costing can become very complicated because some of the part-produced items are complete in terms of say, materials, but incomplete in terms of labour, or else say ⅔ complete for materials and ¼ complete for labour. Although it becomes complicated the principles are no different from that described of calculating equivalent production.

We can now look at an example of process costing in Exhibit 23.2. So that we do not get involved in too many arithmetical complications, we will assume that there are no part completed goods in each process at the start and end of the period considered.

Exhibit 23.3

A bakery making cakes has three processes, process (A) The mixing of the cake ingredients, (B) The baking of the cakes, (C) The packaging of the cakes.

January activity was as follows:

Materials used:	£
Process (A)	4,000
Process (B)	–
Process (C)	1,000
Direct Labour:	
Process (A)	1,500
Process (B)	500
Process (C)	800
Factory Overhead:	
Variable:	
Process (A)	400
Process (B)	1,300
Process (C)	700
Fixed: (allocated to processes)	
Process (A)	600
Process (B)	500
Process (C)	400

During January 100,000 cakes were made.
The Process Cost accounts will appear as:

Process (A)

	£		£
Materials	4,000	Transferred to Process (B)	
Direct Labour	1,500	100,000 units at £0.065	6,500
Variable Overhead	400		
Fixed Overhead	600		
	£6,500		£6,500

Process (B)

	£		£
Transferred from Process (A)		Transferred to Process (C)	
100,000 units at £0.065	6,500	100,000 units at £0.088	8,800
Direct Labour	500		
Variable Overhead	1,300		
Fixed Overhead	500		
	£8,800		£8,800

Process (C)

	£		£
Transferred from Process (B)		Transferred to Finished	
100,000 units at £0.088	8,800	Goods Stock 100,000 units at	
Materials	1,000	£0.117	11,700
Direct Labour	800		
Variable Overhead	700		
Fixed Overhead	400		
	£11,700		£11,700

Other Kinds of Firms

Process costing is found most often in industries such as oil, canning, paint manufacture, steel, textiles, and food processing.

The Problem of Joint Costs

Usually a manufacturing operation results in one simple product. Any excess is regarded as scrap, and the small cost that could be traced to it is ignored, e.g. the manufacture of a suit where the cost is traced to the suit, the small unusable bits of cloth being ignored.

This is not always the case, and where a group of separate products is produced simultaneously, each of the products having relatively substantial sales values, then the products are called 'joint products'. Thus crude oil taken into an oil refinery is processed and the output is in terms of different grades of petrol, paraffin, motor oil etc. This means that in costing terms the costs of the materials and processes etc. have to be split between the joint products.

Many problems exist in this area. Perhaps you will see why when the problem of allocating costs between joint products is concerned with the cutting-up of a cow for beef. From a cow there is rump-steak, the fillet steaks, the T-bone steaks, sirloin, silverside, brisket etc. If the cow cost the butcher £30, then how would you allocate the cost between all of these various joint products? This gives you some idea of the problem which exists, in many industries this becomes involved with complex technological problems.

Assignment Exercises

23.1 A factory has six departments. In departments A, B and C factory overhead is allocated using overhead rates per direct labour hour at A £1.3: B £1.4: C £2.3; Departments D, E and F use an overhead rate per machine hour of D £2.8: E £1.5: F £4.0.

The cost rate of direct labour per hour in the department is A £0.9: B £1.0: C £1.1: D. £1.2: E £0.9: F £1.0.

You are required to calculate the cost of the following jobs:

Job 1001: Dept. A.	Cost of Direct Materials		£118
	Number of direct labour hours		60
Job 1002: Dept. A.	Cost of Direct Materials		£206
	Number of direct labour hours		50
Job 1003: Dept. B.	Cost of Direct Materials		£310
	Number of direct labour hours		71
Job 1004: Dept. C.	Cost of Direct Materials		£205
	Number of direct labour hours		80

Job 1005: Dept. D.	Cost of Direct Materials	£98
	Number of direct labour hours	60
	Number of machine hours	50
Job 1006: Dept. E.	Cost of Direct Materials	£306
	Number of direct labour hours	110
	Number of machine hours	80
Job 1007: Dept. F.	Cost of Direct Materials	£401
	Number of direct labour hours	130
	Number of machine hours	130
Job 1008: Dept. E.	Cost of Direct Materials	£180
	Number of direct labour hours	70
	Number of machine hours	60
	Then passed on to Dept. A to complete where	
	Additional Raw Materials used	£44
	Number of direct labour hours	40
Job 1009: Dept. C.	Cost of Direct Materials	£388
	Number of direct labour hours	50
	then passed to Dept. A where no additional	
	materials used but spent direct labour hours	40
	then passed on to Dept. F. where it was completed	
	Additional materials cost	£68
	Number of direct labour hours	70
	Number of machine hours	59
	(Show your workings)	

23.2A. A factory has five departments. In department J, K and L factory overhead is allocated using an overhead rate per machine hour of J £2.3: K £4.3: L £3.2. Departments M and N use an overhead rate per direct labour hour of M £2.7: N £1.9.

The cost rate of direct labour per hour in the departments is J £1.5: K. £1.3: L. £2.1: M. £1.8: N. £2.0.

You are required to calculate the cost of the following jobs:

Job 1551: Dept. J.	Cost of Direct Materials	£359
	Number of direct labour hours	115
	Number of machine hours	77
Job 1552: Dept. K.	Cost of Direct Materials	£1,498
	Number of direct labour hours	206
	Number of machine hours	117
Job 1553: Dept. L.	Cost of Direct Materials	£115
	Number of direct labour hours	66
	Number of machine hours	66
Job 1554: Dept. M.	Cost of Direct Materials	£110
	Number of direct labour hours	46
	Number of machine hours	24
Job 1555: Dept. N.	Cost of Direct Materials	£1,390
	Number of direct labour hours	279
	Number of machine hours	250

Job 1556: Dept. M.	Cost of Direct Materials	£889
	Number of direct labour hours	104
	Then passed on to Dept. L where Additional	
	Direct Materials cost	£65
	Direct Labour hours	55
	Machine hours	46
Job 1557: Dept. K.	Cost of Direct Materials	£506
	Number of direct labour hours	80
	Number of machine hours	76
	Then passed on to Dept. N where Additional	
	Direct Materials cost	£45
	Direct labour hours	40
	Then passed on to Dept. L where Additional	
	Direct Materials cost	£49
	Direct labour hours	50
	Machine hours	37

(Show your workings)

23.3. In a firm there are 4 types of jobs performed in separate production departments A, B, C and D. In addition there are 3 service departments, K, L and M. Costs have been allocated to the departments as follows:

	Production Departments				Service Departments		
	A	B	C	D	K	L	M
	£	£	£	£	£	£	£
Indirect Labour	4,000	6,000	8,000	2,000	1,500	3,000	4,100
Other Expenses	2,700	3,100	3,600	1,500	4,500	2,000	2,000

The expenses of the Service Departments are to be allocated between other departments as follows:

Dept. K to Depts. A 25 per cent: B 30 per cent: C 20 per cent: D 10 per cent: M 15 per cent.

Dept. L to Depts. A 60 per cent: C 30 per cent: D 10 per cent.

Dept. M to Depts. B 30 per cent: C 50 per cent: D 20 per cent.

In departments A and C the job costing is to use an overhead rate per direct labour hour, whilst in B and D a machine hour rate will be used. The number of direct hours and machine hours per department is expected to be:

	A	B	C	D
Direct labour hours	2,000	4,000	4,450	2,700
Machine hours	1,900	2,600	2,900	2,400

You are required to calculate:

(a) The overhead rates for departments A and C.

(b) The overhead rates for departments B and D.

(Keep your answer — it will be used as a basis for the next question.)

23.4A. In the firm mentioned in 23.3 what would be the costs of the following jobs given that the direct labour costs per hour are Dept. A £2.1: B £1.7: C £2.4: D £2.3.

Job 351: Dept. A.	Direct Materials cost	£190
	Number of direct labour hours	56
	Number of machine hours	40
Job 352: Dept. B.	Direct Materials cost	£1,199
	Number of direct labour hours	178
	Number of machine hours	176
Job 353: Dept. C.	Direct Materials cost	£500
	Number of direct labour hours	130
	Number of machine hours	100
Job 354: Dept. D.	Direct Materials cost	£666
	Number of direct labour hours	90
	Number of machine hours	64
Job 355: Dept. C.	Direct Materials cost	£560
	Number of direct labour hours	160
	Number of machine hours	150
	Job passed on to Dept. B where Additional	
	Direct Materials cost	£68
	Number of direct labour hours	30
	Number of machine hours	20

23.5A. In a firm there are five types of jobs performed in separate production departments P, Q, R, S and T. In addition there are two service departments F and G. Costs have been allocated to the departments as follows:

	Production Departments					Service Departments	
	P	Q	R	S	T	F	G
	£	£	£	£	£	£	£
Indirect Labour	5,000	7,000	3,000	6,000	8,000	10,000	9,000
Other Expenses	500	1,800	1,000	1,200	1,300	6,000	7,000

The expenses of the Service Departments are to be allocated between other departments as follows:

Dept. F to Depts. P 10 per cent: Q 20 per cent: S 30 per cent: T 15 per cent: G 25 per cent.

Dept. G to Depts. P 12.5 per cent: Q 20 per cent: R 25 per cent: S 30 per cent: T 12.5 per cent.

In departments R and T the job costing is to use an overhead rate per direct labour hour, whilst in the other production departments a machine hour rate will be used. The number of direct labour hours and machine hours per department are expected to be:

	P	Q	R	S	T
Direct labour hours	4,000	5,000	3,600	10,000	3,550
Machine hours	3,000	4,000	3,000	8,000	2,800

You are required to calculate:

(a) The overhead rates for departments R and T.

(b) The overhead rates for departments P, Q and S.

(Keep your answer − it will be used for question 23.6.)

23.6A. In the firm mentioned in 23.5 what would be the costs of the following jobs, given that the direct labour rate per hour is Dept. P £1.9: Q £2.5: R. £2.0: S £2.7: T £2.4.

Job 701: Dept. R.	Direct Materials cost	£115
	Number of direct labour hours	35
	Number of machine hours	29
Job 702: Dept. T.	Direct Materials cost	£1,656
	Number of direct labour hours	180
	Number of machine hours	160
Job 703: Dept. P.	Direct Materials cost	£546
	Number of direct labour hours	100
	Number of machine hours	90
Job 704: Dept. S.	Direct Materials cost	£65
	Number of direct labour hours	250
	Number of machine hours	60
Job 705: Dept. Q.	Direct Materials cost	£4,778
	Number of direct labour hours	305
	Number of machine hours	280
Job 706: Dept. P.	Direct Materials cost	£555
	Number of direct labour hours	200
	Number of machine hours	180
	Then passed to Dept. T for completion where	
	Direct Materials cost	£11
	Number of direct labour hours	18
	Number of machine hours	2

23.7A. A factory uses process costing. There are three departments, each concerned with a separate process, called Departments A, B and C. Departments A and C where the labour content predominates, and therefore a labour overhead rate is used. Department B employs a great deal of expensive machinery and a machine hour rate for overhead is in use there.

The following details relate to estimates of overhead:

	Dept. A	Dept. B	Dept. C
	£	£	£
Indirect labour	17,000	2,000	24,000
Other Indirect expenses	3,000	8,000	6,000

The number of labour hours worked will be A 10,000, B 1,000, C 12,000. The number of machine hours in department B will be 500.

Find the cost of producing 100 units which had raw materials costing £3,000 taken into Department A, processed in 200 labour hours, then passed on to Department B where 100 labour hours are spent on them and 45 machine hours, and finished off in Department C where £168 additional materials are incorporated, and 270 labour hours are spent on them. The cost per hour of direct labour is Dept. A £2.2: Dept. B £1.8: Dept. C £2.4.

24

Introduction to Pricing Policy

One thing is clear — that in the long term the revenues of a firm must exceed its costs or else the firm will go out of business. If it was a company it would have to be liquidated, if it was a firm run by a sole trader he might conceivably become bankrupt. On the other hand firms may find that in the short term costs sometimes exceed revenues, in other words the firm makes a net loss. Many firms do make losses from time to time without being forced out of business.

This being so, the way in which the prices are determined of the goods sold by the firm is of paramount importance. You may well expect that there are some definite rules which will be observed by a firm when it fixes its prices, and that these rules are followed by all businesses. Your expectations would, however, be quite wrong.

With pricing, each firm has certain features which may not apply to other firms, and this will affect its pricing policy. For instance, taking a simple illustration, let us look at the price of sugar sold by three different businesses dealing in groceries. The first business (A) is a grocer's shop in a village, it is the only grocer's shop, and the next shop at which the villagers can buy sugar is thirty miles away. The second shop (B) is also a grocer's shop in a town where there are plenty of other shops selling sugar. The last business (C) is a very large supermarket in a city, in a street where there are other large supermarkets. For a bag of sugar you might have to pay, at (A) 20p, (B) 18p, (C) 14p. The sugar may well be of exactly the same quality and be manufactured by the same firm. Firm (A) buys in small quantities, subsequently it pays a higher price than (B) or (C) for its sugar, but it knows that none of its customers want to go thirty miles for sugar. The owner does not want to lose the self-respect by over-charging anyway, so he settles for 20p. He always remembers that if he charged more, then his customers might well buy sugar in large quantities when they went to the market town to shop. Firm (B) makes hardly any profit at all out of his sugar sales, he fears that if his regular customers go elsewhere for their sugar they may well decide to buy other things as well, so that not only would he lose his sugar sales he may lose a great deal of his other sales.

Supermarket (C) sells sugar at a loss — it does this quite deliberately to tempt in customers who come to buy cheap sugar, and then buy other items on which the supermarket makes reasonable profits.

If there can be such differences in the selling price of a bag of sugar sold by three firms, none of whom had in fact produced the sugar, then how much more complex is the position where firms manufacture goods and then have to fix prices. This is where study of economics helps one to get this in better perspective. The elasticity of demand must be considered as well as whether or not the firm has a monopoly, and other factors so that economics gives you a framework in which your thinking can be carried on. It is not the purpose of this book to be an economics text, but you can well see that really the thinking behind pricing relies on economic analysis. We will content ourselves with accepting that this is so, and will merely look at how accounting portrays it.

Although there may be no clearly defined rules on pricing, it can at least be said that views of pricing can be traced to one of two attitudes. These are:

1. Ascertain the cost of the product and then add something to that for profit, the sum being the selling price. This is usually known as "Full-Cost Pricing".

2. Ascertain the price at which similar products are selling, and then attempt to keep costs below that level so as to make a profit.

Many of the problems connected with full-cost pricing are those concerned with absorption costing and marginal costing. In absorption costing the whole of the fixed costs were allocated to products, whereas in marginal costing the "contribution" was found out of which fixed costs would have to come leaving the profit as the difference. The information shown in Exhibit 24.1 has been drawn up on a full-cost basis, using the following philosophy.

A considerable number of firms use the full-cost basis, very likely because it is easy to apply. This is of itself not meant as a criticism — after all the accounting that is used should be the simplest method of achieving the desired ends. There is certainly no virtue at all in using complicated methods when simple ones would be sufficient. Complicated methods means that the accounting system costs more to operate, and if the benefits are no greater than those derived from the simple system, then the accounting system should be scrapped and replaced by the simple system. Using methods just because they are simple can, however, be harmful if they give the wrong data, whereas a more complex system might give the right data. The simple system of full-cost pricing is to find the cost of direct materials and direct labour and then add relevant amounts to represent overheads and profit. The selling price is calculated in a manner similar to the following:

	£
Cost of Direct Materials and Direct Labour	10
Add Variable Manufacturing Overhead	5
Add Share of fixed manufacturing overhead	1
	16
Add Percentage (say 50 per cent in this case) for Selling Administration and Finance Costs	8
	24
Add Percentage for profit (in this case say 25 per cent)	6
	30

The percentage of 50 per cent for selling, administration, and finance costs is probably based on the figures for the previous year, where as a total for the year these figures would have approximated to 50 per cent of the total of direct materials + direct labour + variable manufacturing overhead + fixed manufacturing overhead (i.e. in this case this would have amounted to £16 for one unit). Therefore taking 50 per cent as an addition is really saying that the basic situation is similar to the previous year.

Remember that this was an example, full-cost pricing is not always done in exactly the same manner, but the example just shown is a typical one. As we have seen already in chapter seven the allocation of fixed costs is very arbitrary, yet here the selling price is based upon figures produced as a direct consequence of such arbitrary allocation.

We can now look at Exhibit 24.1 where three firms are making identical products, and for the purpose of illustration we will assume that the variable and fixed costs for each firm are the same. Different accountants use different methods of allocating fixed overhead between products, even though in each case the allocation may seem to be quite rational. There is usually no one 'right' way of allocating fixed overhead, instead there are 'possible' ways. In this Exhibit each of the three firms manufactures two products, and because of the different ways in which they have allocated fixed overhead they have come up with different selling prices for their products.

Exhibit 24.1

	Blue Ltd. Products		Green Ltd. Products		Red Ltd. Products	
	B	A	B	A	B	A
	£	£	£	£	£	£
Direct Labour and Materials	10	12	10	12	10	12
Variable Overhead	16	10	16	10	16	10
Marginal Cost	26	22	26	22	26	22
Fixed Overhead	6	26	22	10	14	18
Full Cost	32	48	48	32	40	40
Add Profit: 12.5 per cent of Full Cost	4	6	6	4	5	5
	36	54	54	36	45	45

238

In real life once the selling prices have been calculated the market prices of similar goods are looked at, and the price fixed on the basis of competition etc. In this case the price might well be adjusted to £45 for both products A and B. In this case, by a coincidence — after all the allocation of fixed overhead has been done on an arbitrary basis — Red Ltd. has managed to get its selling prices calculated to exactly the general market price.

Suppose that the firms had really placed their faith in their selling price calculations. Blue might think that as the full cost of product B was £48 then it would lose £3 for every unit sold of product B. Green Ltd. might, on the other hand, think that as the full cost of Product A is £48 then it would lose £3 on every unit sold of product A. Blue Ltd. might decide to cease production of B, and Green Ltd. decide to cease production of A. If the plans had been for each firm to sell 100 of each of products A and B, then the plans have now altered to Blue Ltd. to produce and sell 100 of A only, Green Ltd. to sell 100 of B only, and Red Ltd. to sell both 100 of A and 100 of B. The summarised profits will now be as shown in Exhibit 24.2.

Exhibit 24.2

	Blue Ltd. £	Green Ltd. £	Red Ltd. £
Sales: 100 of A×£45	4,500		4,500
100 of B×£45		4,500	4,500
Total Revenue	4,500	4,500	9,000
Less Costs: Direct Labour and Materials			
Product A 100×£10	1,000		1,000
Product B 100×£12		1,200	1,200
Variable Overhead:			
Product A 100×£16	1,600		1,600
Product B 100×£10		1,000	1,000
Fixed Overhead: does not change because of cessation of production in Blue Ltd. and Green Ltd. (see text)	3,200	3,200	3,200
Total Costs	5,800	5,400	8,000
Net Profit			1,000
Net Loss	1,300	900	

Exhibit 24.2 shows that Blue Ltd. and Green Ltd. would incur losses if they ceased production of product B and product A respectively. Yet if they had not ceased production they would both have made profits of £1,000 as Red Ltd. has done. After all they are similar firms with exactly the same costs — the only difference was the way they allocated fixed costs. The fixed costs in each firm totalled £3,200. Blue allocated this between products as A £6: B £26: Green allocated it A £22: B £10: C allocated it A £14: B £18. With 100 units of each product this amounted to an allocation of £3,200 for each firm. Fixed overhead does not change just because of ceasing

production of one type of product. The factory rent and rates will remain the same, so will the typists' salaries and other fixed costs.

The question, therefore, arises as to which figure is relevant in deciding whether to continue the manufacture of a certain product or to cease production. The answer to this is that the marginal cost figure is the one that is relevant. If this is less than the selling price, then the difference will be the contribution towards fixed overhead, thus reducing the burden of the fixed overhead on the other products. This can be shown as:

	Product A	Product B
	£	£
Selling Price	45	45
Marginal Cost	26	22
Contribution towards fixed overhead and profit	£19	£23

Just let us test this out with another firm in Exhibit 24.3 which has the following cost and selling information. The firm would sell 100 of each product it manufactured. Total fixed overhead is £4,800 − allocated A £5 (100), B £7 (100), C £11 (100), D £15 (100), E £10 (100), i.e. £4,800 total.

Exhibit 24.3

Violet Ltd.

Products	A	B	C	D	E
Cost: (per unit)	£	£	£	£	£
Direct Labour and Materials	8	9	16	25	11
Variable overhead	7	8	10	13	14
Marginal Cost	15	17	26	38	25
Fixed Overhead	5	7	11	15	10
Full Cost	20	24	37	53	35
Selling Price per unit	30	21	31	80	20

On the full-cost basis only A and D would seem to be profitable. Should therefore, production of B, C and E be discontinued? According to what has been said production should cease only when the selling price is less than marginal cost. In Exhibit 24.4 we will see if following our own advice brings about the greatest profit. We will also see at the same time what would have happened if production was not cut at all.

Exhibit 24.4

	(1) Following full-cost pricing, cease producing B, C and E £	(2) Using marginal costing, cease producing E only £	(3) Ignore costing altogether and produce all items £
Sales: A 100×£30	3,000	3,000	3,000
B 100×£21		2,100	2,100
C 100×£31		3,100	3,100
D 100×£80	8,000	8,000	8,000
E 100×£20			2,000
Total Revenue:	11,000	16,200	18,200
Less Costs: Direct Labour and Materials:			
100×cost per product	(£33) 3,300	(£58) 5,800	(£69) 6,900
Variable Cost: 100×cost per product	(£20) 2,000	(£38) 3,800	(£52) 5,200
Fixed Overhead (does not change)	4,800	4,800	4,800
Total Costs	10,100	14,400	16,900
Net Profit	£900	£1,800	£1,300

The £'s figures in brackets show the cost of each product, e.g. in (1) the Direct labour and Materials are A £8 + D £25 = £33.

As you can see in Exhibit 24.4 it would be just as well if we followed our own advice. This would give a profit of £1,800 compared with £900 using the full-cost method or £1,300 if we disregarded costing altogether. Sometimes the full-cost method will give far better results than ignoring costing altogether, but this case shows that in fact the wrong kind of costing can be even worse than having no costing at all! The marginal costing approach will, however, give the better answer in this sort of situation.

There is, however, a danger in thinking that if the marginal cost of each product is less than the selling price then activities will be profitable. This is certainly not so, and full consideration must be given to the fact that the total contributions from all the products should exceed the fixed costs otherwise the firm will incur an overall loss. Different volumes of activity will affect this. Let us look in Exhibit 24.5 with a two product firm making products A and B given different volumes of activity. Product A has a marginal cost of £10 and a selling price of £14. Product B has a marginal cost of £6 and a selling price of £8. Fixed costs are £1,400.

Exhibit 24.5

Profit, or loss, at different volumes of activity

	A	B	A	B	A	B	A	B
Units sold	100	100	200	200	300	300	400	400
	£	£	£	£	£	£	£	£
Contribution (Selling Price less Marginal cost) A £4 per unit, B £2 per unit	400	200	800	400	1,200	600	1,600	800
Total Contributions		600		1,200		1,800		2,400
Fixed Overhead		1,400		1,400		1,400		1,400
Net Loss		£800		£200				
Net Profit						£400		£1,000

Here the selling price always exceeds marginal cost, but if activity is low the firm will incur a loss.

The main lessons to be learned about selling prices is that:

(a) Selling prices should exceed marginal costs.

(b) In the long term the total contributions at given volumes must exceed the fixed costs of the firm.

Maximisation of Total Contribution

It should be stressed that it is the maximisation of the total contribution from a product that is important. In this the volumes of activity cannot be disregarded. Suppose for instance that a firm could only manufacture two products in future, whereas to date it had manufactured three. It may well be that per unit the contribution may well have been (A) £10, (B) £8 and (C) £6. If a decision was made on this basis only then (C) would be discontinued. However, if the volumes were (A) 20, (B) 15 and (C) 30, then the total contributions would be (A) 20×£10 = £200: (B) 15×£8 = £120: (C) 30×£6 = £180. As (B) has the lowest *total* contribution it should be (B) that is discontinued, not (C).

Assignment Exercises

24.1A. Glasses Ltd. make four different products, Q, R, S and T. They have ascertained the cost of direct materials and direct labour and the variable overhead for each unit of product. An attempt is made to allocate the other costs in a logical manner. When this is done 10 per cent is added for profit.

The cost of direct labour and materials per unit is Q £14; R £28; S £60; T £32.
Variable overheads per unit are Q £4; R £8; S £13; T £12.
Fixed overhead of £1,900 is allocated per unit as Q £2; R £4; S £7; T £6.
You are required:

(a) Calculate the prices at which the units would be sold by Glasses Ltd. if the full-cost system of pricing was adhered to.

(b) What would you advise the company to do if, because of market competition, prices had to be fixed at Q £33; R £39; S £70; T £49?

(c) Assuming production of 100 units of each item per accounting period, what would be the net profit (i) if your advice given in your answer to (b) was followed, (ii) if the firm continued to produce all of the items?

(d) What would you advise the company to do if, because of market competition, prices had to be fixed at Q £17; R £48; S £140; T £39?

(e) Assuming production of 100 units of each item per accounting period, what would be the net profit (i) if your advice given in your answer to (d) was followed, (ii) if the firm continued to produce all of the items.

24.2A. Bottles Ltd. makes six different products, F, G, H, I, J and K. An analysis of costs ascertains the following:

Per Unit	F	G	H	I	J	K
	£	£	£	£	£	£
Direct labour and direct materials	15	17	38	49	62	114
Variable cost	6	11	10	21	22	23

Fixed costs of £11,400 are allocated per unit as F £4; G £7; H £7; I £10; J £16 and K £13.
Using full-cost pricing 20 per cent is to be added per unit for profit.
You are required to:

(a) Calculate the prices that would be charged by Bottles Ltd. if the full- cost pricing system was adhered to.

(b) What advice would you give the company if a survey of the market showed that the prices charged could be F £26; G £26; H £66; I £75; J £80; K £220?

(c) Assuming production of 200 units per period of each unit manufactured what would be the profit of the firm (i) If your advice in (b) was followed, (ii) if the firm continued to produce all of the items?

(d) Suppose that in fact the market survey had revealed instead that the prices charged could F £30; G £33; H £75; I £66; J £145 and K £130, then what would your advice have been to the company?

(e) Assuming that production of each item manufactured was 200 units per month, then what would have been the profit (i) If your advice in (d) had been followed, (ii) if the company chose to continue manufacturing all items?

24.3 Jugs Ltd. make five different products — A, B, C, D and E. These have been costed per unit as:

Direct Materials and Direct Labour: A £16; B £19; C £38; D £44; E £23.
Variable overhead: A £11; B £17; C £23; D £14; E £9.

Fixed overhead totalling £3,600 per period is allocated per unit, on a basis of a production of 100 units of each item per period, as A £3; B £4; C £9; D £12; E £8.
When the total cost is found 10 per cent is added for profit.
You are required to:

(a) Ascertain the selling prices of each item if the full-cost pricing system is used.

(b) Owing to competition and the general state of the market, if prices had to be fixed at A £32; B £49; C £56; D £66; E £48; what would be your advice to the directors of Jugs Ltd?

(c) Assuming production of 100 units per item would what be the net profit or loss (i) If your advice under (b) was adhered to by the company, (ii) If the company continued to produce all the items?

(d) Suppose instead that the state of the market was different, and that the prices had to be fixed at A £24; B £38; C £68; D £64; E £29; what would be your advice to the directors?

(e) Assuming production of 100 units per item, what would be the net profit or loss (i) If your advice under (d) was adhered to by the company, (ii) If the company continued to produce all the items?

24.4. Bunghole Ltd. make four different products: Cork, Plastic, Screwtop and Wedge. They have ascertained the cost of direct materials and direct labour and variable overhead which they state to be: Direct Labour and Materials: Cork £14, Plastic £5, Screwtop £37 and Wedge £23; Variable Overhead: Cork £22, Plastic £13, Screwtop £9 and Wedge £17.

The fixed expenses totalling £3,000 have been allocated between the products per unit produced as: Cork £4, Plastic £2, Screwtop £14 and Wedge £10. When this has been done a figure equal to 10 per cent of the total cost is added for profit.
You are required to:

(a) Calculate the prices at which the products would be sold by Bunghole Ltd. if the full-cost system of pricing was adhered to.

(b) What would you advise the company to do, if, because of competition, prices had to be fixed at: Cork £43, Plastic £16, Screwtop £58, and Wedge £59?

(c) Assuming production and sales of 100 units of each product per period, taking the selling prices in (b) above, find what would be the net profit or loss if the firm followed your advice.

(d) What would you advise the company to do, if because of competition prices had to be fixed at: Cork £49, Plastic £20, Screwtop £55 and Wedge £37?

(e) Assuming production of 100 units of each item per accounting period, what would be the net profit or loss (i) if your advice given in your answer to (d) was followed, (ii) if the firm continued to produce all of the items.

25

Introduction to Relevant Costs

One of the most difficult decisions facing a manager is to choose between alternative courses of action where there are a variety of complex issues involved. Usually one of the key issues he will have to face is one involving costs in which case it is important to make use of the available cost information correctly. Wrong conclusions can easily be drawn from cost information which is presented in ways that do not make clear the assumptions underlying the preparation of those costs. This was clearly seen in Chapter 24 on Pricing Policy.

For example if the estimated costs of Product X next period are:

	£	
Variable Cost	10,000	
Fixed Cost	20,000	
Total Cost	30,000	÷ estimated production of 15,000 units

= £2 per unit.

Simply to state that the cost is £2 may be misleading since the decision may involve changing the number of units produced to 18,000 units and the costs would therefore be

	£	
Variable Cost	12,000 (+ 20%)	
Fixed Cost	20,000 (no change)	
Total Cost	32,000	÷ estimated production of 18,000 units

= £1.78 per unit

In other words costs figures are usually only valid at certain assumed levels of production and cannot be used outside that level.

One of the hardest things to do in practice is to define the problem properly. A manager may be aware of a particular difficulty — for example a component may always cause difficulty through delayed production — but the solution may not always be obvious. The manager may think that the reason for delayed production is faulty machinery which frequently breaks down — in fact the difficulty may lay with the workforce which is inadequately trained — which is the real reason for machine breakdowns and therefore the basic problem. Not only is the definition of the real problem often difficult but also finding the full range of solutions to the problem.

Clearly considering all the possibilities to solve any problem is likely to involve too much work. Some judgement often has to be used to select the most likely winners. Very often what goes on at the present time is used as a basis for comparison with the alternatives to see if a change is worthwhile, i.e. cost effective.

Having collected together the alternative courses of action that look feasiable the next stage is to evaluate all the factors capable of being measured. If machinery is involved — how much will it cost to buy or rent? how much power will it use and therefore cost to operate? what will the cost of wages be? and so on. All of these costs can be totalled for each alternative to provide comparative costs of the choices.

In any set of alternatives it should not be forgotten that there are many things that can't be expressed in quantitative and therefore cost terms. For example the attitude of employees towards new equipment may be crucial — in extreme cases they may refuse to operate it. The benefits of new equipment may be hard to evaluate because they are intangible — though nontheless real. A new computer may speed up information flows and increase the total available sources of information — but what is this worth? Probably only a guess can be made in advance of the decision — however this type of judgement should always be made together with all the hard facts that can be collected in evidence. The cost consequences of decisions should always be considered even though they don't give the complete picture.

The use of marginal costs on decisions about pricing and whether a product line should be dropped or continued was considered in the previous chapter. Another typical example of using cost information in this way is a decision about whether a product should be manufactured internally or bought in from an outside supplier.

Example: A company currently manufactures a valve which is incorporated in another product. The valve costs are as follows:

Unit Cost

	£
Direct Material	1.50
Direct Labour — variable	2.50
Manufacturing Overheads:	
Variable	0.50
Fixed	1.50
	6.00

The fixed costs are based on a total cost estimate of £150,000 with 100,000 valves produced.

The company discovers that it could buy the value outside for £5.00 — should it therefore discontinue manufacture?

We know that the unit variable cost is £5.00 which is below the price of £5.00 we can buy at from outside. The decision is thus not straightforward — it would only be definite if the variable costs were more than £5.00 — when it would clearly pay us to buy in.

The question therefore is whether the 50p per unit difference between the variable cost of £4.50 and the buying price of £5 is in fact a worthwhile contribution to our fixed overheads of £150,000. Often it is useful to express the options in total cost terms rather than in unit costs:

Producing 100,000 Units:	£	Buying in 100,000 units	
Direct Material	150,000	Supplier	500,000
Direct Labour	250,000		
Variable Overhead	50,000		
	450,000		500,000
Fixed Overhead	150,000		?
	600,000		?

The query is how much of the Fixed Overhead will remain to be carried by the firm if manufacture is ceased and the valves bought in. If all the cost remains then the total cost of buying in would be £500,000 + £150,000 = £650,000 which is more than the costs of making ourselves. It is likely however that some element of the Fixed Overhead could be absorbed by expanding some other activity or by economy measures. If the remaining unabsorbed fixed costs fall below £100,000 then it would be worth considering the proposal to buy in.

Cost will not be the only consideration however since once manufacture is ceased the firm may lose control of essential things like quality and reliability of supply. The supplier may quickly put up his price if there is limited competition. These and other non-financial considerations may override the purely financial out-turn.

Scarce Resources

If a firm is operating in circumstances where one or more of its resources are limited — then to produce the maximum contribution the unit contribution for each product must be related to the scarce resource.

Illustration

A firm produces two products A and B. The firm can sell as many units as it can make and neither product is dependent for its market on the other. However the manufacture requires skilled labour and the firm only has 400 labour hours at its disposal. The details of the two products are as follows:

	A	B
	£	£
Unit Selling Price	40	20
Unit Variable Cost	36	18
Contribution per unit	4	2
Labour Hours per unit	4	1

At first glance product A with a unit contribution of £4 appears to be more attactive than B which has a unit contribution of £2. However A needs 4 hours of scarce labour whilst B only requires 1 hour. The contribution per labour hour for A is therefore £1 (£4 ÷ 4 hrs) whilst for B it is £2 (£2 ÷ 1 hr). Thus B appears better in terms of contribution per labour hour. This can also be shown in total terms as follows:

Total Contribution

It total hours are used to produce all A then the units produced

will be $\dfrac{400}{4}$ = 100 units × £4 per unit £400

If total hours are used to produce all B then the units produced

will be $\dfrac{400}{1}$ = 400 units × £2 per unit £800

The problem becomes more complex if the firm faces scarce resources in more than one input. For example if both labour and machine time are scarce then it is probably no longer possible to rank the products on the sample basis of contribution per hour since there are both labour and machine hours involved which may give different results. These problems can however be solved using linear programming techniques – but are not developed in this book.

Opportunity Costs

The real problem we are examining in evaluating decisions is to estimate the influence of the decision on resources available to the firm. Where the resources involved are variable costs like direct materials in current and continual use then the impact of the decision is usually clear – we can measure how much material is being used and what it's current market price is. Where however the resource involved is in some old little used asset how do we assess its value? The only way this can be done is to assess the impact of a particular decision. For example a decision which makes use of an asset should bear the cost of the impact of the decision on the asset. If using it reduces its value because of the wear and tear or usage involved then the cost is the loss in value. The same decision may prevent the asset being sold − since it is not required for any other purpose − the cost of the decision is therefore the price that could be obtained from selling the asset.

The reasoning is:

1) Establish the things which will be required as a consequent of your decision.

2) Determine what the business would do with the things required in 1) in the best available alternative.

3) The cost of the decision can now be assessed since it is the value of the items concerned evaluated by reference to the best alternative use in 2) (Which the business cannot undertake because of its decision).

Example

A business has in stock two raw materials which are suitable for an order enquiry it has just received. Material M of 10 tons originally cost £50 per ton. It costs £60 per ton to replace but has a scrap value if sold of only £20 per ton. Material Q of 8 tons originally cost £30 a ton. It has a replacement cost of £80 per ton and a scrap value of £5 per ton.

The order enquiry involves using 5 tons of M and 6 tons of Q. Material M is in continuous use and on use it is always replaced. Material Q is old stock left over from discontinued processes and if used would not be replaced. It is likely to be scrapped in the near future to release storage space.

Stages 1 and 2 of the decision are clearly set out above. the cost of the decision to take the order would be − for Material M the use of 5 tons at a value of £60 per ton = £300. This must be the cost of the decision since if used the material is replaced. For Material Q the decision is different because the best alternative use is scrap which has a value of £5 per ton which for 6 tons is worth £30. The replacement cost is not relevant since there is no intention to replace this item.

The value of materials implied by the order is therefore £330 and if the price is sufficient to cover this the business should consider it. Notice that the historic cost which for M is £250 (5×£50) and for Q is £180 (6×£30) is not relevant to the decision.

The idea of valuing a resource in terms of its alternative best use is often called opportunity costing, − a concept frequently used in economics. It of course presupposes that the decision taken knows what the best alternatives are.

Management in practice often has to take decisions with very inadequate information. Nonetheless it is better to try to approximate through the correct approach than not to attempt an assessment of this type at all — since a purely historic cost approach is likely to be very misleading.

The ideas discussed here are further developed in Chapter 33.

Assignment Exercises

25.1. Thomas Machines Ltd produces a part used in large assemblies in a special department. The current years' costs have been as follows:

	£
Direct Materials	100,000
Direct Labour	60,000
Variable Overhead	55,000
Fixed Overhead	95,000
	310,000

During the year 1000 parts have been produced. A new contract for the company would involve increasing output to 1,500 parts. This could be done by introducing a work system which would increase direct labour costs by 10%. The cost control department has recently obtained a quotation from an outside supplier to supply the part for £240 each, which is considerably less than the £310 it costs Thomas Machines to manufacture. If the part was sub-contracted £40,000 of fixed overhead could be removed, the balance would remain.

What would you recommend the company to do?

25.2. Zebrite Productions Company produces three products X, Y, and Z all of which use a material called Zebo which is in short supply.

Faced with prospects of further cuts in material supplies with only 1,000 lbs being available it wants to know which products to concentrate on. The products are independent of eachother and have market demands well in excess of available supplies.

Product		X		Y		Z
Direct Material	lbs	£	lbs	£	lbs	£
Zebo	20	200	10	100	5	50
Direct Labour and						
Variable Overhead		50		40		30
Fixed Overhead		30		30		30
Total Unit Cost		280		170		110
Selling Price		560		340		220

25.3. For a special short term project Alexit PLC wants to use the following items:

1. Material 105 which originally cost £5,000 but is no longer used. Its replacement cost would be £10,000 but its realisable value if sold £1,000.

2. A machine originally costing £40,000 now depreciated by £25,000 to a book valueof £15,000. If not used on the project the machine would be sold for £3,000. Its replacement cost is £50,000. At what value should they be charged to the project?

25.4A. The managers' of the Tenco Company are considering whether to continue the manufacture of a sub-assembly or whether to buiy it in from another firm. The costs related to the annual usage of 50,000 are as follows:

	£
Direct Material	150,000
Direct Labour	200,000
Variable Overheads	50,000
Fixed Overhead	300,000
	700,000

If the sub assembly is bought in the variable costs would be expected to reduce by 90% and the fixed costs to reduce by 20%. The quoted price for buying in is £10 per unit.

Should the sub-assembly be bought-in or continue to be manufactured by the company?

25.5A. Ace Zoots Company manufactures a cutting tool assembled from one each of two components A and B. The machinery in use in the workshop can be used to make either component. The workshop currently is working at full capacity − which is determined by the machine time available. 1200 machine hours are available. The details of manufacture are as follows:

	Machine Hours Used	Unit Variable Cost £	Unit Fixed Cost £	Total Cost £
Component A	10	50	20	70
B	20	60	60	120
Assembly Cost		100	40	140
	30	210	120	330
Selling price				500

At the present time the company manufactures 40 units which uses all the machine time (40 units × 30 hours per unit = 1200 hrs). There has been a considerable increase in demand however and the company could sell up to 120 units per annum at the existing price. It can sub-contract Component A at a cost of £80 per unit and Component B at £90 per unit.

Which course of action would you recommend?

25.6A. Alberta Company operates a department producting wooden boxes for packing purposes. It is considering buying the boxes from a specialised supplier. The costs of the department which produces 10,000 boxes per annum are as follows:

	£
Timber at cost	1,000
Nails, Wire etc. at cost	500
Rent or premises	1,500
Depreciation of machine	800
Direct Labour	5,000
Allocated Fixed Cost	2,000
	10,800

The following explanations are related to the costs of the department:

(a) Timber is valued at the current market replacement price for the material used.

(b) Nails, wire etc represents a proportion of the original price paid two years ago for a large supply bought at a liquidation sale. It cost £5,000 and was expected to last for 10 years. Five years supply is left and this at replacement price would cost £4,500. However the current supplies left in stock if sold off would only raise £500.

(c) Rent of premises represents the rent paid on a lease obtained some years ago. The equivalent market rental for similar space is now £2,500 per annum. The company is currently looking for space to rent similar to that occupied by the box department, in order to expand another department.

(d) Depreciation of machine represents the straight line depreciation charge on a machine bought 3 years ago. It cost £8,000 and had an expected life of 10 years and nil scrap value. Its current book value is therefore £5,600 i.e. Cost of £8,000 less Aggregate Depreciation of $3 \times £800 = £2,400$. If the department no longer needs the machine it would be sold at an expected price of £2,000.

(e) Direct Labour is the wages of the operatives in the department. Other departments would take over any operatives if the department shut.

(f) Allocated fixed costs represent general overheads which would not reduce if the department closed.

The company could buy the boxes for 95p each from an outside suppliers. This cost amounting to £9,500 appears cheaper than continuing to manufacture itself. Should it manufacture or buy in?

26

Budgetary Control

In the chapters on Budgetary Control in the first year book *Finance*, the way in which an organisation developed its budgets was described in detail. The ways in which budgetary controls function may be summarised as:

1. Forecasting
2. Planning
3. Measuring
4. Authorising.

This is also described under the Management Process in Chapter 14.

Forecasting

Forecasting is the process of anticipating the future in so far as it affects the organisation. This involves two aspects, firstly the outside environment which determines the overall demand for the organisation's goods or services. It will be determined by political and economic factors; locally, nationally and internationally. Secondly there is the internal situation that is determined by management decisions. The management will always have to react to the outside environment whether good or bad. However it will have a choice as to how far it wishes to attempt to change the external environment by direct action, such as, for example, advertising or other promotional activity. A management seeking to change its fortunes by creating new opportunities is called pro-active, rather than simply responding to the market which is reactive. In practice good managers are both pro-active and reactive.

Forecasts which seek to quantify the future so far as an organisation is concerned need to predict both the outside environment and the organisations planned internal strategies. The area in which this activity is most difficult is in Capital Budgeting where the resources may be invested over many future years. Operational Budgets which usually look only one year ahead are less difficult but nonetheless need a great deal of care.

Forecasting the future can be done best where analysis of past data is a good guide to what is likely to happen in the future. Where there tends to be continuity from one period to another careful analysis of past information about the external market, as well as the organisation's own performance, is undertaken by using accounting and statistical analysis. The aspects of this analysis which are most useful in budgetting are in relation to cost behaviour patterns, which were described in detail in the first year course book *Finance*. Similarly the analysis of friends in Ratios was described in Chapter 13 of this book. In both of these cases a statistical technique such as 'least squares' is used to plot the trend of data over a number of time periods so that, for example, costs at different levels of activity may be accurately predicted. This analysis enables the likely outcomes of planned activities to be forecast with greater confidence than might otherwise be the case. However it can never be overstressed that new factors can arise which completely alter the market. For example new legislation may prevent a product being sold at all in future, or a technical innovation may completely alter the cost structure of an industry in a very short period.

Forecasting therefore uses past data to help anticipate the future − but inevitably must sometimes be based on much more uncertain grounds. Where new products or processes are concerned which will take a number of years to establish themselves − even where they prove successful − the forecasts are more in the nature of 'educated guesses' than a projection of previous experience.

Planning

The process of forecasting leads to the identification of a set of choices which the organisation faces. Planning is the process of deciding which paths to follow and identifying the resources required. Planning is usually divided into long range or strategic planning which is concerned with deciding the overall objectives and direction the organisation should follow. The process of budgetary control however is based on the shorter term translation of strategic plans into operational plans. A budget in this context is concerned with what is expected to happen in the next operating period − usually one year ahead. The main aim to promote efficiency by making sure that labour, materials and capital are available at the right place and time − thus eliminating waste through the anticipation of problems likely to arise. Budgetary control seeks to co-ordinate the resources available in the way that promotes the achievement of an organisation's objectives to best advantage.

Measuring

The comparison of what has been planned in the operational budget with what actually happens in reality is a major element in the use of budgets for control purposes. The analysis of variances on a regular short-term basis (for example monthly) should warn management of any trends developing in actual performance which require replanning. Management have to continually re-evaluate what they are doing in the light of what is happening in the world outside the organisation. Where things are changing fast the budgets may have to be revised frequently. Many firms prepare 'rolling' budgets which means that they continually update the budgets for a fixed period ahead. For example each month an additional month twelve months ahead is added — together with any changes necessary to the intervening eleven months.

The measurement process requires to explain why the budget plan differs from actual. This detailed explanation of variances will be explained under the chapters on standard costing. In addition it is important that those preparing budgets should use past experience to improve future planning activities. This is known as a 'feedback' process, i.e. learning from previous mistakes and successes.

Authorising

An important function of budgetary control which is widely used in large organisations is a method of delegating authority. The approval of a budget for the following period by senior management, authorises lower levels of management to operate within the approved budget without obtaining fresh authority for each transaction. For example an engineer working for a local authority will be authorised to build a new road bridge if it was allowed in his annual budget. Without this 'budget authority' separate authority to spend the money would have to be obtained. Whilst this use of budgets may be very convenient for most routine activities it has also a number of problems. It may for example motivate managers to operate very narrowly within budget confines and pay little attention to opportunities for new initiatives which may, if considered independently, be very attractive.

In its worst manifestations managers will seek to increase the approved budget amount by 'padding' their estimates and ignoring possible ways of immediate cost saving. In this way they feel confident of keeping their actual cost within budget without too much problem.

The essence of successful use of budgeting in the context is therefore to consider how effectively and objectively the budgeted amounts are vetted by top management. Only if careful control is exercised on setting the budgets will this form of budgetary control be successful.

Using Budgets

Budgetary Control is a highly desirable element in the way any but the smallest organisation is managed. In its most basic form the development of a 'Business Plan' to calculate the financial requirements is a fundamental. Virtually all banks and finance companies require such a statement covering the next year in detail and up to another four years in broad terms.

Having started on the process of preparing a business plan, the management usually follows the logical step of breaking down the overall plan into smaller parts which coincide with the responsibility of lower levels of management. This process of informing managers of what they are required to achieve in a clear numerical format is called 'Responsibility Accounting' and is discussed in the next chapter.

Another extension of the budgeting process is to expand the use of planned costs into the costing of products. This process is usually called Standard Costing and is explained in later chapters. Standard Costing is thus a particular form of budgeting which some organisation find useful, particularly where they need access to detailed costs for their products or activities. The analysis of variances developed in these chapters on standard costing could be used in other areas of budgeting.

27

Responsibility Accounting

The development of modern organisations employing many people involves the creation of a management structure which delegates responsibility from one manager to several lower level employees called subordinates. In its simple basic form this type of management structure forms a pyramid with lower levels of management made responsible for limited areas of activity and responding upwards to senior managers for guidance and support where it is required.

Exhibit 27.1
Organisation Chart for Part of an Organisation

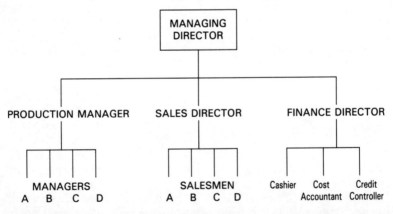

Exhibit 27.1 is a simplified organisation chart which shows that the Managing Director is the top level of management who delegates responsibility to three specialised directors in the areas of Production, Sales and Finance. They in turn delegate to lower levels of management. In a large organisation there can be many levels of delegation and in consequence a very complex organisation chart of relationships. The type of structure shown is called hierarchical because authority is passed down from the top to lower management levels. With the authority goes responsibility – those who are given the power implied by a particular management job are also

required to account for how well they perform the job to those above them. Even the managing director will usually have to account for the whole organisations performance to a board of directors acting for the shareholders.

Some different forms of organisation have evolved to meet the needs of different industries. For example a matrix form of relationship has been evolved in some aerospace industry organisations. The management is organised on one side by functions as in the traditional hierarchical structure, i.e. a sales manager responding to a director in charge of a project. A team of people from different functions are allocated to the firms major projects each under the direction of a project director or leader. Thus the sales manager in addition to responding to his sales director will also respond to the project leader to which he is assigned.

Thus the actual way an organisation is structured will vary considerably in practice. Some will be very formal and hierarchical — others much more informal with authority being shared on a broader basis. The important thing is that in all organisations there needs to be control whatever the actual structure adopted and the basic features of control will remain the same.

Control in this context means influencing people to behave in the way you want them to, rather than in a way that they would themselves prefer. Absence of control means that everybody in the organisation would have complete autonomy — to come and go as they wished to work hard or not at all. The extremes of absolute control where everyone behaves like a programmed machine and total anarchy where everyone does their own thing are not normally found. Most organisations have to find the right level of control which the people in the organisation respond to best. Too much control and people will lose motivation because they feel they are only cogs in a huge machine and are dehumanised. Too little control and there will be waste of resources with no proper coordination of effort.

It is always important to realise that an organisation is nothing other than a collection of people. Organisations do not think — only the people who work in them can do that. An organisation cannot do anything of itself — but will do what the most powerful person or group of people want it to do. This top management group are therefore 'the organisation' for purposes of control and making the crucial decisions about the way in which the organisation should be structured.

In the earlier chapters methods have been described of preparing accounting information to help management. The analysis of costs in order that the products or services of the organisation can be costed is clearly of great importance. Similarly the extension from historic costs into future plans which is worked in budgeting and standard costing provides key information for control. However in these chapters most of the emphasis is on the cost of activities, output or products, rather than the cost of an individual managers area of responsibility.

In a manufacturing business a cost centre is used for collecting costs related to the job or process. This focus of cost collection will often coincide with an area of management responsibility, although not always. In addition focusing on responsibility may be the only way of controlling non-manufacturing costs such as administration and marketing.

A responsibility centre is any part of an organisation for which a manager is responsible. It may be relatively small compared to the whole organisation for example a small department employing only two people on personnel work, but on the other hand a senior manager may be responsible for a major operating division of the organisation which is a major business in its own right. Like the organisation chart the responsibility at the lower levels will be limited and at the top level will cover the whole. Appropriate ways of collecting the information for areas of responsibility will have to be developed.

The following example illustrates the difference between analysis of costs by product and by responsibility center.

Green Company Ltd. manufactures two products X and Y in its small factory. Each product is manufactured in three process departments and in addition there is a packing and distribution department, a sales department and an accounting department.

The costs are analysed in the first instance every three months in terms of each product produced. For the first quarter of 19-1 the figures were:

Product Costs	Product X	Product Y	Total
	£	£	£
Direct Material	8,000	15,000	23,000
Direct Labour	4,000	7,000	11,000
Factory Overheads	3,000	6,000	9,000
Packing & Distribution	2,000	4,000	6,000
Selling	2,000	3,000	5,000
Accounting	1,200	2,000	3,200
	20,200	37,000	57,200
Units Produced	4,000	12,000	
Unit Cost £	5.05	3.09	

However in order to determine responsibility for the costs they are also allocated to Departments which are responsibility centers.

Responsibility Center Costs	Process 1 Dept.	Process 2 Dept.	Process 3 Dept.	Packing & Distribution Dept.	Selling Dept.	Accounting Dept.	Total
	£	£	£	£	£	£	£
Direct Material	9,000	4,000	10,000				23,000
Direct Labour	4,000	3,000	4,000				11,000
Indirect Labour & Salaries	2,000	3,000	1,000	3,000	3,000	2,600	14,600
Sundry Supplies	1,000	1,500	500	2,000	500	600	6,100
Transport				1,000			1,000
Travelling					1,500		1,500
	16,000	11,500	15,500	6,000	5,000	3,200	57,200

At the lower levels of management very often it is only realistic to measure the expenses of a responsibility centre. To measure the output of many departments in monetary terms is not realistic. For example in the personnel department it is straightforward to measure the salary, wages and other costs of the department but the value of the work done in interviewing potential employees, maintaining staff record cards etc. can not be accurately assessed. Responsibility centres where only the costs can be measured are called Expense Centres.

Where the responsibility centre covers a broader section of the organisation it may be possible to measure revenues as well as expenses. Here we are usually talking about an activity which can be viewed as a smaller business within the overall organisation. If we can measure both revenues and expenses then we can prepare a Profit and Loss Account to measure performance. This type of responsibility centre is called a profit centre.

An extension of the Profit Centre is also very common in large organisations where the assets employed in the Profit Centre are exclusive to it. Here the responsibility centre has not only its Profit and Loss Account but its own Balance Sheeet showing the resources invested in the centre. These are known as Investment Centres. Many of the largest companies in the world break down their activities into operating divisions which are Investment Centres.

Control of Profit and Investment Centres is similar to controlling a whole business and will not be further developed in this book. Control of expense centres is important and is relevant to topics covered earlier on cost centres and budgeting.

For purposes of presenting the information to the responsible managers costs are collected for each responsibility center and presented in a format resembling that in Exhibit 27.2.

Department Cost Report for Department B Period: January

	This Month £	Budget for Month £	Year to Date £	Budget Year to Date £	Budget Variance
Direct Materials	5,000	4,800	16,000	14,400	(1,600)
Direct Labour	3,000	3,500	8,500	10,500	2,000
Supervision Cost	1,000	1,200	3,500	3,600	100
Indirect Labour	800	790	2,700	2,370	(330)
Supplies	1,200	1,100	3,400	3,300	(100)
Other Costs	900	900	2,900	2,700	(200)
Total	11,900	12,290	37,000	36,870	130

Exhibit 27.2

The information included in Exhibit 27.2 may be extended to include columns for the previous years figures where this is judged to be useful.

The important thing to determine before a manager is judged on his departments performance is the extent to which he can genuinely influence the costs for that department. Some costs he may control entirely, others may be allocated to him and not be within his power to alter. Part of the solution has already been suggested by the use of flexible budgets. The use of a flexible budget implies that careful thought has been given to varying the figures in line with actual levels of prevailing activity. However this will not entirely solve the problem of costs allocated from outside and care must be taken not to penalise people for things over which they do not have control. Just because a cost is variable does not mean it is automatically controllable. Detailed consideration will have to be given to the facts in each responsibility centre.

Assignment Exercises

27.1A. Explain what is meant by a cost centre and a responsibility centre.

27.2A. What is the difference between expense centres, profit centres and investment centres?

27.3A. What is the significance of 'controllable costs' for management control?

28

Standard Costing: An Introduction

A cost accounting system can be said to be either an actual cost system or a standard cost system. The difference is not in the systems themselves but rather on the kind of costs that are used. In the costing systems already shown we have seen that they have consisted of the actual costs for direct materials and direct labour, and overhead has been charged by reference to a pre-determined overhead rate. Standard costing uses the costs that should have been incurred. So standard costing has costs that should have been incurred, whilst other systems mainly use costs that have been incurred.

In an actual cost accounting system costs are traced through the records as product costs. On the other hand standard costing uses standards of performance and of prices derived from studying operations and of estimating future prices. Each unit being produced can have a standard material cost, a standard direct labour cost and a standard overhead cost. As with any form of management accounting this does not in fact have to be carried out fully, for instance some companies will use standard labour and standard overhead costs but may use actual material costs. In the rest of this chapter we will consider firms that use standard costing system for all items.

As with all management accounting the benefits flowing from using standard costing should exceed the costs of operating it, so that there should be advantages accruing from having a standard costing system, and these are:
1.   Usually it is simpler and needs less work than an actual cost system. This is because once the standards have been set they are adhered to, and the standard costs will remain unchanged for fairly long periods. Other systems need constant recalculations of cost. For instance the average cost method of pricing issues of materials needs a recalculation of the price each time there are further receipts, whereas standard cost of materials will remain at a constant figure. This can bring about a reduction in the costs of clerical work.
2.   The unit costs for each identical product will be the same, whereas this may not be the same with actual costing systems. For instance, in an actual cost system two men making identical units may be paid at different wage rates, the materials issued to one man may have come from a slightly later lot of raw materials received which cost more than the previous lot and

therefore the issue price may be higher, and so on. In a standard costing system the same amount would be charged for each of these men, until such time as the standards were altered.

3. A standard cost system provides a better means of checking on the efficiency with which production is carried on, in that the differences between the standard costs and the actual costs, i.e. the variances throw up the changes in efficiency.

4. One important advantage may be that standard costing might make faster reporting available. This is certainly most important, as generally the later information is received the less useful it will be. Standard costing has a great deal of predetermined data when compared with an actual costing system, therefore entering up job order sheets, job sheets and many other tasks can be speeded up if the actual costs do not have to be waited for.

The costs that will have been flowing through the standard costing system is that of standard costs and as actual costs will normally be different, then the difference or variance if adverse (i.e. actual costs have exceeded standard costs) will be debited to the profit and loss account. If the variance is a favourable one (i.e. actual costs have been less than standard costs) then this would be credited to the profit and loss account. This must be done as all the costs used for the calculation of gross profit etc. have been standard costs, and if the variances were not put in the profit and loss account then the net profit would not be the net profit actually made.

Setting Standards

Standard cost accounting is a classic case of the use of the principle of 'management by exception'. Put roughly this means that when things are going according to plan leave them alone, and concentrate instead on the things that are deviating from planned results. With standard costing the actual results that conform to the standards require little attention. Instead management's interest is centred on the exceptions to standards.

Getting the 'right' standards is, therefore, of prime importance. If the 'wrong' standards are used, not only will a lot of time and money have been wasted, but it may bring worse results than if no standard had been set al all. Standards may be unsuitable because they were not set properly, or else that conditions have changed greatly since they were set.

Standards of one of two types can be used; ideal standards and maintainable standards. These are as follows:

1. Ideal standards. These are set at a maximum level of efficiency, and thus represent conditions that really can very rarely be attained. This approach can be seriously objected to, in that if standards are too high, employees who might otherwise be motivated by standards which are possible to achieve may become discouraged.

2. Attainable standards. It is simple for someone to say that individuals will be motivated to attain standards that they are capable of, that they will not exert very much effort to exceed standards, and that standards outside

the capability of a person will not motivate him. From this follows the also easy conclusion that standards should be neither 'too easy' nor 'too difficult' but should be 'just right'. The difficult part of this is in saying what the 'just right' figures are to ask as standards. There is no doubt that the work of behavioural scientists in this area has brought about a far greater insight into such problems. In a very large firm such specialists may be members of the team setting the standards.

The standards for materials and for labour can be divided between those which are concerned with (i) prices and (ii) quantities. Standard overhead costs are divided between standard variable overhead costs, and standard fixed overhead costs.

Assignment Exercises

28.1A. What are the disadvantages of having an actual cost system compared with a standing costing system?

28.2A. What is 'management by exception'?

28.3A. What harm can 'wrong standards' bring about?

28.4A. What objections are there to 'ideal' standards?

28.5A. What are the benefits of using 'attainable' standards?

29

Introduction to Variance Analysis I: Material Variances

The difference between standard cost and actual cost has already been stated to be a variance. Remember these are classified:

Adverse: Actual cost greater than standard cost.

Favourable: Actual cost less than standard cost.

The use of the words favourable and adverse should not be confused with their meaning in ordinary language usage, they are technical terms. Whether a variance is 'good' or 'bad' can only be determined after the cause(s) of the variance have been fully investigated and ascertained.

There is a great deal of difference between the *computation* of the variances and their *analysis*. The computation is simply the mathematical calculation of the variance. The analysis of the variance is a matter requiring a fair amount of judgement, it just cannot be performed in a mechanical fashion.

We can now look at some computations of variances. In fact there are many variances which can be computed, but we will concentrate on a few of the more important ones. In order that sense can be made of the computations and a reasonable job of analysis done, it will be assumed that the standards set were calculated on a rational basis.

N.B. In the computations of variances which follows this, there are diagrams to illustrate the variances which have been calculated. The lines drawn on the diagrams will be as follows:

Representing standard costs _ _ _ _ _ _ _ _ _ _

Representing actual costs ....

Where actual costs and standards costs are the same __.__.__.__.__.__.__

1. Materials Variances — Computations

(a) *Material Price Variances:*

(i) Favourable variance:

Material J	
Standard price per foot	£4
Standard usage per unit	5 feet
Actual price per foot	£3
Actual usage per unit	5 feet

Usage is the same as standard, therefore the only variance is that of price calculated:

	£
Actual cost per unit 5 × £3	15
Standard cost per unit 5 × £4	20
Variance (favourable)	£5

The diagram illustrates this in that the variance is represented by the shaded area. This is £1 by a quantity of 5, therefore the variance is £5. The variance extends to the price line and not the quantity line, therefore it is a price variance.

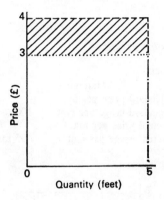

(ii) Adverse variance:

	Material K
Standard price per foot	£9
Standard usage per unit	8 feet
Actual price per foot	£11
Actual usage per unit	8 feet
Variance computed:	£
Actual cost per unit 8 × £11	88
Standard cost per unit 8 × £9	72
Variance (adverse)	£16

The shaded part of the diagram is the variance, this extends £2 times a quantity of 8, therefore the variance is £16. Notice that the shaded area is outside the lines marked ------------ representing standard costs. In the diagrams when the variance is outside the standard cost area as marked by the standard cost lines then it will be an adverse variance. When it is inside the standard cost area as marked by the standard cost lines then it will be a favourable variance.

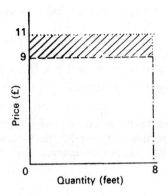

Quantity (feet)

(b) Materials Usage variances

(i) Favourable variance:

	Material L	
Standard price per ton		£5
Standard usage per unit	100 tons	
Actual price per ton		£5
Actual usage per unit	95 tons	

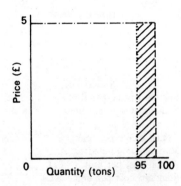

Quantity (tons)

Cost is the same as standard, therefore the only variance is that of usage calculated:

		£
Actual cost per unit 95×£5		475
Standard cost per unit 100×£5		500
Variance (favourable)		25

267

(ii) Adverse variance:

Material M

Standard price per yard		£8
Standard usage per unit		11 yards
Actual price per yard		£8
Actual usage per unit		13 yards
Variance computed:		£
Actual cost per unit 13×£8		104
Standard cost per unit 11×£8		88
Variance (adverse)		16

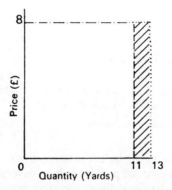

Here again the variances for Materials L and M are shown in diagrams by means of shaded areas. The variances extend to the quantity lines and are, therefore, usage variances. With material L the variance is shown inside the standard cost area, and is, therefore, a favourable variance, whereas material M shows an adverse variance as it is outside the standard cost area.

(c) Combinations of Material and Usage Variances

Most variances are combinations of both material and usage variances. Sometimes one variance will be favourable whilst the other is an adverse one, sometimes both will be adverse variances, and at other times both will be favourable variances.

(i) Favourable and Adverse variances combined:

Material N

Standard price per metre	£6
Standard usage per unit	25 metres
Actual price per metre	£7
Actual usage per metre	24 metres

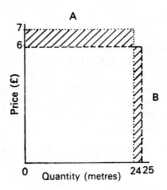

The net variance is calculated as:

	£
Actual cost per unit $24 \times £7$	168
Standard cost per unit $25 \times £6$	150
Variance (adverse)	£18

As the diagram shows this is in fact made up of two variances. The first variance, shown as the shaded portion A, is an adverse price variance (i.e. it is outside the standard cost lines, therefore actual cost has exceeded standard cost). The second variance, shown as the shaded portion B, is a favourable usage variance (i.e. it is inside the standard cost lines, therefore actual usage has been less than standard usage).

The adverse price variance can therefore be seen to be £1 by a quantity of 24 = £24. The favourable usage variance can be seen to be a length of 1 metre by a price of £6 = £6. The net (adverse) variance is therefore made up:

Adverse material price variance	24
Favourable material usage variance	6
Net (adverse) variance	£18

(ii) Both Adverse variances combined:

Material O

Standard price per kilo.	£9
Standard usage per unit	13 kilos
Actual price per kilo.	£11
Actual usage per unit	15 kilos

The net variance is computed:

		£
Actual cost per unit	$15 \times £11$	165
Standard cost per unit	$13 \times £9$	117
Variance (adverse)		£48

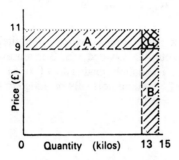

The diagram shows the shaded area A which is definitely a price variance of £2 × 13 = £26 adverse. Shaded area B is definitely a usage variance of 2 × £9 = £18 adverse. This makes up £44 of the variance, but there is the double shaded area, C, of 2 × £2 = £4. This is really an area which is common to both usage and price. Sometimes, although not very often, this would be treated as a separate variance, but as detail is necessarily limited in this book we will just add it to the price variance, making it £26 + £4 = £30, the usage variance being left at £18.

(iii) Both Favourable variances combined:

Material P	
Standard price per ton	£20
Standard usage per unit	15 tons
Actual price per ton	£19
Actual usage per unit	13 tons

The net variance is computed:

		£
Actual cost per unit	$13 \times £19$	247
Standard cost per unit	$15 \times £20$	300
Variance (favourable)		£53

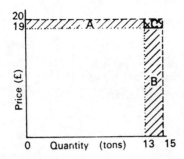

The diagram shows the shaded area A which is definitely a price variance of £1 × 13 = £13 favourable. Shaded area B is a usage variance of 2 × £19 = £38 favourable. The double shaded area C of £1 × 2 = £2, making up the total variance of 53 would normally be added to the usage variance to make it £38 + £2 = £40.

2. Materials Variances — Analysis

(a) Price Variances

The price variance is a simple one in that it is obvious that the purchasing department have not been able to buy at the anticipated price. How far this is completely outside the powers of the purchasing department depends entirely on the facts. It may simply be that the rate of inflation is far greater than it had been possible to foresee, or that special forms of extra taxes have been introduced by the Government. No one can surely blame the purchasing department for not knowing the secrets of the government's budget each year! On the other hand it may have been that poor purchasing control has meant that orders for materials have been placed too late for the firm to manage to get the right price in the market, or that materials which ought to have been bought in bulk have been in fact bought in small lots at uneconomic prices. If there are regular suppliers, a short-term gain by buying a cheaper lot from somewhere else could militate against the firm's benefit in the long run if the firm's regular suppliers took umbrage.

Buying the cheapest materials does not always bring about the achievement of the greatest profit. It may result in more wastages, a greater amount of labour time because the men take longer to do the job with inferior materials, and a unit made up of poor materials may well damage the image of the firm because its products do not last as long as they used to do.

All the same there must be someone to whom the responsibility for the price variance can be traced and he is then accountable for it.

(b) Usage Variances

There are many reasons for excessive use of material. Inferior materials can bring about a lot of waste, so can workers who are not as skilled as they ought to be. Perhaps the machinery is not suitable for the job, or there might even be deliberate wastage of material, e.g. wood wasted so that it can be taken home by workers as fuel etc. The theft of material obviously aggravates a usage variance. Here again responsibility must be traced.

Key Questions of Variances

Before we look at the computation or analysis of any further variances this is a convenient point to raise some fundamental questions about variances. They are:

1. Why do we wish to calculate this particular variance?

2. When it has been calculated what action are we going to take about it?

3. If we are not going to make an effective use of the variance, then why bother at all to calculate it?

Inventory Records under Standard Costing

It is worth noting at this point that when a firm adopts a Standard Costing system it avoids the difficulties described earlier in Chapters 18 and 19 involving FIFO, LIFO or Average Stock methods. In a Standard Costing system all materials received and issued are valued at the Standard Cost in the inventory account. There is no recording problem associated with changing prices during the period since they are separately recorded as variances.

Provided that standards are reviewed sufficiently often this system should ensure that the values of inventories are maintained close to their current value.

Disposition of Variances

The question arises as to how the variances are to be brought into the final accounts of the business. There are, in fact, several methods of dealing with them.

They can be treated entirely as costs (if adverse variances) which are period costs and are, therefore, not included in the valuation of closing stocks of finished goods or work in progress. Alternatively they may be brought in as product costs and therefore used in the valuation of closing stocks. Another variation is to treat those variances which are controllable as period costs, but the uncontrollable variances be treated as product costs. All of these methods are acceptable for the final accounts which are used for external reporting.

Example of Standard Costing in Inventory Records

Using the data from Exhibit 19.1 and assuming the following standard costs which were revised at the beginning of each year:
Year 1   £11 per unit: Year 2   £14 per unit: Year 3   £20 per unit.

	Opening Stock	Price Variance	Receipts	Issues	End of Year Stock
Year 1	Nil	Nil	40×£11=£440	30×£11=£330	10×£11=£110
2	10×£14=£140	Opening Stock F 30			
		Receipts F 10	30×£14=£420	32×£14=£448	8×£14=£112
3	8×£20=£160	Opening Stock F 48			
		Receipts U 6	42×£20=£840	36×£20=£720	14×£20=£280

Note the Price Variances include the adjustment of the opening stock to the new standard at the start of the period, and the difference between standard and actual price of goods received in the period.

Trading and Profit and Loss Accounts

Year	1		2		3	
	£	£	£	£	£	£
Sales		420		512		864
Opening Stock at standard cost	–		140		160	
Purchases	440		420		840	
	440		560		1,000	
Less Closing Stock	110		112		280	
Cost of Goods Sold		330		448		720
Standard Gross Profit		90		64		144
Price Variances		–	F	40	F	42
		90		104		186
Expenses		50		60		80
Net Profits		40		44		106

By comparison the profits for:			
AVCO	40	36	100
FIFO	50	34	120
LIFO	30	22	46
Replacement	40	20	64

The difference between the profits using standard costs and AVCO, FIFO and LIFO depends on the standard price and on the way the price variances are treated. In this example the variances on opening stock are dealt with

273

at the beginning of the period. Often the standards are revised more frequently than annually and thus these variances would be spread through the year.

Assignment Exercises

29.1A. Calculate the material variances from the following data, stating whether they are price variances or usage variances, and whether they are adverse or favourable.

(i)	Material A:	Standard price per ton	£40
		Standard usage per unit	11 tons
		Actual price per ton	£40
		Actual usage per unit	13 tons
(ii)	Material B:	Standard price per metre	£25
		Standard usage per unit	60 metres
		Actual price per metre	£28
		Actual usage per unit	60 metres
(iii)	Material C:	Standard price per lb.	£3
		Standard usage per unit	1,000 lb.
		Actual price per lb.	£3
		Actual usage per unit	973 lb.
(iv)	Material D:	Standard price per yard	£17
		Standard usage per unit	440 yards
		Actual price per yard	£14
		Actual usage per unit	440 yards

(handwritten annotations: "70." beside Material B standard usage; "£5" beside Material C actual price; "500" beside Material D standard usage)

29.2A. Draw graphs from the data in 29.1 letting a shaded area be the variance. Use lines drawn as ---------- to represent standard costs, lines drawn .... representing actual costs, and lines drawn __.__.__.__ where standard costs and actual costs are the same.

29.3A. Calculate the materials variances from the following data.

(i)	Material E:	Standard price per metre	£6
		Standard usage per unit	88 metres
		Actual price per metre	£6
		Actual usage per unit	85 metres
(ii)	Material F:	Standard price per ton	£117
		Standard usage per unit	30 tons
		Actual price per ton	£123
		Actual usage per unit	30 tons
(iii)	Material G:	Standard price per litre	£16
		Standard usage per unit	158 litres
		Actual price per litre	£16
		Actual usage per unit	165 litres

(iv) Material H:	Standard price per foot	£16
	Standard usage per unit	92 feet
	Actual price per foot	£19
	Actual usage per unit	92 feet
(v) Material I:	Standard price per ton	£294
	Standard usage per unit	50 tons
	Actual price per ton	£300
	Actual usage per unit	50 tons
(vi) Material J:	Standard price per kilo	£27.5
	Standard usage per unit	168 kilos
	Actual price per kilo	£27.5
	Actual usage per unit	156 kilos
(vii) Material K:	Standard price per barrel	£44
	Standard usage per unit	23 barrels
	Actual price per barrel	£44
	Actual usage per unit	25 barrels
(viii)Material L:	Standard price per ton	£248
	Standard usage per unit	40 tons
	Actual price per ton	£232
	Actual usage per unit	40 tons

29.4A. Using the same method as in 29.2 draw graphs of the data in 29.3.

29.5A. Calculate the following materials variances:

(i) Material Q:	Standard price per ton	£20
	Standard usage per unit	34 tons
	Actual price per ton	£18
	Actual usage per unit	37 tons
(ii) Material R:	Standard price per yard	£17
	Standard usage per unit	50 yards
	Actual price per yard	£19
	Actual usage per unit	46 yards
(iii) Material S:	Standard price per metre	£12
	Standard usage per unit	15 metres
	Actual price per metre	£14
	Actual usage per unit	18 metres
(iv) Material T:	Standard price per roll	£40
	Standard usage per unit	29 rolls
	Actual price per roll	£37
	Actual usage per unit	27 rolls
(v) Material U:	Standard price per kilo	£7
	Standard usage per unit	145 kilos
	Actual price per kilo	£8
	Actual usage per unit	154 kilos
(vi) Material V:	Standard price per gallon	£25
	Standard usage per unit	10,000 gallons
	Actual price per gallon	£22
	Actual usage per unit	9,850 gallons

29.6A. Using the same method as in 29.2 draw graphs of the data in 29.5.

29.7. Calculate the following materials variances:

(i)	Material AB:	Standard price per roll	£19
		Standard usage per unit	500 rolls
		Actual price per roll	£17
		Actual usage per unit	482 rolls
(ii)	Material CD:	Standard price per gallon	£50
		Standard usage per unit	22 gallons
		Actual price per gallon	£54
		Actual usage per unit	25 gallons
(iii)	Material EF:	Standard price per litre	£12
		Standard usage per unit	180 litres
		Actual price per litre	£12
		Actual usage per unit	191 litres
(iv)	Material GH:	Standard price per metre	£16
		Standard usage per unit	100 metres
		Actual price per metre	£18
		Actual usage per unit	107 metres
(v)	Material IJ:	Standard price per ton	£105
		Standard usage per unit	200 tons
		Actual price per ton	£99
		Actual usage per unit	200 tons
(vi)	Material JK:	Standard price per mile	£1,000
		Standard usage per unit	29 miles
		Actual price per mile	£1,022
		Actual usage per unit	27 miles

29.8A. Using the same method as in 29.2 draw graphs of the data in 29.7.

30

Introduction to Variance Analysis II: Labour Variances

The computation of labour variances is similar to that of material variances. With labour variances the analysis can be broken down into:

(a) Wage rate variances.

(b) Labour efficiency variances.

Because the computation of labour variances is so similar to those of material variances only two examples will be given.

1. Labour Variances — Computations

(a) *Wage Rate Variance*

Product A	
Standard hours to produce	100
Actual hours to produce	100
Standard wage rate per hour	£0.9
Actual wage rate per hour	£1.0

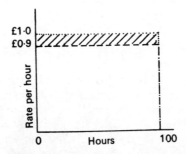

As the actual and standard hours are the same, then the only variance will be a wage rate variance, computed:

		£
Actual cost per unit	100×£1.0	100
Standard cost per unit	100×£0.9	90
Variance (adverse)		£10

The diagram illustrates this in that the variance is represented by the shaded area. This is £0.1 by a quantity of 100, therefore the variance is £10. The variance extends to the wage rate line and it is thus a wage rate variance, and as the shaded area is outside the standard cost lines, indicated by lines marked ------- then it is an adverse variance.

(b) Labour Efficiency Variance

Produce B

Standard hours to produce	400
Actual hours to produce	370
Standard wage rate per hour	£1.0
Actual wage rate per hour	£1.0

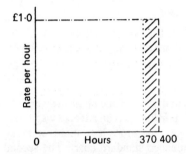

As the actual and standard wage rates are the same, then the only variance will be a labour efficiency variance, computed:

	£
Actual cost per unit 370×£1.0	370
Standard cost per unit 400×£1.0	400
Variance (favourable)	£30

The diagram illustrates this in that the variance is represented by the shaded area. This is a quantity of 30 by a rate of £1.0, therefore the variance is £30. The variance extends to the time line, therefore this is an efficiency variance, as the job has been completed in a different number of hours than standard. As the shaded area is inside the standard cost lines indicated by lines marked ------ then it is a favourable variance.

(c) Combined Wage Rate and Efficiency Variance

Product C

Standard hours to produce	500
Actual hours to produce	460
Standard wage rate per hour	£0.9
Actual wage rate per hour	£1.1

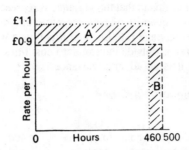

The net variance can be computed as:

	£
Actual cost per unit 460 × £1.1	506
Standard cost per unit 500 × £0.9	450
Variance (adverse)	£56

The diagram shows that this is made up of two variances. The first variance, shown as the shaded portion A, is an adverse wage rate variance (it is outside the standard cost lines, therefore it is an adverse variance because actual cost for this has exceeded standard cost). The second variance, shown as the shaded portion B, is a favourable labour efficiency variance (it is inside the standard cost lines, therefore actual hours have been less than standard hours).

The adverse wage rate variance can, therefore, be seen to be £0.2 by a quantity of 460 = £92. The favourable efficiency variance is a quantity of 40 by a price of £0.9 = £36. The net adverse variance is, therefore, made up of:

	£
Adverse wage rate variance	92
Favourable labour efficiency variance	36
	£56

2. Labour Variances — Analysis

Labour wage rates will probably be set in conjunction with the trade unions involved, so that this variance may not really be subject to control at any other level other than at the bargaining table with the unions involved. Nevertheless such a variance could arise because a higher grade of labour was being used than was necessary, even taking into account trade union needs. It might reflect a job running behind schedule that had to be finished off quickly even though higher grade labour was used. It might have been a rush job that also meant bringing in a higher grade of labour as well. The staffing policy of the firm may have come adrift because they have not recruited sufficient numbers of the various grades of labour.

Labour efficiency variances can be caused by a great number of things. Using unsuitable labour, unsuitable machinery, workers trying to slow work up so that more overtime rates of pay are earned, the day after a bank holiday, or the day before it, can affect performance. The morale of workers, the physical state of workers, using poor materials which slows up production, hold-ups because of bottlenecks in production and so on. The possibilities are almost endless. At the same time if the variance was worth calculating then some form of action should follow, as otherwise there is no point at all in doing the accounting work of calculating such variances.

Assignment Exercises

30.1A. Calculate the labour variances from the following data, stating whether they are rate variances or efficiency variances, and whether they are favourable or adverse.

(i)	Standard hours to produce	20
	Actual hours to produce	22
	Standard wage rate per hour	£1.4
	Actual wage rate per hour	£1.4
(ii)	Standard hours to produce	150
	Actual hours to produce	150
	Standard wage rate per hour	£1.5
	Actual wage rate per hour	£1.6
(iii)	Standard hours to produce	67
	Actual hours to produce	67
	Standard wage rate per hours	£1.7
	Actual wage rate per hour	£1.5
(iv)	Standard hours to produce	200
	Actual hours to produce	189
	Standard wage rate per hour	£1.8
	Actual wage rate per hour	£1.8

30.2A. Draw graphs from the data in 30.1 letting a shaded area be the variance. Use lines drawn as ------- to represent standard costs, lines drawn .... representing actual costs, and lines drawn __.__.__.__.__ where standard costs and actual costs are the same.

30.3A. Calculate the labour variances from the following data:

		Standard hours	Actual hours	Standard wage rate	Actual wage rate
(i)	Job A	220	218	£2.1	£2.1
(ii)	Job B	115	115	£1.7	£1.9
(iii)	Job C	200	240	£1.8	£1.8
(iv)	Job D	120	104	£2.0	£2.0
(v)	Job E	68	68	£1.8	£1.5
(vi)	Job F	30	34	£1.7	£1.7
(vii)	Job G	70	77	£1.6	£1.6
(viii)	Job H	100	100	£1.9	£2.0

30.4A. Using the same method as in 30.2 draw graphs of the data in 30.3.

30.5. Calculate the labour variances from the following data:

		Standard hours	Actual hours	Standard wage rate	Actual wage rate
(i)	Job I	150	142	£2.0	£2.2
(ii)	Job J	220	234	£1.9	£1.7
(iii)	Job K	50	48	£2.0	£1.9
(iv)	Job L	170	176	£2.0	£2.2
(v)	Job M	140	149	£2.1	£1.8
(vi)	Job N	270	263	£1.6	£2.0

30.6A. Using the same method as in 30.2 draw graphs of the data in 30.5.

30.7A. Calculate the labour variances from the following data:

		Standard hours	Actual hours	Standard wage rate	Actual wage rate
(i)	Job P	200	200	£1.9	£2.1
(ii)	Job Q	150	140	£2.0	£1.8
(iii)	Job R	175	169	£1.5	£1.9
(iv)	Job S	180	164	£2.2	£2.2
(v)	Job T	80	69	£2.5	£2.3
(vi)	Job U	70	74	£2.0	£2.1

30.8A. Using the same method as in 30.2 draw graphs of the data in 30.7.

30.9. You are required to calculate the labour variances from the following data:

		Standard hours	Actual hours	Standard wage rate £	Actual wage rate £
(i)	Job A	136	136	3.6	3.0
(ii)	Job B	200	200	3.8	4.0
(iii)	Job C	140	154	1.6	1.6
(iv)	Job D	180	164	2.2	2.2
(v)	Job E	75	70	2.0	1.8
(vi)	Job F	540	526	1.6	2.0
(vii)	Job G	440	468	1.8	1.6
(viii)	Job H	70	74	2.0	2.1
(ix)	Job I	180	214	2.0	2.1

31

Introduction to Variance Analysis III: Overhead Variances

Management of Overheads

In Chapter 21 the problem of allocating manufacturing overheads to jobs or processes, was introduced. In the first instance the costs were collected in cost centres — normally recognisable departments of the organisation. The total costs of these centres is then applied to products or jobs a they pass through the operations of the cost centre.

Suppose that a firm collects costs into three manufacturing departments with these results:

Department	A	B	C
	£	£	£
Fixed Overhead Cost	50,000	40,000	20,000
Variable Overhead Cost	30,000	35,000	40,000
Total Overhead	80,000	75,000	60,000
Direct Labour Hours	10,000	30,000	15,000
Direct Labour Cost	£22,000	£59,000	£35,000
Machine Hours	20,000	2,000	10,000

Exhibit 31.1

A decision has to be taken as to which activity either labour or machine time is the dominant factor in the department and will provide the most sensible basis for allocating the overhead.

In the case of Department A Machine Hours appear to be the major factor and therefore overheads will be charged on the basis $\dfrac{£80,000}{20,000}$ hours = £4 per machine hour. The firm will record for each job or process the number of machine hours taken and the overheads allocated on this total of hours at £4 per hour.

In Department B labour appears to be the dominant feature and therefore overheads will be charged on a labour hour rate calculated at $\dfrac{£75,000}{30,000}$ hours = £2.50 per hour. Department C does not exhibit any dominant activity and could either be expressed in a machine hour rate or a labour hour rate. Some firms where rates of pay in a department are stable and the mix of labour at different rates of pay stays the same prefer to express the overheads as a percentage of labour cost. In Department C it could be $\dfrac{£60,000}{£35,000}$ = 171%.

Thus the labour cost for all work going through Department C would be collected and overheads allocated at 171% of this labour cost figure.

Predetermined Rates

The usual procedure whether using standard costing or not is to predetermine the overhead absorption rates using budgeted figures both for the overhead costs and for the activity measure, whether machine or labour hours or cost. This process has a number of advantages − since not only does it allow proper current estimates to be made for things such as price quotations − but also it avoids the problem of fluctuating overhead rates at different times of the year due to seasonal variations. For example an ice cream manufacturer is likely to be much more active in the summer months than the winter. Because activity is low in winter the rate of absorption is likely to rise steeply since costs will not reduce proportionately. It makes more sense to view the overheads in this type of business on an annual cycle and recover the same amount of overhead in both summer and winter.

Variances in Overhead Recovery

As in all situations where budgeted figures are used there is almost certainly going to be variances at the end of a period. Take figures from Exhibit 31.1 for department A as the budget and compare them with actual performance:

	Department A Budget figures £	Actual figures £
Fixed Overhead	50,000	52,000
Variable Overhead	30,000	37,000
Total Overhead	80,000	89,000
Machine Hours	20,000	25,000
Machine Hour Rate £4		

Exhibit 31.2

The actual machine hours worked of 25,000 will have been used to allocate overheads to production at the rate of £4 per hour and therefore £100,000 will have been allocated. Compared to actual overheads of £89,000 this represents an over-absorption of £11,000. Only if 22,250 machine hours had been worked would the recovery have been exactly equal to actual overhead costs.

In a cost accounting system not using standard costing the over or under absorption of overheads would be either:

1. transferred wholly to cost of goods sold in the profit and loss account for the period.

2. allocated between closing inventories and cost of goods sold

3. carried forward to the next period.

The first choice would be used if the difference was felt to represent a shortfall in achievement for example if the number of hours worked had dropped due to bad management planning. The second would be applied if the differences were felt to be due to poor estimates of the original budgets. The third would only apply to interim accounts — not those at a year end.

Analysing the variances

The Variance between the amount recovered of £100,000 and the actual overhead cost of £89,000 can be analysed into a number of constituent variances in the normal manner of standard costing. In the example we have used the variance can be due to

1. the prices paid for goods and sources being different from original estimates or standards.

2. the volume of activity during the period being different from the original estimate.

These are known as the budget or spending variance for the first and a volume variance for the second reason.

Budget or Spending Variance

This represents the difference between the actual cost of overhead and the budgeted overhead cost adjusted to the actual level of operational activity.

From Exhibit 31.2 the budget figures need to be increased to take account of the fact that activity measured in machine hours has increased from 20,000 to 25,000 hours. This will not of course increase the Fixed Overhead — only the variable overheads which we will assume increase by 25% in line with the hours.

	a Original Budget	b Adjusted Budget	c Actual	b−c Variance
Fixed Overhead	50,000	50,000	52,000	(2,000)
Variable Overhead	30,000	37,500	37,000	500
	80,000	87,500	89,000	(1,500)

Exhibit 31.3

The Actual Expenditure exceeds the Adjusted Budget by £1,500 which represents an adverse Budget or Spending Variance.

Volume Variance

The other factor apart from the cost of the overheads which was budgeted in developing the predetermined standard was the number of machine hours. In the example we estimated that 20,000 machine hours would be worked whereas 25,000 were actually worked. This difference would not matter if all the overheads were variable since the rate per hour would be constant at different activities. Where fixed costs are concerned however increasing the activity will increase the amount recovered above the level required, and if activity is below budget insufficient overhead will be recovered.

In the example the rate is split:

$$\text{Fixed} \quad \frac{50,000}{20,000} = \quad £2.50$$

$$\text{Variable} \quad \frac{30,000}{20,000} = \quad \underline{£1.50}$$

$$£4.00$$

When the machine hours increase from 20,000 to 25,000 we recover $5,000 \times £2.50 = £12,500$ more than required.

An alternative way of viewing this is to compare the amount of overheads recovered at 25,000 hours with the flexible budget for this level of activity:

Recovered 25,000×£4		100,000
Budget Variable Cost 25,000×1.50	37,500	
Fixed Cost	50,000	87,500
Volume variance		12,500

This variance shows that by increasing the utilisation of the fixed resources in a business considerable savings are made. The £12,500 is a favourable variance in terms of the original standard.

Summary of Variances

The analysis so far shows:

	£
Standard Overhead recovered at actual level of activity (25,000×£4)	100,000
Budget or Spending Variance − adverse	1,500
	101,500
Volume Variance − favourable	12,500
Actual level of Manufacturing Overheads	89,000

Assessing Variances

In Standard Costing in an organisation where products are being manufactured it is common for the cost of the overheads to be related to the product. If in the example a Superwidgit is manufactured in Department A which it is estimated requires 2 machine hours per widgit then the standard cost of overhead per Superwidgit will be $2 \times £4 = £8$.

If in the actual period a Superwidgit takes less than two hours to make there will be a favourable variance which will be costed at £4 per hour. Similarly if more than two hours are taken there will be a unfavourable variance.

Using the example and assuming Department A exclusively manufactures Superwidgits, the Original Budget is to make 10,000 Superwidgits and the actual production of Superwidgits in 12,000.

	Department A Original Budget £	Actual £
Total overhead	80,000	89,000
Machine Hours	20,000	25,000
Hours per Superwidgit	2	
Number of Units	10,000	12,000

To produce 12,000 widgits should take 24,000 hours at the standard rate. Since the actual hours are 25,000 there is an adverse variance of 1,000 hours which costs £4 per hour (note this is both fixed and variable overhead in effect being wasted through operating at below expected efficiency). Relating this adverse £4,000 variance to the other overhead variances we get:

	£
Standard Cost of Overheads for 12,000 Actual Superwidgits produced × £8 =	96,000
Efficiency Variance − adverse	4,000
Standard Overhead recovered at Actual Level of Activity	100,000
Budget Variance − adverse	1,500
	101,500
Volume Variance − favourable	12,500
Actual level of Manufacturing Overhead	89,000

A Comprehensive Example

The data set out below refers to a cost centre for a particular period of time:

Budget

Variable Overheads (extract)

	Output		*Cost*
	in units	*in standard hours*	*£*
	9,800	49,000	98,000
	9,900	49,500	99,000
	10,000	50,000	100,000
	10,100	50,500	101,000
	10,200	51,000	102,000
Fixed overheads			150,000

Budgeted volume of production 10,000 units
Standard Labour Hours/Unit = 5

Actual

Variable overhead	£104,000
Fixed overhead	£160,000
Direct labour hours worked	49,000 hours
Units of production	9,900 units

9,900 units of production is the equivalent of 9,900 × 5 = 49,500 standard direct labour hours.

Before making the variance calculations it will be helpful to make some observations on the data given. The flexible budget shows that each unit of production has a standard variable overhead cost of £10. Alternatively, this can be expressed as £10 ÷ 5 = £2 per standard hour of labour. It should not be assumed that this rate of £2 would also apply to levels of production outside the range shown. These may well be step costs, such as additional supervision, which would alter the standard variable overhead rate at higher levels of output.

The fixed costs are thought likely to remain fixed provided the range of output does not extend too far above or below the budgeted volume of production. The fixed standard rate is £150,000 ÷ 50,000 = £3 per standard hour of labour, or £150,000 ÷ 10,000 = £15 per unit.

The Standard Unit Cost for Overhead is thus £10 + £15 = £25 per unit and £2 + £3 = £5 per labour hour.

This budgeted volume of production is likely to be the level of output thought of as being normal and acceptable in the long run. It is frequently referred to as the normal volume of production.

Calculation of variances

Firstly it is helpful to calculate the net variance which is to be analysed. This is developed from the standard cost of the actual units produced:

Standard Cost of Actual Production 9,900 × £25 =		£247,500
Actual Overhead Costs Total		£264,000
Total Variance −	Adverse	16,500

This is broken down into:

Efficiency Variance

Actual Units Produced 9,900 × 5 hours =	49,500	(standard labour hours)	
Actual labour Hours	49,000		
Labour Hours Saved	500		
Efficiency variance at the overhead rate per labour hour £5		Favourable	2,500

Budget Variance

Budgeted Overheads at Actual Labour Hours			
worked of 49,000 − Variable		98,000	
Fixed		150,000	248,000
Actual Overheads			264,000
Budget Variance −	Adverse		16,000

Volume Variance

Budgeted Recovery of Fixed Overheads at standard activity 50,000 hrs × £3		150,000
Actual Recovery of Fixed Overheads at actual activity 49,000 hrs × £3		147,000
Volume Variance −	Adverse	3,000

Summary of Variances

		£
Efficiency	Favourable	2,500
Budget	Adverse	16,000
Volume	Adverse	3,000
		16,500

Reconciliation of Standard and Actual Cost

Standard Cost of Actual Production 9,900 units × £25	247,500
Efficiency Variance − favourable	2,500
Budgeted Level of Overhead Cost on Actual Labour Hours at Standard 49,000 × £5	245,000
Budget Variance − adverse	16,000
	261,000
Volume Variance − adverse	3,000
Actual Cost of Overheads	264,000

Variances and Management Action

The calculation of variances and their explanation to managers is of no value unless the information so revealed is put to use in making decisions which changes subsequent activities. The question then arises as to whether every variance needs some form of action. It is not possible to be dogmatic here, it really does depend on circumstances. With some variance a fairly large variance may be fairly insignificant, whereas with others even a small amount may call for urgent action.

There is no doubt that variance calculations of the right type, transmitted to the right people at the right time, and which have an effect upon subsequent operations, can be of immense use. On the other hand much of the effort put into variance calculation in many firms just goes to waste, as managers do not act on the information. This is very often because a poor "selling" job has been done by the accounting staff to the managers concerned, in that they have not either been able to convince the manager that variance analysis is worthwhile, or possibly that the information provided is not really what the managers requires to enable him to tackle his job properly.

Assignment Exercises

31.1. Calculate the overhead variances from the following data.

(a) Budgeted for £6,000 variable overhead and 1,000 machine hours.

            Actual overhead   £5,840

            Actual machine hours   1,000

(b) Budgeted for £20,000 variable overhead and 5,000 machine hours.

            Actual overhead   £21,230

            Actual machine hours   5,000

(c) Budgeted for £12,000 Fixed overhead and the actual overhead is found to be £11,770.

(d) Budgeted for £40,000 Fixed overhead and the actual overhead is found to be £41,390.

(e) Budgeted production of 2,000 units in 8,000 hours. Standard variable overhead rate is £3 per hour.

     In fact 2,000 units are produced in 7,940 hours.

(f) Budgeted production of 5,000 units in 15,000 hours. Standard variable overhead rate is £4 per hour.

     In fact 4,860 units are produced in 15,000 hours.

31.2. Calculate the overhead variances in the following cases:

(a) Budgeted for £37,000 fixed overhead. The actual fixed overhead turns out to be £36,420.

(b) Budgeted for production of 500 units in 250 hours. The variable overhead rate is £6 per hour. In fact 500 units are produced in 242 hours.

(c) Budgeted for £18,000 variable overhead and 9,000 machine hours. Actual overhead is £18,000 and actual machine hours 8,820.

(d) Budgeted for £9,000 variable overhead and 3,000 machine hours. Actual overhead is £8,790 and actual machine hours 3,000.

(e) Budgeted for £120,000 fixed overhead. The actual fixed overhead turns out to be £129,470.

(f) Budgeted for production of 10,000 units in 30,000 hours. Standard variable overhead rate is £8 an hour. In fact 9,880 units are produced in 30,000 hours.

31.3. Calculate the following overhead variances:

(a) Budgeted fixed overhead is £30,000 and budgeted hours 10,000. Actual fixed overhead turns out to be £30,000 but actual hours were 10,320.

(b) Budgeted fixed overhead is £40,000 and budgeted hours 20,000. Actual overhead turns out to be £39,640 and actual hours worked 20,000.

(c) Budgeted fixed overhead is £5,000 and budgeted hours 10,000. Actual overhead turn out to be £5,000, but the actual hours are 9,600.

(d) Budgeted fixed overhead is £60,000 and budgeted hours 15,000. Actual fixed overhead turns out to be £62,390 and actual hours 15,000.

31.4A. You are required to calculate the overhead variances of Joseph Ltd. The budget is prepared as:

(a) Total budgeted variable overhead £400,000.

(b) Total budgeted fixed overhead £160,000.

(c) Budgeted volume of production 80,000 direct labour hours or 40,000 units.

The actual results turn out to be:

(d) Actual variable overhead £403,600.

(e) Actual fixed overhead £157,200.

(f) Actual volume 78,500 direct labour hours which resulted in 42,000 units of production.

31.5A. You are required to calculate the overhead variances of Raymond Ltd. The budget is prepared as:

(a) Total budgeted variable overhead   £100,000.

(b) Total budgeted fixed overhead   £125,000.

(c) Budgeted volume of production 50,000 direct labour hours of 250,000 units.

The actual results turn out to be:

(d) Actual variable overhead   £96,500.

(e) Actual fixed overhead   £129,400.

(f) Actual volume 52,000 direct labour hours which resulted in 244,000 units.

31.6A. You are required to calculate the overhead variances of Edward Ltd. The budget is prepared as:

(a) Total budgeted variable overhead £500,000.

(b) Total budgeted fixed overhead £200,000.

(c) Budgeted volume of production 200,000 direct labour hours or 100,000 units.

The actual results turn out to be:

(d) Actual variable overhead £508,000.

(e) Actual fixed overhead £211,600.

(f) Actual volume 196,000 hours which resulted in 92,000 units of production.

32

Introduction to Variance Analysis IV: Sales Variances

Sales Variances

The analysis of the difference between budgeted sales levels and actual levels can have an important bearing on the understanding of results. The main factors which are important in analysing sales are

(a) selling price variances
(b) volume variances
(c) mix variances.

The selling price variance measures the overall profit difference caused by budgeted unit selling price and actual unit selling price being different. If the budget was to sell 100 widgits at £5 each and the actual sales were 100 widgits of £4.50 each, there will be a profit reduction of £50 due to the adverse selling price variance of 50p per unit on the 100 units sold.

The Volume Variances in Sales will be measured in terms of the difference in the total quantity being sold between budget and actual. The impact of changes in volume of sales on profit can only be measured if we know the profitability of the sales. This will be dealt with at gross profit level. Thus if the budget is to sell 100 widgits with a unit gross margin of £2 and the actual sales achieved are only 90 widgits then there is an adverse variance of 10 units ath the margin of £2 which represents a loss of profit of £20. If several products are being sold the variance will be worked on total units actually sold in the proportion originally budgeted.

Example

Product	Budget Sales Units	%	Budget Gross Margin £	Total Budget Margin £	Actual Sales Units	Actual Sales in Budget %
X	200	33.3	1	200	250	240
Y	200	33.3	1.50	190	190	240
Z	200	33.3	3.50	260	280	240
	600	100.0		700	720	720

The Volume Variance is calculated by Company Actual Sales in budget percentage mix with the original budget at budget margins:

Product	Budget Sales Units	Actual Sales in Budget % Units	Variance Units	Budget Margin £	Volume Variances
X	200	240	40	1.00	40.00
Y	200	240	40	1.50	60.00
Z	200	240	40	3.50	140.00
	600	720	120		240.00

The Mix Variance arises where more than one product is being sold and the different products have differing profit margins. If the proportions in which the actual sales of the products varies from budget then the overall profit will vary as a consequence.

In the example on volume variance the original budget was compared with actual sales split in the budget mix. For the mix variance these figures of actual sales in budget mix are compared with the actual sales and the differences evaluated at the budgeted gross profit margin.

	Actual Sales Budget % Units	Actual Sales Units	Variance Units	Budget Gross Margin £	Mix Variance
X	240	250	+10	1.00	+ £10
Y	240	190	−50	1.50	− 75
Z	204	280	+40	3.50	+£140
	720	720	−		+ £75.0

The difference in mix between budget and actual has increased profit by £75 due mainly to the influence of more sales of product Z i.e. there is a favourable mix variance of £75.

Example

Product	%	Units	Budget Unit Selling Price £	Budget Unit Gross Profit £	Budget Total Profit £	Actual Units	Actual Unit Selling Price £	Actual Unit Gross Profit £	Actual Total Profit £
A	16.7	100	20	5	500	90	21	6	540
B	33.3	200	25	10	2,000	220	24	9	1,980
C	50	300	10	2	600	350	10	2	700
	100	600			3,100	660			3,220

Total Variance = Actual Profit   3,220
                Budget Profit   3,100

                Favourable Value   120

Firstly eliminate the price variance using the actual units sold as the basis.

	Actual Units Sold	Budget Price	Actual Price	Unit Variance	Total Price Variance
	1	2	3	$3 - 2 = 4$	$1 \times 4 = 5$
		£	£	£	£
A	90	20	21	+ 1	+ 90
B	220	25	24	− 1	− 220
C	350	10	10	−	−
		Adverse Price Variance			− 130

Secondly eliminate the volume variance using the average budgeted gross profit to evaluate the variance.

	Actual Units Sold	Actual Units in Budget %	Budget Units Sold	Variance in Units	Budget Unit Gross Profit	Total Value Variance
	1	2	3	$2 - 2 = 4$	5	$4 \times 5 = 6$
					£	£
A	90	110	100	+ 10	5	+ 50
B	220	220	200	+ 20	10	+ 200
C	350	330	300	+ 30	2	+ 60
	660	660	600	+ 60		
			Favourable Volume Variance			+ 310

Finally eliminate the mix variance. This is done by comparing the actual total units sold in the mix originally budgeted with the actual sales.

	Budget %	Actual Total Sales Split in Budget & Units	Actual Sales Units	Difference $3 - 2 = 4$ Units	Budget Unit Gross Profit	Mix Variance
	1	2	3		5	$4 \times 5 = 6$
					£	
A	16.7	110	90	− 20	5	− 100
B	33.3	220	220	−	10	−
C	50.0	330	350	+ 20	2	+ 40
		660	660			
			Adverse Mix Variance			− 60

Summary of Variance

Adverse Price Variance	− 130
Favourable Volume Variance	+ 310
Adverse Mix Variance	− 60
Favourable total Sales Variance	+ 120

The Gross Profit Margin may change for reasons other than changes in Sales — for example if the cost of materials varies from budgets or wage rates change. This type of variance has however already been dealt with under Material and Labour Variances.

Assignment Exercises

32.1. The Grange Company has the following results for the year to 31 March 19-1. A single product — a toggle was made by the Company.

	Budget	Actual
Sales in units	125,000	150,000
Sales in £	312,500	356,250

The Standard cost of manufacturing each unit was £1.50.
What are the price and volume variances on sales in 19-1.

32.2A. Corporec PLC manufactures a detergent in one of its plants. The information for the year to 30 September 19-2 was as follows:

	Budget	Actual
Sales in gallons	180,000	170,000
Sales in £	540,000	527,000

The Standard Cost of manufacturing a gallonn was £2.
Calculate the price and volume variances for 19-2.

32.3. The following data was collected for Molton Ltd. for the year ended 31 March 19-3.

Product	Budget Selling Price	Budget Sales Units	%	Budget Gross Profit per unit	Budget Gross Profit Total	Actual Selling Price	Actual Sales Units	%	Actual Gross Profit per Unit	Actual Gross Profit Total
	£			£	£	£			£	£
M	5	800	25	1.00	800	5.10	840	30	0.90	756
N	8	1,600	50	1.50	2,400	7.90	1,680	60	1.40	2,352
P	7	800	25	1.20	960	7.30	280	10	1.20	336
		3,200	100		4,160		2,800	100		3,44

Calculate price, volume and mix variances for 19-3.

32.4A. The following information relates to Burton Company for the year to 30 June 19-6.

Product	Budget Units	Sales %	Budget Selling Price Unit	Budget Gross Profit per Unit	Actual Units	Sales %	Actual Unit Selling Price	Actual Unit Gross Profit
			£	£			£	£
A	400	14.3	30	5	500	20.8	29	4
B	600	21.4	25	4	400	16.7	27	5
C	1,800	64.3	40	10	1,500	62.5	39	9
	2,800	100.0			2,400	100.0		

Calculate price, volume and mix variances for 19-6.

33

Accounting Theory I: Introduction

To many students it will seem strange that a discussion of accounting theory has been left until this stage of the course. Logically you could argue that it should have preceded all the practical work.

The reason for not dealing with theory at the beginning is simple. From a practical standpoint of teaching, it could easily have confused you then, and made it more difficult to assimilate the basic rules of accounting. The terms used in theory, such as what is meant in accounting by capital, liabilities, assets, net profit and so on, would not then have been understood. Leaving it until now, if theory points out what is wrong with accounting methods, at least you know those methods. Theory taught in a vacuum is counter-productive for most students.

In the discussion which follows, we want you to remember that this is your first proper look at accounting theory. We do not intend it to be an exhaustive examination, but simply an introduction to give you an overall appreciation.

An overall accepted theory?

It would not be surprising if you were expecting to read now exactly what the overall accepted theory of accounting is, and then proceed to examine the details later. We are afraid there is no such 'accepted' theory. This is much regretted by those accountants who have chosen an academic life. Many 'practical' accountants, and you will meet quite a few of them, are quite pleased that no such theory exists. To them, accounting is what accountants do, and they feel theory has little place in that. Such a narrow view is to be deprecated. Accounting theory provides a general frame of reference by which accounting practices can be judged, and it also guides the way to the development of new practices and procedures.

The lack of an accepted theory of accounting does not mean that it has not been attempted; there have been numerous attempts. At first they consisted of an *inductive* approach. This involved observing and analysing the practices of accountants to see if any consistent behaviour could be detected. Should a general principle be observed, anyone deviating from it could be criticised accordingly. Such attempts failed. First, it was impossible to find consistent patterns of behaviour amongst the mass of practices which had developed over the years. Second, such an approach would not have brought about any important improvements in accounting practices, as it looked at 'what accountants do' rather than 'what accountants *should* be doing'.

A different approach emerged, as recently as the 1950s. It was a *normative* approach, in that it was aimed at the improvement of accounting practice. It also included elements of the inductive approach in attempting to derive rules based on logical reasoning when given a set of objectives. The combination of these approaches has been a valuable and productive one, albeit still in its infancy. For instance, it had an important effect upon current value accounting which we will examine later. The main problem has been that of a general agreement as to the objectives of accounting.

As you might expect, general attention has more recently tended to switch away to a less ambitious approach. This is based, first, on identifying the users of accounts, and then finding out what kind of information they require. Such an approach was used in *The Corporate Report,* produced under the auspices of the Accounting Standards Committee (ASC), and published in 1975. We will look later at the user groups which were identified. The other important report using this approach was that of the Sandilands Committee in 1975. This will also be considered more fully later.

There is still a major problem here. Should accountants give the user groups the information they *are* asking for, or the information for which they *should* be asking? With management accounts this is not such a great problem, as management and accountants get together to agree on what should be produced. The financial accounts present greater problems. First, there is not such a close relationship between the accountant and the user groups. Second, there are the legal and other regulations governing financial accounts which the accountant must observe. Another point which will be considered later is whether only one report should be issued for all user groups, or whether each group should have its own report.

Having had an overall look at how theory construction is proceeding, we can now turn to look at theory in more detail.

Measurement of income

Some books use the word 'income', but the words 'net profit' mean exactly the same. In this book the calculation of net profit is done within fairly strict guidelines. Your earlier studies gave you guidance on the overall concepts ruling such calculations. However, just because the business world and the accounting profession use this basic approach does not mean it is the only one available. We will now consider possible alternatives to the basic method.

Let us start by looking at the simplest possible example of the calculation of profit, where everyone would agree with the way it is calculated. John is starting in business, his only asset being cash £1,000. He rents a stall in the market for the day, costing him £40. He then buys fruit for cash £90, and sells it all during the day for cash £160. At the end of the day John's only asset is still cash: £1,000 − £40 − £90 + £160 = £1,030. Everyone would agree that his profit for that day was £30, i.e. £160 sales − £90 purchases − £40 expenses = £30. In this case his profit equals the increase in his cash.

Suppose that John now changes his style of trading. He buys the market stall, and he also starts selling nuts and dried fruit, of which he can keep a stock from one day to another. It we now want to calculate profit we cannot do it simply in terms of cash, we will also have to place a value both on the stock of fruit and nuts and on his stall, both at the beginning and end of each day.

The argument just put forward assumes that we can all agree that profit represents an increase in wealth or 'well-offness'. It assumes that John will make a profit for a period if either:

(a) he is better off at the end of it than he was at the beginning; or

(b) he would have been better off at the end than the beginning had he not consumed some of the profits by taking drawings.

Sir John Hicks, the economist, expressed this view by saying that the profit was the maximum value which a person could consume during a period and still be as well off at the end of the period as at the beginning.

In terms of a limited company, the Sandilands Committee, which will be mentioned in greater detail later, said that a company's profit for the year is the maximum value which the company can distribute as dividends during the year, and still be as well off at the end of the year as it was at the beginning.

There are some important questions here which need answering. They are:

(a) how can we measure wealth at the beginning and end of a period?

(b) how do you measure the change in wealth over a period?

(c) having measured wealth over a period, how much can be available for consumption and how much should not be consumed?

There are basically two approaches to the measurement of wealth of a business.

(a) Measuring the wealth by finding the values of the individual assets of a business.

(b) Measuring the expectation of future benefits.

In the first year book *Finance* you learnt the technique of discounting. We will use it here to calculate the present value of the expected future net flow of cash into the firm.

We will first look at the different methods of valuation on an individual asset basis.

Asset valuation alternatives
Historical cost

This method is the one you have used so far in the financial accounting in this book. Even in that case there is not always one single figure to represent it. Let us look at a few examples.

(*a*) Depreciation. How do we 'precisely' charge the cost of using an asset to a particular period? As you have already seen, there is no one 'true' answer; the choice of method, expected length of use of the asset, etc., is quite arbitrary.

(*b*) Stocks to be used during the period can be charged out at FIFO, LIFO, AVCO, NIFO, and so on. There is no one 'true' figure.

(*c*) Suppose we buy a block of assets, e.g. we take over the net assets of another organization. How do we allocate the cost exactly? There is no precise way, we simply use a 'fair value' for each asset. Any excess of cost over the total of fair values we call goodwill.

Adjusted historical cost

Because of changes in the value or purchasing power of money, the normal historical cost approach can be very unsatisfactory. Take the case of a buildings account; in it we find that two items have been debited. One was a warehouse bought in 1950 for £100,000 and the other an almost identical warehouse bought in 1985 for £400,000. These two figures are added together to show cost of warehouses £500,000, quite clearly a value which has little significance.

To remedy this defect, the original historical cost of an asset is adjusted for the changes in the value or purchasing power of money over the period from acquisition to the present balance sheet date. The calculations are effected by using a price index.

This method does not mean that the asset itself is revalued. What is revalued is the money for which the asset was originally bought. This method forms the basis of what is known as *current purchasing power* accounting, abbreviated as CPP.

It does not remove the original problems of historical accounting which we have already described. All this does is to take the original historical cost as accurate and then adjust it.

To illustrate this method, let us take an instance which works out precisely, just as the proponents of CPP would wish.

A machine which will last for five years, depreciated using the straight line method, was bought on 1 January 1984 for £5,000. On 1 January 1986 exactly the same kind of machine (there have been no technological improvements) is bought for £6,000. The price index was 100 at 1 January 1984, 120 at 1 January 1986 and 130 at 31 December 1986. The machines would appear in the balance sheet at 31 December 1986 as follows, the workings being shown in *the box alongside.*

	Historical cost £	Conversion factor £		Balance sheet CPP at 31 Dec. 1986 £
Machine 1	5,000	130/100	6,500	
Machine 2	6,000	130/120	6,500	13,000
Less Depreciation				
Machine 1	3,000	130/100	3,900	
Machine 2	1,200	130/120	1,300	5,200
				7,800

You can see that the CPP balance sheet shows two exactly similar machines at the same cost, and each has been depreciated £1,300 for each year of use. In this particular case CPP has achieved exactly what it sets out to do, namely put similar things on a similar basis.

Underlying this method are the problems inherent in the price index used to adjust the historical cost figures. Any drawbacks in the index will result in a distortion of the adjusted historical cost figures.

Replacement cost

Replacement cost, abbreviated as RC, is the estimated amount that would have to be paid to replace the asset at the date of valuation. You will often see it referred to as an 'entry value' as it is the cost of an asset entering the business.

How do we 'estimate' the replacement cost? As we are not in fact replacing the asset we will have to look at the state of the market at the date of valuation. If the asset is exactly the same as those currently being traded, perhaps we can look at suppliers' price lists.

Even with exactly the same item, there are still problems. Until you have actually negotiated a purchase it is impossible to say how much discount you could get — you might guess but you could not be certain. Also, if the asset consists of, say, ten drilling machines, how much discount could you get for buying ten machines instead of one only?

If we have those difficulties looking at identical assets, what happens when we are trying to find out these figures for assets which cannot still be matched on the market? Technological change has greatly speeded up in recent years. If there is a second-hand market, it may be possible to get a valuation. However, in second-hand markets the price is often even more subject to negotiation. It becomes even more complicated when the original asset was specially made and there is no exactly comparable item, new or second-hand.

The difficulties outlined above mean that solutions to valuation can be sought under three headings:

(*a*) Market prices. As already mentioned, there will often be a market, new or second-hand, for the assets. For instance, this is particularly true for motor vehicles. If our asset differs in some way an adjustment may be necessary, thus cutting into the desirable degree of objectivity.

(*b*) Units of service. Where a market price is unobtainable, this being especially so with obsolete assets, a value is placed on the units of service which the asset can provide, rather than trying to value the asset itself.

For instance, assume that a machine has an estimated future production capacity of 1,000 units. A new machine producing the same type of product might have a total future capacity of 5,000 units. If the running costs of the machines are the same, the value of the old machine can be said to be one-fifth of the cost of the new one, as that is the proportion its future capacity bears to the new one. If the running costs were different an adjustment would be made.

(*c*) Cost of inputs. If the asset was made or constructed by the owner, it may be possible to calculate the cost of replacing it at the balance sheet date. Present rates of labour and materials costs could be worked out to give the replacement cost.

Net realizable value

Net realizable value means the estimated amount that would be received from the sale of the asset less the estimated costs on its disposal. The term 'exit value' is often used as it is the amount receivable when an asset leaves the business.

A very important factor affecting such a valuation is the conditions under which the assets are to be sold. To realize in a hurry would often mean accepting a very low price. Look at the sale prices received from stock from bankruptcies — usually very low figures. The standard way of approaching this problem is to value as though the realization were 'in the normal course of business'. This is not capable of an absolutely precise meaning, as economic conditions change and the firm might never sell such an asset 'in the normal course of business'.

The difficulties of establishing an asset's net realizable value are similar to those of the replacement value method when similar assets are not being bought and sold in the market-place. However, the problems are more severe as the units of service approach cannot be used, since that takes the seller's rather than buyer's viewpoint.

Economic value (present value)

As any economist would be delighted to tell you, he/she would value an asset as the sum of the future expected net cash flows associated with the asset, discounted to its present value.

Certainly, if you really did *know* (not guess) the future net cash flows associated with the asset and you had the correct discount rate, your valuation would be absolutely correct. The trouble is that it is impossible to forecast future net cash flows with certainty, neither will we necessarily have chosen the correct discount rate. It is also very difficult to relate cash flows to a particular asset, since a business's assets combine together to generate revenue.

Deprival value

The final concept of value is based on ideas propounded in the USA by Professor Bonbright in the 1930s, and later developed in the UK for profit measurement by Professor W. T. Baxter.

'Deprival value' is based on the concept of the value of an asset being the amount of money the owner would have to receive to compensate him or her exactly for being deprived of it. We had better point out immediately that the owner does not have to be deprived of the asset to ascertain this value, it is a hypothetical exercise.

This leads to a number of consequences.

(*a*) Deprival value cannot exceed replacement cost, since if the owner were deprived of the asset he/she could replace it for a lesser amount. Here we will ignore any costs concerned with a delay in replacement.

(*b*) If the owner feels that the asset is not worth replacing, its replacement cost would be more than its deprival value. He/she simply would not pay the replacement cost, so the value to the owner is less than that figure.

(*c*) If the asset's deprival value is to be taken as its net realizable value, that value must be less than its replacement cost. It would otherwise make sense for someone to sell the asset at net realizable value and buy a replacement at a lower cost. Again, delays in replacement are ignored.

(*d*) Take the case where an owner would not replace the asset, but neither would he/she sell it. It is possible to envisage a fixed asset which has become obsolete but might possibly be used, for example, when other machines break down. It is not worth buying a new machine, as the replacement cost is more than the value of the machine to the business. Such a machine may well have a very low net realizable value.

The benefit to the business of keeping such a machine can be said to be its 'value in use'. This value must be less than its replacement cost, as pointed out above, but more than its net realizable value for otherwise the owner would sell it.

303

It is probably easier to summarize how to find 'deprival value' by means of the diagram in Exhibit 33.1.

Exhibit 33.1

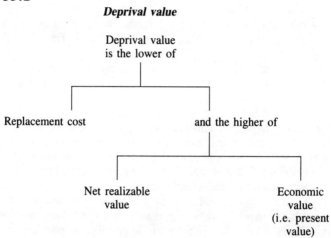

Deprival value

Deprival value
is the lower of

Replacement cost   and the higher of

Net realizable   Economic
value   value
(i.e. present
value)

This can be illustrated by a few examples, using assets A, B and C.

	Asset A £	Asset B £	Asset C £
Replacement cost (RC)	1,000	800	600
Net realizable value (NRV)	900	500	400
Economic value (EV)	2,000	700	300

The deprival values can be explained as follows; check them against Exhibit 54.1.

(a) Asset A. If the firm were deprived of asset A, what would it do? As economic value is greater than replacement cost it would buy another asset A. The deprival value to the business is therefore £1,000, i.e. replacement cost.

(b) Asset B. If deprived of asset B, what would the firm do? It would not replace it, as RC £800 is greater than its value to the business — its economic value £700. If deprived, the firm would therefore lose the present value of future cash flows, i.e. its economic value £700. This then is the deprival value for asset B.

(c) Asset C. With this asset there would be no point in keeping it, as its economic value to the firm is less than the firm could sell it for. Selling it is the logical way, so the deprival value is net realizable value £400.

Capital maintenance

Let us go back to Sir John Hicks's definition of income (profit): 'A man's income is the maximum value which he can consume during a week, and still expect to be as well off at the end of the week as he was at the beginning.'

We have looked at the different ways we could value assets as a preliminary to totalling them to find the wealth or 'well-offness' at a particular date. Before going any further we must examine the problems of measuring the maintenance of wealth (or 'well-offness') over a period. We could call this 'capital maintenance'.

The basic method used in accounting, and described earlier throughout this book, is that of *money capital maintenance*. Using this approach, if a firm has £1,000 in capital or net assets on 1 January 19-1 it must have £1,000 in capital or net assets at 31 December 19-1 to be as well off at the end of the period. This means that, provided no new share capital has been issued and no dividends paid or share capital withdrawn, a company starting with capital of £1,000 on 1 January 19-2 and finishing with capital of £1,600 on 31 December 19-2 must have made a profit of £600, using this approach to capital maintenance.

Such a method would be acceptable to everyone in a period when there is no change in prices. However, most people would agree that the approach is not satisfactory when either prices in general, or specific prices affecting the firm, are changing. In these two cases, to state that £600 profit has been made for 19-2 completely ignores the fact that the £1,000 at 1 January 19-2 and the £1,000 at 31 December 19-2 do not have the same value. From this we can see the possibilities of three different concepts.

(*a*) *Money capital maintenance.* The traditional system of accounting as already described.

(*b*) *Real capital maintenance.* This concept is concerned with maintaining the general purchasing power of the equity shareholders. This takes into account changes in the purchasing power of money as measured by the retail price index.

(*c*) *Maintenance of specific purchasing power of the opening capital of the equity.* This uses a price index which is related to the specific price changes of the goods in which the firm deals.

From these we can look at the following example, which illustrates three different figures of profit being thrown up for a firm.

A worked example

A company has only equity share capital. Its net assets on 1 January 19-5 are £1,000, and on 31 December 19-5 £1,400. There have been no issues or withdrawal of share capital during the year. The general rate of inflation, as measured by the retail price index is ten per cent, whereas the specific rate of price increase for the type of goods in which the company deals, is 15 per cent. The profits for the three measures are as follows:

	(a) Money maintenance of capital	(b) Real capital maintenance	(c) Maintenance of specific purchasing power
	£	£	£
Net assets 31 Dec 19-5	1,400	1,400	1,400
Less what net assets would have to be at 31 Dec 19-5 to be as well off on 1 Jan 19-5			
(a) Money maintenance	1,000		
(b) Real capital 1,000+10%		1,100	
(c) Specific purchasing power maintenance 1,000 + 15%			1,150
Profit	400	300	250

Note that under the three methods:

(a) here the normal accounting method gives £400 profit;

(b) this case recognizes that there has been a fall in the purchasing power of money;

(c) this takes into account that it would cost £1,150 for goods whose value at the start of the year was £1,000.

Combinations of different values and capital maintenance concepts

We have just looked at three ways of calculating profits based on historical cost allied with three capital maintenance concepts. This can be extended by using replacement cost or net realizable value instead. Each of these, when adjusted by each capital maintenance concept, will give three separate figures for profit. Together the three different means of valuation, multiplied by three different concepts of capital maintenance, will give us nine different profit figures.

At this stage in your studies it will be difficult to understand how such different profit measures could be useful for different purposes. However, we can use one simple example to illustrate how using only the traditional way of calculating profits can have dire consequences. The next example shows how this can happen.

A worked example

A company has net assets on 1 January 19-7 of £100,000 financed purely
by equity share capital. During 19-7 there has been no injection or
withdrawal of capital. At 31 December 19-7 net assets have risen to
£115,000. Both the retail price index and the specific price index for the
goods dealt in have risen by 25 per cent. Taxation, based on traditional
historical cost calculations (maintenance of money capital), is at the rate
of 40 per cent. The profit may be calculated as follows.

	Maintenance of money capital	Maintenance of real capital and of specific purchasing power
	£	£
Net assets on 31 Dec 19-7	115,000	115,000
Less net assets needed to be as well off at 31 Dec 19-7 as with £100,000 on 1 Jan 19-7		
(a) Money capital	100,000	
(b) Both real capital and specific purchasing power £100,000 + 25%		125,000
Profit/Loss	15,000	(10,000)

Tax payable is £15,000 × 40% = £6,000. Yet the real capital or that of
specific purchasing power has fallen by £10,000. When tax is paid that would
leave us with net assets of £115,000 − £6,000 = £109,000. Because of
price changes £109,000 could not finance the amount of activity financed
by £100,000 one year before. The operating capacity of the company would
therefore be reduced.

Obviously it is not equitable for a company to have to pay tax on what
is in fact a loss. It is only the traditional way of measuring profits that has
thrown up a profit figure.

Operating capital maintenance concept

This approach looks at the output which could be generated by the initial
holding of assets. A profit will only be made if the assets held at the end
of the period are able to maintain the same level of output.

A very simple example of this is that of a trader who sells only one
product, a particular kind of watch. The only costs the trader incurs are
those of buying the watches. He/she has no assets apart from watches. In
this case the operating capital consists solely of watches.

Using the historical cost concept the trader will recognize a profit if
the revenue from the sale of a watch exceeded the historic cost of it.

However, using the operating capital maintenance concept he will recognize a profit only if the revenue from the sale is greater than the cost of buying another watch to replace the watch sold.

Assignment Exercises

33.1. Contrast the views concerning measurement of income held with that of an economist and by an accountant who believes in historical cost accounts.

33.2. What different ways are there of looking at Capital Maintenance? Describe them briefly.

34

Accounting Theory II: Accounting for Changing Price Levels

As you have seen in the preceding chapter, changes in price levels can lead to both profit and asset valuation figures being far from reality if simple historical cost figure are used. This is not a recently observed phenomenon. As far back as 1938, Sir Ronald Edwards wrote several classic articles which were published in *The Accountant*. You can find these in the book, *Studies in Accounting Theory*, edited by W. T. Baxter and S. Davidson and published by the Institute of Chartered Accountants, London, 1977.

The greater the rate of change in price levels, the greater the distortion. The clamour for changes to simple historical cost accounting is noticeably greater when the inflation rate is high — at such times the deficiencies of historical cost accounts are most obvious. If there were a period of deflation, however, the historical cost accounts would still be misleading.

In certain countries in the world the annual rate of inflation in recent years has been several hundred per cent. Historical cost accounts in those countries would certainly be at odds with accounts adjusted for inflation. In the UK the highest rate in recent years, based on the RPI was 17.8 per cent for 1979, falling to as low as 3.7 per cent for 1986.

We can now look, in outline only, at suggestions made in the UK since 1968 as to methods which could be used to adjust accounts for changing price levels.

Current purchasing power (CPP)

This proposal is something you have already read about. It is the adjustment of historical cost accounting figures by a price index figure to give figures showing what we called real capital maintenance. It will convey more of the problems and uncertainties facing the accounting profession in this regard, if we look at the history of the various proposals.

First came *Accounting for stewardship in a period of inflation*, published in 1968 by the Research Foundation of the Institute of Chartered Accountants in England and Wales (ICAEW). Stemming from this came Exposure Draft No. 8 (ED 8), published in 1973. ED 8 contained the proposal that companies should be required to publish, in addition to their conventional accounts, supplementary statements which would be, in effect, their final accounts amended to conform to CPP principles. In May 1974 a Provisional Statement of Standard Accounting Practice No. 7 (PSSAP 7) was published. Notice the sign of uncertainty, it was a *provisional* standard — the only one yet published. Compared with ED 8 which said that a company should be *required* to publish CPP accounts, PSSAP 7 simply *requested* them to publish such accounts. Many companies would not accede to such a request.

PSSAP 7 stipulated that the price index to be used in the conversion of accounts from historical cost should be the retail price index (RPI). As the actual price index relating to the goods dealt in by the firm might be quite different from RPI, the CPP accounts could well be distant from the current values of the firm itself.

The exact nature of the calculations needed for CPP accounts is not shown here.

Many people, including the government, were completely dissatisfied with the CPP approach. After ED 8 was issued the government set up its own committee of inquiry into inflation accounting. The chairman of the committee was Mr (now Sir) Francis Sandilands. The report, often known as the Sandilands Report, was published in September 1975.

Current cost accounting (CCA)

The Sandilands Committee's approach was quite different from ED 8 and PSSAP 7. The committee recommended a system called 'current cost accounting' (CCA). This basically approved the concept of capital maintenance as the maintenance of operating capacity.

After the Sandilands Report appeared, the accounting bodies, as represented by their own Accounting Standards Committee (ASC), abandoned their proposals in PSSAP 7. A working party, the Inflation Accounting Steering Group (IASG), was set up to prepare a Statement of Standard Accounting Practice based on the Sandilands Report.

This group published ED 18, 'Current cost accounting', in November 1976. It was attacked by many members of the ICAEW, whose members passed, in July 1977, a resolution rejecting compulsory use of CCA. However, the government continued its support, and in November 1977 the accounting profession issued a set of interim recommendations called the Hyde guidelines (named after the chairman of the committee). The second exposure draft, ED 24, was issued in April 1979, followed by SSAP 16 in March 1980. SSAP 16 was to last three years to permit the evaluation of the introduction of CCA. After this, ED 35 was published in July 1984.

In November 1986 the CCAB Accounting Standards Committee published its handbook, 'Accounting for the effects of changing prices'. At the same time presidents of five of the leading accountancy bodies issued the following statement:

'The presidents of five of the leading accountancy bodies welcome the publication by the CCAB Accounting Standards Committee of its Handbook on "Accounting for the effects of changing prices".

The presidents endorse the CCAB Accounting Standards Committee's view that, where a company's results and financial position are materially affected by changing prices, historical cost accounts alone are insufficient and that information on the effects of changing prices is important for an appreciation of the company's results and financial position. The presidents join the Accounting Standards Committee in encouraging companies to appraise and, where material, report the effects of changing prices.

The five bodies have proposed that SSAP 16, "Current cost accounting", which was made non-mandatory by all the CCAB bodies in June 1985, should now be formally withdrawn. They take the view, however, that the subject of accounting for the effects of changing prices is one of great importance. Accordingly, they support the Accounting Standards Committee in its continuing work on the subject and agree that an acceptable accounting standard should be developed.'

The Institute of Chartered Accountants in England and Wales; The Institute of Chartered Accountants of Scotland; The Institute of Chartered Accountants in Ireland; The Chartered Institute of Management Accountants; The Chartered Institute of Public Finance and Accountancy.

So once again the idea of forcing companies to produce accounts adjusted for changing prices has been rejected. The emphasis is now on encouragement, rather than trying to force companies to do it.

The reason why, at this early stage in your studies, we have given you some of the history behind the efforts to compel companies to produce CCA accounts is to illustrate the conflicts that have taken place inside and outside the accountancy profession. Opinions on the merits of CCA accounts are widely divided.

Handbook on 'Accounting for the effects of changing price levels'

We can now look at the main outlines of this handbook. The ASC is now trying to encourage companies to co-operate in an attempt to produce accounts suitable for the effects of changing price levels. In doing this it does not try to recommend any one method, or even recommend one way only of publishing the results. The handbook says that the information may be presented:

(*a*) as the main accounts; or
(*b*) in the notes to the accounts; or
(*c*) as information supplemental to the financial statements.

The handbook first examines the problems.

Problems during a period of changing price levels

Obviously, the greater the rate of change, the greater will be the problems. We can now list some of them.

(a) *Fixing selling prices*. If you can change your prices very quickly, an extreme case being a market trader, this problem hardly exists. For a company setting prices which it is expected to maintain for a reasonably long period, the problems are severe. It dare not price too highly, as early demand may be reduced by an excessive price; on the other hand, the company has to guess how prices are going to change over a period so that sufficient profit is made.

(b) *Financial planning*. As it is so difficult to guess how prices are going to change over a period, planning the firm's finances becomes particularly trying. Obviously, it would be better if the plans were revised frequently as conditions changed.

(c) *Paying taxation and replacing assets*. We have seen earlier how, during a period of inflation, traditional historic accounting will tend to overstate profits. Such artificial 'profits' are then taxed. Unless various supplementary tax allowances are given, the taxation paid is both excessive and more than true profits, adjusted for inflation, can bear easily. This tends to lead to companies being short of cash, too much having been taken in tax. Therefore, when assets which have risen in price have to be replaced, adequate finance may not be available.

(d) *Monetary assets*. If stocks of goods are held, they will tend to rise in money terms during a period of inflation. On the other hand, holding monetary assets, e.g. cash, bank and debtors, will be counter-productive. A bank balance of £1,000 held for six months, during which the purchasing power of money has fallen ten per cent, will in real terms be worth only 90 per cent of its value six months before. Similarly, in real terms debt of £5,000 owed continually over that same period will have seen its real value fall by ten per cent.

(e) *Dividend distribution*. Just as it is difficult to calculate profits, so is it equally difficult to decide how much to pay as dividends without impairing the efficiency and operating capability of the company. At the same time the shareholders will be looking to payment of adequate dividends.

Solutions to the problems

The handbook recommends the use of one of two concepts. These will now be examined fairly briefly.

Profit under the operating capital maintenance concept

This has been mentioned previously, with a simple example given of a trader buying and selling watches. Under this concept several adjustments are needed to the profit calculated on the historical cost basis. Each adjustment is now considered.

Adjustment 1: holding gains and operating gains

Nearly all companies hold fixed assets and stocks. For each of these assets the opportunity cost will bear little relationship to its historic cost. Instead it is the asset's value to the business at date of consumption, and this is usually the replacement cost of the asset.

Accordingly the historic cost profit, which was based on money capital maintenance, can be divided into two parts.

(a) Current cost profit, or operating gains. This is the difference between sales revenue and the replacement cost of the assets.

(b) Holding gains. This is the replacement cost of the assets less historical cost of those assets.

For example, a company buys an asset for £1,000 on 1 January 19-4. It holds it for one year and sells it for £1,600 when the replacement cost is £1,200. There has been a historical cost profit of £600. This can be analysed as in Exhibit 34.1:

Exhibit 34.1

Profit for 19-4

	£
Historical cost profit (£1,600−£1,000)	600
Less holding gain (£1,200−£1,000)	200
Current cost profit (or operating gain)	400

To put it another way, the company makes £200 historical profit by simply holding the asset from when its replacement cost (i.e. original cost) was £1,000, until the date of sale when its replacement cost was £1,200. The actual current cost profit at point of sale must reflect conditions at date of sale, i.e. the company has sold for £1,600 something which would currently cost £1,200 to replace. The current cost profit is therefore £400.

The holding gains are often described as a cost of sales adjustment (COSA).

Adjustment 2: depreciation

Depreciation is to be adjusted to current replacement cost values. Without going into complicated examples, this means that if the historical cost of depreciation is £4,000 and the current cost of depreciation, based on current replacement cost values, is £7,000, the adjustment should be £3,000 as follows:

	£
Depreciation based on historical cost	4,000
Adjustment needed to bring depreciation charge to CCA basis	3,000
CCA depreciation	7,000

Adjustment 3: monetary working capital adjustment

The monetary working capital needed to support the operating capability of the business will be affected by inflation. An adjustment will be needed to the historic profits in respect of this.

Adjustment 4: gearing adjustment

If we borrow £1,000 now, and have to pay back exactly £1,000 in five years, we will gain during a period of inflation. We will be able to put the £1,000 to use at current purchasing power. In five years' time, if £1 now is worth only 60p by then, we will have gained because we will only be giving up £600 of current purchasing power now. The gearing adjustment is an attempt to adjust current cost operating profits for this factor.

Profit and loss account based on the operating capital maintenance concept

A general idea how such a profit and loss account could appear can now be given.

R.S.T. Ltd.
Profit and Loss Account incorporating Operating Capital
Maintenance Concept adjustments

	£	£
Profit on the historical cost basis, before interest and taxation		100,000
Less current cost operating adjustments:		
(1) Holding gains (COSA)	15,000	
(2) Depreciation	10,000	
(3) Monetary working capital	5,000	30,000
Current cost operating profit		70,000
(4) Gearing adjustment	(2,000)	
Interest payable less receivable	6,000	4,000
Current cost profit before taxation		66,000
Taxation		25,000
Current cost profit attributable to shareholders		41,000
Dividends		30,000
Retained current cost profit for the year		11,000

Profit under the financial capital maintenance concept

According to the handbook this method is sometimes known as the 'real terms' system of accounting. The steps by which the profit is calculated can be summarized as:

(*a*) calculate shareholders' funds at the *beginning* of the period, based on current cost asset values; then

(*b*) restate *opening* amount in terms of pounds at the end of the period, by adjusteding (*a*) by the relevant change in a general price index (e.g. RPI); then

(*c*) calculate shareholders' funds *at the end* of the period, based on current cost values.

Assuming that there have been no introductions or withdrawals of capital, including dividends, if (*c*) is greater than (*b*) a 'real terms' profit will have been made. Otherwise a loss will have been incurred.

Allowance will have to be made in steps (*a*) to (*c*) above where there have been introductions or withdrawals of capital, or where there have been dividends.

The calculation of 'real terms' profit, as described, has been by way of comparing opening and closing balance sheets. Suppose that the 'real terms' profit figure had been £10,000, it could in fact have been calculated in the following manner:

	£	£
Historical cost profit		7,800
Add holding gains: the amount by which the current costs of the assets have increased over the period	3,400	
Less inflation adjustment: the amount by which general inflation has eroded shareholders' funds	1,200	
Real holding gains		2,200
Total real gains		10,000

The balance sheet approach was described first, as it is probably the easier to understand in the first instance. Obviously the link between opening and closing balance sheets can be traced to total real gains, which can also be explained using the profit and loss account concept.

Current cost balance sheet

The two main differences between a current cost balance sheet and a historical cost balance sheet are as follows:

(*a*) assets are shown at value to the business on the balance sheet date, rather than at any figure based on historical cost or at any previous revaluation;

(*b*) obviously the balance sheet would not balance if asset values were altered without an amendment somewhere else. A current cost reserve account is opened, additions to historical cost account values are debited to each asset account, whilst a credit will be made in the current cost reserve account. Entries are also made here to complete the double entry in respect of the four adjustments in the current cost profit and loss account. As a result, all double entry adjustments are made in this account and so the balance sheet will now balance.

Assignment Exercises

34.1. Explain how profits can be split between holding gains and operating gains.

34.2. Briefly state the stages of development in the accountancy profession during the past 20 years in its attempt to deal with the effects of inflation on final accounts.

35

Objectives of Financial Statements

In Chapter 33, Accounting theory I, we pointed out that a recent development in accounting theory had been towards identifying the users of accounts, and then finding out the type of information they require. Both *The Corporate Report 1975* and the 1975 *Sandilands Report* were directed in this fashion.

Users of accounts

The main users of published accounts of large companies are now identified with the main reasons they require the accounts.

(a) *Shareholders of the company,* both existing and potential, will want to know how effectively the directors are performing their stewardship function. They will use the accounts as a base for decisions to dispose of some or all of their shares, or to buy some.

(b) *The loan-creditor group.* This consists of existing and potential debenture and loan stock holders, and providers of short-term secured funds. They will want to ensure that interest payments will be made promptly and capital repayments will be made as agreed. Debenture and loan stock holders, whether redeemable or irredeemable, will also want to be able to assess how easily they may dispose of their debentures or loan stocks, should they so wish.

(c) *Employee groups,* including existing, potential and past employees. These can include trade unions whose members are employees. Past employees will be mainly concerned with ensuring that any pensions, etc. paid by the company are maintained. Present employees will be interested in ensuring that the company is able to keep on operating, so maintaining their jobs and paying them acceptable wages, and that any pension contributions are maintained. In addition, they may want to ensure that the company is being fair to them, so that they get a reasonable share of the profits accruing to the firm from their efforts. Trade unions will be upholding the interests of their members, and will possibly use the accounts in wage and pension negotiations. Potential employees will be interested in assessing whether or not it would be worth seeking employment with the company.

(d) *Bankers.* Where the bank has not given a loan or granted an overdraft, there will be no great need to see the accounts. Where money is owed to the banks, they will want to ensure that payments of interest will be made when due, and that the firm will be able to repay the loan or overdraft at the correct time.

(e) *The business contact group.* This includes trade creditors and suppliers, who will want to know whether or not they will continue to be paid, and the prospects for a profitable future association. Customers are included, since they will want to know whether or not the company is a secure source of supply. Business rivals in this group will be trying to assess their own position compared with the firm. Potential takeover bidders, or those interested in a merger will want to assess the desirability of any such move.

(f) *The analyst/adviser group.* These will need information for their clients or their readers. Financial journalists need information for their readers. Stockbrokers need it to advise investors. Credit agencies want it to be able to advise present and possible suppliers of goods and services to the company as to its creditworthiness.

(g) *The Inland Revenue* will need the accounts to assess the tax payable by the company.

(h) *Other official agencies.* Various organizations concerned with the supervision of industry and commerce may want the accounts for their purposes.

(i) *Management.* In addition to the internally produced management accounts the management is also vitally concerned with any published accounts. It has to consider the effect of such published accounts on the world at large.

(j) *The public.* This consists of groups such as ratepayers, taxpayers, political parties, pressure groups and consumers. The needs of these parties will vary accordingly.

Characteristics of useful information

From the various reports which have appeared since 1975 the following characteristics have been noted.

(a) *Relevance.* This is regarded as one of the two main qualities. The information supplied should be that which will satisfy the needs of its users.

(b) *Reliability.* This is regarded as the other main quality. Obviously, if such information is also subject to an independent check, such as that of the auditor, this will considerably enhance the reliance people can place on the information.

(c) *Objectivity.* Information which is free from bias will increase the reliance people place on it. It is, therefore, essential that the information is prepared as objectively as possible. Management may often tend to give a better picture of its own performance that is warranted, and is therefore subjective. It is the auditor's task to counter this view, and to ensure objectivity in the accounts.

(d) *Ability to be understood.* Information is not much use to a recipient if it is presented in such a manner that no one can understand it. This is not necessarily the same as simplicity.

(e) *Comparability.* Recipients of accounts will want to compare them both with previous accounts of that company and with the results of other companies; without comparability the accounts would be of little use.

(f) *Realism.* This can be largely covered by the fact that accounts should show a 'true and fair' view. It has also been contended that accounts should not give a sense of absolute precision when such precision cannot exist.

(g) *Consistency.* This is one of the basic concepts, but it is not to be followed slavishly if new and improved accounting techniques indicate a change in methods.

(h) *Timeliness.* Up-to-date information is of more use to recipients than outdated news.

(i) *Economy of presentation.* Too much detail can obscure the important factors in accounts and cause difficulties in understanding them.

(j) *Completeness.* A rounded picture of the company's activities is needed.

Problems of information production in accounting

You have seen that a company's profit and loss account and balance sheet produced for general publication is a multi-purpose document. The present state of the art of accounting is such that we have not yet arrived at producing specific financial reports for each group of users, tailored to their special needs.

At times, companies do produce special reports for certain groups of users. A bank, for instance, will almost certainly want to see a forecast of future cash flows before granting a loan or overdraft. The Inland Revenue will often require various analyses in order to agree the tax position. Some companies produce special reports for the use of their employees. In total, such extra reports are a very small part of the reports which could be issued.

Of course, producing reports is not costless. To produce special reports, exactly tailored to every possible group of users, would be extremely costly and time-consuming. It is hardly likely that any existing company would wish to do so. There is, however, no doubt that this is the way things are moving and will continue to move.

For the present, however, most companies produce one set of accounts for all the possible users, with the exception that management will have produced its own management accounts for its own internal purposes. Obviously such a multi-purpose document cannot satisfy all the users. In fact, it will almost certainly not fully satisfy the needs of any one user group — save that it must satisfy the legal requirements of the Companies Act.

Published accounts are, therefore, a compromise between the requirements of users and the maintenance of accounting concepts, subject to the overriding scrutiny of the auditor. Judgement forms so much a part of presenting information, that it can be said that if it were possible to have two large companies with identical share capitals, numbers of employees, fixed assets, turnover, costs, etc., the published accounts of the two companies would not be identical. Just a few straightforward items will suffice to show why there would be differences. Depreciation methods and policies may vary, as may stock valuation assessments, bad debt provisions, figures for revaluation of properties, and so on. There will probably be rather more subtle distinctions, many of which you will come across in the later stages of your studies.

Assignment Exercises

35.1. Who are the main users of accounts? Very briefly list their individual requirements.

35.2. Give a list of the main characteristics of useful information in accounting.

35.3. A normative approach to accounting theory is one which:
(A) you would expect a normal man to understand
(B) attempts to derive rules based on logic
(C) is aimed at the improvement of accounting practice
(D) ignores present accounting practice.

35.4. A period of inflation is likely to have the following effect on monetary assets and fixed assets
(A) real assets only will maintain their purchasing power
(B) monetary assets only will maintain their purchasing power
(C) both kinds of assets will lose some of their purchasing power
(D) both kinds of assets will gain some purchasing power.

Questions 35.5, 35.6 and 35.7 are based on the following information.

	Asset R £	Asset S £	Asset T £
Net Realizable Value	4,200	4,000	3,000
Economic Value	2,800	2,500	2,700
Replacement Cost	2,100	3,500	6,000

35.5. The deprival value of Asset R is:
(A) £6,000
(B) £3,000
(C) £2,700
(D) another figure.

35.6. The deprival value of Asset S is:
(A) £2,500
(B) £3,000
(C) £4,000
(D) £3,500.

35.7. The deprival value of Asset T is:
(A) £3,000
(B) £6,000
(C) £2,700
(D) another figure.

35.8. The costs in the use of scientific or technical knowledge towards producing new or substantially improved materials, devices, products, processes, systems or services are known as:
(A) applied research expenditure
(B) technical research expenditure
(C) development expenditure
(D) intangible asset development expenditure.

35.9. Real Capital Maintenance is concerned with:
(A) the maintenance of the specific purchasing power of the opening capital of the equity
(B) maintaining the general purchasing power of the equity shareholders
(C) the idea of capital change as propounded in the first 21 chapters of this study-pack
(D) maintaining the operating capability of the organization.

35.10. In a Current Cost Balance Sheet:
(A) assets are shown at historic cost adjusted by reference to changes in the Retail Price Index
(B) assets are shown at what they would have cost if the very best prices had been obtained on purchase
(C) assets are shown at their value to the business on the balance sheet date
(D) the current cost reserve account is cancelled by a transfer against the profit and loss account balance.

35.11. Fungible assets:
(A) can never be turned into cash
(B) are deducted from current liabilities
(C) are intangible by nature
(D) are mainly indistinguishable one from another.

36

Accounting in Different Forms of Organisation

Accounting is used in organisations of very diverse characteristics and objectives. Even in the manufacturing sector there are vast differences between companies which make aeroplanes, quarry for stone, make clothes, process food, print books and so on. However in the manufacturing sector most organisations have in common the fact that they produce a tangible product and have a main objective to earn profits.

Despite the areas of common interest even manufacturing organisations in the same industry may have quite distinct management styles which are reflected in different approaches to their management accounting. The techniques discussed in this book are those which have been distilled from the practice of organisations which have been successful over many years. Not every organisation applies all the techniques in exactly the same way. When you visit or work for a particular business, you will have to look carefully to see how the general principles have been adapted to the particular needs of that business.

Much the same can be said about organisations in the Service Sector. The only thing that distinguishes Service from Manufacturing is the absence of a tangible end product in the service sector. However the services provided by Banks, Insurance Companies, Building Societies, Airlines, Taxi Companies, Solicitors, Accountants and so on, are just as susceptible to being costed and budgeted as a manufactured product.

It is true to say however that in the service area it is possible to find a significant number of organisations which provide services but do not sell these services for an economic price. The types of organisation which provide services without having a profit objective would include local and national government organisations, the national health service and a wide variety of charities.

In organisations where profit is not calculated because there is no sales figure, there will nonetheless be costs of operation and a limit to the financial resources of the organisation. Whilst the measurement of profit does provide one very useful index of performance for an organisation, it is still necessary to prepare management accounts where the profit is not calculable. These accounts will be concerned to prepare budgets of all activities and seek to obtain measures to ensure that the benefits obtained from the service outputs are as high as possible given the level of cost inputs. This type of process is often called Cost-Benefit analysis, and is one way of ensuring that non-profit service organisations do not become inefficient and unresponsive to the needs of people who are supposed to be served.

The formal methods of accounting for organisations in the public sector were disussed in the first year book *Finance*. There are also special requirements for charities laid down by the Charity Commissioners, and for friendly societies, mutual societies and building societies which have special requirements of accounts from the Registrar of Friendly Societies. Many organisations under these headings control very large amounts of resource. There needs for good management accounting are very similar to a fully profit oriented business.

37

Managing Financial Resources

In the Management of an organisation's resources it is necessary to balance a complex set of flows into and out of the available funds of cash. Cash provides the starting point and common resource requirements for an organisation to carry on its affairs. This is not to say that a large positive bank balance is necessary. Many organisations carry on their activities with an overdrawn bank account. They can only do this however where the banker is confident that the organisation can readily repay what it owes when called on to do so.

Ultimately management must ensure that when they acquire assets, the returns from that investment will be positive. In profit oriented business this means that prior to buying any asset the manager must be confident that it will make a positive contribution either to a profit or some other positive objective of the organisation. It is fairly obvious that a trading company which buys goods for £10 must positively expect to sell them for considerably more than £10 if it hopes to stay in business.

The problem about investing in assets however profitably and maintaining adequate cash balances is essentially one of timing. In the study of cash budgets in the first course book *Finance* the technique of calculating cash requirements in each period was shown as part of budgeting.

The preparation of budgets whether of operations or of capital does not in itself ensure the proper use of resources. Managers need to monitor the performance that is actually taking place against what the budgets show ought to be happening. From experience many firms find that they have to take particular care in the monitoring and control of working capital.

Working Capital Management

The flows involved in a manufacturing business are shown in Exhibit 37.1.

324

Exhibit 37.1
Working capital flow in a manufacturing firm

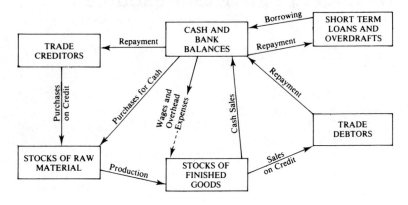

The essential flow of working capital in Exhibit 37.1 shows a cycle of cash flowing out in the production of goods which are then converted back into cash through sales. In trying to balance this process the manager must therefore firstly keep in control the production process which includes buying materials and stocking them, keeping employees and machinery at work and stocking finished goods prior to sale. Secondly the selling process must also be kept in closely co-ordinated check with production.

The production manager's job would be made easier if he could buy much more material than he is likely to need and similarly he would have more machinery and labour. However, whilst having large supplies of the productive resources to hand will make the job of production easier, it will be costly to carry stocks of items that will not be absolutely necessary. Carrying stocks of material will involve the following types of cost which increase as more stock is held:

1. Storage charges for rental of warehouses
2. Handling charges
3. Damage, Deterioration and Obsolescence of goods during storage
4. Security costs
5. Interest charges on funds tied up in stocks.

If these costs just shown increase with the amount of stock held there will also be some costs which will be reduced:

1. Ordering costs (a few large orders are cheaper than many small ones)
2. Buying prices may be reduced for large quantities ordered in a delivery
3. Stock out costs, which are costs which result when production is halted for lack of material and will include costs of idle machines and staff as well as customer badwill.

The overall effect of these two types of cost can best be illustrated on a graph (*see* Exhibit 37.2). Line A shows costs which increase as more stock is held. Line B shows the costs which reduce as more stock is held.

Line C represents the total cost = A + B. The total cost line C has a minimum point equivalent on the graph to quantity X and cost of holding stock £Y. This is the point where a firm should seek to fix the quantity of stock it holds, since the total cost is lowest at this point.

Exhibit 37.2

Total costs of carrying stock-in-trade

Number of units in stock		25	50	100	200	250	300	400
A Annual cost of carrying stock @ £1 per unit	£	25	50	100	200	250	300	400
B Average cost of placing orders and stockout cost	£	2,000	1,000	500	250	200	165	125
C Total cost of holding stock at each level		2,025	1,050	600	450	450	465	525

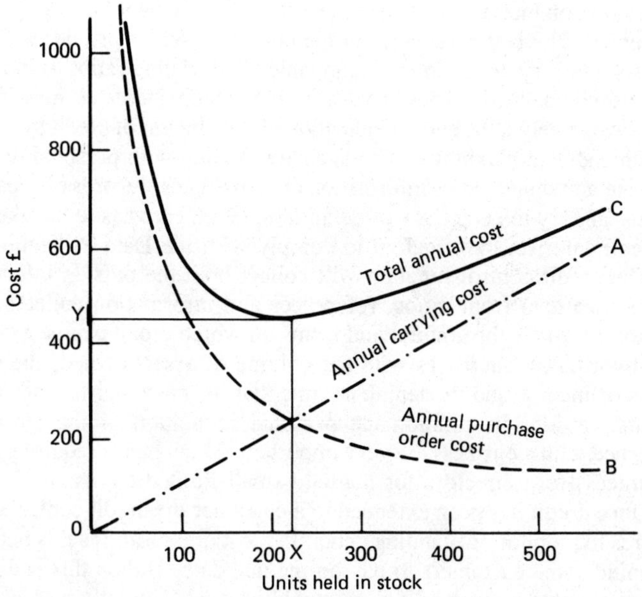

The basic principles shown in Exhibit 37.2 will apply to all assets, for example machinery, buildings or cash itself. Some costs will reduce the more of the asset that is held, whereas others will increase. The objective of management should be to find the optimal point for total costs.

The way in which management will decide on the quantity of assets to hold can be helped by using the cost information to develop a model to calculate the optimal point. This type of model is very frequently applied to control inventory levels. These stock control models are not dealt with in this book, but are very helpful in many organisations in limiting the financial resource tied up in working capital.

The other aspect of working capital that needs special management attention arises in the area of sales and debtors. When any orgnisation is asked to supply goods or services on credit to another organisation it involves the risk of either non-payment of the debt or more frequently delayed repayment. This type of problem prompts many organisations to employ special Credit Control Departments to monitor all transactions where credit is extended to customers.

Credit control starts most logically prior to a transaction taking place. This normally involves credit rating a potential customer. In order to do this most organisations will employ some outside agency to give information, as well as making their own assessment.

The outside agencies which exist in the market usually specialise in either corporate credit rating of companies and businesses or collecting credit information on individuals who seek to borrow from banks or hire purchase companies. The better agencies in the corporate sector provide a detailed analysis of a very wide range of companies, calculating ratios as indicators of financial viability. They give a rating which indicates how risky a company is likely to be and an indication of the amount of credit they would recommend as a maximum. The agencies dealing with personal debts try to collate a vast amount of information on individuals' records of repayment of loans and try to keep track of defaulters. Great care has to be taken now with computerised information to comply with the Data Protection Act.

The credit control function will collect both the outside information and its own data from ratios, references and information collected from a customer, to fix the amount and terms on which credit can be extended. Creditworthiness increases with the volume of assets owned, the size of profits or income and the length of time that the customer has been in the business or job. In addition the personal reputation of the individuals concerned with a business are very important. Many banks require personal guarantees from directors for loans to small limited companies.

Once credit has been extended to a customer the credit control section requires to monitor outstanding debts. In most organisations it is necessary to remind some customers to pay on the due date. Unless this is done the volume of debtors outstanding can quickly mount − greatly increasing the required working capital. At the end of the line Credit Control will have to decide when to take formal steps to recover unpaid debts, using debt collection agencies or the courts. Most organisations do not want to get to this final stage; it is much better to avoid bad debts than to attempt to collect them.

Effective credit control requires an efficient accounting system, which keeps the personal accounts of customers up to date. Salesmen need to be able to check whether a customer is within his credit limit or whether a payment is needed before more sales can be made. If the accounts are not kept properly, effective credit control is very difficult.

Fixed Asset Management

The management of Fixed Assets as distinct from Current Assets, which are part of Working Capital, is simply one of the time factor and the scale of resources to be invested. In the chapters in the first book *Finance* dealing with Capital Budgeting the way in which spending on Fixed Assets are evaluated was discussed in detail. Since fixed assets usually have a life involving many years it is normal to include the interest cost of the funds invested in the assets concerned. This 'cost of capital' is in reality an important consideration in many other decisions. For example it was included as part of the costs considered in this chapter in deciding on the optimal level of investment in stock-in-trade. The idea of calculating the Cost of Capital for use in Capital Budgets and decisions relating to the use of a firm's resources is developed in the next set of chapters.

38

Capital Expenditure Evaluation and Uncertainty

In the first year course book *Finance* the budgets of capital expenditures were based on an assumption of average certainty. In reality however different types of project have widely different levels of uncertainty attached to their outcomes. The outcomes of replacement of machinery on an existing product line is likely to be much easier to estimate than the result of investment in a totally new product line of an innovatory kind. Methods need to be developed to deal with uncertainty in this type of situation. Some of the most common methods of allowing for uncertainty are described below.

Scaling down benefits and scaling up uncertain costs

Perhaps the commonest method of allowing for uncertainty is to adopt a very conservative approach to the estimated data used in capital budgets. This may simply mean reducing estimates of revenues by a fixed percentage and increasing estimates of costs likewise. Perhaps a more useful approach is to obtain from the estimates a range of likely outcomes which might range over

'Best	'Most	'Worst
Likely	Likely	Likely
Outcome',	Outcome',	Outcome'.

Continual vigilance is necessary in preparing estimates for capital budgets since people become highly committed to projects and tend to produce figures to prove their case, rather than objective estimates.

Adjusting the cut-off rate

Another common method of allowing for uncertainty is to increase the rate of return required from a project. Most businesses find that the actual rate of return earned by the business as a whole falls short of the returns promised by individual projects. It is always hard after the event to effectively trace what happens — although post-auditing of capital budgets is very desirable in principle. In practice therefore businesses tend to fix cut off rates some way higher than then estimated cost of capital to allow for shortfalls from the budget. Different cut-off rates are also often applied to projects in different classes of uncertainty. Replacement of existing plant will require a lower cut-off than investment in a new and untried development.

Estimates using subjective probabilities

Some organisations have used estimating techniques which require the estimators to consider the range of likely outcomes and relate to them a subjective assessment of the probability of occurence. For example instead of a single estimate of sales the likely range is associated with its probability.

1 Sale Estimates £	2 Probability of Outcome	$3 = 1 \times 2$ Expected Sales
1,000	0.1	100
2,000	0.3	600
3,000	0.4	1,200
4,000	0.2	800
	1.0	2,700

The probability of the outcome in the second column is assigned by the estimator to the range of sales estimates in column one. The probabilities add to one as they cover the full range of likely outcomes. The expected sales from this estimate amount to £2,700.

This type of approach is only likely to prove better than other methods if there is reasonable basis for assigning the probability of outcome — based on analysis of previous experience for example.

Sensitivity Analysis

When the data to be analysed has been assembled — particularly if it is to be analysed on a computer — it may be helpful to run the calculation through a number of times — each time varying an item of input to the budget. For example on the first run using the best estimate figures — the present value may be positive. On the second run the sales estimates may be reduced by 10% and the new result compared with the first run. If the second outcome shows a negative present value it is clear that the result is sensitive to the estimates of sales. In this way all the items crucial to the success of the project can be identified and special additional scrutiny given to their validity.

Assignment Exercises

38.1. What are the main ways in which organisations allow for uncertainty in evaluating investment decisions?

38.2. The marketing managers have been asked to estimate the likely sales of a new product by applying their subjective judgement to the probability of achieving a range of estimates of sales. The probabilities they apply as a percentage must add to 100% since it is certain that some level of sales will be achieved. Their estimates are totalled and summarised as follows:

Estimated Sales in Units	Probability of achievement %
100,000	5
200,000	20
250,000	30
300,000	40
350,000	5
	100

What is the expected level of sales in units?

38.3A. The following estimates of cash flows are made in respect of a new project:

Period	Capital Investment outlay	Sales	Expenses	Net Cash Flow
0	45,000	–	–	45,000
1		(40,000)	22,000	(18,000)
2		(40,000)	22,000	(18,000)
3	(2,000)	(40,000)	22,000	(20,000)

(Figures in brackets are cash inflows)
Show the effect of the following events happening separately
(a) Capital Investment increase + 10%
(b) Sales reducing − 10%
(c) Expenses increasing + 5%.
Start from the original estimates calculating the NPV at an interest rate of 10%.

39

Risk and Accounting Structure

In the first year course book *Finance* the ideas of Break Even Analysis were introduced. The Break Even Chart shows clearly how risk emanates from variations in sales in relation to costs. Risk is usually defined in terms of the variability in profits and of course ultimately in the likelihood of failure, implied in bankruptcy or liquidations. A Business with a high proportion of fixed cost will show a much higher rate of increase in profit as sales rise above break- even compared to one with a high proportion of variable cost. Correspondingly the high fixed cost company will show a much more dramatic decline into loss as sales reduce.

Exhibit 39.1

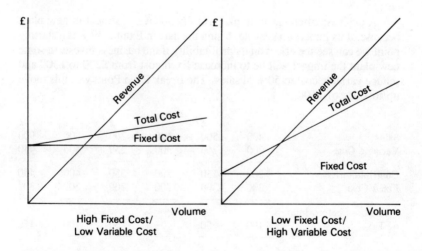

High Fixed Cost/
Low Variable Cost

Low Fixed Cost/
High Variable Cost

In numerical terms this can be illustrated as follows:

Fixed Costs are £200 and Variable Costs are 60% of Sales. The Break Even Point is therefore at Sales of £500. The Break Even is worked out from the fact that we know Fixed Cost is £200 and that the contribution is: Sales

− 60% Sales = 40% Sales. Thus every £1 sold will make a contribution of 40p. The point of break even is where contribution equals fixed costs i.e.

$$\frac{200}{.4} = £500 \text{ sales.}$$

	£	£	£	£	£	£
Sales	400	500	600	700	800	900
Variable Cost	240	300	360	420	480	540
Contribution	160	200	240	280	320	360
Fixed Cost	200	200	200	200	200	200
Profit/Loss Before Interest and Tax	−40	−	40	80	120	160

Exhibit 39.2

The impact of changes in sales level can be seen to have a more than proportional impact on profit −

Sales Increase from £600 to £700 = + 16.7%
Profit Increase   £40 to £80 = +100.0%
Sales Increase from £600 to £800 = + 33.3%
Profit Increase   £40 to £120 = +200.0%

The effect of the level of fixed cost on the returns of a business is called gearing. A highly geared company is one with a high proportion of fixed cost.

A business often has to think carefully about investment in new plant because of its impact on gearing. Using the data in Exhibit 39.2 as a starting point we can see the effect on its profitability if the business invests in some new plant the impact will be to increase fixed cost from £200 to £300 and reduce variable cost to 50% of sales. The Break Even Point will this move up to sales of £600.

	£	£	£	£	£	£
Sales	400	500	600	700	800	900
Variable Cost	200	250	300	350	400	450
Contribution	200	250	300	350	400	450
Fixed Cost	300	300	300	300	300	300
Profit/Loss before Interest or Tax	−100	− 50	−	50	100	150

The impact of the new investment has been to increase the Break Even Sales from £500 to £600 in exchange for which the rate of profitability has increased. This can best be seen on the graph Exhibit 39.1 where a higher geared situation shows the widest angle between the Revenue and Total Cost Line.

In numerical terms increasing sales from £700 to £800, i.e. 14.3% increases profits from £50 to £100, i.e. 100%.

The analysis we have examined which relates to the change in gearing from operating factors does not in itself indicate whether the investment is a good one or not. It does however show that new investment can have a significant impact on the operational risk of the business. The decision will have to be taken as to whether the increased profitability justifies the increase in break even position. If sales are hard to come by, this may not be justified.

Financial Gearing

The impact of a firm borrowing money and paying interest on it, rather than funding itself entirely from its equity capital is very similar in effect to operational gearing. The interest on borrowing is the same in its impact as a fixed cost.

To illustrate this the data from Exhibit 39.2 will be taken.

	£	£	£	£	£	£
Sales	400	500	600	700	800	900
Profit/Loss before Interest and Tax	− 40	0	40	80	120	160

If the business is funded entirely from Ordinary Share Capital amounting to £1,000, then if we ignore tax the rates of return would be

	£	£	£	£	£	£
Sales	400	500	600	700	800	900
Return = Profit/Loss = Share Capital of £1,000	4%	0	4%	8%	12%	16%

If instead of funding entirely from ordinary shares. If the business raised its £1,000 funds − £600 from Ordinary Shares and £400 from a 10% Loan then the returns amend be as follows:

	£	£	£	£	£	£
Sales	400	500	600	700	800	900
Profit/Loss before Interest and Tax	− 40	0	40	80	120	160
Interest	− 40	− 40	− 40	− 40	− 40	− 40
Net Profit before tax	− 80	− 40	0	40	80	120
Return = Profit/Loss = Share Capital of £600	13.3%	−6.7%	0	6.7%	13.3%	20%

The impact of borrowing money on the return to the Ordinary Shareholders is to increase the return to him beyond the point where operating profits exceed a return of 10% on the capital, i.e. Sales of £150. After this point the returns to the ordinary shareholder accelerate. Notice however the significant increase in Break Even Point from £500 to £600 and that sales must in fact exceed £750 before the shareholder is better off.

Quite apart from the increased risk from gearing the introduction of borrowing brings a legal risk that the lender may − if for example interest is not paid on time − take a legal charge over the company's assets.

The net cost of borrowing is reduced if tax is taken into account, since the interest charge is deductible from profit subject to tax. If we assumed a 50% tax rate the figures would be as follows:

100% Share Capital

	£	£	£	£	£	£
Sales	400	500	600	700	800	900
Net of Tax Profit/Loss	− 20	0	20	40	60	80
Return	− 2%	0	2%	4%	6%	8%

60% Share Capital

Net of Tax Profit	− 40%	− 20	0	20	40	60
Return	−6.7%	−3.3%	0	3.3%	6.7%	10%

The Measurement of Gearing is also covered in Chapter 12 on Ratio Analysis. The ratios give an indication of the level of gearing in a company both measured from the Balance Sheet and the Profit and Loss Account. In this chapter we have examined the impact of the gearing on risk.

Assignment Exercises

39.1. Plant A has fixed costs of £30,000 p.a. and its variable costs are 50% of Sales. Plant B has fixed costs of £20,000 p.a. and its variable costs are 60% of Sales.

Both plants produce the same product. Compare the returns from the two plants and say which appears to be most risky.

39.2A. Using the data for plant A show the return on Ordinary Shares by assuming that the plant is owned by
(a) a Company whose capital consists of £100,000 Ordinary Shares.
(b) a Company whose capital consists of £60,000 Ordinary Shares and £40,000 10% Loan Stock.
What other differences does the introduction of borrowed capital introduce?

39.3A. The Exmoor Company produces a single product which it sells at £10, per unit and which has a variable cost of £4 per unit. The fixed costs per annum are £42,000 and its current levels of operation are funded from share capital and reserves amounting to £70,000. It currently sells 10,000 units a year at full capacity but could expand this to 15,000 by investing £10,000 which it would have to borrow at 15% interest. Fixed Cost would be increased by £2,000 p.a. but variable cost would stay the same. Show the impact of the increase on break even and return on share capital.

40

Cost of Capital I

The Cost of Capital to an organisation is the rate of return which must be earned if it is to meet its obligations to lenders and the expectations of investors who are thinking of buying shares or other securities in the organisation. If it is to increase the wealth of its owners it will need to earn more profit than the cost of its capital.

The Cost of Capital covers the return required by the whole range of its Ordinary Shares, Preference Shares, Debentures and Loan Stock as well as Overdrafts and other Creditors. The whole range will be combined to give an average cost for the whole organisations capital. Before this is done however the cost to the organisation of the individual sources of capital will be discussed.

Short Term Borrowing

Short terms loans come mainly in the form of loans and overdrafts from banks and other financial institutions. The interest rates charged on these accounts are normally based on the daily balance of the account, in which case the interest charged is a 'real' rate. If some other basis of charging interest is used the equivalent real rate must now by law be quoted. This is called the Annual Percentage Rate (APR).

The rates of interest charged on overdrafts fluctuate with the central bank base lending rate. How much more than the base rate a bank charges is based on the creditworthiness and size of the borrower. This type of lending is only normally made in 'low-geared' situations where the bank feels it has adequate security for the loan.

Short term funds may also be obtained by issuing Bills of Exchange − which are promises to pay a fixed sum at a specified future date. The Bill of Exchange can, provided the signatory is creditworthy, be discounted for immediate cash. The real rate of interest is different from the nominal rate − in this type of transaction.

Since interest charged will be deductible from taxable profit the net cost of interest will be reduced by the rate of tax paid by the company. If the tax rate is 42% the net cost will be 58% of the gross amount i.e. £100 gross interest would only cost £58 after taking the tax into account.

In more formal terms the net cost of the loan is: The gross interest $\times$ (1 −tax rate). Example if the gross interest is 10% and tax rate 42%, the net cost is 10% $\times$ (1 −.42) = 5.8%.

Intermediate Term Loans

Banks and other Financial Institutions offer term loans usually for specific developments or projects over periods from 5 to 10 years. The arrangements for making the loan usually require repayment by instalments in the later years of the loan period. Interest is again based on a predetermined formula − often calculated at the amount owing at the start of each year − the real rate of interest has therefore to be calculated.

Trade Creditors and accruals

Trade creditors and accruals do not normally involve interest payments and are often described as costless forms of finance. In considering the overall cost of capital it is convenient to treat these current liabilities as a deduction from current assets. This is in line with the calculation of return on capital employed described in Chapter 12, where current liabilities excluding overdrafts are deducted from current assets. If this method is used the cost of capital is directly comparable with the return on capital employed.

Debentures and Long Term Loan Stock

A company may be fortunate enough to have sold debentures at a time in the past when interest rates were low. The actual rate of interest paid may thus be well below the current market rates. For example if a company issued debentures ten years ago carrying interest of 5% − the current rate of interest today required being 10% − what will happen to the market price of the debenture? Taking a £100 unit of Debenture the interest paid will be £5 per annum. An investor to expects a yield of 10% − therefore he will only pay such a price for the debenture as will yield him 10%. Let x = the market price of the debenture. Then

$$\frac{£5}{x} \times \frac{100}{1} = 5\%$$

Then x = £50

The investor will thus only pay £50 for £100 face or par value of debentures. It is the yield on this market value which represents the real cost of the debentures. In this example the cost of debentures would be 10% less the tax rate adjustment.

If the company pays tax at 52% on profits the net cost of the borrowing is 10% $\times$ (1 −.52) = 4.8%.

Preference Share Capital

The difference between Preference Share Capital and Debentures is in two main respects. Firstly a dividend does not have to be declared if the directors consider it inadvisable or there are insufficient profits, and there are no legal remedies for the preference shareholder when dividends are not paid. If interest is not paid then the company is defaulting on its debt and the debenture holder can obtain legal redress. In every other respect however the payment of a fixed preference dividend has the same impact on gearing as the payment of interest — taking a fixed amount of the profit each year it is paid. In a normally successful business — preference dividends are paid as a matter of course since no dividend on other shares can be paid until they have received their dues.

The other difference between preference dividend and interest is that for tax purposes the dividend is paid out of taxed profit and is not allowable as a deduction for tax purposes. The cost of a preference share is therefore the yield of its dividend over the market price without adjustment for tax.

Example: A company has £1 Preference Shares which pay a fixed dividend of 10p per share. The market value of the shares is 80p. The cost of this capital is therefore $\dfrac{10p}{80p} = 12.5\%$.

Some Financing Decisions

When issuing shares, debentures or loans, a company will have to decide on the precise terms of the issue. It can choose whether they should be issued at par, at a premium or at a discount. It can in the case of redeemable preference shares, debentures or loans decide both on the rate of interest to be paid, and a date for redemption. While all the factors involved are complex and cannot be considered here, by applying interest calculations a proper decision can be made on the basis of financial costs.

Example. A company needs £500,000 cash for a ten-year period. The company's financial advisers have made the following offers:

> 14 per cent Ten-year debentures at 110
> 12 per cent Ten-year debentures at 100
> 10 per cent Ten-year debentures at 90

Repayment at par will be made at the end of ten years.

Which offer should be accepted on cost considerations alone?

In order to consider the cost of the various issues, each will have to be converted to its present value at the date of issue. In order to do this a rate of interest will have to be used in the calculations. For this example since 12 per cent is the rate when debentures are issued at par this will be assumed to be the Market rate of interest. The present value of the issues will comprise:

1. The present value of the interest payments to be made over ten years.

2. The present value of the capital repayment at the date of redemption ten years hence.

The nominal value of debentures issued will vary according to the terms of issue:

(a) 14 per cent Debentures at 110

$$\frac{£500,000}{1} \times \frac{100}{110} = £454,545$$

$$\begin{array}{r} £ \\ Check\ 454,545 \\ Add\ 10\ per\ cent\ \underline{45,455} \\ \underline{500,000} \end{array}$$

(b) 12 per cent Debentures at 100

$$\frac{£500,000}{1} \times \frac{100}{100} = £500,000$$

(c) 10 per cent Debentures at 90

$$\frac{£500,000}{1} \times \frac{100}{90} = £555,556$$

$$\begin{array}{r} £ \\ Check\ 555,556 \\ Less\ 10\ per\ cent\ \underline{55,556} \\ \underline{500,000} \end{array}$$

The interest payments on the bonds sold will be:

			£
(a)	Nominal Value £454,545 at 14 per cent =	63,636
(b)	Nominal Value £500,000 at 12 per cent =	60,000
(c)	Nominal Value £555,556 at 10 per cent =	55,556

Calculation of the Present Value of the Capital Sum and Interest:

(a) 14 per cent Debentures   £
Capital Sum £454,545 at 12 per cent = £454,545×0.322 =   146,363
Interest of 63,636 at 12 per cent = 63,636×5.650   =   359,543

    505,906

Present Value of £1 table = 0.322
Present Value of an Annuity of £1 table = 5.650

(b) 12 per cent Debenture   £
Capital Sum £500,000 at 12 per cent = £500,000×0.322 =   161,000
Interest of £60,00 at 12 per cent = £60,000×5.650   =   339,000

    500,000

(c) 10 per cent Debenture   £
     Capital Sum £555,556 at 12 per cent = £555,556×0.322 =   178,889
     Interest of £55,556 at 12 per cent = £55,556×5.650   =   313,891
     _____
                                                              492,780
     ========

In this example, therefore, the 10 per cent debenture is the cheapest.

Assignment Exercises

40.1. A Bill of Exchange for 90 days with a face value of £100,000 is discounted at the prime market rate of 12%. What is the real rate of interest?

40.2A. What would the real rate of interest have been if the Bill of Exchange had been for six months?

40.3. A company has some non redeemable debentures which pay 5% interest on each £100 unit of stock. The debentures currently sell on the market for £40 a unit. What is the market yield on these debentures?

40.4. If the company pays corporation tax at 52% on its profits, what is the net of tax market rate for the debentures in question 40.3?

40.5A. A Company has issued £1 6% Preference Shares. The Market price for these shares is currently £0.35. What is the cost of this Preference Share Capital?

40.6A. If the Company pays corporation tax at 52% on its profits, what is the net of tax market rate for its preference shares as detailed in question 40.5A.?

40.7A. A company is seeking to raise £200,000. It has been offered the choice of issuing debentures with a ten year life either at

(a) 15% interest and issued at 105 redeemable at par
(b) 13% interest and issued at 97.5 redeemable at par

   The current market rate for debentures is 14% which option should the company choose?

41

Cost of Capital II − Ordinary Shares

The cost of capital for borrowing is relatively easy to establish because there is a fixed rate of interest determined for each security. If we establish the price for the security then the yield is established. With ordinary share capital there is no established rate for dividends − other than the hope of investors that the company will continue to prosper.

When an investor buys an ordinary share he anticipates a return based not only on the dividends he receives but also on capital gains he hopes to make when he sells the share, i.e. that the value of the share will rise.

For example Mr. X buys a share in Y Ltd. for £2. He expects a dividend of 50p at the end of a year, at which time he also expects to sell the share for £2.50. The return is therefore:

Value at the end of year 50p + £2.50 =	£3.00
Cost	2.00
Gain	1.00

$$\text{Return} = \frac{\text{Gain}}{\text{Cost of Investment}} = \frac{£1}{£2} = 50\%.$$

If the dividend and capital gain were not to be received until the end of the second year the rate of return would be reduced to 22%.

$$\frac{A}{(1+r)^n} = P$$

$$\frac{3.00}{(1+r)^2} = 2$$

$$r = \sqrt{\frac{3}{2}} - 1$$

$$r = .22 \text{ or } 22\%.$$

To develop this line of approach to the valuation of a share we will refer back to the methods of Present Value in the first year book Finance where the basic formula $P = \dfrac{A}{(1+r)^n}$ was stated where P is the Principal or present value and A the future amount.

If we want to value a share at its present value P then we need to estimate the future amounts we expect to receive from it and the rate of return expected from a share of this type. The value P will equal the future Dividend and the future Sale Price, discounted at the market rate. Using the data in the earlier example the value of a share where the dividend in the first year is expected to be 50p and the value at the end £2.50 with a required rate of return of 50% then

$$P_0 = \frac{D_1}{(1+r)^1} + \frac{P_1}{(1+r)^1}$$

Where P_0 is the share price now
D_1 is the dividend in year 1
P_1 is the share price in year 1

$$P_0 = \frac{0.5}{1+0.5} + \frac{2.50}{1+0.5}$$

$$P_0 = \quad .333 \quad + \quad 1.667 \quad = £2.00.$$

If the dividend in year 1 is nil but expected to be 50p at the end of year 2 and a sale price of £2.50 at the end of year 2 then: –

$$P_0 = \frac{D_1}{(1+r)^1} + \frac{D_2}{(1+r)^2} + \frac{P_2}{(1+r)^2}$$

$$= \frac{0}{(1+0.5)^1} + \frac{0.5}{(1+0.5)^2} + \frac{2.50}{(1+.05)^2}$$

$$= \quad 0 \quad + \quad 0.22 \quad + \quad 1.11$$

$$= £1.33$$

(Note the price would be £2 if the required return was 22%).

If we start with the one year horizon of

$$P_0 = \frac{D_1}{(1+r)^1} + \frac{P_1}{(1+r)^1}$$

and then consider that

$$P_1 = \frac{D_2}{(1+r)^2} + \frac{P_2}{(1+r)^2} \quad \text{and} \quad P_2 = \frac{D_3}{(1+r)^3} + \frac{P_3}{(1+r)^3} \quad \text{and so on}$$

then in place of the P_1 and P_2 etc. we can substitute dividend flows with only a terminal Price at the end of the series: –

$$P_0 = \frac{D_1}{(1+r)^1} + \frac{D_2}{(1+r)^2} + \frac{D_3}{(1+r)^3} + \frac{D_4}{(1+r)^4} + \ldots\ldots + \frac{D_n}{(1+r)^n} + \frac{P_n}{(1+r)^n}$$

where n is a large number. At this point the impact of discounting with large numbers will reduce the value of P_n to something very small and insignificant – which for practical purposes may be ignored. Thus the present price may be considered to represent the discounted value of future dividends.

In anticipating future dividends it is common in an established and stable business to estimate the rate of growth after the first year as a percentage rather than estimate each dividend separately. If the dividend is expected to grow at 5% per annum then in year 2 the dividend will be $D_1 \times (1+.05)$ and in year 3 the dividend will be $D_1 \times (1+.05)(1+.05)$ or $D_1(1+.05)^2$. If we use g as the growth rate rather than 5% then we can express the general formula to value a share as follows: −

$$P_0 = \frac{D_1}{(1+r)^1} + \frac{D_1(1+g)}{(1+r)^2} + \frac{D_1(1+g)^2}{(1+r)^3} + \frac{D_1(1+g)^3}{(1+r)^4} + \ldots \ldots + \frac{D_1(1+g)^{n-1}}{(1+r)^n}$$

If we make the assumption from that the growth rate will continue constantly to infinity then the above expression can be reduced mathematically to

$$\cdot P_0 = \frac{D}{r-g} \text{ provided that } r > g.$$

If g is higher than r then the full formula must be used. Example: The current dividend on a share is 50p. The rate of return expected on similar shares is 8% and the growth rate of dividends is expected to be 3% per annum.

$$P_0 = \frac{50}{.08-.03} = \frac{50}{.05} = 1000p.$$

The current price expected would be £10 per share.

Note that if there were no growth rate expected − as for instance would be the case for fixed interest securities the formula can still be used e.g. facts as before but nil growth.

$$P_0 = \frac{50}{.08-0} = \frac{50}{.08} = 625p.$$

The current price is reduced to £6.25 with no growth. Since in this chapter we are concerned with the cost of capital the formula just developed can be expressed in terms of a rate of interest

$$P = \frac{D}{r-g} \text{ is equivalent to}$$

$$r = \frac{D}{p} + g$$

Expressing this in words we have earlier in the book in Chapter 12 defined $\frac{D}{p}$ as the Dividend Yield. Thus the rate of return is the Dividend Yield plus growth rate.

Some analysts prefer to consider share prices from the profits basis rather than dividends. The commonest way of expressing this is through the Price Earnings ratio which was introduced in the Chapter on Ratio Analysis. The Price Earnings ratio represents the capitalisation factor that

343

the market applies to a firms profits to arrive at the Share Price. Thus if a firm has a P/E ratio of 9 and Earnings per share of £3 then the Market Price of the share will be £27. The capitalisation factor will be related both to the particular firms rating for risk and performance and also the general market rates of return. In order to use the P/E ratio for predicting prices it is therefore necessary to predict both the future pattern of the ratio as well as the future pattern of earnings.

Example

The data for Alpa Ltd. relating to EPS and P/E ratio was as follows:

	EPS	P/E ratio
19-1	20p	8.1
19-2	22p	8.4
19-3	25p	8.3
19-4	28p	8.5

The analyst expects earnings for 19-5 to increase by 10% and the P/E ratio to remain constant. The expected market price for 19-5 will therefore be

EPS 28+2.8 × P/E 8.5 = 261.8p.

This type of prediction of share price is most likely to be useful for short term prediction of less than one year, since there is no adequate way of forecasting the longer term factors when market conditions are unstable.

Relating the Price Earnings ratio to the Dividend approach developed earlier in this chapter is possible if the proposition of earnings distributed as dividends is expected to remain constant so that

$D = aE$ where D = Dividends
  E = Earnings
  a = The proportion of earnings paid out as dividends.

The rate of return formula expressed earlier was:

$$r = \frac{D}{P} + g$$

if we replace D by a E in this formula then

$$r = \frac{aE}{P} + g$$

$\dfrac{aE}{P}$ is the same as $\dfrac{a}{\frac{P}{E}} = \dfrac{a}{\text{P/E ratio}}$

$$\therefore r = \frac{a}{\text{P/E ratio}} + g$$

or P/E ratio = $\dfrac{a}{(r-g)}$

The P/E ratio is thus dependent on the proportion of profit paid out as dividend, the expected rate of return on the investment and the growth rate.

Example if a company pays out 50% of its profit as dividends, the expected rate of return is 10% and the growth rate of dividends is expected to be 5% p.a. then

$$P/E = \dfrac{0.5}{(.1-.05)} = 10 \text{ times}$$

The methods of valuing shares discussed in this chapter will only be helpful in periods of stability. Where markets are fluctuating it becomes very difficult to predict the future and hence the simple models based on established trends are no longer helpful.

Assignment Exercises

41.1. An analyst estimates that the return on a share will be £1.00 in year 1, £2.00 in year 2 and it can be sold at the end of year 2 for £5.00. What is the share worth now if the market rate of interest is 12%?

41.2A. What would the price have been for the share in 41.1 if the market rate of interest were 15%?

41.3. A share in Company X currently pays a dividend of £0.60 per annum. The dividend paid have grown at a rate of 5% p.a. for many years and are expected to continue at the same rate in future. The market rates of return for such shares are 10%. What price should a share in company X be?

41.4. If no growth rate were expected in dividends on the shares of Company C in question 41.2 what would the price be?

41.5A. A share priced at £5 pays a dividend of £0.60 per annum. The growth rate expected to coninue on dividends is 2% p.a. What rate of return is implied?

41.6. The expected earnings per share in a security is £0.13 in the coming year. The Price Earnings ratio is expected to remain at current level of 9.2. What is the expected price?

41.7A. If a company pays out 60% of its profit as dividends and the rate of return on its shares is expected to be 15% with a growth rate in dividends of 4% what would you expect its P/E ratio to be?

42

Cost of Capital III – Weighted Average Cost of Capital

Chapters 40 and 41 considered different elements in the Capital Structure of a Company. In order to arrive at an overall cost of capital for the firm these different parts – share capital and loans need to be combined. Ideally a company should be seeking to create a capital structure that produces the lowest overall cost of capital that it can achieve. There is however no simple way of achieving this nor is it possible to provide any correct method of measuring the actual cost of capital. This is because of the dynamic nature of the markets within which companies operate. Only if we could predict the future with certainty could we say for sure what the risks and returns were and therefore the associated costs.

Nonetheless it is very important for a firm to estimate its cost of capital since this provides a minimum level below which capital project returns may not be allowed to fall. Many firms as we have already indicated set a cut-off rate somewhat higher than estimated cost of capital. Nonetheless it is useful to know what the base is – rather than plucking a figure from pure guesswork.

In combining the various elements of capital structure some weighting of the different components has to be used. The most easily obtained weighting is the book value from the Balance Sheet of the different items.

Example:

	Balance Sheet Book Value £	Weights
Share Capital	100,000	.67
Debentures	50,000	.33
	150,000	1.00

The Weights obtained would then be applied to the cost of capital rates.

Example

	Cost of Capital %	Weight	Weighted Average %
Share Capital	9.8	.67	6.57
Debentures	6.5	.33	2.15
		1.00	8.72

The calculated weighted average cost of capital at 8.72% would give an approximate idea of the basis for capital budgeting decisions.

Rather than use the book value of the capital there is a strong argument for using the market values of the capital sources in the Balance Sheet. For example for Ordinary Shares if the company has 100,000 Ordinary Shares outstanding and the market price per share is £2.30 then the weighting for Ordinary Shares and the Reserves would be 100,000 × £2.30 = £230,000.

In calculating the weighted average cost of capital it is convenient to combine together various components where a company has whole variety of different sources. The following headings are normal:

Equity: Ordinary Share Capital and all Reserves

Preference Share Capital.

Debt: All debentures and loans both short and long term.

If a company has debentures or other securities which may at some future time be converted to ordinary shares, they should be included in Equity.

Exhibit 42.1

Combine the following balance sheet items to calculate weights based on book value:

Share Capital 100,000 £1 shares		100,000
Reserves		
Retained Profits	75,000	
Share Premium Account	25,000	
		100,000
Preference Shares 50,000 10% £1 shares		50,000
8% Debenture Stock		70,000
Short Term Loans		20,000

			Weight %
Equity 100,000 + 100,000 =		200,000	58.8
Preference		50,000	14.7
Debt 70,000 + 20,000		90,000	26.5
		340,000	100.0

Using the information in Exhibit 42.1 with Market Values it would change the weightings. If the market price for

Ordinary Shares =	£2.50
Preference Shares =	£0.90
Debenture Stock =	95
Short Term Loan	par

			Weight %
Then	Equity (100,000×2.50)	250,000	65.5
	Preference	45,000	11.8
	Debt (66,500+20,000)	86,500	22.7
		381,500	100.0

Exhibit 42.2

If the market rate for Equity is 10% for Preference Share 14% and Debt 12% calculate the weighted average cost of capital using book balues as in Exhibit 42.1 and Market Values from Exhibit 42.2.

	Book Value Weight %	Market Value Weight %	Market Rate	Book Value WACC	Market Value WACC
Equity	58.8	65.5	.10	5.88	6.55
Preference	14.7	11.8	.14	2.06	1.65
Debt	26.5	22.7	.12	3.18	2.72
	100.0	100.0		11.12%	10.92%

When considering the rate of interest to use as a cut off on projects it is important to remember that the items comprising the total sources of funds are interdependent. A company can only borrow funds if it has an adequate equity base. The lenders of funds will only tolerate certain levels of gearing which depend on the riskiness of the business in which it operates. Thus it is for most purposes appropriate to use the average cost of capital in assessing projects. However the marginal cost of raising funds is always important and any major investment which will require large scale fund raising should also be assessed against the specific cost of those funds raised.

Assignment Exercises

42.1. Glory Company Ltd has the following sources of capital as extracted from the balance sheet:

		£
500,000 £1 Ordinary Shares		500,000
250,000 £1 6% Preference Shares		250,000
Reserves		
Retained Profit	170,000	
Revaluation Reserve	50,000	
Share Premium Account	60,000	
		280,000
Long Term Loan Stock (12%)		100,000
Short Term Loan (15%)		50,000
		1,180,000

Calculate the weighting factors to establish the weighted average cost of capital based on book values.

42.2. The market value of sources capital for Glory Co. Ltd. in 42.1 is as follows:

Ordinary Shares	£2.50
Preference Shares	£0.50
Long Term Loan	95
Short Term Loan	par.

What are the weighting factors using the market values?

42.3. Using the weighting factors based on book values calculated in 42.1 and 42.2 establish what the WACC is based on book value weighting and market value weighting using the following rates:

Equity	12%
Preference	15%
Debt	14%

42.4A. Emperor Glass Fittings Ltd has the following extract from its balance sheet a sources of capital:

	£
1,000,000 £0.50 Ordinary Shares	500,000
100,000 £2 7% Preference Shares	200,000
Reserves	
Profit and Loss Account	400,000
	1,100,000
Debentures − 10%	600,000
Short Term Loan 12%	100,000
	1,800,000

The Quoted Price of its Ordinary Shares which yield 10% is £3 per share. The Preference Shares are quoted at £1 per share. Debentures are quoted at 80 and Short Term Loan at par.

The company is taxed at 40%.

What is its weighted average cost of capital.

43

Valuing a Business

In order to value a business with a view to buying or selling it there are two main parts to be evaluated. Firstly there are the tangible assets which the business owns such as buildings, machinery or stock in trade. Secondly there is the particular ability which this business has to earn profits. This second part arises from a variety of reasons such good employees, patents and so forth which give it special advantages. It is the combination of the two values for assets and profitability which creates the total worth of a business.

In the position where a business has been unsuccessful and trading at a loss the second element may be worthless. The value of the assets is then no more than they can be sold for in the market. Assets can be auctioned item by item in a public sale. If the assets are of good quality in general demand they may reach prices which are comparable with the market replacement price for similar items. Often however specialized items such as machinery may only reach scrap values to dealers. Ideally the seller of assets would like to sell to an eager buyer who will pay the equivalent of the market price with a buyer setting up a new business would pay for replacing all the assets. The knockdown price for assets sold piecemeal at an auction is usually the last resort. It is impossible to be much more specific about the value that such assets will be worth since they differ to much in kind.

In current cost accounting assets are valued in terms of their 'value to the business'. This means the value of assets in their current use expressed in terms of the best alternative means of supplying that use.

For example a Widgit Machine Mark A which originally cost £10,000 has been owned for six years is to be valued in current cost terms it is depreciated at £1000 per annum over 10 years. The firm would decide on the facts surrounding the particular asset. If the machine were to be destroyed what would happen in the following circumstances:

(a) Because the machine is in current use it would be replaced by an exactly comparable machine which is the best available equipment. The current value is thus the current market replacement value of the machine now £15,000 less allowance for depreciation based on six years wear and tear, $15,000 \times \frac{9}{10} = £9,000$ depreciation. the net value is thus £6,000.

(*b*)   Because the machine is obsolete and it is not in current use, its replacement value is not relevant. Its only value to the firm is its realisation value − what it can be sold for, in this case £500.

(*c*)   The machine is in current use, but is no longer the best equipment for the job. However it is not considered economic to replace the existing equipment. The value of the existing equipment will be based on the new equipment values. If the new equipment is superior because it is cheaper to buy now only £8,000 but does the same job − then the value of the old equipment will simply be reduced to the new lower replacement price less depreciation for the six years use, i.e. £8,000 less $\frac{6}{10}$ = £3,200.

(*d*)   Using the circumstances as in (*c*) but assuming that the new equipment is superior because it produces the goods at a lower cost for materials − then the value will have to be adjusted. The starting point would be the value of the new machine since this is the best current choice this would cost £16,000. The existing equipment however costs £1,000 per annum more to run − which disadvantage will reduce its value. By working out the present value of the extra costs, the amount to be deducted from the new equipment replacement value can be worked out. Assuming the existing equipment will last for five years and a 10% cost of capital the present value of the extra cost disadvantage would be £1,000 × 3.791 = £3,791. The net value to the business of the existing machine would be:

$$£16,000 − \tfrac{6}{10} = 9,600 \text{ less } £3,791 = £5,809$$

A business may own assets like leaseholds whose value van be readily ascertained in the market. If for example a lease is owned which entitles the business to receive rentals of £5,000 per year for 15 years then the value is the present value of this set of cash flows. If the market interest rate is 12% then £5,000 × 6.811 = £34,055 for the value of the lease.

In summary therefore the value of assets to a business may be either:

Replacement: where the business is a successful going concern and the asset if lost would be replaced.

Realisation: where the business is unsuccessful and assets will have to be sold off or if the assets are no longer useful

Present Value: particularly where there is a clear right to future cash flows from an asset such as a lease.

The ability of a firm to earn profits which are better than its competitors will entitle it to a price in excess of its asset value if it is sold. The term Goodwill is frequently used for the amount paid for this benefit of what are often called super profits. Goodwill is discussed in Chapter 11.

Example

XYZ Company is expected to earn the following profits for the next five years in comparison to standard profits for the industry:

Year	1	2	3	4	5
XYZ profit	500,000	550,000	600,000	660,000	700,000
Standard profit	200,000	250,000	300,000	400,000	600,000
Extra Profit of XYZ	+300,000	+300,000	+300,000	+260,000	+100,000

After five years the special patents which give XYZ is advantage expire. What is the current value now of its advantage.

The extra profits can be discounted back to a present value at the market rate of return expected from companies like XYZ — say 15%. The Goodwill is therefore worth:

Year	Extra Profit £	P.V. factor at 15%	Net Present Value £
1	300,000	.870	261,000
2	300,000	.756	226,800
3	300,000	.658	197,400
4	260,000	.572	148,720
5	100,000	.497	49,700
			£883,620

The business will therefore be valued at Goodwill £883,620 plus the market value to the business of its assets, evaluated in much the same terms as for current cost accounting.

Another approach to the valuation of a business is to consider it in much the same way that was used with regard to ordinary shares in Chapter 41. The approach so far as a share was concerned was to estimate future returns from the investment in the form of dividends and sales proceeds.

$$P_0 \quad \frac{D_1}{(1+r)} + \frac{D_2}{(1+r)^r} + \ldots + \frac{D_n}{(1+r)^n} + \frac{P_n}{(1+r)^n}$$

If the whole company is bought then cash generated from the company replace dividends and the terminal price the amount the business will eventually he sold off for.

Example: A take over bidder estimates that if he buys X Ltd he will hold it for three years and in each year withdraw cash of £50,000. At the end of the three years he will sell it off to £100,000. The market rate for this type of venture is 25%. What is X Ltd worth?

$$P_0 = \frac{50,000}{1.25} + \frac{50,000}{(1.25)^2} + \frac{50,000}{(1.25)^3} + \frac{100,000}{(1.25)^3} = £148,000$$

In practice the price actually paid will depend a great deal on the competition in the market to buy the company. The methods described of using asset value and goodwill and valuing on cash returns expected do provide some

352

basis from which to judge a reasonable price. Where these two methods produce different answers as they inevitably do working from different bases some businessmen work from an average of the two although this is purely expedient.

Many takeover situations develop into an auction and the price offered to buy a business, or supply a majority of its shares may escalate more in response to the competetiveness of the bidders than any rational evaluation of the business's worth. The reverse situation also exists where a company in financial difficulty may find very few bidders and a buyer may acquire it at well below its current operating values for assets.

The price quoted on the Stock Exchange for a share does not represent the price of obtaining a majority of the shares in that company, it is a price only for buying a small holding at current conditions of supply and demand. A sudden increase in demand will change the situation considerably. In addition the Stock Exchange operates a special code of conduct for takeover bidders to protect the interest of small shareholders who may be tempted to sell before they know of a bid.

For small businesses, not quoted on the market there are frequently customary methods which are applied to establish the value of a business. For example the price is quoted as: 'stock in trade and other assets at valuation plus two years purchase of the net profits'. This type of valuation may be satisfactory if the business concerned is of a very standard kind. However it only a short cut tot he more detailed evaluation of value previously discussed and the short cut may produce a seriously incorrect solution.

Assignment Exercises

43.1. What factors are likely to contribute to a business being able to earn super-profits?

43.2. A company owns a machine which cost £50,000 and is now written down by 50%. A new but identical machine which would have to be bought if the current machine were destroyed would cost £80,000. What is the current value to the business of the existing machine?

43.3A. A machine which cost £90,000 and has been depreciated by £60,000 and has a remaining life of 3 years it would be replaced if lost by a new machine which costs £100,000. The new machine produces labour savings of £2,000 p.a. compared to the old machine. What is the current value to the business of the existing machine if cost of capital is 10%?

43.4. A company owns a licence which will entitle it to royalties of £60,000 for the next 5 years. If cost of capital is 10% what it the licence worth?

43.5A. Logo Company is expected to earn a profit of £600,000 p.a. for the next ten years which is twice the profit rate for other firms in the industry. Using a cost of capital rate of 16% what are the super profits worth?

43.6A. The Cash generated by Long Ltd. is estimated currently to be £50,000 p.a., and growing into the foreseeable future at 5% per annum. If the rate of return required is 12% what is Long Ltd. worth?

44

Computer Hardware and Applications Software

The five basic components of the computer have already been mentioned in the first year course book *'Finance'*.

Exhibit 44.1

A computer configuration

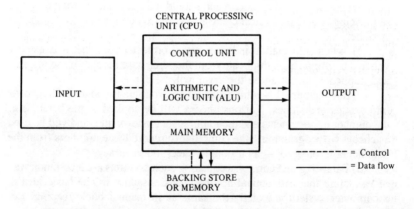

The dotted control lines indicate the issue of operating instructions from the CPU to peripheral equipment, such as printers.

Each of these elements in the computer hardware will be discussed in turn in relation to its accounting implications.

Input

We have already indicated that the main input devices to a computer are the keyboard for direct input (or in some systems optical character recognition — OCR) or, for indirect input, the information is first recorded on an input medium such as magnetic tape, disk or punched cards. Two important aspects of control need to be considered in respect of all input:

(*a*) is the data correct?

(*b*) is the input authorised?

Control in this context does not imply operating instructions, but rather the operation of internal control systems intended to safeguard the assets of the organization from wrongful waste or misappropriation. The official definition of an 'internal control system' is:

> 'The whole system of controls, financial and otherwise, established by the management in order to carry on the business of the enterprise in an orderly and efficient manner, ensure adherence to management policies, safeguard the assets and secure as far as possible the completeness and accuracy of the records.'

The necessity for this type of control has been emphasized by some spectacular errors and frauds on computer-based systems.

To try to ensure that the data entered is correct, most organizations have checks which are intended to eliminate error and discourage fraud. The following methods are commonly used for large volumes of accounting data.

(*a*) Control on source documents. These should be consecutively numbered. Any spoiled document should be retained to maintain full sequencing. Careful physical control is exercised over stocks of numbered stationery.

(*b*) When information is being keyed on to tape or disk it is usually verified by preparing a duplicate from the same base record. If the original and duplicate do not agree the error will be exposed.

(*c*) Batch controls — which operate by grouping homogeneous records into groups or batches. Various checks will be applied to the batch, e.g. the number of documents and their aggregate money value, and will be used as checks by programming the computer to record these numbers from the data actually entered — as a double check on accuracy.

(*d*) Balancing and control accounts — such accounts are a common way of validating the arithmetical accuracy of transactions. The basic idea in a computer system is exactly the same as in manual book-keeping, i.e. Opening balances + or − Input transactions = Closing balances.

(*e*) Audit trail of transactions. Any good system should be able to trace a trail of transactions in retrospect. The actual processes which are undertaken in the CPU of a computer may not be permanently recorded. However, it is possible to make sure that input and output records are maintained to enable information which may have been lost to be recreated.

With a well-designed system it is usually possible to restrict clerical or recording errors in input data to levels that are acceptable to management. A zero level of error would probably be too expensive to operate! However, the control of unauthorized inputs presents a very much more difficult and potentially dangerous element. Here the organization may be faced with a deliberate attempt by someone either inside or outside the organization to corrupt the organization's database — either for personal gain or simply for malicious reasons.

Control is centred on limiting access to input points to the computer. This may be done by physical means, i.e. locking the rooms in which input devices are kept, or by locking individual keyboards and only issuing keys to authorized personnel. This may be practical in a small system, but in many large organizations the requirements for widespread input points makes physical control difficult. Many systems allocate passwords or code numbers to users. A good example is the cashcard used for issuing cash to customers of the main banks and building societies. The customer has a plastic key and is given an individual code number. In theory these systems should be foolproof but human nature provides a weak link (with help from faulty machinery) which leads to the many problems with these systems frequently commented on in the press.

The effects of the 'hacker' to gain unauthorized access to computer systems imposes a considerable need for care. Together with the possibility of accidental damage, this should make the development of back-up systems and duplicated information — as well as care in controlling access — essential features in the design of even small computer systems.

Central processing unit

The CPU contains three main parts:
- (a) control unit;
- (b) arithmetic and logic unit (ALU);
- (c) main memory.

Control unit

The control unit consists of circuitry which will perform these functions:
- (a) read stored program instructions;
- (b) decode the program instructions;
- (c) cause the instructions to be executed;
- (d) obtain the next instruction in sequence.

Arithmetic logic unit

The ALU performs two main functions:

- (a) arithmetic functions such as addition and multiplication;
- (b) logical decision-making.

Main memory

The memory included in the CPU is known as primary storage. It is divided in two.

(a) Random access memory (RAM) is a volatile form of storage which only operates when the electric power is switched on. When the power goes off RAM is lost. When working with the power switched on information can be read and written to it at high speed.

(b) Read only memory (ROM), as its name implies, can only have information read from it. It is non-volatile which means that the information is retained even when the power is switched off. Thus, frequently used programs can be loaded in at time of manufacture without fear of being deleted.

Both ROM and RAM can be accessed at electronic speeds — unlike information on tape or disks which will be relatively slow to access.

When working with computers the memory capacity is often used to define a computer's power. The capacity is measured in kilobytes, usually abbreviated to K, i.e. a computer may be described as having a capacity of 256K.

To understand this measurement it is necessary to understand how data is stored in a computer. The most elementary piece of data is known as a *bit*. A bit can take on only one of two possible values, either 0 or 1. A single bit is not very useful but when linked with other bits more useful data can be stored.

The following combinations illustrate this:

Two bits put together have four combinations:
00, 01, 10, 11

Three bits put together have eight combinations:
000, 001, 010, 011, 100, 101, 110, 111

or, put another way:

2 to the power 2 combinations = 2^2 = 4 for 2 bits
2 to the power 3 combinations = 2^3 = 8 for 3 bits
2 to the power 4 combinations = 2^4 = 16 for 4 bits
etc.

In general there are 2^n combinations for *n* bits.

A byte consists of eight bits. Thus, a byte will contain 2^8 = 256 combinations of data. Each combination could represent a different letter, digit or special character such as a full stop, comma, etc. For example:

1 0 0 0 0 0 0 0 may represent the letter A
1 0 0 0 0 0 0 1 may represent the letter B
etc.

The storage capacity of a computer is usually measured in kilobytes rather than bytes. A kilobyte consists of 1,024 bytes. However, it is often convenient to think of a kilobyte as 1,000 bytes, i.e. a 512K computer has a memory of approximately 512,000 bytes. Very large computers may have their memory measured in megabytes (M) where M = 1,024K.

As a rule of thumb, one megabyte is taken as equivalent to one million bytes.

The output of a computer may be visually displayed on a visual display unit (VDU) or television monitor screen — these are either monochrome or in colour. If hard copy is required there is a wide variety of different printers available — some relatively slow and giving a poor print, others very fast and of high quality. The output can be transmitted over telephone wires via a modem (modulator/demodulator) which translates the digital signal of a computer into the analogue signal carried on telephone wires and then retranslates the message into a recovery computer. If it is needed for future reference the information in the output will normally be retained by recording it on tapes or disks which can then be retained for as long as necessary. Important output material which would cause major problems if lost should be duplicated and one copy kept in a separate safe location. Security of the backing store of information is of great importance.

Small computers or large?

Recent advances in technology have blurred the traditional distinction between small (micro), medium-sized (mini) and large (mainframe) computers. There is now a continuous range from very small to very large systems.

At the smaller end of the market the personal computer (PC) has made the major breakthrough in business computing at the office level. PCs — usually with at least 256K of memory — have the great advantage of flexibility in that they can act as stand-alone computers capable of processing significant amounts of data, but can also be used as input devices to a larger mainframe system. The feature which has most helped to gain such a large market for PCs has been the concurrent introduction of generally accepted systems software and good applications software. There are basically two kinds of software — systems software and applications software. Systems software is concerned to make the computer operate as easily as possible. Examples are operating systems and programming languages such as BASIC. Applications software is written to solve particular problems, e.g. wage systems, sales ledger routines, etc.

Operating systems

An operating system is a program that provides a basis upon which the computer user and applications programs can work. The operating system is the interface with the hardware, and must make it workable by those users and applications programmers who are not fully aware of its intricacies. A single command to the operating system will allow a detailed set of procedures to be followed — for example, keeping track of the location of data on a floppy disk. The main breakthrough in PCs was the acceptance by manufacturers of standard disk operating systems (DOS) which made it possible for applications software to be used on a very wide range of different manufacturers' hardware. Whilst the users of mainframe computers will employ specialist staff to adapt the specialist systems software to their particular requirements, the smaller user cannot afford the same resource.

However, a well-established DOS together with applications programs which, if not wholly suitable immediately, can be altered through the use of a simple programming language such as BASIC make the computer viable to the small firm.

Applications programs

Applications programs can be written to solve one particular problem or class of problems. Some particular problems for which programs are frequently written include nominal ledger, sales and purchase ledgers, payroll and inventory control. In addition, some programs are written to help solve a more general class of problems. These are spreadsheets and database and word processing programs.

Electronic spreadsheets

These are an automated version of the manual analysis worksheet. They allow for quick and accurate analysis of information, which is very useful in an office and accounting environment. More sophisticated packages incorporate facilities to produce graphical material as well as text, and multiple commands concerning the calculations involved.

Database programs

These programs allow the easy manipulation of large bodies of data. It is particularly useful, for example, for storing information about an organization's customers. The file can be searched and reports printed to extract any desired information. Similarly, a database system may be very useful for handling large volumes of data on inventories or products in the sales list.

Word processing

Word processing is part of a trend to automate office procedures. The real strength of word processing lies in its ability to allow easy editing of typed material, since corrections on the computer do not necessitate manually retyping a whole document. It also allows the convenient use of standard documents and letters.

Finally, before finishing this section on software it is important to refer again to the control aspect. Just as inputs can be wrong either through error or deliberate act, so too can the software. Considerable care must be taken to ensure the integrity of the programs used. This implies physical security as well as proper audit procedures. To be confident that a sophisticated computer thief or mischief-maker is not at work may be an expensive requirement — but none the less a necessity!

Assignment Exercises

44.1. Explain what you understand by 'internal control' in relation to the use of computers in the accounting context.

44.2. How is a computer's memory defined?

Answers to Assignment Exercises

1.1   Cash at Bank 678 + Unpresented cheques 256 + Credit transfers 56 *less* Lodgement not recorded 115 = Balance per bank statement 875.

1.3   (a) To enter up Dr Walters 54, Cr Bank Charges 22, New balance c/d 1,863.
   (b) Balance per C.B. 1,863 + Unpresented cheque 115 − Bankings not entered 427 = Balance per B.S. 1,551 or in a reverse fashion.

1.5   (a) To enter up Dr Saunders 180, Cr Mercantile 200, Bank Charges 65, New balance c/d (overdraft) 4,007.
   (b) Bank Overdraft per C.B. 4,007 + Bankings not entered 211 − Unpresented cheque 84 = Bank Overdraft per B.S. 4,134.

2.1 (i) J. Harris   Dr. 678 : J. Hart   Cr. 678
   (ii) Machinery   Dr. 4,390 : L. Pyle   Cr. 4,390
   (iii) Motor Van   Dr. 3,800 : Motor Expenses   Cr. 3,800
   (iv) E. Fitzwilliam   Dr. 9 : Sales   Cr. 9
   (v) Sales   Dr. 257 : Commissions Received Cr. 257
   (vi) Cash   Dr. 154 : T. Heath   Cr. 154
   needs double the amount.
   (vii) Purchases   Dr. 189 : Drawings   Cr. 189
   (viii) Discounts Allowed   Dr. 366 : Discounts Received   Cr. 366

3.1   (a) (i) Suspense Dr 100, Sales Cr 100 (ii) Cantrell Dr 250, Cochrane Cr 250 (iii) Rent Dr 70, Suspense Cr 70, (iv) Suspense Dr 300, Discounts Received Cr 300 (v) Sales Dr 360, Motor Disposal Cr 360. (b) Suspense A/c Dr: Sales 100, Discounts Received 300 Cr: Balance b/f 330, Rent 70, (c) Net Profit per accounts 7,900 + Sales undercast 100 + Discounts undercast 300 − Rent 70 − Sales 360 = Corrected Net Profit 7,870.

3.3   (a) Bank Charges Dr 7, Suspense Cr 7; Suspense Dr 9, Depreciation Cr 9; Furniture Dr 20, Suspense Cr 20; Suspense Dr 18, Bell Cr 18; Suspense Dr 2, Tate Cr 2; Suspense Dr 10, Muir Cr 10.
   (b) *Profit and Loss:* Cr Net profit as before 2,970, Overcharged depreciation 9, Dr Bank charges 7, corrected Net profit 2,972.
   (c) Furniture 490 + Motors 1,430 = 1,920, Curret Assets, Stock 3,146 + Debtors 2,114 + Cash 1,862 − C.L. Creditors 2,477 = W.C. 4,645 = Total 6,565. Capial 6,093 + Net Profit 2,972 − Drawings 2,500 = 6,565.

4.1 Dr Balance b/f 4,936, Sales Journal 49,916. totals 54,852. Cr Returns In 1,139, Cheques 46,490. Discounts 1,455, Balance c/d 5,768.

4.2 Dr Returns Out 1,098, Bank 38,765, Discounts 887, Balance c/d 5,183, Totals 45,933. Cr Balances b/f 3,676, Purcases 42,257.

4.3 Purchases Ledger Control: Dr: Returns Outwards 5,044, Bank 290,600. Petty Cash 99, Discounts 4,216, Set-offs 2,916, Balances c/d 21,247. Cr: Balances b/fwd 21,926, Purchases 302,196. Totals 324,122. Sales Ledger Control: Dr: Balances b/fwd 37,404, Sales 401,384, Dishonoured Cheques 88. Total 438,876. Cr: Returns Inwards 9,212, Cash & Bank 374,216. Discounts 10,984, Bad Debts 605, Set-offs 2,916, Balances c/fwd 40,643. Total 438,576. Therefore difference of £300 exists in the Sales Ledger.

5.1 F.A. 2,800 − 550, C.A. Stock 3,950, Debtors 4,970, Prepaid 170, Bank 2,564, Cash 55 − C.L. Creditors 1,030, Expenses Owing 470 = Working Capital 10,209. Totals 12,459. Capital 10,000 + (C) ? = (B) ? − 5,673 = (A) ? By deduction (A) = 12,459, (B) = 18,132, (C) = 8,132.

5.3 Sales 47,159 − C.G.S. Opening Stock 13,862 + Purchase 34,246 − Closing Stock 15,144 = 32,964, Gross Profit 14,195, less Wages 5,472, Rent 1,500, Rates 875, Sundries 375, Depreciation 250, = Net Profit 5,723. Balance Sheet: F.A. Fixtures 2,500 − 250, C.A. Stock 15,144, Debtors 8,624, Prepaid 225 − C.L. Creditors 7,389, Bank Overdraft 602 = Working Capital 16,002. Totals 18,252. Capital 20,234 + Profit 5,723 − Drawings 7,705 = 18,252.

5.5 Trading Dr: Opening Stock 40,000, + Purchases 50,000 − Closing Stock 20,000 = Cost of Goods Sold 70,000, Gross Profit 30,000: Cr: Sales 100,000: Profit & Loss: Dr: Admin. 7,000, Selling 10,000, Discounts Allowed 1,000, Depreciation 5,000, Net Profit 8,000. Cr: Gross Profit 30,000, Discounts Received 1,000. Balance Sheet: Balance Sheet totals 68,700. Fixed Assets 80,000 − Depreciation 45,000, Stock 20,000. Debtors 12,500, Bank 1,200 = 33,700 − Creditors 17,500 = 16,200 = Total 51,200. Capital 48,000 + Net Profit 8,000 − Drawings 4,800 = 51,200.

5.7 Trading: Dr: Opening Stock 10,500 add Purchases 47,737, less Closing Stock 11,370 = Cost of Goods Sold 46,867, Gross Profit 29,903. Cr: Sales 76,770. Profit & Loss: Dr: Rent & Rates 4,073, Motor Expenses 4,739, General 1,553, Loan Interest 40, Depreciation, Motors 1,125, Fixtures 550, Net Profit 17,823. Cr: Gross Profit 29,903. Balance Sheet: Capital 25,100 + Net Profit 17,823 + Cash Introduced 3,000 − Drawings 7,434 = 38,489. Loan 500. Total 38,989. Motors 8,000 − Depreciation 4,625 = 3,375, Fixtures 5,500 − Depreciation 1,150 = 4,350, Stock 11,370, Debtors 19,385, Bank 5,092, Cash 112 − Creditors 4,187 − Expenses Owing 508 = Totals 38,989.

6.1 Figures show in order Electrical, Furniture, Leisure Goods. Sales 29,840: 73,060: 39,581 − Opening Stock 6,080: 17,298: 14,370 + Purchases 18,195: 54,632: 27,388 − Closing Stock 7,920: 16,150: 22,395, Gross Profit 13,485: 17,280: 20,218.

6.2 Figures shown Department A then B.
Sales 15,000: 10,000 − C.G.S. Opening Stock 250: 200, + Purchases 11,800: 8,200 − Closing Stock 300: 150 = Gross Profits 3,250: 1,750 − Expenses, Wages 1,000: 750, Delivery 150: −, Salaries 450: 300, Rates 26: 104, Insurance 10: 40, Lighting 24: 96, Repairs 5: 20, Telephone 5: 20, Cleaning 6: 24, Accounting 72: 48, General 36: 24, Net Profit 1,466: 324.

7.1 Columnar Sales Day Book: Total 11,650, VAT 1,030, Hi Fi 5,200, TV 5,100, Sundries 302. Ledger accounts obvious.

7.2 Purchases Analysis Book: Total 2,252, Purchases 1,346, Light 246, Motor 376, Stationery 137, Carriage In 147.

7.3 Debit each total to appropriate expense account. Ledger accounts obvious.

8.1 (a) Bills Receivable Dr: 2,460 & 1,500. Cr: 3,960, Bank Dr. 3,960, Cr. 145 & 1,500 & 6. R. Johnson Dr 2,460, Cr. 2,460, Scarlet Dr. 1,500 & 1,500 & 6, Cr. 1,500 Discounting Charges Dr. 145 (b) JOHNSON'S BOOKS: Bills Payable Dr 1,500, Cr. 1,500, N. Gudgeon Dr. 1,500, Cr 1,500 & 1,500 & 6. Noting charges Dr. 6, SCARLET'S BOOKS: Bills Payable Dr 2,460, Cr. 2,460. Gudgeon Dr. 2,460, Cr. 2,460, Bank Cr 2,460.

8.3 K.C. − Dr Balance b/f 960, Bank 960, Cr Bill Received 960, Bank 360, Bad debts 600.
Bills receivable − Dr KC 960, Cr Bank 960.
Bank − Dr Bill receivable 960, KC 360, Cr Discounting charges 12, KC (discounted bill) 960.
Discounting Charges − Dr Bank 12.
Bad Debts − Dr KC 600.

8.4 Debits 12,370 − 16,904 + 177 + 88 = 29,539.
Credit 105 + 407 + 15,970 + 1,230 + 306 + 129 + 604 + Balances c/d 10,788 + 29,539.

9.1 Source: N. Profit 13,500 + Depreciation 4,000 + Loan 5,000 + Reduction in Stock 7,500 + Reduction in Debtors 3,000 = 33,000, Less Applications: Drawings 8,000, Fixed Assets bought 25,000, Reduction in Creditors 8,500 = 41,500. Reduction in Bank Funds 8,500.

9.3 Source: Profit 2,200 + Depreciation 260 + 200 = Total Generated 2,660 + Loan 1,000 − Application, Drawings 1,500, Plant bought 1,000 = 1,160. Increase in Working Capital 600 to 1,760 = 1,160.

10.2 Sales 123,650 − Cost of Goods Sold, Opening Stock 41,979 + Purchases 85,416 − Closing Stock 56,340 = 71,055, Gross Profit 52,595 + Reduction Provision B.D. 80 − Expenses: Salaries 19,117, Office 2,512, Carriage 1,288, Discounts 115, Bad Debts 503, Loan Interest 4,000, Depreciation Fixtures 770 Buildings 1,000 = Net Profit 23,370 + Interest on Drawings (Me) 180 (Ma) 120 − Interest on Capitals (Me) 3,500 (Ma) 2,950, Salary (Me) 800 = 16,420 shared (Me) 8,210 (Ma) 8,210.

Balance Sheet: F.A. Buildings 75,000 − 26,000, Fixtures 11,000 − 4,070, C.A. Stock 56,340, Debtors 16,243 − Provision 320. Bank 677 − C.L. Creditors 11,150 − Expenses Owing 296 = Working Capital 61,494. Totals 117,424.

Capitals (Me) 35,000 (Ma) 29,500 = 64,500. Current Accounts, Balance (Me) 1,306 (Ma) 298 + Interest on Capital (Me) 3,500 (Ma) 2,950, Salary (Me) 800, Balance of Profit (Me) 8,210 (Ma) 8,210 − Drawings (Me) 6,400 (Ma) 5,650 − Interest on Drawings (Me) 180 (Ma) 120 = 12,924, Loan 40,000.

10.3 Sales 28,797 − Returns In 110 = 28,687 − Cost of Goods Sold, Opening Stock 2,395 + Purchases 19,388 − Returns 286 + Carriage In 216 − Closing Stock 5,623 = 16,090 = Gross Profit 12,597 + Discounts 404 − Expenses: Wages 4,389, Rent 542, Insurance 104, Delivery 309, Motor 635, General 204, Loan Interest 140, Discounts 392, Depreciation 187, Provision B.D. 320 = Net Profit 5,779 + Interest on Drawings (P) 58 (H) 39 − Salary (H) 300 − Interest on Capital (P) 450 (H) 240 = 4,886 Shared (P) 2,932 (H) 1,954.

Balance Sheet: F.A. Motors 2,500 − 817, C.A. Stock 5,623, Debtors 8,462 − Provision 320, Prepaid 12, bank 5,241, Cash 180 − C.L. Creditors 1,899, Expenses Owing 197 = Working Capital 17,102, Totals 18,785. Capitals (P) 9,000 (H) 4,800 = 13,800. Current Accounts: Balances (P) 880 (H) 120 + Share of Profits (P) 2,932 (H) 1,954 + Interest on Capital (P) 450 (H) 240 − Drawings (P) 1,825 (H) 1,429 − Interest on Drawings (P) 58 (H) 39 = (P) 2,379 (H) 606 = 2,985, Loan 2,000.

12.2 (a) On the assumption that Creditors and Debtors are paid are approximately the same time, it is an indication of the company's ability to meet its current liabilities from liquid current assets.

(b) The profit return on all longer term sources of capital to the business plus bank overdrafts. The profit is before charging any return on the sources of capital.

(c) It enables an assessment to be made of the actual period of credit allowed to customers by comparison with the official period and comparative firms.

(d) By showing what stake the shareholders have in the Total Assets, suppliers of other sources of capital can assess the amount of cover for their debts in the event of failure.

(e) This indicates how many times the profits could have covered this dividend and is therefore some guide to the likely stability of dividends. It also indicates how much profit is retained in the business.

12.4 1. A, C, E.
     2. A, C, E.
     3. E.
     4. D, F (assuming current assets exceed current liabilities)
     5. No Effect.

12.6

$$a = \frac{.1}{1.5} = 6.7\%$$

$$b = \frac{15.000}{100.000} = \text{£}.15 \text{ per share}$$

$$c = \frac{1.5}{.15} = 10.0$$

12.8 Selection of five from:

Current Ratio 1.89:1; Acid Test Ratio .78:1 (Note Only Bank and Debtor Balances included) Gross Profit/Sales 33⅓ % Net Profit/Sales (no tax assumed) 13.3%. Net operating Profit/Capital Employed

$$\frac{20 + \text{Debenture Interest } 3}{200} = 11.5\%$$

Net Profit/Owners Equity $\frac{18}{140}$ = 14.3% Stock Turnover $\frac{120}{30}$ = 3.3 times. Sales/Fixed Assets $\frac{150}{120}$ = 1.3 times. Days Sales in Debtors = 122. Net Worth/Total Assets $\frac{140}{290}$ = 48.3% Fixed Assets/Net Worth $\frac{120}{140}$ = 85.7%. Coverage of Fixed Charges $\frac{20+3}{3}$ = 7.7 times.

12.10 Current Ratios 1) 2.4:1 2) 2.4:1, Acid Test Ratio 1) 1.2:1 2) 1.2:1 Gross Profit/Sales 1) 21.3 2) 20.3 Net Profit/Sales 1) 5% 2) 4.5% Operating Profit/Capital Employed:

1) $\frac{30,000}{200,000}$ = 15% 2) $\frac{38,000}{294,000}$ = 12.9% Net Profit/Owners Equity:

1) $\frac{30,000}{200,000}$ = 15% 2) $\frac{34,000}{234,000}$ = 14.5% Stock Turn (using year end

figures 1) $\frac{472}{120}$ = 3.9 times 2) $\frac{596}{188}$ = 3.2 times. Sales/Fixed Assets

1) $\frac{600}{60}$ = 10 times 2) $\frac{748}{80}$ = 93 times. Collection Period for Debtors

1) = 60.8 days 2) = 80 days Net Worth/Total Assets 1) $\frac{200}{300}$ = .67

2) $\frac{234}{446}$ = .52 Coverage of fixed charges. 1) n/a 2) $\frac{38,000}{300}$ = 9.5

12.12 (a) 1:1
  (b) 5.2 times
  (c) 9.2%
  (d) 34.1 days
  (e) 3.31 times.

13.4 A central key ratio is explained in terms of subsidiary ratios branching from it. Each subsidiary is similarly dealt with until a pyramid develops with the base showing very details ratios and the top the final overall summary ratio.

The presentation allows the overall picture to be easily visualised, and key ratios to be quickly spotted.

13.7 *Liquidity*

The substantial increase in the previous four years on Current ratio shows a reduction in 19-1 to 2.5 which is in part accounted for by reduction in Acid Test ratio from 1.22 to 1. The change probably reflects management policy to reverse a trend towards inefficient use of liquid resources.

Profitability

The steady decline in the ratio of Net Profit/Owners Equity indicates a general reduction in the company's profitibility rather than any temporary decline. The adequacy of this level of return must be judged against other comparable companies.

Use of Assets

The collection period for debtors has lengthened during the four years but reduced a little in the current period. The trend is in sympathy with the liquidity ratio and probably reflects management's difficulties with declining profitability, i.e. attracting customers.

Stock Turnover has reduced in every period. This is an unsatisfactory trend when taken in conjunction with all the other indicators.

Capital Structure

Times Interest changes covered. This ratio has not changed must and indicates that the company is not in immediate difficulties so far as covering interest payments is concerned. With declining profits this is at least some encouragement.

Summary

All the main indicators are showing adverse trends, i.e. Liquidity, Profitability and Use of Assets. From the evidence we have this tends to support a feeling that management has not been effective. Fortunately the company is not too highly geared and may survive to do better.

13.9

		19-2
(1)	Gross Profit % Sales	8.8%
	Net Profit % Sales	0.9%
	Current Ratio	3.2:1
	Acid Test Ratio	1.5:1
	Debtors − Collection Period in Days	16.8 Days
	Stock Turnover	13.9 Days
	Net Worth as % of Total Assets	64.9%
	Number of Times Fixed Charges Earned	8.0 times
	Operating Profit/Capital Employed	6.9%
	Earning per Ordinary Share	£.20
	Price Earnings Ratio	7.5 times
	Dividend Yield	3.3%

(2) Comments:

Gross Profit − tending to follow industry pattern but only third in rank.

Net Profit − following Gross Profit trend, second in rank, but overall the return seems low.

Current and Acid Test Ratios − nothing exceptional on interfirm basis although the level appears high for general standards.

Debtors − only one company is substantially better but may be setting a desirable standard.

Stock Turnover − some improvement is possible as evidenced by A and C.

Net Worth as % Total Assets − Both A and B appear to be more highly geared than P, which may indicate that future borrowing maybe a good source of raising funds.

Number of Times Fixed Charges Covered − Only one company has a better cover which reinforces the previous point.

Operating Profit/Capital Employed − P is showing well in 19.2 at this level, compared to the other companies, but this is not a satisfactory return when borrowing on 8% Debentures.

Earnings per Ordinary Share − Despite earning the highest return on capital employed the ordinary shareholders are not benefiting, possibly because A is paying higher interest charges than A or C.

Price Earnings Ratio − P seem to be very much undervalued in comparison with A or C. There must be special external factors.

Dividend Yield − P seems to be average.

14.1 (a) Limited Companies
(b) Little
(c) Objectives
(d) Efficient Objectives

14.3 (a) F
(b) F
(c) T
(d) T

15.2 Raw Materials 210,000 + Direct Labour 120,000 = PRIME COST 330,000 − Factory Overhead: Factory Indirect Labour 110,000, Other Factory Indirect Expenses 66,000, Firms Canteen Expenses ¾ 6,000, Depreciation Machinery in Factory 6,000 = PRODUCTION COST 518,000 + Selling & Distribution Expenses: Wages, lorry drivers 2,500, Salaries: Salesman 7,000 Commission on Sales 1,200, Depreciation: Delivery Vehicles 1,500, Showroom Equipment 100, Administration Expenses: Salaries, Employees in Admin Block 80,000, Firms Canteen Expenses ¼ 2,000, Depreciation, Accounting Machinery 500, Finance Expenses: Interest on loans 2,000 = TOTAL COST 614,800.

15.4 (i) f, h (ii) m (iii) a, c, e, g, j, 4/5ths of n.t.v. ¾ of w, x. (iv) b.d.i. 1/5th of n, p, q, part of ¼ of w (v) l, r, s, z, part of ¼ of w (vi) o, k, u, y.

15.6 Raw Mats 120,000 + 400,000 − 160,000 = 360,000 + Haulage Costs 4,000, Direct Labour (70% × 220,000) 154,000, Royalties 1,600 = (a) PRIME COST £519,000: Factory Overhead: Factory Indirect Labour 66,000, Other Factory Indirect Exps 58,000, Travelling Expenses 100, Depreciation Factory Machinery 38,000, Firm's canteen expenses 4,000 = (b) PRODUCTION COST 685,700: Administration Expenses: Salaries 72,000, Travelling Expenses 200, Firms Canteen Expenses 2,000, Depreciation Accounting & Office Mac'nery 2,000 + Cars of Admin. Staff 1,600, Other Admin Expenses 42,000, Selling & Distribution Expenses: Salaries 8,000, Commission 1,400, Travelling Expenses 2,900, Depreciation Equipment 300 + Salesmen's Cars 3,800, Other Selling Expenses 65,000, Carriage Costs on Sales 7,800: Finance Costs 3,800 (c) TOTAL COST 898,500.

15.7 (i) c, e (ii) d, q, w, (iii) i, m, t, v, z, x (iv) a, g, k, n, u, y (v) b, f, j, l, o, s, (vi) h, p, r.

16.1 Manufacturing A/c: Dr Opening Stock Raw Materials 18,450, + Purchases 64,300 + Carriage Inwards 1,605 − Closing Stock Raw Materials 20,210 = Cost of Raw Materials Consumed 64,145 + Direct Labour 65,810 = Prime Cost 129,955, Factory Overhead Expenses: Fuel & Power 5,920, Rent and Rates ⅔rds 1,800, Depreciation: Machinery 8,300, + Work in Progress 1.1.19-7, 23,600, + Work in Progress 31.12.19-7, 17,390 = Production Cost of Goods Completed c/d 152,185. Trading A/c: Opening Stock Finished Goods 17,470 + Production Cost of Goods Completed 152,185, less Closing Stock Finished Goods 21,485 = Cost of Goods Sold 148,170; Gross Profit 52,430; Cr. side: Sales 200,600. Profit & Loss: Dr. Office Salaries 16,920, Rent & Rates ⅓ 900, Lighting & Heating 5,760, Depreciation: Office Equipment 1,950, Net Profit 26,900.

16.3 Manufacturing A/c: Dr. Opening Stock Raw Materials 8,565, + Purchases 39,054 less Closing Stock Raw Materials 9,050 = Cost of Raw Materials Consumed 38,569, Manufacturing Wages 45,775 = PRIME COST 84,344, Factory Overhead Expenses: Rates 4,800, General Expenses 5,640, Light & Heat 2,859, Depreciation 2,000 = Cr: Production Cost of Goods Completed c/d 99,643. Trading: Dr. Opening Stock Finished Goods 29,480. + Production Cost of Goods Completed b/d 99,643 − Closing Stock Finished Goods 31,200 = Cost of Goods Sold 97,923, Gross Profit c/d, 38,577, Cr. Sales 136,500. Profit & Loss: Dr. Administration Expenses: Office Salaries 6,285, Light & Heat 1,110, General Expenses 1,950, Rates 2,200, Depreciation: Office Equipment 1,500 = 13,045, Selling & Distribution Expenses: Advertising 1,758, Salesmens Commission 7,860, Delivery Van Expenses 2,500 + 12,118, Net Profit 13,414. Cr. Gross Profit b/d 38,577. Balance Sheet: Capital 137,456 + Net Profit 13,414 − Drawings 8,560 = 142,310. Current Liabilities: Creditors 19,450, Accrued Expenses 305 = 19,755. Totals 162,065. Fixed Assets: Premises 40,000, Machinery 50,000 less depreciation 19,500 = 30,500, Office Equipment 15,000 less depreciation 5,500 = 9,500. Current Assets: Stocks, Raw Materials 9,050, Finished Goods 31,200, Debtors 28,370, Prepayments 108, Bank 13,337.

17.1 C. Dean: Trading: Dr Purchases 100,000 − Closing Stock (800 units) 16,000 = Cost of Goods Soled 84,000, Gross Profit 126,000, Cr. Sales 210,000. Profit & Loss: Dr Wages & Salaries 50,000, Rent & Rates 9,000. Other Expenses 40,000,l Finance Expenses 1,000, Net Profit 26,000, Cr. Gross Profit b/d 126,000.

D. Warren: Trading: Dr. Cost of Raw Materials 100,000, Direct Wages 28,000 = Prime Cost 128,000, Factory Indirect Expenses 38,000, Indirect Factory Labour 8,000, Cr: Factory Cost Goods Completed c/d 174,000. Profit & Loss, Dr: Factory Cost Goods Completed 174,000, less Closing Stock Finished Goods (800/5,000 × 174,000) 27,840 = Cost of Goods Sold 146,160, Gross Profit 63,840, Cr: Sales 210,000. Profit & Loss: Dr. Salaries Admin 10,000, Salaries Salesman 4,000, Other Selling & Admin. 11,000. Finance Expenses 1,000, Net Profit 37,840. Cr. Gross Profit 63,840.

17.3 C. Dean: Trading: Dr: Opening Stock 16,000, Add Purchases 120,000 less Closing Stock (1,200 units) 24,000 = Cost of Goods Sold 112,000, Gross Profit c/d 168,000, Cr. Sales 280,000. Profit & Loss: Dr. Wages 53,000, Rent & Rates 9,000, Other Expenses 42,000, Finance Expenses 2,000, Net Profit 62,000, Cr: Gross Profit b/d 168,000.

D. Warren: Manufacturing A/c: Dr: Raw Materials 120,000, Direct Wages 30,000 = Prime Cost 150,000, Factory Indirect 39,000, Factory Indirect Labour 9,000. Cr: Factory Cost Goods Completed c/d 198,000.

Trading A/c: Dr: Opening Stock Finished Goods 27,840, Add Factory Cost of Goods Completed 198,000, less Closing Stock Finished Goods (1,200/6,000 × 198,000) 39,600, Cost of Goods Sold 186,240, Gross Profit c/d 93,760. Cr: Sales 280,000, Profit & Loss: Dr. Salaries, Administration 10,000, Salaries, Salesmen 4,000, Other selling 8,000, Other Admin. Expenses 4,000, Finance Expenses 2,000, Net Profit 65,760. Cr: Gross Profit b/d 93,760.

18.1 (i) FIFO Stock 800 (ii) LIFO Stock 688 (iii) AVCO Stock 740.

18.2 In each case Sales 1,040, Purchases 1,440, Gross Profit: FIFO 400, LIFO 288, AVCO 340.

18.5 None at all. There can be one but there doesn't have to be one.

18.7 (a) (i) FIFO 6 units at £13 each = £78, (ii) LIFO 6 units at £10 each = £60, (iii) AVCO 6 units at £12.50 each = £75. (b) Sales in each case 1,092, Purchases in each case 830, less different amounts for stock so that Gross Profit become (i) FIFO 340, (ii) LIFO 322, (iii) AVCO 337.

19.1 FIFO Stocks: end Year (1) 280, Year (2) 180, Year (3) 336.

19.2 LIFO Stocks: end Year (1) 240, Year (2) 120, Year (3) 234.

19.3 AVCO Stocks: end Year (1) 260, Year (2) 170, Year (3) 320.

19.4 Trading Accounts each method: Sales: Year (1) 660, Year (2) 1120, Year (3) 1324. Purchases: Year (1) 780, Year (2) 700, (3) 1200.
(i) FIFO Gross profits Year (1) 160, (2) 320, (3) 280.
(ii) LIFO Gross Profits Year (1) 120, (2) 300, (3) 238.
(iii) AVCO Gross Profits Year (1) 140, (2) 330, (3) 274.

19.5 The answer would be exactly the same as in 5.1. It makes not difference as to whether the perpetual or the periodic method is in use.

19.6 Year (1) 20 × £12 = £240, (2) 10 × £12 = £120, (3) 10 × £12 + 6 × £19 = £234.

19.7 Year (1) Average cost is £780 ÷ 60 = £13. Closing Stock is 20 × £13 = £260. Year (2) Average cost is £960 ÷ 60 = £16. Closing Stock is 10 × £16 = £160. Year (3) Average cost is £1360 ÷ 70 = £19.43. Closing Stock is 16 × £19.43 = £310.88.

19.8 The Trading Accounts for FIFO and LIFO would have been exactly the same as in 5.4. The AVCO figures would give gross profits of Year (1) 140, (2) 320, (3) 252.

19.22 Gross Operating Profits, Year 1 £150   Year 2 £220   Year 3 £271.

19.23 Gross Operating Profits, Year 1 £330   Year 2 £196   Year 3 £347.

20.1

Employee number	Standard hours of actual output	Actual hours	Hours saved	Bonus at £2 hour £	Minimum wage £	Gross wage £
1002	2,000 ÷ 50 = 40	35	5	10	200	210
1003	2,000 ÷ 50 = 40	37	3	6	200	206
1005	1,650 ÷ 50 = 33	35	–	–	200	200

20.2

Employee number	Hours worked	Units produced in standard hours	Time saved	Employee's ⅓ share	Total hours for payment	Wages at £4 per hour
						£
205	40	70	30	10	50	200
208	40	50	10	3⅓	43⅓	173.33
226	36	38	2	⅔	36⅔	146.67

21.1

	P_1	P_2	P_3	S_1	S_2	Total	
						£	
Rent	1,500	1,500	1,500	750	750	6,000	floor space
Heating	923	923	692	231	231	3,000	cubic capacity
Power	5,000	2,000	1,000	1,667	333	10,000	machine h.p.
Depreciation	2,000	800	800	1,200	5,200	10,000	machine values
Indirect Labour	4,000	4,000	6,000	2,000	2,000	18,000	labour hours
Miscellaneous	667	667	1,000	333	333	3,000	labour hours
	14,090	9,890	10,992	6,181	8,847	50,000	

21.2

	P_1	P_2	P_3	S_1	S_2	Total	
	2,472	1,236	1,236	–	1,237	6,181	S1
	3,361	3,361	3,362	–	–	1,237 +8,847	S2
	5,833	4,597	4,598			15,028	

P_1 19,923 + P_2 14,487 + P_3 15,590 = 50,000

22.1 (A) Marginal cost per unit: Direct Labour 3 + Direct Materials 3.5 + Variable 2.25 = 8.75. Price offered is £9. It will therefore increase the profit of the firm to accept the order. Could give proof showing total costs if order not accepted 20,000, Sales 22,000 = Net Profit 2,000 compared with if order accepted, total costs 20,875, Sales 22,900 = Net profit 2,025.

(B) Marginal cost per unit: Direct Labour 3 + Direct Materials 3.5 + Variable costs 2.25 + Depreciation extra machine £3,000 ÷ 150 units = £2 + Running costs extra machine £600 p.a. ÷ 150 = £4. Total 14.75.

Variable costs more than selling price, therefore do not accept order. Proof would show total costs if order not accepted 20,000, Sales 22,000 = Net Profit 2,000. If order accepted total costs 22,212, Sales 23,500, = Net Profit 1,288.

22.5 Marginal cost per unit under normal production, Direct Labour £4 + Direct Materials £5.25 + Factory Indirect Expenses (£9,000 × ⅔ ÷ 4,000) £1.50 = £10.75. Under normal production therefore (all things being equal) extra sales at a figure above £10.75 will bring in extra profit.

(a) Special case − not normal production. Marginal cost per unit as above £10.75 + Extra machine costs: Running cost (£1,800 ÷ 200) £9 = Depreciation (£3,000 − £200 = £2,800 ÷ 800) £3.50 = total £23.25. Selling price £13 is above marginal cost on normal production therefore ACCEPT.
(b) Selling price £13 is above marginal cost on normal production therefore ACCEPT. Advice qualified under (a) and (b) − depends on effect on sales to other customers, existing sales to customer under (b) etc. Price-cutting wars with other producers etc. etc.

22.6 With both methods the figures of sales per year and of Direct Labour, Materials, Variable overhead and Fixed Overhead will remain the same. What will vary will be the calculation of the figures for stocks, and thus profits. Year 1, Sales 144,000, Direct Labour 40,000, Direct Materials 30,000, Variable Overhead 50,000, Fixed Overhead 16,000. Marginal method, closing stock (£120,000 × 1,000/10,000) 12,000, Gross Profit 20,000. Absorption method, closing stock (£136,000 × 1,000/10,000) 13,600, Gross Profit 21,600. Year 2, Sales 160,000, Direct Labour 48,000, Materials 36,000, Variable Overhead 60,000, Fixed Overhead 16,000. Marginal method Opening stock b/fwd 12,000, Closing stock (£144,000 × 3,000/12,000) 36,000, Gross profit £24,000. Absorption method Opening stock b/fwd 13,600. Closing stock £160,000 × 3,000/12,000) 40,000. Gross Profit 26,400. Year 3, Sales 240,000, Direct Labour 64,000. Materials 48,000, Variable Overhead 80,000, Fixed Overhead 16,000. Marginal method, Opening stock b/fwd 36,000, Closing stock (£192,000 × 4,000/16,000) 48,000, Gross profit 44,000. Absorption method, Opening stock b/fwd 40,000, Closing stock (£208,000 × 4,000/16,000) 52,000, Gross Profit 44,000.

23.1

	Materials	Direct Labour	Factory Overhead	Total
Job 1001	118	60×£0.9= 54	60×£1.3= 78	250
Job 1002	206	50×£0.9= 45	50×£1.3= 65	316
Job 1003	310	71×£1.0= 71	71×£1.4= 99.4	480.4
Job 1004	205	80×£1.1= 88	80×£2.3=184	477
Job 1005	98	60×£1.2= 72	50×£2.8=140	310
Job 1006	306	110×£0.9= 99	80×£1.5=120	525
Job 1007	401	130×£1.0=130	130×£4 =520	1051
Job 1008 Dept. E	180	70×£0.9= 63	60×£1.5= 63	
Dept. A	44	40×£0.9= 36	40×£1.3= 52	465
Job 1009 Dept. C	388	50×£1.1= 55	50×£2.3=115	
Dept. A	−	40×£0.9= 36	40×£1.3= 52	
Dept. F	68	70×£1.0= 70	59×£4 =236	1,020

23.3

	Production Departments				Service Departments		
	A	B	C	D	K	L	M
Indirect Labour	4,000	6,000	8,000	2,000	1,500	3,000	4,100
Other Expenses	2,700	3,100	3,600	1,500	4,500	2,000	2,000
	6,700	9,100	11,600	3,500	6,000	5,000	6,100
Apportionment of costs:							
Dept. K	1,500	1,800	1,200	600	(6,000)		900
Dept. L	3,000		1,500	500		(5,000)	
							7,000
Dept. M		2,100	3,500	1,400			(7,000)
	£11,200	13,000	17,800	6,000	–	–	–

(a) Overhead rate per direct labour hour

Department A $\dfrac{£11,200}{2,000} = £5.6$

Department C $\dfrac{£17,800}{4,450} = £4.0$

(b) Overhead rate per machine hour

Department A $\dfrac{£13,000}{2,600} = £5.0$

Department A $\dfrac{£6,200}{24,000} = £2.5$

24.3 (a) Selling prices A 33: B 44: C 77: D 77: E 44.

(b) Discontinue C.

(c) (i) Followed your advice. Sales A 3,200 + B 4,900 + D 6,600 + E 4,800 = 19,500. Less Costs: Direct Materials & Labour (16 + 19 + 44 + 23) × 100 = 10,200: Variable Costs (11 + 17 + 14 + 9) × 100 = 5,100: Fixed Costs 3,600. Total Costs 18,900. Net Profit 600.
(ii) Produced all items. Sales A 3,200 + B 4,900 + C 5,600 × D 6,600 + E 4,800 = 25,100. Less Costs: Direct Materials and Labour (16 + 19 + 38 + 33 + 23) × 100 = 14,000: Variable Costs (11 + 17 + 23 + 14 + 9) × 100 = 7,400: Fixed Costs 3,600. Total Costs 25,000. Net Profit 100.

(d) Discontinue A and E.

(e)   (i) Followed your advice. Sales B 3,800 + C 6,800 + D 6,4000 = 17,000. Less Costs: Direct Materials & Labour (19 + 38 + 44) × 100 = 10,100: Variable Costs (17 + 23 + 14) × 100 = 5,400; Fixed Costs 3,600. Total Costs 19,100. Net Loss 2,100.

(ii) Produced all items. Sales S 2,400 + B 3,800 + C 6,800 + D 6,400 + E 2,900 = 22,300. Less Costs: Direct Labour and Material (16 + 19 + 38 + 44 + 23) × 100 = 14,000: Variable Costs (11 + 17 + 23 + 14 + 9) × 100 = 7,400: Fixed Costs 3,600 = Total Costs 25,000. Net Loss 2,700.

24.4 (a) Cork: Labour & Materials 14, Variable o/h 22, Marginal cost 36, Fixed Costs 4, Full Cost 40 + Profit 10% 4 = Selling Price 44. Plastic: Labour & Materials 5, Variable o/h 13, Marginal Cost 18, Fixed Costs 2, Full cost 20, Add Profit 10% 2 = Selling Price 22. Screwtop: Labour & Materials 37, Variable o/h 9, Marginal Cost 46, Fixed Costs 14, Full cost 60, Add Profit 10% 6 = Selling Price 66. Wedge: Labour & Materials 23, Variable o/h 17, Marginal Cost 40, Fixed Costs 10, Full Cost 50, Add Profit 10% 5 = Selling Price 55. (b) Discontinue only those products which are selling at less than marginal cost, i.e. Plastic. (c) Sales: Cork 100 × £43 = £4,300, Screwtop 100 × £58 = £5,800. Wedge 100 × £59 = £5,900, Total Sales 16,000. Less: Direct Labour Cork 1,400, Screwtop 3,700, Wedge 2,300, Total 7,400, Variable o/h Cork 2,200, Screwtop 900, Wedge 1,700, Total 4,800, Fixed Costs 3,000, Profit 800. (d) Discontinue Wedge. (e) (i) Sales: Cork 4,900, Plastic 2,000, Screwtop 5,500, Total 12,400, Less: Direct Labour & Materials, Cork 1,400, Plastic 500, Screwtop 3,700, Total 5,600, Variable o/h Cork 2,200, Plastic 1,300, Screwtop 900, Total 4,400, Fixed Costs 3,000, Loss 600. (e) (ii) Sales, Cork 4,900, Plastic 2,000, Screwtop 5,500, Wedge 3,700, Total 16,100. Less: Direct Labour & Materials, Cork 1,400, Plastic 500, Screwtop 3,700, Wedge 2,300, Total 7,900, Variable o/h, Cork 2,200, Plastic 1,300, Screwtop 900, Wedge 1,700, Total 6,100, Fixed Costs 3,000, Loss 900.

25.1 To manufacture 1,500 parts would cost:

	£
Direct Material (+50%)	150,000
Direct Labour (+50%+10%)	99,000
Variable Overhead (+50%)	82,500
Fixed Overhead	95,000
	426,500

To buy in the 1500 parts would cost:—

1,500×£240	360,000
Unabsorbed Fixed Overhead	55,000
	415,000

The company could save £11,500 by sub-contracting, and obtain the advantage of releasing some working and fixed capital as well as management time. Against this it might lose control of delivery and quality. Also future price quotations may not be so competitive.

25.2

	X	Y	Z
Contributions are:	£	£	£
Sales Price	560	340	220
less:	250	140	80
Contribution per unit	310	200	140
lbs of Zebo per unit	20	10	5
∴ Contribution per lb of Zebo	£15.50	£20.00	£28.00

∴ Chose Z then Y then X.

Total Contributions would be based in 1000 lbs of Zebo.
producing:

$$200 \text{ of } Z = \text{£28,000}$$
$$100 \text{ of } Y = \text{£20,000}$$
$$50 \text{ of } X = \text{£15,500}$$

Note: It might be advisable in terms of longer term planning of markets to sell all three products even though reducing current levels of profit — particularly if the material shortage is only likely to be short lived.

25.3 If the project is a one-off — with no continuing commitment to a price then both items would be charged at the realisable value:

	£
Material 105	1,000
Machine	3,000
	4,000

If the information were to be the basis for a contract price into the future, then the appropriate values would be based on replacement cost.

	£
Material 105	10,000
Machine	50,000
	60,000

29.5 (i) Price Variance (F) 68, Usage (A) 54, Net (F) 14, (ii) Usage (F) 68, Price (A) 92, Net (A) 24, (iii) Price (A) 36, Usage (A) 36, Total (A) 72, (iv) Price (F) 81, Usage (F) 74, Total (F) 155. (v) Price (A) 154, Material (A) 63, Total (A) 217, (vi) Price $9,850 \times £3 = 29,550$ (F), Usage $150 \times £22 = 3,300$ (F) Total (F) 32,850.

29.7 (i) Price Variance (F) 964, Usage (F) 306, Total (F) 1,270. (ii) Price (A) 100, Usage (A) 150, Total (A) 250. (iii) Actual cost 2,292, Standard cost 2,160 = (A) 132. (iv) Price (A) 214, Usage (A) 112, Total (A) 326. (v) Actual cost 19,800, Standard cost 21,000 = (F) 1,200. (vi) Usage (F) 2,000, Price (A) 594 = Net (F) 1,406.

30.5 (i) Efficiency variance (F) 16, Wage (A) 28.4 = Net (A) 12.4. (ii) Rate (F) 44, Efficiency (A) 23.8, Net (F) 20.2. (iii) Rate (F) 4.8, Efficiency (F) 3.8, = Total (F) 8.6. (iv) Rate (A) 35.2, Efficiency (A) 12.0 = Total (A) 47.2. (v) Rate (F) 42, Efficiency (A) 16.2 = Net (F) 25.8. (vi) Efficiency (F) 11.2, Rate (A) 105.2 = Net (A) 94.

30.9 Standard cost 136 × £3.6 = 489.60, Actual cost 136 × £3 = 408.00. Fav. wage rate variance 81.60, (ii) Standard cost 200 × £3.8 = 760.00, Actual cost 200 × £4 = 800.00. Adv wage rate variance 40.00. (iii) Standard cost 140 × £1.6 = 224.00, Actual cost 154 × £1.6 = 246.40. Adv. labour efficiency variance 22.40. (iv) Standard cost 180 × £2.2 = 396.00, Actual cost 164 × £2.2 = 360.80. Fav. Labour efficiency variance 35.20. (v) Fav. wage rate variance £0.2 × 70 = 14.00, Fav. labour efficiency £2 × 5 = 10.00, Total £24.00. Compares with standard cost 75 × £2 = 150.00, Actual cost 70 × £1.8 = 126.00, Variance 24.00. (vi) Fav. labour efficiency variance 14 × £1.60 = 22.40. Adv. wage rate variance 526 × £0.40 = 210.40. Net Adv. labour variance 188.00. (vii) Fav. wage rate variance 468 × £0.20 = £93.60. Adv. labour efficiency variance 28 × £1.80 = 50.40. Net fav. labour variance 43.20. (viii) Adv. wage rate variance 74 × £0.10 = 7.40. Adv. labour efficiency variance 4 × £2.0 = £8.00. Total adv. labour variance 15.40. (ix) Adv. wage rate variance 214 × £0.10 = 21.40. Adv. labour efficiency variance 34 × £2.0 = 68.00. Total Adv. labour variance 89.40.

31.1

(a)	Actual overhead		5,840
	Overhead applied to production × £6		6,000
	Favourable budget (or spending) variance	£	160
(b)	Actual overhead		21,230
	Overhead applied to production 5,000×£4		20,000
	Adverse budget (or spending) variance	£	1,230
(c)	Actual Fixed Overhead		11,770
	Budgeted Fixed Overhead		12,000
	Favourable Fixed Overhead Spending Variance	£	230
(d)	Actual Fixed Overhead		41,390
	Budgeted Fixed Overhead		40,000
	Adverse Fixed Overhead Spending Variance	£	1,390
(e)	Actual hours × standard rate (7,940 × £3)		23,820
	Budgeted hours × standard rate (8,000 × £3)		24,000
	Favourable efficiency variance	£	180
(f)	Actual hours × standard rate (15,000 × £4)		60,000
	Budgeted hours (4,800×3) × standard rate (14,580×£4)		58,320
	Adverse efficiency variance	£	1,680

33.2 Give notes on:
(a) Money Capital Maintenance
(b) Real Capital Maintenance
(c) Maintenance of Specific Purchasing Power of the opening capital of the equity
(d) Operating Capital Maintenance Concept.

31.2 (a)

Actual Fixed Overhead		36,420
Budgeted Fixed Overhead		37,000
Favourable Fixed Overhead Spending Variance		£ 580

(b)

Actual hours × standard rate (242 × £6)	1,452
Budgeted hours × standard rate (250 × £6)	1,500
Favourable efficiency variance	£ 48

(c)

Actual overhead	18,000
Overhead applied to production (8,820 × £)	17,640
Budget (or spending) variance	£ 360

(d)

Actual overhead	8,790
Overhead applied to production (3,000 × £3)	9,000
Favourable budget (or spending) variance	£ 210

(e)

Actual Fixed Overehad	129,470
Budgeted Fixed Overhead	120,000
Adverse Fixed Overhead Spending Variances	£ 9,470

(f)

Actual hours × standard rate (30,000 × £8)	240,000
Budgeted hours (9,880 × 3) × standard rate £8	237,120
Adverse efficiency variance	£ 2,880

31.3 (a)

Actual hours × standard rate 10,320 × £3	30,960
Budgeted hours × standard rate 10,000 × £3	30,000
Favourable volume variance	£ 960

(b)

Actual Fixed Overhead	39,640
Budgeted Fixed Overhead	40,000
Favourable Fixed Overhead Spending Variance	£ 360

(c)

Actual hours × standard rate 9,600 × £0.5	4,800
Budgeted hours × standard rate 10,000 × £0.5	5,000
Adverse volume variance	£ 220

(d)

Actual Fixed Overhead	62,390
Budgeted Fixed Overhead	60,000
Adverse Fixed Overhead Spending Variance	£ 2,390

32.1 Adverse Price Variance £18,750 Favourable Volume Variance £25,000.

32.3 Price Variance − nil − Adverse Volume Variance £520 Favourable Mix Variance £56.

35.3 C   **35.4** A   **35.5** A   **35.6** D   **35.7** A   **35.8** C

35.9 B   **35.10** C   **35.11** D.

38.1 As per the Chapter − scaling down estimates of gains, benefits or revenues and scaling up estimates of cost. The cut off rate of return may also be increased above the cost of capital. To improve judgement a number of profiles may be taken − Best, Most Likely and Worst so that a range of outcomes can be seen, which may be further extended by sensitivity analysis − where varying assumptions about individual components will indicate how important they are for success. The estimates of items such as sales may be helped by using subjective probability to produce an expected outcome from a range of estimates.

38.2

Units	Probability	Expected unit sales
100,000	.05	5,000
200,000	.20	40,000
250,000	.30	75,000
300,000	.40	120,000
350,000	.05	17,500
	1.00	Total 257,000

39.1

$$\text{Break even for Plant A} = \frac{\text{F.C.}}{\text{Contribution per £ Sales £0.50}} = \frac{30,000}{£0.50} = \frac{£60,000}{\text{Sales}}$$

$$\text{Plant B} = \frac{20,000}{£0.40} = \frac{£50,000}{\text{Sales}}$$

Profitability of Plant A

	£	£	£	£	£	£	£
Sales	40,000	50,000	60,000	70,000	80,000	90,000	100,000
Variable Cost	20,000	25,000	30,000	35,000	40,000	45,000	50,000
Contribution	20,000	25,000	30,000	35,000	40,000	45,000	50,000
Fixed Cost	30,000	30,000	30,000	30,000	30,000	30,000	30,000
Net Profit (Loss)	(10,000)	(5,000)	0	5,000	10,000	15,000	20,000

Profitability of Plant B

Sales	40,000	50,000	60,000	70,000	80,000	90,000	100,000
Variable Cost	24,000	30,000	36,000	42,000	48,000	54,000	60,000
Contribution	16,000	20,000	24,000	28,000	32,000	36,000	40,000
Fixed Cost	20,000	20,000	20,000	20,000	20,000	20,000	20,000
Net Profit (Loss)	(4,000)	0	4,000	8,000	12,000	16,000	20,000

Plant A has a higher break even point and only produces higher profits than Plant B when sales in excess of £100,000 p.a. are achieved. The relative riskiness depends on how strong the market demand is for the product. Unless there is a very high level of demand in excess of £100,000 Plant A is inherently more risky than plant B.

39.2

	£	£	£	£	£	£	£
Sales	40,000	50,000	60,000	70,000	80,000	90,000	100,000

(a)

Net Profit (Loss)	(10,000)	(5,000)	0	5,000	10,000	15,000	20,000
Return on Shares of £100,000	(10%)	(5%)	0	5%	10%	15%	20%

(b)

Contribution	20,000	25,000	30,000	35,000	40,000	45,000	50,000

Interest £4,000
Fixed Cost £30,000

34,000	34,000	34,000	34,000	34,000	34,000	34,000

Net Profit (Loss)	(14,000)	(9,000)	(4,000)	1,000	6,000	11,000	16,000
Return on Shares of £60,000	(23.3)%	(15)%	(6.7)%	1.7%	10%	18.3%	26.7%

The introduction of borrowed capital increases the break even point from sales of £60,000, to sales of £68,000 ($\frac{£34,000}{£0.50}$). On Sales of £80,000 the rate of return 10% is the same under both funding situations and equal to the loan rate. On Sales above £80,000 the return to Ordinary Shareholders is higher with the loan capital since they take profits in excess of £10,000.

40.1 The company receives £100,000 − £2,959 = £97,041 immediately (£100,000 $\times .12 \times \frac{19}{365}$ = £2,959)

The real rate of interest is: −

$$\frac{2,959}{97,041 \times \frac{90}{365}} = 12.37\%$$

40.3 $\frac{\text{Interest}}{\text{Market Price}} = \frac{5}{40} = 12.5\%.$

40.4 $12.5\% \times (1 - .52) = 6\%.$

41.1

$$P = \frac{1}{(1 + .12)} + \frac{2}{(1 + .12)^2} + \frac{5}{(1 + .12)^2} = £6.47$$

41.3

$$P = \frac{D}{K - 9} = \frac{.60}{.1 - .05} = £12.00$$

41.4 $\frac{.60}{.1 - 0} = £6.00$

41.6 $£0.13 \times 9.2 = £1.20.$

42.1

			£	% weight
Equity	500+280	=	780	66.1
Preference		=	250	21.2
Debt	100+ 50	=	150	12.7
			1180	100.0

42.2

		£	% weight
Equity	500,000×2.50	1,250,000	82.2
Preference		125,000	8.2
Debt	95,000		
	50,000	145,000	9.6
		1,520,000	100.0

42.3

	Rate of Return	Book Weighting	Book WACC %	Market Weighting	Market WACC %
Equity	.12	66.1	7.93	82.2	9.86
Preference	.15	21.2	3.18	8.2	1.23
Debt	.14	12.7	1.78	9.6	1.34
		100.0	12.89	100.0	12.43

43.1 Good management, Patents, Trade Marks and special know how. Trading reputation, good or unique trading situation etc.

43.2 50% × £80,000 = £40,000.

43.4 £60,000 × 3.791 = £227,460

Index